TOURISM MANAGEMENT

Managing for change

Second edition

Stephen J. Page

ELSEVIER

AMSTERDAM • BOSTON • HEIDELBERG • LONDON • NEW YORK • OXFORD
PARIS • SAN DIEGO • SAN FRANCISCO • SINGAPORE • SYDNEY • TOKYO
Butterworth-Heinemann is an imprint of Elsevier

Butterworth-Heinemann is an imprint of Elsevier
Linacre House, Jordan Hill, Oxford OX2 8DP
30 Corporate Drive, Suite 400, Burlington, MA 01803, USA

First edition 2003
Second edition 2007

British Library Cataloguing in Publication Data
A catalogue record for this book is available from the British Library

Library of Congress Cataloguing in Publication Data
A catalogue record for this book is available from the Library of Congress

ISBN–13: 978-0-7506-8205-3
ISBN–10: 0-7506-8205-1

For information on all Butterworth-Heinemann publications visit our
web site at http://books.elsevier.com

Printed and bound in Italy
06 07 08 09 10   10 9 8 7 6 5 4 3 2 1

TOURISM MANAGEMENT

Contents

Figures

Plates

Tables

Preface

This book is written as a simple, plain language introduction to tourism and assumes no prior knowledge of what tourism is and how it affects our everyday lives. To read it you need to ask one question: why is there so much interest in tourism? If you are inquisitive about tourism and how it has developed as a business then read on. This is a book which looks at what the tourism industry is and does, and why it is such an important global business. In simple terms it shows how tourism is organized, run and managed – and how our desire to take holidays and use our leisure time creates an industry which is expanding and is sometimes seen as out of control. This book does not pull any punches: it is not full of jargon, buzzwords and academic goobledegook – there are far too many books like that which fail to convey the excitement that tourism engenders. It tells a story chapter by chapter about how tourism has developed, what tourism is and how specialist businesses meet the insatiable demand for holidays and travel. Where technical terminology is used, it is explained in lay terms for the general reader. The book offers many insights into a fascinating business which is changing so fast that even commentators find it hard to keep abreast of it.

The book takes a global look at what tourism is with examples from various countries and places, and asks: *If tourism is so important to our economies and society, what can we do to manage it? Whose responsibility is it? Is it too late to control it?* Such questions can only be answered after explaining how the tourism industry exists as a large unwieldy set of interests that are united by one key principle: making money from the visitor and their pursuit of pleasure or travel. The book is comprehensive in the way it treats the different elements of the tourism sector and questions what the challenges of managing tourism are.

Tourism Management: Managing for change will be essential reading for anyone interested in tourism – including tourists – and who want to understand how the business works, how it makes profits and what are the effects of its activities on destinations. The book examines all the key trends now affecting the tourism industry from the impact of technology to the way low-cost airlines have transformed the market for leisure travel.

We are all living in an age of major social and economic transformation, and tourism is part of that transformation. Reading this book will at least help you understand what is driving these changes in tourism and what is likely to stimulate future changes. For the tourism manager, the book will undoubtedly spell out a few home truths. For the general reader, it will show how difficult being a manager in tourism actually is – and the problems that we, the travelling public – *the tourists* – actually pose for businesses – as well as the opportunities and the challenges.

I hope you enjoy reading this book. It is certainly not the largest book ever written on tourism, but it is a clear, lucid and frank assessment which is easy to follow and above all shows how everything fits together – since tourism is not a simple business, all about holidays – or is it? Why not read on and find out! Happy reading.

Stephen J. Page is Scottish Enterprise Forth Valley Professor of Tourism Management in the Department of Marketing, at the University of Stirling, Scotland

Acknowledgements

A number of people have helped with this book in one way or another. They are Neil McLaren and Sharon Martin in the Department of Marketing at the University of Stirling. A number of organizations and individuals have granted copyright permission to use illustrations including: Eric Laws, Elsevier, Stagecoach, Airports Council International, the German Tourist Board, Michael Hall and Simon McArthur, Mintel, the Civil Aviation Authority, John Brown at the Scottish Executive, Brian Hay (formerly of VisitScotland), David Edgell, Multilingual Matters, easyJet, the Association of Asia Pacific Airlines and the European Travel Commission.

I would like to thank Sally North at Butterworth-Heinemann who commissioned this new edition of the book and her interest in developing something which is more accessible to a wide range of readers. I am also indebted to Thomas Mavrodontis for his detailed and meticulous translation of the first edition and the help with removing a number of errors.

Last but not least, Jo and Rosie made a big difference – not least all the hours of fun and enjoyment – when I was not writing. My book would not be complete without a mention of someone special who always encouraged me in writing – my mum whose memory will always be with me. This book is dedicated to your memory.

Abbreviations

Throughout this book, the term WTO is used to signify the World Tourism Organization. Since writing the book, the World Tourism Organization has received United Nations status, and so the correct attribution is now UN-WTO. This is noted so that readers are aware of the recent change.

Chapter **1**

Tourism today: Why is it a global phenomenon embracing all our lives?

Learning outcomes

This chapter provides an overview of tourism as a subject of study and after reading the chapter you should be able to understand:

- why tourism has emerged as a major leisure activity
- how tourism can be defined as an human activity
- how to distinguish between domestic and international tourism
- why tourism has to be measured and the importance of tourism statistics
- the scale and importance of tourism at a global scale and some of the reasons for its growth
- why tourism is a difficult activity to manage.

Introduction

The new millennium has witnessed the continued growth of interest in how people spend their spare time, especially their leisure time and non-work time. Some commentators have gone as far as to suggest that it is leisure time – how we use it and its meaning to individuals and families – that defines our lives, as a focus for non-work activity. This reflects a growing interest in what people consume in these non-work periods, particularly those times that are dedicated to travel and holidays which are more concentrated periods of leisure time. This interest is becoming an international phenomenon known as 'tourism': the use of this leisure time to visit different places, destinations and localities which often (but not exclusively) feature in the holidays and trips people take in. For example, in 2005 the World Travel and Tourism Council (WTTC) estimated that travel and tourism as economic activities generated US$6201 billion which is expected to grow to US$10 678.5 billion by 2015. This equates to a 4.6 per cent growth in the demand for travel and tourism per annum, which is far in excess of the scale and pace of growth in the economies of most countries. At a global scale, the economic effects of travel and tourism are estimated by WTTC to be responsible for 214 000 000 jobs: this is equivalent to 8.3 per cent of world employment. In 2005 tourism represented 10.4 per cent of total personal consumption, while it accounted for over 9 per cent of all global capital investment and 10 per cent of world GDP.

Therefore, the growing international significance of tourism can be explained in many ways. In an introductory text such as this, it is important to stress at the outset the following types of factors and processes in order to illustrate the reasons why tourism assumes an important role not only in our lives but also globally:

- *Tourism is a discretionary activity* (people are not required to undertake it as a basic need to survive, unlike consuming food and water).
- *Tourism is of growing economic significance* at a global scale, with growth rates in excess of the rate of economic growth for many countries.
- *Many governments see tourism as offering new employment opportunities* in a growing sector that is focused on service industries and may assist in developing and modernizing the economy.
- *Tourism is increasingly becoming associated with quality of life issues* as it offers people the opportunity to take a break away from the complexities and stresses

of everyday life and work – it provides the context for rest, relaxation and an opportunity to do something different in a new environment.

- *Tourism is becoming seen as a basic right in the developed, Westernized industrialized countries* and it is enshrined in legislation regarding holiday entitlement – the result is many people associate holiday entitlement with the propensity (i.e. the potential to engage in) to generate tourism.
- *In some less developed countries, tourism is being advocated as a possible solution to poverty* (this is described as 'pro-poor' tourism strategies), with local people benefiting from this form of economic activity.
- *Holidays are a defining feature of non-work* for many workers.
- *Global travel is becoming more accessible* in the developed world for all classes of people with the rise of low-cost airlines and cut-price travel fuelling a new wave of demand for tourism in the new millennium. This is potentially replicating the demand in the 1960s and 1970s for new popular forms of mass tourism. Much of that earlier growth was fuelled by access to transport (i.e. the car and air travel) and this provided new leisure opportunities in the Western world.
- *Consumer spending on discretionary items such as travel and tourism is being perceived as a less costly item in household budgets.* It is also much easier to finance tourism with the rapid rise in credit card spending in developed countries, increasing access to travel opportunities and participation in tourism.
- *Technology such as the internet has made booking travel-related products easy* and placed it within the reach of a new generation of computer-literate consumers who are willing to get rid of much of the traditional ritual of going to a travel agent to book the annual holiday to Lanzarote or Ibiza. Such technology now opens many possibilities for national and international travel at the click of a computer mouse.

From this brief list of possible reasons why tourism is now assuming a major role in the lives of people, it is evident that tourism is also becoming a powerful process affecting all parts of the globe. It is not only embraced by various people as a new trend, a characteristic or defining feature of people's lives, but is also an activity in which the masses can now partake (subject to their access to discretionary forms of spending). This discretionary activity is part of wider post-war changes in Western society with the rise in disposable income and spending on consumer goods and services. The first major wave of growth was in home ownership, then in car ownership and, last, in accessing tourism and international travel. In fact international travel (and domestic travel, i.e. within a country) is a defining feature of the consumer society. Whilst the car has given more people access to tourism and leisure opportunities within their own country, reductions in the price of aeroplane tickets has made international travel and tourism products and services more widely available. For example, in the UK the number of air travellers is expected to rise from around 180 million in 2004 to 475 million by 2030. This is not without its environmental cost.

Tourism in this respect is a phenomenon that is constantly evolving, developing and reformulating itself as a consumer activity. Tourism, as a consumer activity, is constantly being developed by the tourism industry and individual businesses, as marketing is used to develop new ideas, products and services and destinations. This is reflected in the international interest in developing niche products: holidays focused on specific interests and activities. Examples of niche products are nature-based or ecotourism excursions, such as nature watching in the Galapagos Islands, and wine- and food-based tourism. Both of these types of holiday are increasing in popularity, reflecting as they do people's interests and hobbies. Tourism appeals to the human imagination. As an activity it knows no bounds: it is global and it affects the environment it occurs in, the people who host it, the economies it seeks to benefit and the tourists who consume it as an experience, product and an element of their lives. With tourism having this all-embracing role, it is no surprise that many commentators, researchers and governments have agreed on the need to manage it as a process and activity, especially since it has the potential to snowball and grow out of proportion if it is not. Therein lies the basic proposition of this book – tourism needs managing if it is to be successful and beneficial rather than a modern-day scourge.

Yet one of the fundamental problems in seeking to manage tourism is in trying to understand *what it is*: how it occurs, why it occurs where it does, the people and environments that are affected by it and why it is a volatile activity that can cease as quick as it can start. These types of question are what this book seeks to address. It will also look at why tourism as a consumer activity is built on dreams, images and what people like to do; this is notoriously difficult to understand as it involves entering the realms of psychology and the mind of the individual tourist. Furthermore, these psychological elements are bound up in notions of enjoyment, feelings, emotions and seemingly intangible and unseen characteristics. The issue is further complicated by the way in which an individual's tastes and interests change throughout their life. In other words, being a tourist is based on the principle of non-work and enjoyment of one's free time in a different locality, and results in an experience, a treasured memory and something personal. Consequently, understanding what tourism is, how it operates, what it means to people and how it should be managed are key challenges for any locality in the new millennium with the global growth of tourism activity.

Why study tourism? Is it just about enjoyment and holidays?

Tourism and its analysis have become a relatively recent field of study among academics, researchers and commentators. Some of the very early textbooks on tourism (which are detailed in the further reading section at the end of this chapter) can be dated to the early 1970s, with a second wave being produced in the 1980s and then a massive explosion in the late 1980s and 1990s as tourism education and training expanded worldwide. There are a range of commonly recognized problems in studying tourism, a number of which are important to the way in which we understand whether it is just about enjoyment and holidaytaking:

- Tourism is a multidisciplinary subject which means that a wide range of other subjects, such as psychology, geography, economics, to name but a few, examine it and bring to it a range of ideas and methods of studying it. This means that there is no overarching academic agreement on how to approach the study of tourism – it really depends on how you are looking at tourism, and the perspective you adopt which determines the issues you are interested in studying.
- This has led to a lack of clarity and definition in how to study tourism, something that other researchers have defined as *reductionism*. What this means is that tourism is normally defined by reducing it (hence 'reductionism') to a simple range of activities or transactions (i.e. *What types of holidays do people choose?* or *How do people purchase those holidays?*) rather than by focusing on the framework needed to give a wider perspective or overview of tourism as a dynamic and important subject.

These problems often compound the way people view tourism as a subject, emphasizing the holiday or enjoyment aspects of travelling (in one's spare time or on business) as the defining features or reference point of tourism. To the general public tourism is something everyone knows about – it is something many have engaged in and so have an opinion on what it is, its effects and widespread development.

Those involved in the study of tourism face similar situations within the institutions and organizations they work within, since many academics and researchers have a broad awareness of tourism similar to that of the general public and so have prejudices and opinions about it as a subject. Therein lies one of the continual problems facing the student of tourism: anyone who is charged with the study of pleasure, enjoyment and the use of leisure time cannot be engaged in serious academic study – can they? Other researchers in science, the arts and humanities work in long-established disciplines and have generations of literature, knowledge and a tradition of studying serious problems in society such as disease control, homelessness, poverty; the negative aspects of life and their improvement. So tourism is not perceived a serious subject, as it does not address societal problems. In reality, these prejudices and attitudes are fundamentally flawed, outdated and ill informed in a society where the consumption of leisure and pleasure are now key elements in the quality of life of the population. For example, a recent project I undertook with VisitScotland, the National Tourism Organization for Scotland examined the impact of a flu pandemic on Scottish tourism, highlighting that tourism was now one of the biggest sectors of its economy, worth £4.5 billion. A flu pandemic could devastate the economy and thereby the wider economic and social structure of Scotland. So tourism and its study do matter, especially where it is an integral part of the national economy. Admittedly, tourism is about pleasure and enjoyment, but its global growth and expansion are now creating serious societal problems and issues; a fundamental understanding of tourism is required if we are to manage and control the impacts and problems it can cause. One way of beginning to understand that tourism is more than holidays and enjoyment is to think about why tourism is so important in modern society (i.e. its social, cultural and economic significance) by looking at an important process which has led to the demand for it – the rise of the leisure society.

The leisure society

Tourism is now widely acknowledged as a social phenomenon, as the nature of society in most advanced developed countries has now changed from one which has traditionally had an economy based on manufacturing and production, to one where the dominant form of employment is services and consumer industries (i.e. those based on producing consumer goods and services). At the same time, many countries have seen the amount of leisure time and paid holiday entitlement for their workers increase in the post-war period so that workers now have the opportunity to engage in the new forms of consumption such as tourism. These changes have been described as being part of what has been termed as the *leisure society*, a term coined in the 1970s by sociologists. They were examining the future of work and the way in which society was changing, as traditional forms of employment were disappearing and new service-related employment, increased leisure time and new working habits emerged (e.g. flexi-time and part-time work). Some commentators described this as a 'leisure shock' in the 1980s since many workers were still not prepared for the rise in leisure time and how to use it.

As society has passed from the stage of industrialization to one now described as post-industrial, where new technologies and ways of communicating and working have evolved, sociologists such as Baudrillard (1998), in *The Consumer Society: Myths and Structures*, have argued that we have moved from a society where work and production has been replaced by one which leisure and consumption now dominate. This has been reflected in social changes, such as the rise of new middle classes in many developed and developing countries, and these middle classes have a defining feature, which is the concern with leisure lifestyles and consumption. The new-found wealth among the growing middle class has been increasingly spent on leisure items and tourism is an element of this (e.g. in 1911, 1 per cent of the population had 70 per cent of wealth; this dropped to 40 per cent in 1960 and 23 per cent in 2002 in the UK). The international growth in holidaytaking is directly related to this new middle class. The increasing mobility of this group has been reflected in a sixfold increase in air passengers travelling in the UK 1971–2003 and households that own one car rising from 52 per cent in 1971 to 74 per cent in 2004. But the greatest growth has been in the two-car households, rising from 8 per cent in 1971 to 29 per cent in 2003. If the UK is fairly representative of changes in other countries, then recent changes in consumer expenditure illustrate the growth of this leisure society:

• Cheaper air fares and changing patterns of personal expenditure recorded in *The Family Spending Survey 2003–2004* (www.statistics.gov.uk) by the Office for National Statistics found that household spending in the UK included £57 a week on recreation and culture, ranked second to transport. This recreational spending included £11.60 a week spent on overseas package holidays and 0.80p on UK-based package holidays: four times the amount spent in real terms in 1968. In contrast, £5 a week was spent on sport fees and £2 a week on cinema, theatre and museum admissions.

- This spending varied by age group: in households where the main respondent was aged 30–50 years, they spent £70.80 a week on recreation and culture; those aged 50–65 spent £64.20 a week and those aged over 75 years spent only £22.40 a week.
- The amount spent on overseas holidays has increased sevenfold since 1971, when 6.7 million trips were taken. This has grown to 41 million trips worth £26.7 billion in 2004 with those in managerial and professional employment (the new middle classes) spending double that of other employed classes.
- In the period 1993–2003, there was a 79 per cent growth in domestic air passengers at UK airports due to low-cost air travel. The volume of outbound trips was three times that of domestic travel, with two thirds of outbound trips to 15 EU countries, 30 per cent (30 million) being to Spain and 18per cent to France.

This snapshot of the UK shows that tourism is a major element of the leisure spending of households, reflected in what researchers have described as 'leisure lifestyles'. Interest in tourism in Europe, North America and other parts of the world has been given an added boost by the impact of new technology such as the internet and the worldwide web, which has rendered knowledge and awareness of tourism and the opportunities to travel worldwide more accessible. The worldwide web has been used as a medium to portray travel options and the product offerings of destinations, so that people can search and explore travel options at a global scale from the ease of a computer terminal. In Europe, the impact of this new technology in the early years of the twenty-first century has generated a new tourism boom akin to the rise in international tourism in the 1970s, with new forms of technology and the supply of cheaper forms of travel (i.e. the low-cost airlines) fostering this demand. For example, Jersey European Airways rebranded itself in 2000 Flybe and in 2002 adopted a low-cost model of operation (see Chapter 6 for more detail) to compete with other carriers. Its growth since 2002 can be attributed to its low-cost model and it has grown its online bookings from 6 per cent in 2002 to over 85 per cent in 2005, for an airline now carrying over 5.5 million passengers a year. Whilst this figure of 85 per cent of bookings online has been exceeded by other low-cost airlines, it does illustrate the power of the internet and its role in reaching a new customer base in the tourism sector. This has given rise to the rise of *e-tourism*, which is the digitization of all elements in the tourism supply chain (see Chapter 4 for more detail), whereby the supply and demand for tourism can be met through new virtual forms of distribution such as the worldwide web, as opposed to conventional methods such as travel agents and paper brochures. This has certainly revolutionized tourism and the access to travel knowledge and information, hitherto largely within the confines of travel agents and travel organizers: now everyone can be their own travel agent if they have access to the technology. According to the European Travel Commission in 2005, some of the key trends which reflect this growth are:

- Almost 60 million people in the USA use internet search engines every day (and travel features as major element of what they look at in terms of internet content).
- According to the Association of British Travel Agents, almost 40 per cent of consumers in the UK purchased their holidays online.
- In Poland, 30 per cent of the population over the age of 15 use the internet, and this may offer growth prospects for future travel.
- In the Baltic States, around 15 per cent of the population use the internet, a 50 per cent growth since 2000, providing future growth potential for travel and tourism markets.
- By 2010, the worldwide population of internet users will reach 1.8 billion, rising from 1.08 billion in 2005.
- In November 2005, the world's leading top ten internet users in terms of volume of users and in order of importance were the USA, China, Japan, Germany, India, the UK, South Korea, Italy, France and Brazil, illustrating not only the importance of some mature developed countries but also the significance of emerging countries with major outbound travel potential such as China.
- The rate of broadband internet usage is set to rise from 215 million users in 2005 to 500 million in 2010, expanding the opportunities and access of internet users who may use the internet to book travel.

Source: Compiled from the European Travel Commission, www.etc-corporate.org, © European Travel Commission

What emerges from these trends is that access to internet technology is increasing and one important feature which many studies confirm is that this technology is increasingly used to search out and peruse travel options as well as for making bookings. With these issues in mind, attention now turns to what is meant by the terms 'tourism', 'tourist' and 'travel'.

Concepts – tourism, the tourist and travel

Attempts to define tourism are numerous and very often the terms 'travel' and 'tourism' are used interchangeably. According to the international organization responsible for tourism, the World Tourism Organization (UN-WTO):

> Tourism is defined as the activities of persons travelling to and staying in places outside their usual environment for not more than one consecutive year for leisure, business and other purposes not related to the exercise of an activity remunerated from within the place visited. The use of this broad concept makes it possible to identify tourism between countries as well as tourism within a country. 'Tourism' refers to all activities of visitors, including both 'tourists (overnight visitors)' and 'same-day visitors'. (www.world-tourism.org)

This seemingly straightforward definition has created a great deal of debate. In fact, controversy has surrounded the development of acceptable definitions since the League of Nations' attempt to define a tourist in 1937 and subsequent attempts by the United Nations conference in 1963 which considered definitions proposed by the then IUOTO (now UN-WTO). There have also been attempts to clarify what is meant by the term 'visitor' as opposed to 'tourist' and the distinction between tourists who travel within their own country (domestic tourists) and those who travel to other countries (international tourists). What the debates on defining tourism at a technical level show is that it is far from an easy task in agreeing what constitutes a 'tourist'. For example, should we include someone who is a visitor staying in a second home: they are technically away from their homes, but are staying in an other form of property they own? Similarly, how far away from your home area must you travel before your activity is deemed tourism? A further problem is associated with the category of cruise ship passengers who dock at a port and visit briefly, not staying overnight, or cross-Channel trippers who may cross an international boundary but then return within a day and do not stay overnight.

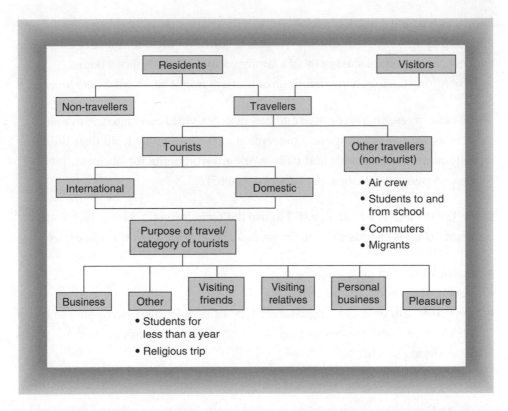

Figure 1.1   The classification of tourists (developed and modified from Chadwick, 1994)

To try and encompass many of these anomalies and problems, the UN-WTO produced guidelines and a useful categorization for defining a tourist, which is shown in Figure 1.1. What is increasingly obvious is that new forms of research on tourism are needed to understand how the phenomenon loosely defined as tourism is evolving as it is far from static. For example, research on tourism and migration has identified the short-term migration of the elderly who winter in warmer climates – such as the UK pensioners who overwinter in the Mediterranean – as a new type of tourist. These patterns of tourism migration incorporate owners of second homes, tourists and seasonal visitors who spend two to six months overseas in locations such as Tuscany, Malta and Spain. For example, in the UK 328 000 people own a second home in the UK and 178 000 have purchased overseas properties. In the USA estimates of domestic second-home ownership ranges between 3.6 million and 9.2 million properties, the majority of which are located in coastal or rural areas. This pattern of seasonal tourism and migration also generates flows of people

known as 'visiting friends and relatives', and these are somewhat different to the conventional images of package holidaymakers destined for these locations in Europe. In
the USA, a long-established trend of a family vacation is the holiday home.

Therefore, the following definition of tourism might be useful where tourism is

> the field of research on human and business activities associated with one or
> more aspects of the temporary movement of persons away from their imme-
> diate home communities and daily work environments for business, pleas-
> ure and personal reasons. (Chadwick 1994: 65)

In the USA, there is a tendency still to use the term 'travel' when in fact 'tourism'
is meant. What is clear is that tourism is associated with three specific issues:

- 'the movement of people;
- a sector of the economy or an industry;
- a broad system of interacting relationships of people, their needs [sic] to travel
  outside their communities and services that attempt to respond to these needs
  by supplying products'.

Source: After Chadwick (1994: 65)

From this initial starting point, one can begin to explore some of the complex
issues in arriving at a working definition of the terms 'tourism' and 'tourist'.

Probably the most useful work to provide an introduction to tourism as a concept and the relationship with travel is Burkart and Medlik's (1981) seminal study
Tourism: Past Present and Future. This identified the following characteristics associated with tourism:

- tourism arises from the movement of people to and their stay in various
  destinations
- there are two elements in all tourism: the journey to the destination and the stay
  including activities at the destination
- the journey and the stay take place outside the normal place of residence and
  work, so that tourism gives rise to activities that are distinct from those of the
  resident and working populations of the places through which tourists travel
  and in which they stay
- the movement to destinations is of a temporary, short-term character, with
  intention to return within a few days, weeks or months

- destinations are visited for purposes other than the taking up of permanent residence or of employment remunerated from within the places visited.

Source: Burkart and Medlik (1981: 42)

All tourism includes some travel but not all travel is tourism, while the temporary and short-term nature of most tourist trips distinguishes it from migration. But how does tourism fit together – in other words how can we understand the disparate elements? One approach is to look at tourism as an integrated system, which means that one has to ask how tourism is organized and what the defining features are.

An organizing framework for the analysis of tourism

The most widely used framework is that developed by Leiper (1990) who identified a tourism system as comprising a tourist, a traveller-generating region, tourism destination regions; transit routes for tourists travelling between generating and destination areas, and the travel and tourism industry (e.g. accommodation, transport, the firms and organizations supplying services and products to tourists). This is illustrated in Figure 1.2 and shows that transport forms an integral part of the tourism system, connecting the tourist-generating and destination region together. Thus, a 'tourism system' is a framework which enables one to understand the overall process

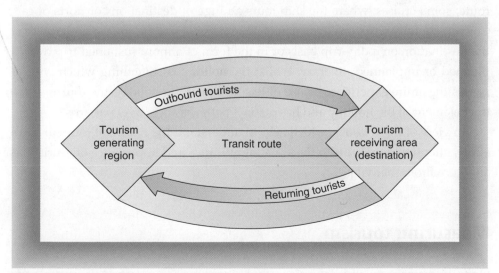

Figure 1.2 Leiper's tourism system (redrawn from Page, 1995; based on and modified from Leiper, 1990)

of tourist travel from both the supplier and purchaser's perspective (known respectively as 'supply' and 'demand') while identifying the organizations which influence and regulate tourism. It also allows one to understand where the links exist between different elements of tourism, from where the tourist interacts with the travel organizer (travel agent or retailer), the travel provider (airline, or mode of transport), the destination area and tourism sector within the destination. This approach is also helpful for understanding how many elements are assembled by the tourism sector to create an experience of tourism. One major element in this experience of tourism is the tour, which is a feature of holidays and the use of leisure time.

The tour, holidays and leisure time

What is evident from Leiper's model of the tourism system is that the tour – which is a trip, travel anywhere for pleasure or leisure – is a vital element. The tour is an underpinning feature of tourism, a prerequisite for tourism to occur, since the consumer has to be brought to the product or experience, has to travel, and is a reciprocal event – the traveller travels out and back. Transport and single or multiple destinations are involved. The conventional definition of tour inevitably implies travel to one or more places, called 'destinations'. There are various forms of tour: the excursion by road or rail which may have a scenic element known as a touring route; some cruises, where the ship tours a range of destinations or ports of call. Conversely, the excursion element may be something that the tourist undertakes at the destination on a day-trip basis or in the form of a more sustained trip, with a planned or unplanned itinerary. Whilst the holiday is something which encompasses the entire experience or use of leisure time for a holiday, the tour is a distinct element of the holiday and has distinct patterns and travel patterns.

In view of these issues, which help to understand the nature of tourism as an entity, attention now turns to the scale, significance and importance of tourism as an international activity.

Measuring tourism

Once we agree a general definition of what tourism is, we can look for methods that add precision to the scale, volume and significance of tourism as a global activity. Measuring tourism also helps to understand some of the problems which planners and decision-makers need to address in planning for tourism and future growth scenarios. There are three basic considerations in trying to define tourism as an activity, which are:

1 What is the purpose of travel (e.g. business travel, holidaymaking, visits to friends and relatives)?
2 What time dimension is involved in the tourism visit, which requires a minimum and a maximum period of time spent away from the home area and the time spent at the destination? In most cases, this would involve a minimum stay of more than 24 hours away from home and less than a year as a maximum.
3 What situations exist where some countries may or may not choose to include travellers, such as cruise passengers, travellers in transit at a particular point of embarkation/departure and excursionists who stay less than 24 hours at a destination, as tourists?

There are five main reasons why measuring tourism is important:

1 to understand why and how significant it is for certain destinations, countries and regions in terms of the scale and value of the visitors
2 to understand how important it is for countries in terms of their balance of payments, as it is an invisible export that generates foreign currency and income
3 to assist the tourism industry and governments in planning for and anticipating the type of infrastructure which is required for tourism to grow and prosper
4 to assist in understanding what type of marketing is needed to reach the tourist as a consumer, and what factors will influence tourists to visit a country or destination
5 to help the tourism industry make decisions about what type of action is needed to develop tourism businesses and further develop in this area.

At a general level, measuring tourism through the collection, analysis and interpretation of statistics is essential to the measurement of the volume, scale, impact and value of tourism at different geographical scales from the global to the country level down to the individual destination. At the simplest level, this is shown in Figure 1.3, which demonstrates the trends in global tourism since 1950. This uses the UN-WTO arrival statistics for each year and shows that international tourist arrivals have not simply grown year on year. A number of downturns have occurred in tourist arrivals, more recently caused by the impact of Foot and Mouth in the UK, the 11 September 2001 and Bali (September 2002) terrorist events and

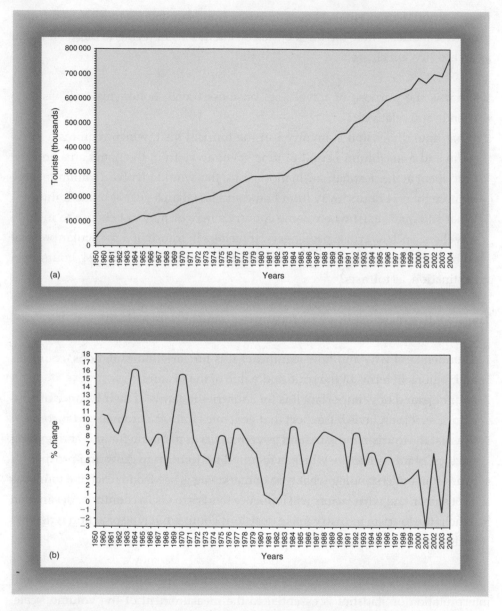

Figure 1.3 The growth of international tourism since 1950: (a) total visitor arrivals; (b) percentage change year on year (source: UN-WTO data)

other factors (e.g. the economic crisis in Argentina, the strength of the US dollar, conflict in the Middle East and the SARS (Severe Acute Respiratory Syndrome) outbreak. One could term the period since 2000 as one in which international tourism has operated in 'turbulent times'. Part of this turbulence, as Glaeßer (2006)

Table 1.1 International tourist arrivals by region of arrival in 2001, 2003 and 2004 (source: modified from UN-WTO)

Region	Million arrivals		
	2001	**2003**	**2004**
Africa	28.5	30.8	33.2
Americas	122.2	113.8	125.8
Asia and the Pacific	120.5	119.3	152.5
Europe	387.8	399.0	416.4
Middle East	24.0	28.8	35.4
World	688.5	690.9	763.0

notes, is the impact of natural catastrophes on tourism. For example, in the twentieth century there have been 50 000 natural disasters but between 1990 and 2005 there have been 500–700 such catastrophes each year causing losses of US$650 billion between 1990 and 1999. These events have periodically interrupted or at worst devastated the tourism industry (e.g. Hurricane Rita in the USA in 2005), contributing to the notion of turbulence in tourism activity. In other words, a range of factors impact upon visitor arrivals at an international level, because tourism is a very fickle activity (i.e. it is very vulnerable to the external factors mentioned above which act as deterrents to travel) and adverse events can act as shock waves which send ripples across the world and impact upon people's willingness to travel for pleasure reasons. At the same time, major religious events can be a major stimulus to tourist travel such as pilgrimages to locations such as Lourdes in France, where its waters are seen as having healing properties. Other religious events such as the Pope's Christmas message attract large audiences in Rome while other religious faiths have similar examples. At a global scale, Table 1.1 shows the recent patterns of arrivals by UN-WTO region for 2001–2003 and some of the local trends in international tourism. The findings can be summarized as follows:

- international tourism is dominated by western European destinations
- new areas for tourism activity, such as Asia and the Pacific (including the growing economies of Singapore, Thailand, South Korea, Taiwan and China) are beginning to develop their volume of visitor arrivals at the global scale despite the impact of SARS

- the dominant destinations worldwide in terms of arrivals in 2003 were France, Spain, the USA and Italy, followed by China
- more established destinations in north-western Europe and the USA have seen slow to sluggish growth.

But one of the enduring problems which Table 1.1 does not show is that, far from being comprehensive, tourism statistics are an incomplete source of information because they are often only an estimate of the total pattern of tourism. In addition, such statistics are often dated when they are published because there is a significant time lag in their generation, analysis, presentation and dissemination. This is because many published tourism statistics are derived from sample surveys with the results being weighted or statistically manipulated to derive a measure which is supposedly representative of the real-world situation. Hence, many tourism statistics at a country or regional level often state they are estimates of tourism for this reason. In reality, this often means that tourism statistics may be subject to significant errors depending on the size of the sample.

The typical problems associated with measuring tourism are as follows:

- tourists are a transient and highly mobile population making statistical sampling procedures difficult when trying to ensure statistical accuracy and rigour in methodological terms
- interviewing mobile populations such as tourists is often undertaken in a strange environment, typically at ports or points of departure or arrival where there is background noise which may influence responses
- other variables such as the weather may affect the responses.

Source: Latham (1989)

Even where sampling and survey-related problems can be minimized, such tourism statistics have to be treated carefully as they may be influenced by how the tourist was measured and the type of approach used, and you need to know these factors. The main ways of measuring tourists through surveys are as follows:

- pre-travel studies of tourists' intended travel habits and likely choice of destination (intentional studies)

- studies of tourists in transit to provide information on their actual behaviour and plans for the remainder of their holiday or journey (actual and intended studies)
- studies of tourists at the destination or at specific tourist attractions and sites, to provide information on their actual behaviour, levels of satisfaction, impacts and future intentions (actual and intended studies)
- post-travel studies of tourists on their return journey from their destination or on-site experience, or once they have returned to their place of residence (post-travel measures).

Such studies can also be used to examine different facets of the tourist as the following three approaches suggest:

- measurement of tourist volume, enumerating arrivals, departures and the number of visits and stays
- expenditure-based surveys which quantify the value of tourist spending at the destination and during the journey
- measurement of the characteristics and features of tourists to construct a profile of the different markets and segments visiting a destination.

In the commercial world, tourism data are also collated by organizations that specialize in its collection and analysis including market research companies. Tourism consultants may also be commissioned specifically to collect data for feasibility studies of tourism developments or new business opportunities and much of the information remains confidential to the client due to its commercial sensitivity. But in most cases, national governments collate tourism statistics through studies of domestic and international tourism. International tourism is more widely studied and this is normally passed to the UN-WTO and the Organization for Economic Co-operation and Development (OECD) collate and publish international travel statistics from member nations.

Once we have an understanding of how tourism is measured and collated, then we can begin to think about what the patterns and trends in tourism mean at a global level and what the implications are, particularly in terms of the more critical issues of what forces are affecting tourism as a global activity.

New forces affecting tourism – globalization, inequality and the developed and developing world

When one looks at the patterns of tourism, and those areas which are growing in terms of international tourism, it is evident that the majority of outbound travellers are from the developed countries of Europe and North America, Australasia and the new middle class in many developing countries. In some cases, the tourists are travelling to developing countries where the standard of living often means the majority of the population lives at subsistence level or at a much lower standard than the visitor. The contrast in wealth between visitor and host is often very large and it highlights a clear inequality between those who have the disposable income to enjoy the luxury of international and domestic travel and the tourism employees who are working at low wage rates and in low-paid, unskilled jobs. This situation is made worse by the growing impact of globalization.

Globalization is a process associated with the growth of large international companies and corporations, which control various forms of economic development and production internationally from their host country, making goods and delivering services at a lower cost using low overheads and cheap labour in developing countries. Tourism is no exception to this: large multinational hotel chains and tour operators use developing countries and destinations as the basis for their tourist product. In these situations, the economic linkages with the local community are limited, so that low-skill jobs and low economic benefits are traded off against the profits and economic benefits of tourism development being expropriated (i.e. returned) to the country of origin of the multinational firm. In many cases, the weakly developed nature of local economic linkages in developing countries' tourism economies mean they are often trapped into such exploitative relationships because they do not have the indigenous capital or entrepreneurs to set up tourism businesses. A lack of education, know-how and power to negotiate with multinationals to maximize the benefits for local people means that tourism can develop as a form of exploitation for such communities. This may mean that rather than importing foodstuffs, such as internationally recognizable brands, to meet the tastes of tourists, but where local products are developed to nurture the linkages with the local economy, local people may benefit.

Tourists bring their leisure lifestyles with them on holiday and these are increasingly consumptive and conspicuous. Their spending power could be harnessed for the benefit of the local economy. A growing problem in many tourism destinations worldwide is that the growth of tourism and expropriation of its profits means that the environmental resource base which is used to attract tourists (e.g. attractive beaches, wildlife and the cultural and built environment) is not invested in and may be spoilt. More and more, attention is turning to the extent to which tourism is a sustainable economic, social and environmentally based activity. That we should use the environment without conserving it for future generations is one of the central arguments in the sustainable tourism debate. This also raises the issue of inequalities related to tourism; for example, tourist use of local resources required by residents can destroy those resources and environmental quality. This means that local people, governments and international agencies have a responsibility to lobby and take action to ensure that tourism development which occurs in different countries and locations is not only sustainable but seeks to minimize negative impacts as far as possible. It should not marginalize vulnerable groups such as children and the local workforce: the International Labour Organization (ILO) has estimated that between 10–15 per cent of the tourism workforce worldwide is comprised of children who do not enjoy appropriate standards of labour and employment conditions.

Tourism needs to be developed in an ethical manner so that exploitation is not its hallmark. This is a theme which will be returned to later in the book; at this point it is enough to emphasize that tourism development and activity not only needs to be socially and environmentally responsible, it must be sustainable and long-term rather than short-term and exploitative (so that the goose that lays the golden egg is not killed off). The tourism industry needs to work with communities, local bodies and people to ensure that tourism is a win–win activity for everyone and is integrated into the local community rather than just exploiting its local assets. This may require a significant change in emphasis in the way tourism is developed and managed but it is an enduring theme, which is worth highlighting at different points in the book. Tourists and tourism businesses have a greater responsibility to ensure that tourism is promoted as an activity which will not only enhance global understanding and interaction between people of different cultures and societies, but which will also promote dialogue, benefits and opportunities for the tourist, the host and the environment. So, in some situations, tourism may be a way of providing the stimulus and means for preserving and conserving endangered species and environments as well as providing benefits beyond those, which normally accrue to the tourism industry. Tourism has to operate as a profitable activity, but for its long-term future, mutually beneficial relationships and links between the industry, people and the environment must exist to bring financial and sustainable benefits for all and enhance the reputation and image of tourism as a global phenomenon. This is the underlying basis of the pro-poor tourism lobby. In this way the welfare and benefits of tourism to tourists can also be extended to the host population and help to address many of the global inequalities which exist in the growing globalization of tourism activity as multinational enterprises seek to exercise greater control of the choice and nature of tourism being offered to consumers. Although this book will not be able to address all of these issues, it is hoped that they will be at the forefront of the reader's mind so that they are aware of the implications of the tourism industry and its activities at a global, national and local level throughout the book.

A framework for the book

The title of this book is *Tourism Management* and therefore it is useful to present an organizing framework for the book and what is meant by the term 'tourism management'. By this stage, it is evident that the focus of the book and subject matter is tourism. What is often seen and used as an ambiguous term is the word 'management'. Therefore, in this section, the relationship of tourism with management and its meaning in the context of this book is examined.

Tourism and management as a focus for the book

At a very general level, the word 'management' as applied to tourism could be taken as how tourism needs to be managed as a growing activity at a global, national and local level in order that its often contradictory forces (i.e. the pursuit of profit as a private sector activity and impact on the resource base it uses such as a beautiful coastline on a Pacific island) are reconciled and balanced so that tourism develops and is pursued in a sustainable and balanced manner. Whilst this is an overriding concern for readers of this book, there is also a need to examine the basic principles associated with the term 'management' and how these elements of management can be integrated with the study of tourism as an activity. The basic functions associated with management as an activity are concerned with:

1 *Planning,* so that goals are set out and the means of achieving the goals are recognized.
2 *Organizing,* whereby the work functions are broken down into a series of tasks and linked to some form of structure. These tasks then have to be assigned to individuals.
3 *Leading,* which is the method of motivating and influencing staff so that they perform their tasks effectively. This is essential if organizational goals are to be achieved.
4 *Controlling,* which is the method by which information is gathered about what has to be done.

Each of these functions involves decision-making by managers, businesses, tourist destinations or organizations so that they can be harnessed to achieve the objectives and tasks associated with managing tourism. The word 'organization' is often used as an all-embracing term to refer to the type of tourism entity which is involved with tourism as a business or other level. These businesses are motivated by their involvement in tourism to make a profit and, therefore, the efficient organization and management of their activities is essential to ensure that company or organizational objectives are met. There is a school of management thought which argues that management only occurs when chaos occurs and that the function of management is to impose order and structure on that chaos. Within organizations dealing with the tourism sector (e.g. travel agents, airlines, tour operators and associated businesses), resources are harnessed (e.g. employees, finance, capital, technology, equipment and knowledge) to provide an output, which in the case of tourism is normally a product or experience consumed by the tourist or service. This output is achieved through the management of the resources.

There is also a debate among tourism researchers who argue that tourism is a unique sector in that it displays characteristics of partial industrialization which are explained more fully by Leiper (1990: 25) where:

> only certain organisations providing goods and services directly to tourists are in the tourism industry. The proportion of (a) goods and services stemming from that industry to (b) total goods and services used by tourists can be termed the index of industrialisation, theoretically ranging from 100 per cent

(wholly industrialised) to zero (tourists present and spending money, but no tourism industry).

What Leiper's approach to the tourism sector shows is that managing the broad phenomenon called 'tourism' is complex for a number of reasons:

- The tourism industry is not a homogenous sector or segment of the economy: it is made up of various organizations directly involved in tourism (i.e. those which directly service tourist needs) and those indirectly involved and so may be described as allied industries (i.e. food suppliers, retailers and other service providers).
- Some of the organizations directly involved in tourism are responsible for encouraging and promoting tourism development and marketing.
- The allied industries do not always see themselves as tourism-related enterprises.
- The destination or area which the tourists visit is not the sole responsibility of one business or group of businesses; usually the public sector intervenes to ensure that business objectives (i.e. profit and increasing tourism numbers and revenue) are balanced with local needs and business interests (known as 'stakeholder interests') in relation to the resource base which tourism utilizes (i.e. beaches, attractions, the infrastructure and overall environment).
- The public sector is responsible for trying to liaise, plan and manage these diverse group of interests that are associated with tourism as a phenomenon as well as having an underlying responsibility in many cases for the marketing and promotion of the destination.

Therefore, one can see how complex the management of tourism is when the interests and variety of organizations involved in tourism are considered and then the concept of partial industrialization is introduced.

From this discussion, who is responsible for tourism management can be examined at a number of levels, although this is not an exclusive list but a range of illustrations:

- At the individual business level the manager(s) is (are) involved with the functioning and running of the enterprise.
- At the destination level, responsibility often lies with a public sector led agency such as a tourism department (either as a stand-alone body or as part of a local

authority department). In extreme situations where a destination is deluged with tourists due to its popularity, the public sector may lead with a public–private sector partnership involving business interests to manage the visitors on the ground.

- At the country level, it is the national tourism organizations, funded by the public sector through taxes and sometimes with private sector members, who promote and market the country as a place to visit and attempt to manage the diverse interests involved in tourism.
- At each level, be it the individual business, destination or country, a complex web of interactions and interrelationships exist which need to be taken into account in the decisions, interests and actions taken to manage tourism.

In each of these illustrations, the functions of management are harnessed. Tourism management as a pursuit, however, is further complicated in that there is a great debate as to what tourism is, what needs to be managed and who should be responsible. The fact that tourism can be seen as an experience based on the pursuit of pleasure and profit raises many complex issues such as whether the tourist is consuming a product, experience or service, and it leads to many debates on what to manage and how far management controls should be exercised by the tourism industry and public sector.

So what how does this book address these questions?

One way is to view the managerial process of tourism as a multilayered process, in which the various organizations and stakeholders involved in tourism engage at different levels through time. Figure 1.4 demonstrates this. The focus begins with the individual business and the management processes (controlling, planning, leading and organizing) are continuous through the interconnected stakeholder groups from the individual business through to the various interests known as the tourism industry. These interests and the connections between management at different levels and between groups means that, in reality, these groups also have to be aware of external factors that will impact upon management such as the visitor, the business environment, consumer trends, the growth of the leisure society and political processes affecting tourism at government level. The book is organized in such a way that these issues are explained in a manner where the links between different elements of the tourism sector are addressed through examples and case studies. Each chapter builds upon the one preceding to develop the knowledge and understanding of what the tourism industry is, the management

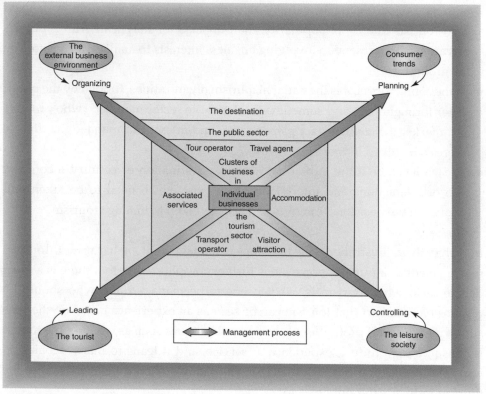

Figure 1.4   A framework for tourism management

challenges facing each sector and how tourism affects changes in different contexts. Accommodating, anticipating and responding to that level of change is one of the major challenges for tourism management in the new millennium.

This book seeks to examine how the tourism phenomenon has emerged as a part of modern society, as a prelude to discussing tourism as a business activity in Chapter 2. This is then followed by a review of why people engage in tourism in Chapter 3, focusing on the demand for tourism experiences. In Chapter 4, the discussion focuses on how the demand for tourism is met by the tourism industry and this provides an organizing framework for Chapters 5 to 8 which examine various facets of the tourism industry, namely transportation (the airline sector in Chapter 5), land-based transport (Chapter 6), the provision of accommodation and hospitality services (Chapter 7) and tour operations and retailing in Chapter 8. In Chapter 9, the significance of visitor attractions is discussed which provide a context for visitor activity and spending in destinations. In Chapter 10, the theme of tourism management is returned to as a context for understanding how tourism is organized, managed and developed in specific environments. This theme is pursued in a public sector context in Chapter 11. Both Chapters 10 and 11 provide the underpinning for Chapter 12, which discusses some of the practical issues and problems associated with managing visitors and sites of tourist activity. In Chapter 13, the future of tourism activity in a global context is reviewed, highlighting future issues and trends in the development of tourism.

References

Baudrillard, J. (1998) *The Consumer Society: Myths and Structures*. London: Sage.

Burkart, A. and Medlik, S. (1981) *Tourism, Past Present and Future*, 2nd edn. London: Heinemann.

Chadwick, R. (1994) Concepts, definitions and measures used in travel and tourism research. In J.R. Brent Ritchie and C. Goeldner (eds) *Travel, Tourism and Hospitality Research: A Handbook for Managers and Researchers*, 2nd edn. New York: Wiley.

Glaeßer, D. (2006) *Crisis Management in the Tourism Industry*. Oxford: Butterworth Heinemann.

Latham, J. (1989) The statistical measurement of tourism. In C.P. Cooper (ed.) *Progress in Tourism, Recreation and Hospitality Management, Vol. 1*. London: Belhaven.

Leiper, N. (1990) *Tourism Systems: An Interdisciplinary Perspective*. Palmerston North, New Zealand: Department of Management Systems Occasional Paper 2, Massey University.

Page, S. J. (1995) *Urban Tourism*. London: Routledge.

Further reading

The best international overview of tourism can be found in:

Page, S. J. and Connell, J. (2006) *Tourism: A Modern Synthesis*, 2nd edn. London: Thomson Learning.

Questions

1 Why is tourism such an important activity in the twenty-first century?

2 How would you classify tourists?

3 Why is tourism management important for a business operating in the tourism sector?

4 How stable is tourism as an economic activity?

2

Tourism: Its origins, growth and future

Learning outcomes

This chapter provides an historical perspective of the evolution of tourism as a business activity through the ages and some of the management challenges it has faced. After reading the chapter you should be able to understand:

- the underlying processes affecting tourism: continuity and change
- the importance of the resort life cycle
- the role of coastal resorts in leisure and tourism during the nineteenth and twentieth centuries
- the role of historical sources such as diaries in reconstructing past patterns of tourism activity
- the evolution of tourism in the post-war period
- the factors associated with the future trends in tourism development such as space tourism.

Introduction

Tourism is not a recent phenomenon. Whilst it was argued in the last chapter that tourism has become a widely accessible product in the consumer-led leisure society, the historical roots of tourism can be traced back almost to the origins of civilization. What the historical study of tourism indicates is that the nature of what tourists do in their leisure time may have changed, as technology has expanded the opportunities for travel. At the same time, tourism has evolved from being an activity which was the preserve of the 'leisured classes' (i.e. the aristocracy) who had both the leisure time and means to engage in travel, to a mass phenomenon. Throughout history, and even to a degree today, what distinguishes the higher social classes' experience of tourism from a mass product, is its highly individualized consumption when compared to the communal consumption of accommodation and transport, in particular, of the mass market experience. This chapter will show that through history tourism has varied in terms of its accessibility to different groups in society through history, and that the development of a leisure ethic and increased prosperity have created new tourism opportunities.

In any historical overview of tourism, two underlying themes are important: *continuity* and *change*. Continuity means that tourism has continued to be an important process, which remained influential in the leisure lifestyles of certain social classes. Change on the other hand characterizes the evolution of tourism through the ages, since tourism is a dynamic, ever-changing phenomenon. Much of the change is based upon the interaction between the demand for and supply of tourism opportunities through time. In terms of supply, key factors promoting the development of tourism can be explained by the role of innovations (i.e. new ideas) that have generated new products, experiences and destinations and released a latent or pent-up demand for tourism. Part of this change in tourism resulted from the innovations of individual entrepreneurs such as Thomas Cook in the nineteenth century, the introduction of new technology (e.g. the railway, the car and jet aircraft) in expanding the endless possibilities for tourist travel. In simple terms, destinations were developed for tourists and tourists visited them, creating an interaction which is implicit in all forms of tourism: a movement from origin area to destination and vice versa. The discovery and development of these destinations also exhibits elements of continuity and change through time as tourism is a dynamic activity which rarely remains static.

There are comparatively few studies documenting the long-term history of tourism, with many studies focused on specific eras or epochs in time. Much of historians' attention has focused on the evolution of mass tourism in both a domestic setting (i.e. the rise and demise of the English seaside resort) and international setting (i.e. the post-war growth and development of the package holiday). But equally important is the historical evolution of tourism from classical times since it established many of the principles of today's use of leisure time for holidays and travel.

Tourism in classical times

The ancient civilization of Greece was not so much important for any major development of tourism, but more for the Greek philosophers' recognition, endorsement and promotion of the concept of leisure, upon which tourism is based. Aristotle considered leisure to be a key element of the Greek lifestyle, where slaves and other people should do the work required and the Greek freemen should put their leisure time to good use.

This positive leisure doctrine may well have been the original 'leisure lifestyle', encouraged the pursuit of music, philosophy, non-work and measures of self-development as elements of Greek society. The development of the Olympic Games after 776 BC did provide a vital stimulus for tourism based upon a major sporting event. Greeks travelled to the site of the Olympic Games and were housed in tented encampments, creating a tourism event. International travel in Greek times was limited due to the Greek wars.

In contrast, the rise of Rome and the Roman Empire was based upon the twin elements of military conquest and administration. The state and private individuals created leisure facilities (i.e. spas, baths and resorts) and enjoyed similar leisure lifestyles to the Greeks. The construction of colosseums for events and spectator sports, as epitomized in the recent film *Gladiator*, created the supply of tourism-related facilities. Therefore, two elements of tourism can be discerned in Roman society: first, domestic tourism focused on urban places where the resorts and facilities/events existed, so that the middle classes in Roman society had somewhere to spend their 200 holidays a year. Second, the conquest of overseas territories and their administration created a demand for business-related travel related to the territorial management and control of these peoples. The middle classes also had expanded opportunities to travel afforded by new territories, trade and the provision of roads linking the Roman origin area to seaside resorts, summer villas and historical sites, which might be visited for health, pleasure and spiritual reasons.

Rome also emerged as an important urban tourism destination because of its capital city function. To service tourist needs, inns, bars and tour guides as well as souvenir sellers developed. In this respect, many elements of modern tourism were established in Roman times, which were mainly made possible by the political stability and provision of infrastructure and facilities and were stimulated by a prosperity among the middle classes who enjoyed travel for leisure and business.

The Middle Ages

In the years following the demise of the Roman Empire, historians have described the years from 500 AD through to the accession of Henry VII in 1485 as the Middle Ages. The early part of this period has also been described as the Dark Ages, a time when the civilization and progress of the Roman era declined. In place of the pleasure-seeking society of the Roman era, the rise of Christianity and the development of monastic orders saw a society evolve which was based on landed estates, a feudal system of peasants and nobility. Yet even in these seemingly dark times, tourism can be discerned with the emergence of festival and event-based tourism stimulated by the activities of the nobility and knights. Jousting tournaments and spectatorship from peasants and other nobility saw a demand emerge for temporary accommodation and travel to these events.

From the later part of the Middle Ages, pilgrims to the Holy Land emerged. Travel was difficult due to the poor quality of access, although this poor access created a demand for accommodation and hospitality services (e.g. food, drink and entertainment) en route. The limited amounts of business travel to centres of commerce across Europe and farther afield were modest in comparison with the present.

The Renaissance and Reformation

The Renaissance originated in Italy after 1350 and reached its zenith in England during Elizabethan times. The earlier trends in festivals and fairs continued, again forming a nucleus of domestic tourism activity. The rise of travelling theatres and the patronage of the arts created opportunities for travel. The Reformation, in contrast, emerged after 1500 with the ideas of Luther and Calvin with their religious zeal that created what has been termed the Protestant work ethic. This is a notable turning point in the history of leisure and thereby tourism, as these Lutheran and Calvinistic ideas questioned the value of leisure, portraying it as idleness, when individuals should devote themselves to a life of good work rather than leisure and enjoyment of pleasure. These ideas can be seen more clearly in the rise of the industrial society, where leisure was denigrated by the capitalists and entrepreneurs who needed to create a more profitable economy.

However, throughout the history of tourism, women remain generally hidden as tourists in the same way that in Europe, the leisure and tourism activities of different social classes began to be separated. In one of the most influential studies of the history of tourism, Towner (1996) explains how the upper classes withdrew from popular culture (i.e. popular activities, pastimes and travel). Likewise the affluent also began to move from town to country for tourism purposes (rest and relaxation) on both a short-term and a long-term basis. This led to the building of rural villas from the Roman period to the Renaissance and again in the eighteenth and nineteenth centuries, creating exclusive forms of rural recreation. In Italy, this process of withdrawing to a country villa was called *villeggiatura* during the Renaissance. In England, the sale of Church lands after the dissolution of the monasteries by Henry VIII freed vast areas of land that provided the basis for country estates as places for recreation and tourism.

Another important development in tourism that originated in the sixteenth century was the Grand Tour, which emerged as an aristocratic form of tourism.

The European Grand Tour

The 'Grand Tour' was a traveller's circuit of key destinations and places to visit in Europe, mainly by the wealthy, aristocratic and privileged classes in pursuit of culture, education and pleasure. The origins of such tours can be discerned in those elements of Roman society that travelled to Greece in pursuit of culture and education. As a form of tourism, it reached its peak in the eighteenth century. Some commentators have gone as far as to suggest it was the forerunner of the modern overseas holiday.

Within western Europe, the Grand Tour is recounted in the diaries, letters and memoirs of travellers as well as being documented in guidebooks and historical records associated with tourism. According to the most detailed research on the Grand Tour by Towner (1985, 1996) the typical tourists in the sixteenth century were young aristocrats who were accompanied by tutors, although this may be an oversimplification. By the eighteenth century, the emerging middle classes formed a growing element of Grand Tourists. Towner (1985) estimated that in the mid-eighteenth century between 15 000 and 20 000 British participants toured continental Europe, around 0.2–0.7 per cent of the population.

Much of the interest in the Grand Tour can be related to the Renaissance and emergence of interest in classical antiques, promoted by learning and developments in philosophy that encouraged travel to expand the human mind. This emerging travel culture which was centred on mainland Europe saw a growing link to knowledge and interest in the classics, art and the appreciation of architecture and an intellectual thought prior to the expansion of mass forms of education and learning. The Grand Tour was far from a static entity as ideas from Europe were imparted back to England and changing fashions and tastes in the interests of Grand Tourists can also be discerned between 1550s and early 1800s. For example, the emergence of interest in landscape and scenery viewing from the 1760s and a wider range of pursuits characterized such tours. The coming of the railway in each area combined with the expansion of the tourism industry. Figures 2.1 and 2.2 illustrate some of the typical Grand Tour routes taken in Europe and the dominance of certain centres (i.e. Paris, Turin, Florence, Naples and Rome). The rise in popularity of Switzerland as a consequence of this pursuit of scenery was also notable, with new modes of transport on land, inland waterways and rivers (e.g. the appearance of steamers on Swiss lakes in the 1820s) creating opportunities for scenic tourism. In the UK, travellers such as Celia Fiennes during the 1680s and Daniel Defoe in the 1720s reflected the traits of the European Grand Tour in their changing attitudes to landscapes and scenery as elements of tourism. The Romantic poets, including Wordsworth, spearheaded the discovery of England's Lake District in the 1790s onwards while Walter Scott's novels glamorized Scotland. Writers and artists were drawn to these landscapes with their scenic qualities. A similar interest in landscape and wilderness can be observed in the new world (i.e. the USA) in the same period, and after 1830 this was popularized by American literature (e.g. *The Last of the Mohicans* in 1826) and the concept of the Western frontier.

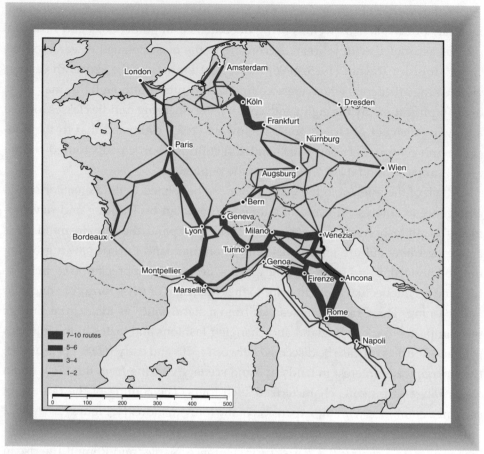

Figure 2.1   Grand Tour routes in Europe, 1661–1700 (© Elsevier). Reprinted from *Annals of Tourism Research*, vol. 12, J. Towner, The Grand Tour: A key phase in the history of tourism: 297–333 © 1985 with permission from Elsevier

An enduring theme from Elizabethan times was the growth of spas as a form of tourism development and it reflects both the continuity and change in the history of tourism.

Some researchers have attempted to explain the growth, stagnation and decline of tourist resorts such as spas in terms of a resort life cycle. The work of Butler, published in 1980, suggested that resorts follow a specific cycle of growth. The initial exploration by tourists is followed by a period of involvement, often with patronage by a royal figure who started a trend towards visitation (e.g. King George III visiting Weymouth in England) or by its wider popularization as a resort for the

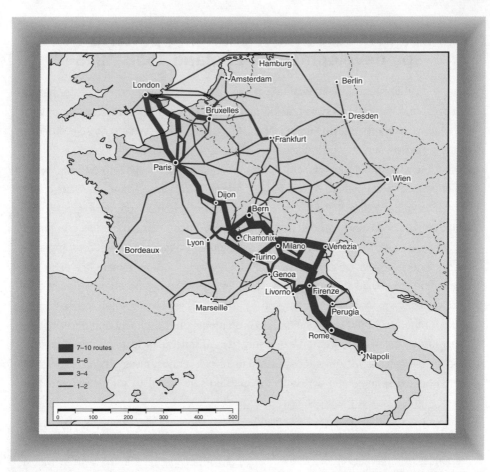

Figure 2.2   Grand Tour routes in Europe, 1814–1820 (© Elsevier). Reprinted from *Annals of Tourism Research*, vol. 12, J. Towner, The Grand Tour: A key phase in the history of tourism: 297–333 © 1985 with permission from Elsevier

elite to visit. This set the stage and created tourism tastes and fashions emulated by the visitors. The next stage of Butler's model is development, followed by consolidation and then stagnation. At this point, the resort may decline or action may be taken by agents of development (i.e. an entrepreneur, the public sector or a combination of both) to rejuvenate the resort, and this rejuvenation is the last stage of the model. Figure 2.3 illustrates this pattern through time and shows the creation (i.e. birth) and decline (i.e. death) of resorts. Although such models are highly generalized and simplify the reality of resort development, they are a starting point for the analyses of resorts such as spas through history.

Box 2.1 Case Study: Changing patterns of spa development in England 1558–1815

There is a long historical tradition of taking mineral waters during tourist trips for health and pleasure in Western society that can be dated back to Roman times. These *aquae*, as they were known, were distributed throughout the Roman territories. What is notable, in terms of the continuity and change in the history of tourism, is that they declined after Roman times (i.e. changed) but formed the basis for the future growth of spa resorts in later times (i.e. continued). Examples are Bath in the UK, Aquae Calidae in Vichy, Aquae Mattiacae in Germany and hot springs in the Bay of Naples. Whilst many Roman spas were less exclusive than those designed for later users, in some countries (Hungary), spas continued in use from Roman times to the Middle Ages. But why did spas develop as sites for tourist consumption?

At a general level, certain factors were a prerequisite for development: the existence of a spring to provide the waters, individuals or agents to promote development and favourable conditions relating to accessibility and trends which promoted spa visiting. In addition, the associated development of accommodation, hospitality and ancillary services, often coalesced to comprise a distinct spa resort. In fact, in colonial America, Philadelphia had spas at Abington, Bristol and Yellow Springs; these urban centres supported nearby springs, and access to the outlying springs led to the development of resorts and facilities in the urban centres.

In many spas that developed in England between 1660 and 1815, patronage by royalty, the nobility and the growing affluent classes stimulated demand. Entrepreneurs, public authorities or a partnership of both led to the growth of spas (e.g. Bath), with individual landowners amongst the gentry or aristocracy providing the land and thus the basis for tourism-based speculative development. In Harrogate in Yorkshire, public-sector promotion by the Corporation in the 1720s provided the basis for development as did the Federal Parks Department in Canada at Radium Hot Springs in the 1920s. In some cases, such as Rotorua in New Zealand, the advances in spa-based health treatments (e.g. hydropathy) saw the New Zealand Tourism and Publicity Department manage and promote the major facilities as a basis to stimulate tourism development. In Scotland, however, late Victorian and Edwardian entrepreneurs created a range of successful and unsuccessful hydro hotels providing the focal point of a spa and health tourism at locations such as Dunblane and Crieff.

What these examples illustrate is that spa development has a longevity in historical terms, whilst factors promoting the growth of some resorts (e.g. the advent of the railway age) led to the continued prosperity of some resorts such as Buxton, Harrogate and Llandrindod Wells whilst others declined due to reduced access, changing tastes and oversupply, particularly those offering niche products such as hydrotherapy.

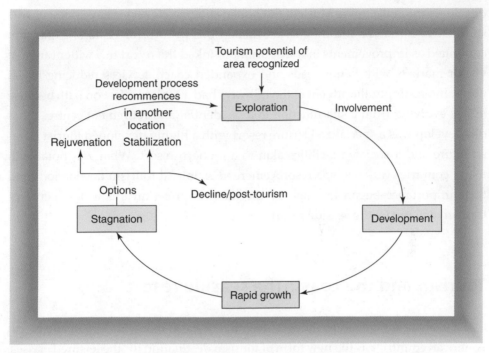

Figure 2.3   The resort life cycle (developed and modified from R. Butler, 1980)

For example, in England, 173 rural spas were created between 1558 and 1815, many of which had a short existence compared to their urban counterparts. Whilst certain spas had an enduring history (i.e. Buxton and Bath), others such as Wellingborough were in existence in the late 1600s but had disappeared by 1711. Probably the most well-known example of spa development is Bath in England. It emerged from its Roman origins with an enduring pattern of visitation during the Middle Ages due to the medicinal value of its waters. One illustration of its rapid expansion was its rise in population from under 2000 in the 1660s to 13 000 in the 1760s and 33 000 in 1801 mainly as the spa-based growth of the town continued. Patronage of Bath initially, in the sixteenth century, was by visitors from London and southern England, then gradually expanded to a national market that included courtiers, the aristocracy, gentry, clergy and professional classes (both the infirm and those of good health seeking cures and preventative medicine). Some estimates of visitor numbers suggest that 8000 tourists visited annually in the early 1700s, rising to 12 000 by the 1750s and 40 000 by 1800. The visiting season was expanded (initially July to mid-August), providing the basis for further investment and development in the town. Much of the public and private sector development was speculative in nature and the market fuelled this in turn for visitors. Expansion continued as improvements in transportation linked the resort to a wider range of visitor markets with better roads and expanded coach services reducing travel times. Interestingly, the advent of the railways had a limited effect on Bath because it was evolving from a spa function to a residential and retirement centre. What did develop was a specialized leisure resort with a highly developed tourist infrastructure and associated facilities akin to a modern resort. What was notable in many countries was that spa resorts emerged as inland tourism destinations and their importance began to wane by the nineteenth century as a new genre of tourism emerged – the seaside resort.

Tourism and the coast: The seaside resort

Coastal areas emerged in the late eighteenth century in many European and North American countries as the new form of tourism destination for the leisured classes. This was at a time when spas and other inland resorts were still expanding, as Figure 2.4 shows in the case of the eastern seaboard of the USA. The coast up to the eighteenth century had been a revered landscape, where religious ideals, cultural attitudes and tastes had not encouraged coastal visiting: on the contrary, the coast was considered an environment to avoid due to the forces of nature and evil. During the eighteenth century, the impact of poets, artists (such as Constable) and romanticists led to the beach and coastline being discovered as a site for pleasure, a place for spiritual fulfilment and for tourism as bathing slowly developed as a social and leisure activity between 1750 and 1840.

A number of key landmarks in the early history of coastal tourism can be recognized, including:

- Dr Russell's (1752) treatise on the use of seawater for health reasons as well as bathing
- the popularization of sea-bathing by royal patronage (e.g. George III bathing at Weymouth in the late eighteenth century)
- royal patronage of resorts (e.g. Brighton by the Prince Regent)
- the combining of health reasons to visit with pleasure and fashion

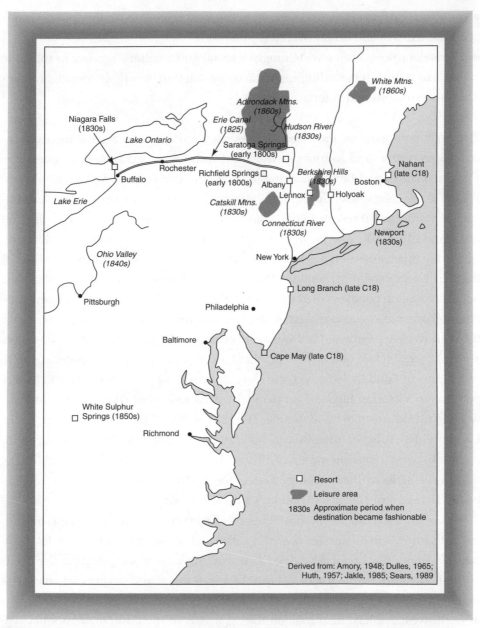

Figure 2.4 The development of selected leisure destinations in the eastern USA by the mid-nineteenth century (source: *An Historical Geography of Recreation and Tourism*, J. Towner, 1996. © John Wiley and Sons Ltd. Reproduced with permission)

- the search by Europe's social elite, from the late eighteenth century onwards, for more exclusive and undiscovered destinations
- the rise of resorts with a wide range of social and ancillary services to meet the needs of visitors (i.e. reading rooms, accommodation, assembly rooms, promenades, excursions and entertainment).

The early patronage by the upper classes soon gave way to a growing access to coastal recreation and tourism as transport technology made resorts accessible. The provision of paddle steamers in the 1820s between London and the Kent coast resorts is one example of this. The railway era, from the 1840s onwards, also connected many coastal resorts to the main sources of demand – the urban industrial heartland of the UK. The major cities provided the principal sources of demand. But while much attention has focused on the growth in coastal tourism, in the UK the 1851 Great Exhibition heralded the early establishment of the package holiday. Some six million people visited the Great Exhibition in 1851 in London, many purchasing organized accommodation and travel from travel clubs (by saving up through weekly payments) or from agents such as Thomas Cook. Some travellers arrived by rail while others from Scotland journeyed by steamer, spending up to two nights in London. However, the real sustained changes to tourism and leisure patterns in Victorian England (in parallel with many other countries worldwide) was the introduction of holiday time. The 1871 and 1875 Bank Holiday Acts in the UK provided four statutory days' holiday, giving workers the opportunity to engage in coastal tourism more fully. These Acts made the coastal resorts in the UK more accessible to the working classes; the middle-class workers had already begun to take more extensive holidays from the 1850s.

A social differentiation in coastal resorts also existed, where developers, municipal authorities and businesses positively attracted certain types of visitor. In northwest England, Blackpool developed as a working-class resort, meeting the needs of the Lancashire textile towns, where cheap rail travel and savings schemes promoted holidaytaking. The different timings of industrial holidays in various towns in north-west England also enabled resorts to extend the traditional summer season, so that accommodation and hospitality services had a wider range of business opportunities and resorts such as Blackpool developed a highly specialized tourism industry.

In terms of the supply of coastal resorts in England and Wales, no major population centre was more than 70–80 miles from a coastal area. In the eighteenth century, a number of early resorts such as Scarborough combined a spa and coastal tourism trade; the majority of resorts were in southern England due to their proximity to London and its large population. During the industrialization and urbanization of England in the late eighteenth and early nineteenth century, a number of other regional markets developed in south-west England and in a limited number of northern and Welsh locations. By 1851, a continuous growth of resorts from Devon to Kent emerged in southern England, complemented by the rising popularity of the Isle of Wight, Wales, north-west and eastern England. By 1881 growing access to the coast led to more specialized resorts, with specific markets emerging, and the growing social divide of visitors to certain resorts (i.e. the middle classes went to Bournemouth and the working classes to Southend, Margate and Blackpool). By 1911, the current-day pattern of resorts was well established, although oversupply and seasonality were common problems for the holiday trade in these resorts. In Scotland, resort development in western districts dependent upon the urban population of Glasgow provided a wide range of opportunities, where the integration of rail and steamers provided a complex system of destinations by the 1880s.

Running parallel to the mass tourism phenomenon of the coastal resorts were the origins of the modern tourism industry, with the emergence of commercially organized tourism by Thomas Cook. Cook organized the first package tours, initially utilizing the Victorian railway system (Leicester to Loughborough in 1841), with railway tours to Scotland in 1848 and overseas tours in the 1850s. In 1866, Cook organized his first tours to America and passenger cruises on the River Nile in the 1880s. Other entrepreneurs, including Henry Lunn, also organized overseas packages for skiing in Switzerland in the 1880s and the upper and middle classes engaged in new overseas tours as well as domestic tourism to coastal resorts.

Tourism in the Edwardian and inter-war years

By the 1900s, coastal tourism, overseas travel by passenger liner and the rise of socially segregated travel offered a wider range of international holiday options to the elite in Western society. The imperial trade of many European powers also created a demand for business travel and limited volumes of recreational travel. For example, by 1914 up to 150 000 American visitors entered the UK each year. The Edwardian years saw the continued expenditure of the middle classes on overseas travel and a growing fascination with rural and scenic areas, popularized by the pursuit of outdoor activities such as shooting and hunting in the Highlands of Scotland and cycling. Almost 10 per cent of *Black's Shilling Guide to Scotland* (1906) was devoted to cycling, using hotels and other accommodation establishments. The railway extended access to mountain climbing activities in the Highlands (i.e. the Ladies Scottish Climbing Club was founded in 1908), reflecting the growing emancipation of women and their role of travellers in Edwardian society. Hiking also emerged as a popular activity, with the rise of the Scottish Youth Hostels Association in 1931. The emergence of sleeper services on long-distance rail routes encouraged middle classes to travel further afield.

One of the historical sources that enables us to understand how and where the Edwardians travelled is the guidebooks. An interesting example is the *Queens Newspaper Book of Travel* (1910), which had been published annually since 1903 and was compiled by a travel editor who was a geographer. This provides descriptions of places visitors from the UK might visit domestically and overseas, or where they might be stationed in the British Empire. It has candid insights as this extract on visiting Rangoon, in Imperial Burma, shows:

> A damp place; and the first feeling on arrival is generally one of prostration, followed by slight ague and fever; but this in robust people soon passes away, and although Rangoon is not regarded as a healthy station, yet of late years sanitary improvements have somewhat bettered its climate … All clothing should be packed in airtight cases. One requires an abundant supply of Indian gauze underclothing (not less than three changes a day, even to corsets).

Guidebooks like this also highlight a neglected feature of tourism history: the development of business travel to manage colonies. They also reveal the travel activities of the colonists, such as the seasonal migration of British in India to hill settlements in the summer to avoid the high temperatures of the lowland cities. Similarly, the rise of tourism between the colonial mother country and the colonies has not been accorded much attention, although it tends to follow the resort life cycle: following the exploration and colonization, tourism developed initially through business travel, then visits to family and relatives and then trips to different destinations. These patterns would appear to have developed across the colonial continents of Africa, Asia and the Pacific islands in parallel with the overt exploitation of the indigenous labour and resource base.

The guidebook is also useful in providing detailed itineraries published from actual tours taken by users of the Guide Book. For example Box 2.2, entitled 'A Tour of Scotland', is a diary of a trip and places visited during that trip. It highlights a diversity of transport modes and was clearly an extensive tour by someone

Box 2.2 Diary of a tour of Scotland

Departs London *August 14th*, heading to Glasgow *August 15th*, visited Glasgow Cathedral, parks and the Art Gallery.

August 16th, made a trip by rail from Glasgow Central Station and then by steamer from Weymss Bay to Ardishaig; lunch and tea on board.

August 17th, left Glasgow Central by rail for Loch Lomond, steamer to the Inversnaid Hotel; many fishermen staying in the hotel; sport fair in the loch.

August 18th, drove to Stronachlacher, thence by steamer and coach to the Trossachs Hotel; lunched there, and thence to Callander by coach – a most enjoyable trip. Took train via St Fillians to Crieff (Drummond Arms Hotel), and stayed one night there.

August 19th, by early train to Loch Awe (via Loch Earn Side – an enchanting journey). We then took the steamer from Loch Awe Station and Hotel; thence a short journey by train to Oban.

August 20th, spent Sunday in Oban.

August 21st, by early steamer to Fort William (Prince Charlie's country), and thence through the Caledonian Canal to Inverness; Palace Hotel (good bedrooms).

August 22nd, left for train to Aberdeen. In Aberdeen, the Grand Hotel is at present time looked upon as the best.

August 23rd, by train to Ballater (lunch), and thence by motor omnibus to Braemar (Invercauld Arms), where we met with every attention; good food, pleasant rooms.

August 24th, by coach across Spital of Glenshee to Blairgowrie, and on to Dunkeld. The Birman Hotel is excellent.

August 25th, in Dunkeld.

August 26th, by rail to Aberfeldy, coach to Kenmore, thence by steamer down Loch Tay to Killin, where we again took the train for Callander (Dreadnought Hotel).

August 27th, in Callander (Sunday).

August 28th, by rail from Callander to Edinburgh (Princes Street) (Caledonian Railway Company's Station Hotel).

August 29th, left Edinburgh (Princes Street section) for London by West Coast Mail Route.

Source: Queens Newspaper Book of Travel (1910: 106)

from the leisured classes as it is over two weeks in duration – a luxury that many of the working classes could not afford in Edwardian Britain.

Such itineraries were encouraged by the railway companies, who published illustrated guides, such as the *Through Scotland* (priced 3d and produced by the Caledonian Railway Company), which was 170 pages and illustrated, as well as free hotel and furnished lodgings guides. Advertisers in the *Queens Newspaper Book of Travel* also promoted hotels and accommodation as well as travel products.

The First World War (1914–1918) slowed the growth of international tourism, although domestic tourism continued in a number of countries, as its R&R (rest and recuperation) function after the ravages of war provided a renewed boost for many resorts. A report in the *The Times* newspaper on 2 December 1918 entitled 'Crowded Out', observed the shortage of accommodation for soldiers visiting London on leave and outlined the arrangements the military had made for obtaining hotel rooms for them. It described the prices fixed by the military and the agreement for officers staying in the West End of London for 6s 6d through to the cost of first-class hotels in the same district of between 10s 6d and 12s 6d. These rates covered the cost of 'bed, lights, bath and breakfast', whilst for 5s a further 5000 rooms had been made available in London by families for troops on domestic home leave. There is a widespread debate on the impact of the war on global travel as most studies of tourism assume it curtailed travel other than troop movements, since this is how researchers depict the impact of war on tourist travel. Yet what is interesting is that *The Times* carried daily advertisements for travel between the UK and many of the colonies and dominion on cruise liners owned by White Star, Cunard Line, Union Line, Nippon Yasen Kaisha, the Orient Line, P&O and City and Hall Lines, for example, as well as Royal Mail steamers, to New Zealand, Australia, South Africa, Hong Kong, Singapore, the USA, Canada and the Mediterranean. These advertisements were not related to troop movements, but to travel for business and pleasure. Therefore, tourism did not cease although *The Times* on 10 December 1918 carried an article advising people against travel on the cross-channel routes to France and Belgium due to congestion on these routes from troop movements.

The depression in industrial economies during the 1920s and 1930s suppressed the demand for international and domestic tourism from all those but the wealthiest, although recreational pursuits replaced some of the demand for travel and new forms of low-cost tourism such as working holidays emerged among poorer working-class families (e.g. Londoners from the East End picking hops in Kent in the autumn). Mechanization in the post-war period gradually removed some of these tourism opportunities, but also created new ones. The construction of second homes on plots of land in the green belt or coastal areas by the working classes in the 1930s was a new, chaotic and unplanned form of domestic tourism. Many such dwellings were subsequently removed by planning acts in the 1930s and 1940s.

Statistical accounts of tourism from the Edwardian and inter-war period give a number of insights about those who were able to travel abroad. An interesting study published in 1933 by Ogilvie, *The Tourist Movement: An Economic Study*, is one of the first systematic studies of the statistical analysis of tourism in the UK tracing tourist movements back to the Edwardian period. It also contains a wealth of data on tourism in other European countries and much of the detail which historians of tourism require to trace the development of tourism as an economic activity. For example, it analyses the problem of measuring tourist numbers and much of the discussion pre-dates the latter discussion of tourist definitions by bodies like the World Tourism Organization (UN-WTO). Using Board of Trade figures, Table 2.1 identifies the flow of British subjects living in the UK who travelled to Europe between 1913 and 1931 and the problems of measurement. It also shows that the flow of travel between the UK and Europe (excluding the First World War) was roughly equal in each direction and grew from around 760 000 to just over a million trips by 1931. Estimates of overseas British visitors (typically from colonial countries) and overseas visitors from other countries who travelled to the UK are shown in Table 2.2. Again, the estimates show that around 500 000–600 000 trips were made to the UK in the 1920s and early 1930s.

In terms of outbound travel from the UK, Table 2.3 shows that British residents and overseas residents trips overseas are not dramatically dissimilar to many of the patterns we observe today. Around 80 per cent of trips were to Europe and the Mediterranean and around 20 per cent were further afield, with much of this travel being dependent upon shipping routes and cruise lines (see also Plates 2.1 and 2.2). Ogilvie (1933) also indicated that these patterns of travel were highly seasonal with the summer (June to September) accounting for around 40 per cent of all trips. The limited growth of air traffic was evident from the records beginning in 1924 when 9563 outbound UK-to-Europe trips were made which grew to 11 295 in 1925, to 22 388 in 1928 and 24 294 in 1931. Similarly, the growth in use of the car as a form of travel to Europe by British residents is apparent from records of the Royal Automobile Club (RAC) and Automobile Association (AA) with around 15 000 overseas travellers crossing to and from Europe and 50 000–60 000 British residents making the same crossing. Ogilvie also documented the rise of

Table 2.1 British subjects, resident in the United Kingdom or overseas, travelling between the United Kingdom and Europe, 1913 and 1921–1931 (source: Ogilvie, 1933)

Year	Inward from Europe	Outward to Europe	Balance inward
1913	763 420	761 019	2 401
1921	561 903	553 099	8 804
1922	640 392	639 050	1 342
1923 (a)	783 644	777 191	6 453
1924	826 684	811 880	14 804
1925	927 618	924 083	3 535
1926	969 712	959 559	10 153
1927	1 002 350	976 494	25 856
1928	1 113 831	1 093 715	20 116
1929	1 115 100	1 093 798	21 302
1930 (b)	1 151 688	1 125 125	26 563
1931	1 077 477	1 029 991	47 486

(a) From 1 April 1923, the figures exclude traffic with the Irish Free State.
(b) Tables I, V, and VI of the annual *Statistics in regard to alien passengers*. In the *Board of Trade Journal* of March 3, 1932, p. 306, the number of British passengers inward in 1930 is given as 1 138 881, the result of subtracting 411 110 aliens from a total of 1 549 991 passengers. This figure for aliens, however, is 12 807 too high, the compiler having apparently added together aliens from Europe (373 757) and *all* transmigrants inward (37 353), instead of only transmigrants *from Europe* (24 546), as had been correctly done for 1929 and previous years. The same *Journal* gives the number of British passengers outward in 1930 as 1 100 377, based upon an aliens total of 404 480, which I do not understand; the correct total of aliens, including transmigrants *to Europe*, being 379 732 (which is adopted for the calculation in the text) and the incorrect total resulting from the inclusion of *all* outward transmigrants being 404 350.

sea traffic between mainland UK and the Irish Free State (Eire, which was formed in 1923) which grew from around 250 000 trips a year in 1923 to 370 000 by 1931.

In the 1930s, a number of interesting insights into the tourism activities of the population are provided by Rowntree's (1941) *Poverty and Progress: A Second Social Survey of York* based on research from 1935. Rowntree found, among a largely working-class population in the town of York, that there was a growth in interest in the Youth Hostel Association among those under 25 years of age, with 4753 guest nights spent in York's youth hostel each year. The research also showed the importance of worker organizations, such as the Cooperative Holiday Association and its later off-shoot, the Cooperative Holiday Fellowship, in promoting holidays in the outdoors

Table 2.2 Visitors to the United Kingdom, 1921–1931 (source: Ogilvie, 1933)

Year	Foreigners	Overseas – British	Total
1921	318 463	131 400	449 863
1922	299 313	143 361	442 674
1923	331 822	168 039	499 861
1924	380 472	201 375	581 847
1925	365 568	199 492	565 060
1926	366 224	206 251	572 475
1927	418 485	214 729	633 214
1928	441 243	237 987	679 230
1929	451 659	240 345	692 004
1930	444 479	243 617	688 096
1931	351 338	217 808	569 146

as part of the health and fitness movement. Some of this was attributed by Rowntree to the reduction in working hours since 1900 from a typical 54-hour week in a factory to a 44- to 48-hour week. A similarly rich source of historical evidence on the holiday habits, activities and behaviour of the British population in the late 1930s is the Mass-Observation project. The Mass-Observation social research organization was set up in 1937 to collate an anthropology of the British population using a wide range of survey methods, including participant observation. The records along with other sources such as diaries are kept at the University of Sussex, UK. One interesting feature of this project was that it confirms what many historians suggest, that holidays were firmly embedded in working-class culture. For example, when a sample of the population were asked what they would economize on, holidays (irrespective of social class) were deemed to be important elements not to be sacrificed.

Probably the most influential development in the 1930s was the rise of the holiday camp, epitomized by the entrepreneur Billy Butlin. In 1936 Butlin bought a plot of 40 acres of land in Skegness and built the first holiday camp, with holidays at between 35 shillings and £3 a week advertised in the *Daily Express* newspaper. In the 1920s only 17 per cent of the population had paid holidays and during the 1930s only three million of the population had holiday with pay. This had changed

Plate 2.1　Thomas Cook provided ever more adventurous travel options for British citizens in the 1920s and 1930s to the Far East reflecting the growing network of cruises and shipping networks

Plate 2.2   1930s Thomas Cook Nile voyage, which was rediscovered and re-promoted in the 1980s and 1990s with great success by the company

Table 2.3 United Kingdom residents abroad, 1921–1931 (source: Ogilvie, 1933)

Year	British residents		Foreign residents returning	Total
	Returning from outside Europe	Crossing to Europe and the Mediterranean		
1921	19 488	480 165	60 252	559 905
1922	20 095	555 974	61 117	637 186
1923	22 334	676 156	59 521	758 011
1924	21 928	698 217	53 404	773 549
1925	26 453	803 952	53 272	883 677
1926	27 170	834 816	53 601	915 587
1927	29 261	849 550	51 005	929 816
1928	31 935	951 532	51 486	1 034 953
1929	32 717	951 604	48 701	1 033 022
1930	32 451	978 859	47 626	1 058 936
1931	27 970	896 092	42 441	966 503

by 1939 when 11 million people in the UK received holidays with pay and Butlins attracted almost 100 000 visitors to Skegness and to a second camp at Clacton in Essex. It is estimated that by 1948 one in twenty holidaymakers stayed at Butlins camps. The origins of the holiday camp concept can be traced to the organized workers associations cycling and tent camps earlier in the twentieth century. By 1939, a wide range of such camps emerged as planned commercialized resorts which provided a fantasy world and offered relatively cheap domestic holidays. At the same time, second homes developed as a more widespread phenomenon in many countries. Greater advertising, promotion and marketing by tour operators, resorts, transport providers (i.e. the railways and shipping companies), combined with the popularization of travel in guidebooks, saw inter-war tourism begin to acquire many of the hallmarks of commercialized travel that continued into the post-war period.

The Second World War impeded the growth of international tourism. Yet even on the eve of the Second World War in 1939, fewer than 50 per cent of the British population spent more than one night away from home. However, the number of car owners had risen from 200 000 people in 1920 to two million in 1939. Other notable developments were the emergence of embryonic passenger airline services challenging the dominant passenger liners, and providing the seeds of the post-war transformation of many societies to adopt the overseas travel bug. In other parts of the world, such as communist Russia, the state used tourism as an organized form of R&R for workers, with sanatoria and resorts developed along the Black Sea and in other locations. For the elite, holiday homes (dachas) near the urban centres were also developed.

Access to new forms of transport (notably road-based) in the inter-war period, opened up the countryside and a wider range of domestic tourism destinations to the population in many countries. The emergence of new forms of domestic tourism (i.e. the holiday camp), cruise liners and air travel led to changing tastes and trends in holidaytaking. Whilst many resorts and transport providers responded to a widening range of opportunities for travel and holidaying, with the use of marketing and promotion, the real rise of mass tourism was a post-war phenomenon.

Post-war tourism: Towards international mass tourism

In Chapter 1 the trend in international tourism, dating back to the 1950s, illustrated the phenomenal growth in international travel, which was punctuated by drops and troughs in demand. Many of the current trends in tourism can be dated to the post-war period, particularly the rise in demand for holidays. This period saw a growth in income, leisure time and opportunities for international travel. In the immediate post-war period, surplus military aircraft were converted to passenger services and the 1950s saw the introduction of jet airliners. As airlines bought new jets, older aircraft became available to charter holiday companies to operate services to holiday destinations. In the UK Vladimir Raitz is credited with offering the first air-related package holiday, subsequently developing Horizon Holidays (now part of Thomson Holidays) and he was soon followed by a number of other tour operators. By 1959, 2.25 million Britons took foreign trips, 76 769 of which were to Spain. In 1966, 94 per cent of these overseas trips were to Europe; this number dropped to 86 per cent in 1974 as other destinations were developed.

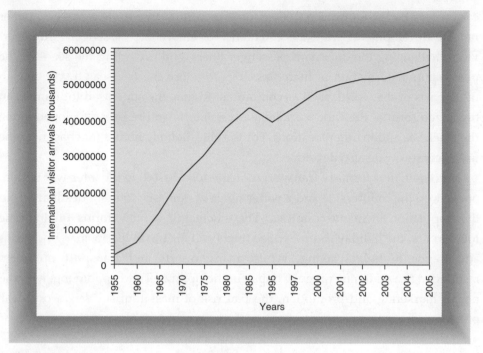

Figure 2.5 The growth of tourism in Spain

Figure 2.5 shows the rise of the package holiday in Spain, which led to the growth of Mediterranean resorts. By 1965, Spain had become Europe's leading tourism destination with 14 million visitors a year (which had grown to nearly 48 million in 2001). Spain saw its share of the UK holiday market rise from 6 per cent in 1951 to 30 per cent in 1968. In the late 1960s package holidays to Mallorca cost £30, which was equivalent to a week's salary. The ill-fated Clarkson's tour operator saw the number of its clients grow from 16 000 in 1966 to 90 000 in 1967, a sign of the massive growth in package holidays. Consumer spending on domestic holidays rose by 80 per cent between 1951 and 1968, and on overseas holidays by 400 per cent. In 1951 a UK holiday cost on average £11, a foreign holiday £41. By 1968 the prices were £20 and £62 respectively and the numbers of Clarkson's clients had risen to 175 000. However, the oil crisis in the 1970s, Arab–Israeli war and the oil embargo of 1973 saw fuel price increases which led to a massive drop in tourist travel. In 1974, Clarkson's collapsed with tourists stranded in 75 resorts in 26 coastal areas. This resulted, in part, from a sustained price war among tour operators in the UK.

During the 1960s the numbers taking foreign holidays was set to rise by 230 per cent and by 1967 there were five million British holidaymakers going abroad.

This rose to 7.25 million in 1971 and 8.5 million in 1972 but dropped to 6.75 million in 1974 due to the oil crisis. Yet throughout this period, the proportion of the population *not* taking a holiday remained almost constant at around 40 per cent and this is similar to the proportion recorded in the 1990s.

In the 1970s, 1980s and 1990s there was an increasing proliferation of tourism products and experiences, and a growing global reach for travel. The growth in leisure time, however, did not lead to a major change in the proportion of people taking holidays. For example, in the UK the proportion of people taking a holiday of four days or more (a long holiday) stayed constant from 1971–1998. What has changed is the number taking two or more holidays: this has risen 15 per cent to 25 per cent in that period. In the period 1950–1988 UK spending on holidays increased sixfold in real terms. Therefore, changes in supply (i.e. by the tourism industry) and demand have seized upon the rise in consumer spending and associated factors such as:

- changes in demand for domestic and international travel, particularly business travel, new markets in visiting friends and relatives (VFR) (e.g. reunions among migrant groups) and the pursuit of new travel experiences
- transportation improvements, especially the introduction of jet aircraft, the wide-bodied jet (i.e. the DC10 and Boeing 747 jumbo jet), and the proliferation of high-speed trains and larger aircraft such as the new Airbus A380
- the development of new forms of holiday accommodation (i.e. the change from the holiday camp to timeshare, self-catering and second homes)
- innovations by tour operators, including the rise of the holiday brochure, new forms of retailing such as direct selling, buying via the internet, more competitive pricing and the evolution of one-stop shop retailing (i.e. the package, insurance, holiday currency, airport transfers and pre-flight accommodation and car parking)
- greater availability of information on destinations to visit from the media, brochures, guidebooks, the internet and travel programmes
- increased promotion of destinations by governments, growing consumer protection to ensure greater regulation and resort promotion in the media and via the internet.

These factors certainly promoted the development of mass tourism in the Western industrialized nations in the post-war period, especially in the 1960s and 1970s. Many of the trends identified in the UK are part of a wider change in Western society towards consumption of tourism products. Looking at the past is interesting because many of the issues we face in modern tourism may already have existed in the past, and so are not necessarily new. Even so, the past may not always be a guide to the future, especially given the speed of change in society, the rapid pace of technological innovations and the effect of wider societal trends. For this reason, no discussion of the origins and growth of tourism is complete without some consideration of the future.

The future of tourism

Anticipating changes in tourism has attracted a great deal of interest from economists who seek to model the changes in demand based on past and future growth assumptions. But this approach alone ignores some of the underlying changes in the nature of society that shape the tourist of the future. For this reason, some consideration of the following key trends over the next decade will help to understand how tourism consumption and development may be affected:

- the ageing of society in the Western industrialized nations, with the over-50 age group – the 'new old' who are active and far from elderly and uninterested in tourism – which is a growing market sector
- a growth in single households, with later marriage and child-bearing as well as increased rates of divorce and single parenthood
- information technology becoming an all-embracing element of our lives, increasingly used by consumers and part of the globalized society
- consumers becoming more environmentally conscious; this will be balanced by increased searches for hedonistic experiences and more flexible leisure time
- tourism consumers looking for greater convenience and ease of access, with the media playing a much greater role in shaping our tastes and preferences.

In fact some of the most important issues affecting world tourism in 2006 are shown in Table 2.4 which ranks a number of key features that will shape consumer behaviour.

One potential approach used by some futurologists to understand future changes in tourism has been the use of scenario planning (see Chapter 13): stories or possible views on what might happen at a future point in time. This approach seeks to use creative thinking to understand how future changes and events may shape the unknown, building a picture of what the tourism consumer of 2015 might look like. In essence, looking at the future is about grappling with uncertainty, beyond the

Table 2.4 The ten important world tourism issues in 2006 (source: Edgell, 2005, personal communication)

1. Safety and security in tourism
2. Impact of the world's economy on tourism
3. Managing sustainable tourism
4. Tourism policy and strategic planning
5. Utilizing e-commerce tools in tourism
6. Tourism education and training
7. New tourism products
8. Quality tourism experience (value/money)
9. Partnerships and strategic alliances in tourism
10. Impact of health issues/natural disasters on tourism

planning horizon of most individuals and businesses. In contrast the approach used by economists, namely econometrics – using past trends and future growth assumptions to forecast changes – is seen as more scientific and precise. The problem in many cases, is that forecasts are rarely achieved. To illustrate how the scenario and forecasting approach have been used, the example of New Zealand's international tourism prospects is reviewed in Box 2.3 because it is an example of where many growth forecasts were achieved.

Box 2.3 Case study: Forecasting international growth in New Zealand

New Zealand's international tourism market depends upon long-haul markets and Australia as sources of tourism demand. Research commissioned by the government's Foundation for Research, Science and Technology (FRST) – set out to forecast overseas visitor arrivals as an approximation of likely growth targets for the new millennium. Table 2.5 shows that 1992 was the milestone year for New Zealand with tourism exceeding one million arrivals and 2003 saw the two million mark exceeded. After 2003, the forecast was for a rise to three million visitors by 2010, according to research by McDermott Fairgray (who completed the initial forecasting work in Table 2.5).

In view of the need to constantly review the accuracy of forecasts, and of the changing market conditions which impact upon visitor arrivals (i.e. economic factors, crises, exchange rates and tastes), the Tourism Research Council of New Zealand commissioned a review of

Table 2.5 International arrivals and visitor forecasts for New Zealand 1966–2010 (source: FRST; Tourism Council of New Zealand)

Year	Visitor arrivals	Visitor arrivals forecasts 2004–2010
1966	100 000	
1971	200 000	
1974	300 000	
1978	400 000	
1983	500 000	
1992	1 000 000	
1996	1 500 000	
2003	2 000 000* (2 104 000 actual arrivals)	
2004		2 338 000
2005		2 482 000
2006		2 611 000
2007	2 500 000*	2 741 000
2008		2 862 000
2009		2 992 000
2010	3 000 000*	3 120 000

*McDermott Fairgray Forecast

international visitor arrivals 2004–2010. What is notable from Table 2.5 is the accuracy of the original McDermott Fairgray forecast for 2003. In 2003, international arrivals were dominated by Australia (33 per cent), the Americas (13 per cent), Japan (7 per cent), North-East Asia (11 per cent) and UK/Nordic countries/Ireland (15 per cent). Table 2.6 describes the economic prospects (i.e. growth assumptions for forecasting), scenarios and expected growth rates. These will help us understand traveller behaviour and factors affecting future growth more fully. Table 2.6 is also interesting because it highlights concerns surrounding economic forecasts, notably crises such as SARS, political instability and the growing global uncertainty associated with terrorism and political issues. Even so, the forecasts for 2004–2010 indicate an expected growth rate of 5.8 per cent per annum in total visitor arrivals, tripling international tourism since 1992 and doubling arrivals in the period 2003–2010.

Table 2.6 Summary of international tourism prospects for New Zealand (NZ) (source: Tourism Research Council of New Zealand, 2004, *International Visitor Arrival Forecasts*, www.trcnz.govt.nz, accessed on 27 January 2005)

	Economic prospects	Tourism prospects	2003–2010 arrivals annual average growth (%)	
Australia	• GDP growth of 3.5 per cent per annum over forecast period • No clear winner in upcoming election • Australia benefiting from higher commodity prices	• NZ viewed as a safe, high-quality destination • Tourism NZ is marketing aggressively in Australia • Lower airfares and increase capacity should ensure continued growth	Holiday VFR Business Education Rest Total	4.6 5.0 5.0 2.3 4.1 4.8
Americas	• The upcoming presidential election may cause short term weakness • Record US trade deficit recorded in the March quarter • There are signs of a US-led economic recovery in the region	• NZ benefiting from its isolation and US-friendly stance • Strong $NZ does not seem to be affecting tourist numbers, but it is having an impact on spend • Tourism NZ is marketing aggressively in the US market	Holiday VFR Business Education Rest Total	3.7 5.5 2.4 3.5 2.5 3.9
Japan	• GDP growth of 1.3 per cent per annum over forecast period • Approval for Koizumi fell following his decision to keep	• Strong growth is expected post-SARS, despite ongoing economic difficulties • Tourism NZ is refocusing its efforts in Japan, which should boost visitor	Holiday VFR Business Education	4.8 8.6 1.7 4.9

(continued)

Table 2.6 (*Continued*)

	Economic prospects	Tourism prospects	2003–2010 arrivals annual average growth (%)	
	troops in Iraq • Unemployment is at a 3-year high	numbers and higher yields	Rest Total	7.6 5.1
North-East Asia	• Strong economic growth expected in this region, particularly in China • Rapid growth is creating inflationary fears • Relations between Taiwan and China remain uncertain	• The education market has suffered a major setback in the past year • Major growth is expected in the South Korean and Chinese markets • Stronger trade links bode well for tourism	Holiday VFR Business Education Rest Total	10.5 6.7 11.0 7.8 11.0 9.7
Rest of Asia	• Strong economic growth expected in this region, particularly in India • The post-SARS recovery has been relatively strong and swift • Some political instability in Thailand and Indonesia	• Most markets in this region are quite mature, with the exception of India which has considerable growth potential • The education market may take some time to recover • Air capacity is an issue for the high potential Indian market	Holiday VFR Business Education Rest Total	9.5 7.6 5.2 2.3 6.5 8.3
UK/Nordic/Ireland	• Steady growth in GDP expected, with the possibility of an economic upturn in the near future	• A mature, diversified and high-yielding source region • There is a strong and stable VFR market	Holiday VFR Business	7.6 6.9 2.4

Region				
	• Markets in this region are characterized by stable politics and sound fundamentals	• The strength of the pound should continue to make NZ a desirable long-haul destination	Education	2.3
			Rest	3.6
			Total	7.0
Rest of Europe	• Moderate growth in GDP of around 2.0 per cent per annum expected in this region	• The recent growth in German arrivals is encouraging	Holiday	4.1
			VFR	5.7
	• Germany is showing some signs of recovery, although businesses and consumers remain pessimistic	• Moderate growth is expected from most markets in this region	Business	4.4
			Education	3.9
		• Air capacity and distance is an issue in some markets	Rest	3.7
			Total	4.3
Rest of the world	• Moderate GDP growth potential	• Reasonable growth potential, but very volatile in some markets	Holiday	4.5
	• Some markets in this region are more influenced by politics than economic policy		VFR	5.2
		• The pacific markets are good low-risk growth prospects, but tend to be low yielding	Business	3.7
			Education	3.3
	• Considerable instability in some of the markets in this region	• Growth depends heavily on the state of the world	Rest	4.6
			Total	4.7

Whilst the forecasts of future tourism illustrates the importance of looking ahead in trying to anticipate changes, one new trend which is emerging as a potential growth area is space tourism.

Space tourism

Since a member of the public joined a Russian space flight in 2001, there has been a growing interest in the future growth of space tourism. However, interest in space tourism is not new, with NASA publishing various reports on space tourism in the 1990s, particularly its 1998 report *General Public Space Travel and Tourism*. In the USA, 12 million people per year visit NASA's Air and Space Museum in Washington, the Kennedy Space Center in Florida and the Johnson Space Center in Texas, while two million a year visit Space World in Japan.

In market research studies, the market for space travel in the USA alone is estimated to be US$40 billion a year. Much of the future potential market is dependent upon reusable launch vehicles that can carry commercial passengers. Research indicates that once ticket prices can be generated at US$10 000, the market will be expanded. However, this is some way off, with the Russian launch vehicle costing US$10 million. Some commentators consider that it will be possible to achieve space tourism in the next 50 years based on short sub-orbital flights. In the longer term, other possibilities may include:

- short earth orbital flights using reusable spacecraft
- orbital tourism in space hotels located around the earth's orbit
- moon and Mars tourism.

For the tourist, seeing the earth from 100 km above its surface will provide a lifetime memory. There will also be a leisure space for activities such as weddings, sports and games. Yet engineers recognize that for technology to advance, major developments in propulsion systems are required. For the tourist, certain medical and physical preparations will be necessary, including familiarization with short sub-orbital flights, an ability to perform emergency procedures and learning coping strategies to deal with claustrophobia, isolation and personal hygiene. Policy changes may also be necessary to modify the Liability Convention (1971) of the

UN that makes the launching country liable for compensation for losses or damage. However, the existing investment by governments in the USA, Europe and Japan of US$20 billion in space agencies indicates that state funding has already underwritten an element of the investment costs in space tourism, and it has a potential to generate an economic return.

In 2005, space tourism moved a step nearer to reality when British entrepreneur Richard Branson signed a £14 million agreement to build five spaceliners in the USA, with Mojave Aerospace Ventures to utilize the technology devised for SpaceShipOne. This space craft reached an altitude of 112 km (368 000 ft) equivalent to 69.6 miles above the earth's surface in 2005. Virgin are planning flights in 2008 at a cost of £100 000 each and they estimate that 3000 people are prepared to pay this price. The Virgin Spaceship will have five passengers, involving a week of pre-flight training, and will last three hours. The highlight will be three minutes of weightlessness.

The future demand for space tourism as a luxury travel experience could grow from a conservative estimate of 150 000 trips a year on 1500 flights (generating revenue of US$10.8 billion with a ticket price of US$72 000) to 950 000 trips on 9500 flights (with a ticket price of US$12 000). The flights would rendezvous with a space hotel, unload incoming passengers and transport returning passengers to earth. What is evident is that in the early years of space tourism the demand will be low and price will be high. This will change as the activity becomes more acceptable – similar to any product life cycle.

Conclusion

The history of tourism can be characterized by continuity and change in the form, nature and extent of tourism activity. The growing globalization and global extent of tourism activity can be explained by wider social access to travel, enabled by a range of factors promoting travel (i.e. income and leisure time). The impact of innovations and entrepreneurs has significantly changed the course of the history of tourism, and the example of Richard Branson's Virgin Galactic is likely to change it again.

The emergence of mass tourism in the period since the 1960s is a dominant feature of the international expansion of world travel. There has also been a fundamental shift in tourism since the 1960s, as the 1990s saw a move from industry-based, standardized packages towards a greater individuality and flexible itineraries, a difference in the nature of experiences sought and concern with issues such as the environment and sustainability. A greater range of niche products has been developed and marketed to fulfil the demand for increasingly sophisticated travel tastes. At the same time, with ageing populations in many countries, earlier retirement and increasing longevity, longer holidays have seen a resurgence (in the 1930s they were the preserve of the wealthy and upper classes).

With the prospect of space travel now a reality, along with more exploratory forms of marine tourism to the ocean's depths, tourism continues to push the bounds of humanity's endurance and quest for discovery and something new. Underwater hotels already exist: futurist notions of underwater tourism are now a reality. What is clear is that tourism has continued to develop and evolve through time, and many current trends will wane as new ones emerge, although these may use existing resources, places and experiences. In some cases new environments, places and experiences will continue to be developed. Tourism is always changing, and the challenge for the tourism manager and entrepreneur is to anticipate new trends and tastes and to meet them.

References

Butler, R. (1980) The concept of the tourist area cycle of evolution: Implications for the evolution of resources. *Canadian Geographer*, 24 (1): 5–12.

Ogilvie, I. (1933) *The Tourist Movement*. London: Staples Press.

Towner, J. (1985) The Grand Tour: A key phase in the history of tourism. *Annals of Tourism Research*, 12 (3): 297–333.

Towner, J. (1996) *An Historical Geography of Recreation and Tourism in the Western World 1540–1940*. Chichester: Wiley.

Further reading

There are a number of excellent sources available on the historical development of tourism including:

Walton, J. (1983) *The English Seaside Resort: A Social History 1750–1914*. Leicester: Leicester University Press.

Walton, J. (2000) The hospitality trades: A social history. In C. Lashley and A. Morrison (eds) *In Search of Hospitality: Theoretical Perspectives and Debates*. Oxford: Butterworth-Heinemann.

Walton, J. (2000) *The British Seaside: Holidays and Resorts in the Twentieth Century*. Manchester: Manchester University Press.

Walton, J. and Smith, (1996) The first century of beach tourism in Spain: San Sebastian and the Playas del Norte from the 1830s to the 1930s. In M. Barke, J. Towner and M. Newton (eds) *Tourism in Spain: Critical Issues*. Wallingford: CAB International.

Ward, C. and Hardy, D. (1986) *Goodnight Campers: The History of the British Holiday Camp*. London: Mansell.

Questions

1 Why is the historical study of tourism useful in understanding the management problems many destinations face in the new millennium?

2 How can you explain the continuity and change in the historical development of tourism?

3 What is the value of the resort life cycle model in explaining tourism growth and development?

4 What are the future prospects for space tourism?

3

Demand: Why do people engage in tourism?

Learning outcomes

This chapter examines the reasons why people go on holiday and the explanations developed to understand the motivating factors associated with leisure travel. After reading this chapter, you should be able to understand:

- the concept of tourism demand and the ways it may be defined
- the role of motivation studies in explaining why people go on holiday
- the different motives used to develop classifications of tourism
- the role of consumer behaviour in explaining why people select certain holiday products.

Introduction

Understanding why people choose to travel and to become tourists seems at first sight a very simple issue. In fact it is a very complex area and, whilst we can all think of simple reasons why people choose to go on holiday, the area has also been extensively studied by psychologists (who study how humans behave, interact and react to external and internal stimuli) trying to derive explanations that apply to groups and individuals to the perennial question: *why do people go on holiday?* Theoretical research has sought to classify travellers into groups in order to generalize the reasons for being involved in tourism. However, there needs to be a recognition that not all tourists are the same. They are diverse and have a wide range of motivations to travel which vary by wealth, age, stage in the life cycle, lifestyle and personal and group preferences. As the tourism industry relies upon travellers choosing to go holiday, understanding what motivates them to visit to specific places and resorts has major economic consequences.

The explanation of why people travel for pleasure, business and other reasons has become further clouded by a fundamental problem: psychologists attempt to develop theories about why people choose to travel but these theories are detached from the way the tourism industry uses very practical marketing-based approaches to understand the same question. One of the distinguishing features of the tourist is that they are an outsider in the places they visit, not an integral element of the fabric of the society and environment. Tourism is also somewhat different to other forms of consumption but there is a tendency to treat tourists in the same vein as we would other consumers, and to apply the same methods of study which are used in the area of consumer behaviour from the field of marketing. However, as Pearce (2005: 9) argues, 'There are several critical dimensions that create differences between tourist behaviour and consumer behaviour. One such major difference lies in the extended phases that surround tourist activities'. These include:

- an anticipation or pre-purchase stage
- an on-site experience
- a return travel component
- the extended recall and recollection stage.

In this respect, the essential feature of the tourist experience, even in the pre-purchase and recall stage, is about being somewhere (notably somewhere else than at home).

Unlike many other consumer purchases, a tourism experience may be enduring, having a long-lasting impact in terms of reflection and psychological enrichment of one's life. In contrast to other tangible goods such as a car, a holiday is more about our dreams, expectations of enjoyment and satisfaction. The nature of the experience in terms of this meaning, value and people-to-people contact distinguishes the consumption of tourism from the way many other products are purchased.

This chapter explores the way in which the academic study and practical application of principles associated with tourism demand have been applied to understanding what motivates tourists as consumers. Motivation is important in terms of the personal satisfaction which the tourist derives from consuming the experience; it is also a component of visitors' perceptions of destinations and should affect how those marketing and promoting a destination present it.

Attempts to classify and group tourists into categories or to develop a model of tourist motivators are fraught with problems, as motivation is a highly individualized element of human behaviour. It affects and conditions how people react and behave as well as their attitudes to tourism as something they consume. In other words, while a range of motivating factors can be considered in promoting travel, a range of highly personal and individualized elements still exist beyond these. There is no universal agreement on how to approach the tourist demand for travel products and services, although this chapter will explore a number of approaches and possible reasons why human beings engage in tourism as a recreational activity. If we understand what prompts people to leave their home area and to travel to other places, then we may be able to develop approaches that help us to manage these visitors and their impacts. It may be possible to help plan for a more enjoyable experience at the place(s) they visit. More fundamentally, understanding tourist motivation in relation to Chapter 2 may help to explain why certain places developed as successful tourism destinations and then continued to grow, stagnated or declined as tastes, fashions and perceptions of tourism changed. One interesting way to view the wider significance of tourist behaviour, as mapped out by Pearce (2005) is to consider the tourist, their motives in choosing a destination and a mode of transport, and their interaction with the destination (Figure 3.1). By understanding these, we can manage the interactions the tourist has with the society, culture and environment in the destination and begin to comprehend the complex outcomes which arise from tourists' behaviour and activity, to improve those features affecting the tourist, host society and setting. But our starting point in this journey to understand why tourists travel has to be

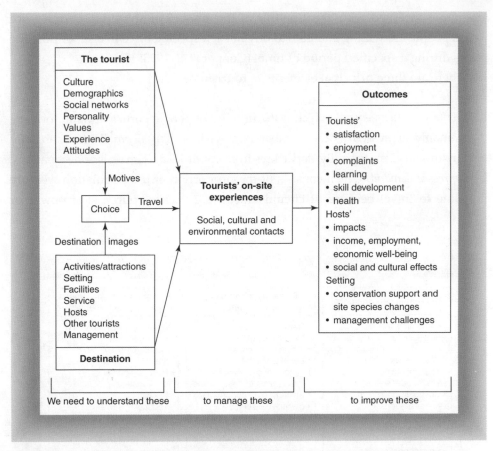

Figure 3.1 Concept map for understanding tourist behaviour (source: *Tourist Behaviour*, P. Pearce, 2005 © Channel View Publishers). Reproduced with permission

what is meant by tourism demand as it drives the growth, development and change in tourism businesses and resorts.

What is tourism demand?

Tourism demand has been defined in numerous ways, including 'the total number of persons who travel, or wish to travel, to use tourist facilities and services at places away from their places of work and residence' (Mathieson and Wall 1982: 1) and 'the relationship between individuals' motivation [to travel] and their ability to do so' (Pearce 1995: 18). In contrast, more economic-focused definitions of demand are more concerned with 'the schedule of the amount of any product or service which people are willing and able to buy at each specific price in a set of possible prices during a specified period of time' (Cooper *et al.* 1993: 15).

There are three principal elements to tourism demand:

1 *Effective* or *actual demand*, which is the number of people participating in tourism, commonly expressed as the number of travellers. It is normally measured by tourism statistics – typically, departures from countries and arrivals at destinations.
2 *Suppressed demand*, which consists of the proportion of the population who are unable to travel because of circumstances (e.g. lack of purchasing power or

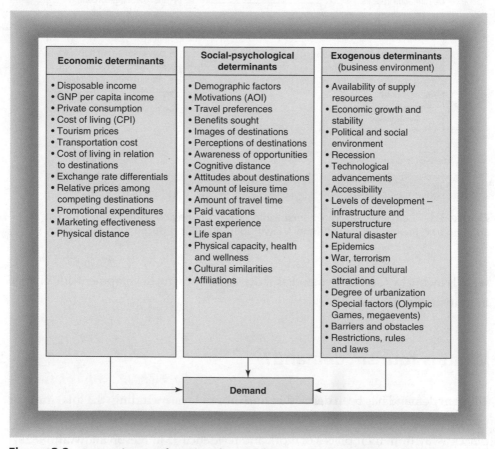

Economic determinants	Social-psychological determinants	Exogenous determinants (business environment)
• Disposable income • GNP per capita income • Private consumption • Cost of living (CPI) • Tourism prices • Transportation cost • Cost of living in relation to destinations • Exchange rate differentials • Relative prices among competing destinations • Promotional expenditures • Marketing effectiveness • Physical distance	• Demographic factors • Motivations (AOI) • Travel preferences • Benefits sought • Images of destinations • Perceptions of destinations • Awareness of opportunities • Cognitive distance • Attitudes about destinations • Amount of leisure time • Amount of travel time • Paid vacations • Past experience • Life span • Physical capacity, health and wellness • Cultural similarities • Affiliations	• Availability of supply resources • Economic growth and stability • Political and social environment • Recession • Technological advancements • Accessibility • Levels of development – infrastructure and superstructure • Natural disaster • Epidemics • War, terrorism • Social and cultural attractions • Degree of urbanization • Special factors (Olympic Games, megaevents) • Barriers and obstacles • Restrictions, rules and laws

Demand

Figure 3.2   Determinants of tourism demand (source: Uysal, 1998 © Routledge). Reproduced from D. Ioannides and K. Debbage (eds), *The Economic Geography of the Tourist Industry*, p. 87, Fig. 5.2, Routledge, 1988

limited holiday entitlement). It is sometimes referred to as 'potential demand'. Potential demand can be converted to effective demand if the circumstances change. There is also 'deferred demand' where constraints (e.g. lack of tourism supply such as a shortage of bedspaces) can also be converted to effective demand if a destination or locality can accommodate the demand.

3 *No demand*, is a distinct category for those members of the population who have no desire to travel and those who are unable to travel due to family commitments or illness.

An interesting study by Uysal (1998) summarized the main determinants of demand (see Figure 3.2): economic, social-psychological and exogenous factors (i.e. the business environment). This useful overview provides a general context for tourism demand and many of the factors help to illustrate the complexity of demand, but does not adequately explain how and why people decide to select and participate in specific forms of tourism, which is associated with the area of motivation.

The motivation dichotomy: Why do people go on holiday?

In a very comprehensive assessment of tourist motivation, Mountinho (1987: 16) defined motivation as a 'state of need, a condition that exerts a push on the individual towards certain types of action that are seen as likely to bring satisfaction'. This means that demand is about using tourism as a form of consumption to achieve a level of satisfaction for an individual, and involves understanding their behaviour and actions and what shape these human characteristics. This seeks to combine what the tourist desires, needs and seeks from the process of consuming a tourism experience that involves an investment of time and money. The expectations a tourist has as a consumer in purchasing and consuming a tourism product or experience is ultimately shaped by a wide range of social and economic factors which Uysal (1998) listed above and which are shaped by an individual's attitudes and perception of tourism.

Yet tourist motivation is a complex area dominated by the social psychologists with their concern for the behaviour, attitudes and thoughts of people as consumers of tourism. A very influential study published in 1993 by Phillip Pearce suggested that in any attempt to understand tourist motivation we must consider how to develop a concept of motivation in tourism, how to communicate this to students and researchers who do not understand social psychology and what practical measures need to be developed to measure people's motivation for travel, particularly the existence of multi-motivation situations (i.e. more than one factor influencing the desire to engage in tourism). Pearce (1993) also discussed the need to distinguish between intrinsic and extrinsic forces shaping the motivation to become a tourist; he explored these issues further in *Tourist Behaviour* (2005).

Intrinsic and extrinsic motivation

There is no all-embracing theory of tourist motivation due to the problem of simplifying complex psychological factors and behaviour into a universally acceptable theory that can be tested and proved in various tourism contexts. One immediate complication is the problem of understanding what drives an individual to travel. For example, while a business traveller is obviously travelling primarily for a work-related reason, there are also covert (or less overt) reasons which are related to that individual's needs and wants. The individual is a central component of tourism demand, as:

> no two individuals are alike, and differences in attitudes, perceptions and motivation have an important influence on travel decisions [where] attitudes depend on an individual's perception of the world. Perceptions are mental impressions of … a place or travel company and are determined by many factors, which include childhood, family and work experiences. However, attitudes and perceptions in themselves do not explain why people want to travel. The inner urges which initiate travel demand are called travel motivators. (Cooper *et al*. 1993: 20).

What this illustrates is that the individual and the forces affecting their need to be a tourist is important. These forces can be broken down into *intrinsic* and *extrinsic* approaches to motivation. The intrinsic motivation approach recognizes that individuals have unique personal needs that stimulate or arouse them to pursue tourism. Some of these needs are associated with the desire to satisfy individual or internal needs – for example, becoming a tourist for self-improvement or what is termed 'self-realization', so as to achieve a state of happiness. It may also help boost one's ego (a feature termed ego enhancement) because of the personal confidence building that travel can encourage. In contrast, the extrinsic motivational approach examines the broader conditioning factors that shape individuals' attitudes, preferences and perceptions but are more externally determined – for example, the society and culture one lives in will affect how tourism is viewed. In the former Soviet Union tourism was a functional relationship that was conditioned by the state that sent workers for rest and recreation so they could return refreshed to improve output and productivity. In contrast, in a free market economy the individual is much freer to choose how and where they wish to travel, within certain constraints (e.g. time, income and awareness of opportunities).

At a general level, tourism may allow the individual to escape the mundane, thereby achieving their goals of physical recreation and spiritual refreshment as well as enjoying social goals such as being with family or friends. In this respect, extrinsic influences on the tourist may be family, society with its standards and norms of behaviour, the peer pressure from social groups, and the dominant culture. For example, one of the cultural motivators of outbound travel from New Zealand among youth travellers (those aged under 30 years of age) is the desire to do the 'Overseas Experience' (the 'big OE'). This often gives travellers a chance to engage in a cultural form of tourism by visiting Europe, seeing relatives and friends and achieves a number of social goals. The big OE also has an intrinsic function as a long-haul trip and a sustained time away from the home environment encourages independence, self-reliance and greater confidence in one's own ability and judgement, and will contribute to ego enhancement. In the UK there has also been a trend towards a similar experience before commencing study at university; it is known as the 'gap year' and a similar style of travel, working holiday, voluntary activity or round-the-world trip takes place.

While analysis of tourist motivation is about the underlying psychological value and features of being a tourist, actual tourism demand at a practical level is derived through a consumer decision-making process. From this process, it is possible to describe three elements, which condition demand:

1 *energizers of demand*, which are factors that promote an individual to decide on a holiday
2 *filterers of demand*, which are constraints on demand that can exist in economic, sociological or psychological terms despite the desire to go on holiday or travel

3 *affecters*, which are a range of factors that may heighten or suppress the energizers that promote consumer interest or choice in tourism.

These factors directly condition and affect the tourist's process of travel decision-making although they do not explain why people choose to travel. For this reason, it is useful to understand how individuals' desires and need for tourism fit into their wider life. This partly reflects upon the intrinsic motivations, and one useful framework devised to understand this is Maslow's hierarchy of human needs.

Maslow's hierarchy model and tourist motivation

Maslow's (1954) hierarchy of needs remains one of the most widely discussed ideas on motivation. It is based on the principle of a ranking or hierarchy of individual needs (Figure 3.3), based on the premise that self-actualization is a level to which people should aspire. Maslow argued that if the lower needs in the hierarchy were

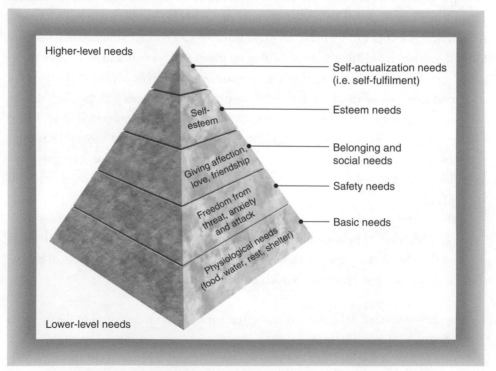

Figure 3.3   Maslow's hierarchy of individual need

not fulfilled then these would dominate human behaviour. Once these were satisfied, the individual would be motivated by the needs of the next level of the hierarchy. In the motivation sequence, Maslow identified 'deficiency or tension-reducing motives' and 'inductive or arousal-seeking motives' (Cooper *et al.* 1993: 21), arguing that the model could be applied to work and non-work contexts, such as tourism and leisure. Yet how and why Maslow selected five basic needs remains unclear, although it appears to have a relevance in understanding how human action is related to understandable and predictable aspects of action compared to research that argues that human behaviour is essentially irrational and unpredictable. Maslow's model is not necessarily ideal, since needs are not hierarchical in reality because some needs may occur simultaneously. But such a model does emphasize the development needs of humans, with individuals striving towards personal growth, and these can be understood in a tourism context.

Maslow's work has also been developed since the 1950s when work on specific motivations beyond the concept of needing 'to get away from it all'. For example, 'push' factors that motivate individuals to seek a holiday have been researched and compared with 'pull' factors (e.g. promotion by tourist resorts), which act as attractors. Ryan's (1991: 25–9) analysis of tourist travel motivators (excluding business travel) identified a range of reasons commonly cited to explain why people travel to tourist destinations for holidays:

- a desire to escape from a mundane environment
- the pursuit of relaxation and recuperation functions
- an opportunity for play
- the strengthening of family bonds
- prestige, since different destinations can enable one to gain social enhancement among peers
- social interaction
- educational opportunities
- wish fulfilment
- shopping.

From this list, it is evident that

tourism is unique in that it involves real physical escape reflected in travelling to one or more destination regions where the leisure experience transpires... [thus] a holiday trip allows changes that are multi-dimensional: place, pace, faces, lifestyle, behaviour, attitude. It allows a person temporary withdrawal from many of the environments affecting day to day existence. (Leiper, 1984, cited in Pearce 1995: 19)

The tourism tradition of motivation studies: Classifying and understanding tourist motives

There are a large number of studies of tourist motivation, dating back to the 1970s, which took many of Maslow's ideas forward and then applied more socio-psychological ideas in a tourism context. In most of the studies of tourist motivation, a common range of factors tends to emerge. For example, Crompton (1979) emphasized that socio-psychological motives can be located along a continuum which explains why certain tourists undertake certain types of travel. In contrast, Dann's (1981) conceptualization is one of the most useful attempts to simplify the principal elements of tourist motivation into a series of propositions (i.e. general statements which characterize tourists) including:

- travel as a response to what is lacking yet desired
- destination pull is in response to motivational push
- motivation may have a classified purpose (this was the focus of many of the earlier studies of motivation)
- motivation typologies
- motivation and tourist experiences.

This was simplified a stage further by McIntosh and Goeldner (1990) into:

- physical motivators
- cultural motivators
- interpersonal motivators
- status and prestige motivators.

On the basis of motivation and using the type of experiences tourists seek, Cohen (1974) distinguished between four types of travellers:

1 *the organized mass tourist*, on a package holiday, who is highly organized and whose contact with the host community in a destination is minimal

2 *the individual mass tourist*, who uses similar facilities to the organized mass tourist but also desires to visit other sights not covered on organized tours in the destination

3 *the explorers*, who arrange their travel independently and who wish to experience the social and cultural lifestyle of the destination

4 *the drifters*, who do not seek any contact with other tourists or their accommodation, wishing to live with the host community.

Clearly, such a classification is fraught with problems, since it does not take into account the increasing diversity of holidays undertaken nor the inconsistencies in tourist behaviour. Other researchers suggest that one way of overcoming this difficulty is to consider the different destinations tourists choose to visit and then establish a sliding scale that is similar to Cohen's (1972) typology, but without such an absolute classification.

One such attempt was by Plog (1974), who devised a classification of the US population into psychographic types, with travellers distributed along a continuum from psychocentrism to allocentrism (see Figure 3.4). The psychocentrics are the anxious, inhibited and less adventurous travellers while at the other extreme the allocentrics are adventurous, outgoing, seeking out new experiences due to their inquisitive personalities and interest in travel and adventure. This means that, through time, some tourists may seek out new destinations, while others will follow the more adventurous as the destinations develop and appear safe and secure. But some of the criticisms of Plog's model are that it is difficult to use because it fails to distinguish between extrinsic and intrinsic motivations. It also fails to include a dynamic element to encompass the changing nature of individual tourists. Pearce (1993) suggested that individuals have a 'career' in their travel behaviour where people:

start at different levels, they are likely to change levels during their life-cycle and they can be prevented from moving by money, health and other people. They may also retire from their travel career or not take holidays at all and therefore not be part of the system. (Pearce, 1993: 125)

Pearce (2005) has argued that a travel career is a dynamic element in a tourist's holidaytaking habits, influenced by travel experience, stage in the life cycle and age. Initially he developed the idea of a travel career ladder (Pearce, 1993),

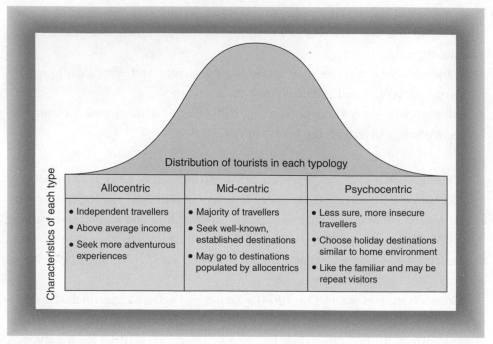

Figure 3.4   Plog's psychographic traveller types (developed and modified from Plog, 1974)

which was built on Maslow's hierarchial system and had five motivational levels:

1 biological needs
2 safety and security needs
3 relationship development and extension needs
4 special interest and self-development needs
5 fulfilment or self-actualization needs.

Later Pearce (2005) de-emphasized the hierarchical elements of a ladder in favour of a reformulated travel career pattern (TCP) approach. The TCP placed a greater emphasis on how motivations form patterns which may link to the notion of travel careers. The notion of the TCP is that tourists will have different motivating patterns over their life cycle which will be impacted upon by their experience of travelling. This reflects better the complexity of understanding tourist motivation, although studies of this have suggested a tourist's experience of domestic and international travel and age were important factors in identifying influences on TCPs. What Pearce (2005) concludes is that we may discern three layers of travel motivation:

- *Layer 1*, the common motives at the core of the TCP: novelty, escape, relaxation, enhancing and maintaining human relationships
- *Layer 2*, a series of moderately important motivators related to self-actualization (i.e. focused on the inner self) that surround this core set of motivations and a number of externally focused motives such as interaction with the host society and environment
- *Layer 3*, an outer layer with lesser importance including motives such as nostalgia and social status.

These factors may also vary in importance according to the culture of the travellers, and the relative significance of these motives may also change during the TCP of individuals.

From the discussion of motivation, it is apparent that:

- Tourism is a combination of products and experiences which meet a diverse range of needs.
- Tourists are not always conscious of their deep psychological needs and ideas. Even when they do know what they are, they may not reveal them to researchers, family and friends.
- Tourism motives may be multiple and contradictory with some working in harmony and others working in direct opposition (i.e. push and pull factors).
- Motives may change over time and be inextricably linked together (e.g. perception, learning, personality and culture are often separated out but they are all bound up together).
- Dynamic models of tourist motivation such as Pearce's (2005) TCP are crucial to understanding not only the role of motivation but also the way that such motives will evolve, change and be conditioned by changes in lifestyle, life cycle and personal growth and development.

The important point here is that motivation is about how a general need/want (in this case the desire to travel) is translated in a context where it can be fulfilled. This is often simplified to push and pull factors but it does raises issues about the ways in

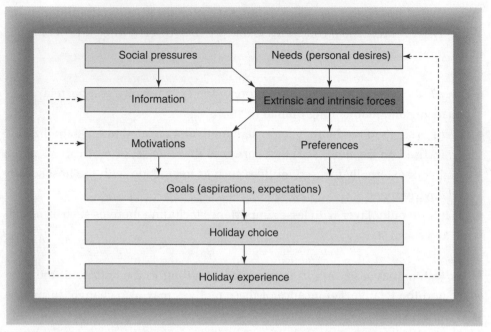

Figure 3.5   The relationship between needs, motivations, preferences and goals in individual holiday choice (source: 'Understanding holiday choice', B. Goodall in C. Cooper (ed.) *Progress in Tourism, Recreation and Hospitality Management*, vol. 3, 1991. © John Wiley & Sons Limited). Reproduced with permission

which tourists as consumers respond to specific stimuli that encourage them to engage in tourism. Goodall (1991) identified the relationship between needs, wants and preferences and goals amongst travellers, where push and pull factors existed as shown in Figure 3.5. Much of Figure 3.5 is focused on consumer behaviour and the role of marketing in providing the stimuli that lead people to choose specific motivations for going on holiday. For this reason, the role of consumer behaviour in tourism is important in understanding the practical ways consumers choose to become tourists.

Consumer behaviour and tourism

Consumer behaviour concerns the way tourists as purchasers of products and services behave in terms of spending, their attitudes and values towards what they buy. Their age, sex, marital status, educational background, amount of disposable income, where they live and other factors such as their interest in travel directly affect this. For marketers who sell and promote tourism products and services, these factors are crucial to the way they divide tourists into groups as consumers so that they can provide specific products that appeal to each group. One frequent approach used by tourism marketers to achieve this goal is 'market segmentation' (i.e. how all the above factors can be used to describe different groups of consumers).

There are a range of approaches one can use in market segmentation though the most commonly used is *demographic or socio-economic segmentation*, which occurs where statistical data such as the census are used together with other statistical information to identify the scale and volume of potential tourists likely to visit a destination. Key factors such as age and income are important determinants of the demand. For example, the amount of paid holidays and an individual or family's income both have an important bearing on demand. One powerful factor shaping demand in a demographic context is social class, which is related to income, social standing and the way status evolves from these factors. Social class is widely used by marketers as a way of identifying the spending potential of tourists. In the UK, the Institute of Practitioners in Advertising uses the following socio-economic grouping of the population with six groups:

A   Higher managerial, administrative or professional
B   Middle managerial, administrative or professional
C1 Supervisory, clerical or managerial
C2 Skilled manual workers
D   Semi- and unskilled manual workers
E   Pensioners, the unemployed, casual or lowest grade workers
After Holloway and Plant (1988)

although other classifications have been devised with various emphases in different countries. The key point to stress from any classification is how social class, employment or economic status impact upon participation in tourism. In most cases, professionals enjoy higher incomes and this affects their consumption of tourism in general terms. However, other factors may come into play, the stage in the family life cycle may inhibit a young professional with children while a working couple in another occupational group may have fewer constraints and therefore more money to spend on holidays. Many studies of income and social class indicate that those in

Classes AB have a greater propensity to take overseas holidays than those in groups DE. This also raises wider social debates about how income and class can contribute to social exclusion of those groups unable to participate in tourism. As discussed in Chapter 2, around 40 per cent of the population in the UK do not take a holiday in any given year. Two other notable factors which impact upon tourism in terms of consumer behaviour are gender and ethnicity.

Gender and ethnicity

Gender has a powerful impact on participation in tourism, since many studies indicate that women in households are the holiday decision-makers. Yet with changes in the existing composition of two-parent households and the growth in single-parent households, the notion of the nuclear family is changing in many Western societies. The consequences are that many tourism providers are having to rethink the nature of the traditional family holiday. Similarly, new trends in holiday consumption can be discerned with children exerting greater pressure on parents in the selection holiday destinations (e.g. pester power), demanding visits to child-oriented destinations (e.g. Disneyland) and locations associated with children's television series (e.g. the Isle of Mull in Scotland where the fictitious *Balamory* BBC Television series is filmed has been receiving up to 250 000 visitors a year, a significant proportion generated by pester power).

Gender has also become a defining feature in the identification of the gay and lesbian market. In the USA this comprises 10 per cent of the tourism market and they are now wooed as a high-spending group (this has led to the use of terms such as the 'Pink Pound' in the UK). In the USA, 75 per cent of such households have income above the national average of US$40 000, with 30 per cent earning in excess of US$100 000; 84 per cent have passports and 82 per cent are university graduates. Over 55 per cent hold management posts and the Tourism Industry Association (TIA) in the USA estimate this market is worth US$54.1 billion a year. However, the gay and lesbian market is also very discerning and seeks destinations with a gay or lesbian involvement that is integrated in the community. Among the top reasons to visit a destination are: holidaying with a boyfriend/girlfriend; attending Gay Pride festivals; holidaying with a group of friends; purchasing a holiday package and taking advantage of internet travel specials. In the USA, the top destinations for gay men in order of preference are New York, San Francisco, Hawaii,

Palm Springs, Fort Lauderdale, West Hollywood, Miami/South Beach and Key West. Lesbians travelled to San Francisco, Provincetown, New York, Hawaii, Key West, West Hollywood, Miami/South Beach, Fort Lauderdale and Palm Springs.

Ethnicity has also been identified as an important factor shaping tourist travel behaviour and consumption patterns. Many Western societies now have multicultural populations, with race and ethnicity assuming a more prominent role in travel markets. According to the TIA in the USA, the emerging Hispanic travel market now accounts for 13.7 per cent of the national population, equivalent to 39.8 million in 2000 which is set to grow to 162.6 million (around 25 per cent) of the US population by 2050. With a buying power of US$653 billion, this is a substantial market despite their low average household incomes of US$33 000 (which are growing steadily). The Hispanic groups in the USA have made a growing use of the internet although there are differences in consumer behaviour between native-born and recent Hispanic migrants. In terms of tourism, the US Hispanic market comprises 77.1 million trips a year, growing at around 20 per cent a year, with 34 per cent of all Hispanic purchasing concentrated in California and Texas. The majority of their travel is for leisure, especially to see family, friends and relatives. Popular domestic destinations in the USA are California, Texas, Florida, Nevada, Arizona and New Mexico, and Hispanics spend around US$480 on a trip. Therefore the examples of gender and ethnicity show that it is important for the tourism sector to understand how consumers can be broken down into discrete groups or segments.

Psychographic segmentation

A more sophisticated approach to segmentation (which was discussed above in the motivation study by Plog, 1974) is *psychographic segmentation* which is often introduced to complement more simplistic approaches based on socio-economic or geographic data. It involves using socio-economic and life-cycle data to predict a range of consumer behaviours or purchasing patterns associated with each stage. Examining the psychological profile of consumers to establish their traits or characteristics in relation to different market segments further develops this. The VALS (Value and Lifestyles) research conducted by the Stanford Research Institute in North America used socio-economic data, and the aspirations, self-images, values and consumption patterns of Americans, to establish nine lifestyles which people could move through. For example, the US tourism industry is a US$1.3 trillion industry and around 2.6 million bedspaces are sold every day in the US while US$94 billion is spent by international travellers in the USA. The tourism industry needs to employ tools such as lifestyle marketing and segmentation to begin to understand the tourist as a consumer, their needs and purchasing behaviour. What the VALS research and subsequent studies have tried to achieve is to reduce the complexity and reality of the market for products and services into a series of identifiable groupings. It uses variables related to consumers' lifestyles (i.e. their interests, hobbies, spending patterns) as well as more personalized variables such as attitudes, opinions and feelings towards travel and tourism. In other words, by combining the behaviour of tourists and their value system comprising their beliefs and how these affect their decision to purchase, the marketers can communicate more effectively with potential consumers by understanding what motivates their decision to purchase certain types of products and services. One example of psychographic segmentation is a specialized product such as ecotourism (travelling to engage in wildlife viewing, visiting natural areas and having a concern with the natural environment); here, segmentation is possible using a range of variables such as the age profile of the ecotourists, how they choose to travel, how they book their holidays, what type of budget they have and their motivation for being an ecotourist.

Once the supplier of the services or products has considered these issues, the next stage to examine is how tourists decide to purchase certain products – particularly the most frequent purchase, which is the holiday.

Purchasing a holiday

A study undertaken in Canada in March 2002 by TripAdvisor found that consumers often take as long as a month to purchase quite complex holiday products online and that illustrates how important it is for businesses to understand how consumers select products both online and from more traditional distribution channels such as travel agents. It also highlights the importance of marketing efforts by tourism businesses to tempt the consumer to book a product. Goodall (1991) constructed a simple model of how consumers select a holiday which involved a number of stages and answers to questions on what they want from the holiday. This concluded that consumers have a range of holiday options available at specific points in time which is based on the preferences of the individual, family and other groups. The following factors exert a powerful influence on the decision to purchase tourism products and services:

- the personality of the purchaser
- the point of purchase
- the role of the sales person
- whether the individual is a frequent or infrequent purchaser of holiday products
- prior experience.

Any explanation of consumer behaviour in tourism also needs to be aware of the motivations, desires, needs, expectations, and personal and social factors affecting travel behaviour. These are in turn affected by stimuli which promote travel (i.e. marketing and promotion), images of the places being visited, previous travel experiences, and time and cost constraints. What this type of debate on tourists as consumers shows is that marketing and promotion are fundamental in a business which seeks to create a four-step process which takes the consumer from a stage of unawareness of a product or service through to a point where they want to consume it. Within marketing, much of the attention focuses on using well-known brands and household names in travel (i.e. Thomson Holidays in the UK and other World of TUI brands in Germany and other European countries) to promote the awareness. Marketers describe this process as the AIDA model: (**A**wareness, **I**nterest, **D**esire, **A**ction).

The AIDA process has been used by the mayor in the Maipo River region, an area just outside the Chilean capital Santiago, to create a unique tourism destination – a UFO tourism zone. The Awareness has been created by UFO sightings over two decades, while the Interest has resulted from increased publicity. To stimulate and satisfy the Desire to visit, the Action is based on plans to erect two observation centres, signposts of sightings and the provision of workshops. A similar scheme was proposed in Bonnybridge, Stirlingshire (Scotland), where a number of UFO sightings have created an interest in developing a visitor centre to promote visits around this specialist interest.

Much of the efforts in marketing are focused on consumer behaviour, seeking to understand how individuals perceive things and digest the information and messages that advertising and promotion use to develop a tourism image. These images impact not only upon the holiday selection process and decision to go on holiday but also, and more importantly, upon destinations – the specific places tourists will visit.

The tourist image of products and places

It is generally acknowledged that many consumers will select a range of destinations (often three to five) when considering where to go on holiday. A major element in the decision to select a specific destination is the image of the place. The tourist(s) select the destination through a process of elimination but this is not a straight linear process from A to B to C. Often, people will look at options, re-evaluate them and reconsider specific places based on their knowledge, the images portrayed in the media and the opinions of individual(s) and group members. This can make travel decisions a lengthy and complex process based on compromise. For example, the 11 September 2001 attack on the USA and terrorist threats created widespread negative images of international travel and one immediate beneficiary of this was the growth of domestic tourism in many countries. This required government and tourism agencies to promote not only 'business as usual' in New York to encourage people to travel again, but to restore negative images portrayed by the media.

Image can be a powerful process where destinations (such as London and Paris) have memorable elements in the landscape which feature as icons to promote awareness and travel to the destination (e.g. the Eiffel Tower in Paris), leading to tourists associating positive reasons to travel with well-known icons that are safe and popular. In some cases, over-popular images of destinations or specific attractions may mean that a degree of caution has to be used to downplay the destination in peak season; this is sometimes called 'de-marketing'. In addition, destinations have to create images of their tourism offerings and locality that help to differentiate them from the competition. In Australia, there has been a rise in wine and food tourism based on local products, and specialist producers in areas such as Margaret River in Western Australia have helped regions to emerge as newly created and re-imaged, with emphasis being placed on the uniqueness of the place. Another example is a desolate area in northern China on the Tibet–Qinghai plateau, where attempts by local government in 2002 have begun to turn a former nuclear weapons research centre (No. 221 Plant, owned by the China Nuclear Industry Corporation) into a tourist attraction. Established in 1958, the site was used to test nuclear bombs and nuclear waste is buried there. Some 16 nuclear tests were carried out over a 30-year period. Negative images and publicity present a major challenge to those creating positive images of the region for visitors, which the Qinghai Provincial Tourism Association are basing on the region's cultural heritage (Tibetan culture and architecture) and the natural environment (varying from snow-capped mountains to desert-style dunes). To attract visitors, a number of festivals have been staged based on horse racing and Buddhist rituals.

Yet much of the image of a destination is not concerned with the tangible elements, since tourism is a combination of tangible perceptions of place and emotional feelings about locations. Even when rational feelings question the logic of visiting somewhere, the desire to see something may override rational concerns. This is related to risk behaviour in holiday purchases. Risk is a complex topic, not least because it is very personal to individuals, and may create certain types of behaviour in tourists. The low-risk tourist will book early, reducing the perceived barriers to travel, and may return to the same resort or country due to the apparent feelings of safety and security. In contrast, risk takers will be less worried about the impact of tourist-related crime, will be less concerned about the stability and certainty offered by booking a package holiday and may choose to be independent travellers organizing their travel and itinerary themselves. Tourists seeking to minimize risks will seek out well-known brands that guarantee quality experiences. Often, these groups prefer the reassurance of booking at travel agents where the face-to-face contact and positive reinforcement of what the experience will offer encourages the purchaser to go ahead. With these issues in mind, our attention now turns to the case study in Box 3.1 and one of the most discussed markets in outbound tourism – the Chinese.

This example of China illustrates that the demand for tourism is variable. Although demand may perform in a constant manner, the overall effect of demand factors is that they are constantly under review by consumers and some fluctuations will inevitably occur when adverse events such as 11 September occur.

Box 3.1 Case study: The Chinese outbound tourism market

Outbound tourism from China has existed since the formation of the People's Republic of China (PRC) in 1949 but it was largely restricted to approved travel for business. Much of the travel was to former communist states. A landmark change in this policy occurred in 1983 when the government allowed Chinese residents to travel to Hong Kong and

Macau, as long as they were booked by designated travel agencies and friends and relations in the destination paid their expenses. Outbound trips were typically organized by the government-run China Travel Service. The scale of change after 1983 led to regulations allowing outbound travel to three South East Asian countries in 1990 (Thailand, Singapore and Malaysia), again if the travel was sponsored by overseas relatives. In 1992, the Philippines was also added; then permission was granted for cross-border trips to Russia, North Korea, Mongolia, Vietnam, Cambodia, Laos, Myanmar and other Soviet-controlled countries. In 1998, Australia and New Zealand received Approved Destination Status (ADS), with European countries recently being added. In 2005, 90 countries had ADS, of which 25 were in Europe.

The scale of travel against this very recent history of outbound travel is significant, as outbound travel grew from 620 000 trips in 1990 to 3.73 million in 1994, 5.32 million in 1997, 10.4 million in 2000 and 29 million in 2004. Some forecasts suggest that, by 2020, China could be the world's largest outbound market with 115 million trips a year. The principal outbound destinations for Chinese travellers are East Asia Pacific destinations, including Hong Kong, Macau, Thailand, Japan and South Korea, and 80 per cent of tourists visit these places. The Russian Federation also attracts a large volume of cross-border trips to places such as Vladivostok. The proportion of official travel is around 40 per cent and private travel accounts for almost 60 per cent; this last category continues to grow at around 20 per cent a year.

The typical profile of an outbound traveller is a person aged 25 to 44 years of age, with higher educational qualifications; affluent and holding a managerial post. In Chinese culture, travel is seen as adding to one's wisdom and experience. Much of the growth in tourism is fuelled by China's booming export economy, changing demographic profiles, reduced barriers to travel and people saving for travel. Much of the initial travel by Chinese tourists embarking on their Travel Career Pattern is to Macau and Hong Kong: they account for 75 per cent of arrivals. With the further relaxation of travel restrictions in 2003 allowing travel to these two destinations without government involvement, they experienced a tourism boom. With Hong Kong Disneyland open in 2005 and a hotel boom in Macau, the Chinese market was directly responsible for 300 000 jobs in Hong Kong's tourism industry. Much of the Chinese tourists' spending is not on luxury accommodation, but on attractions, shopping, eating out and sightseeing. Analysts have divided the Chinese outbound market into the high-volume, low-margin travellers to Macau and Hong Kong who typically earn US$4000–15 000 and the remaining groups earning in excess of US$30 000 a year. For leisure travel, many of the travellers used Air China, staying around five days in Hong Kong or Macau.

Many analysts view Europe as the next region to experience the Chinese travel boom as the USA did not have ADS at the time of writing. Among the new outbound markets which are developing are the upwardly mobile working women and students travelling overseas for education. The regulation of passports, management of travel by state travel agencies and control of travel by package tours rather than independent travel, will continue to add some degree of restraint to outbound travel. Nevertheless, the growth potential of this market over the next decade, its increasing affluence, disposable income and susceptibility to the 'travel bug', will make China a major market for growth.

The future of tourism demand

The growth of domestic and international tourism demand depends on a wide range of factors, some of which have been discussed in this chapter. The example of the Chinese outbound market vividly illustrates the scale of tourism growth that has occurred in a relatively short time frame (i.e. since 1983) and the prospects of it becoming the major outbound market by 2020.

Irrespective of these trends, are more profound changes which are occurring among tourism consumers. Whilst the Chinese are a young and buoyant outbound and domestic market, many other industrialized countries have recognized that their tourists now have much higher expectations of what they purchase and consume as tourists and are somewhat 'mature' markets. For this reason it is interesting to reflect upon some of the consumer trends now affecting tourist consumption which may shape the quality as well as the nature of tourism demand in the next decade:

- Consumers are more discerning of tourism purchases, irrespective of what they pay, and have high expectations of quality.
- In a postmodern society, some researchers argue that the consumer gains as much satisfaction from the process of purchasing as they do from consumption, implying that the purchase process needs to meet these raised expectations.
- Many consumers across the globe are now more e-savvy and able to use technology to establish the range and extent of travel and holiday options, leading to a greater demand for value-adding in the purchase and consumption process.
- More experienced travellers are seeking more innovative, unusual and targeted products which fit with their lifestyles, perception of their lifestyle and needs.

The traditional annual holiday of one to two weeks, purchased through a travel agent from a mass produced brochure, will no longer be the norm.

- The tourism industry will be faced with more discerning clients, a proportion of whom will be willing to purchase a portfolio of products that appeal to their time-poor, cash-rich lifestyles. Ease of consumption will be the new buzzword: the holiday or trip will be an opportunity to de-stress and will not commence with stress, disorganization and lack of attention to detail.
- Marketing techniques which allow targeting, segmentation and client identification to capture the individual needs of the traveller, will provide premium profits for the tourism provider.
- Low-cost, high-volume mass products such as low-cost airline travel will continue to fill a niche for independent price-sensitive travellers without any restrictions from government.
- Consumers are continuing to be heavily influenced by branding, brands and advertising which create an image of the market position, consumer benefits and promise made by tourism products. This trend is likely to continue, with destinations and operators using the brand image to create a unique appeal to certain markets and groups.
- New product development to appeal to individualized aspects of demand (e.g. health and wellness tourism) will see further growth, as niche products aimed at specific groups with these interests are developed.

Conclusion

The reasons why people choose to engage in tourism are diverse and multifaceted. No one simple explanation can be advanced to attribute motivation for tourism. Instead it is a process of understanding the psychology of tourist decision-making based upon the reasons why they wish to travel and take holidays. To simplify some of the reasons, researchers have developed lists of factors and typologies of tourists to try and suggest how humans can be grouped into common types of consumers of tourism. Yet even this is difficult when the ultimate arbiter of motivation, especially of human needs and wants that can be fulfilled through tourism experiences, is the individual. Understanding the individual is a time-consuming process that is not easily reduced to questionnaire surveys or face-to-face interviews on the beach asking tourists why they are there. The tourist has to be understood like an onion: they comprise a number of layers which need to be peeled away to uncover the extrinsic and intrinsic motivational forces. To continue the analogy, over-analysing the tourist may mean that removing all the layers leaves nothing to be eaten and digested; and while slicing the onion in half may reveal the complex thinking and factors shaping human behaviour associated with tourism, predictable and rational behaviour is not necessarily revealed. Consequently, a range of motivational approaches may provide conflicting information. However, what is certain is that taking a holiday and travelling are firmly embedded in modern society and although fashions, tastes and changes in travel habits may alter outward motivation, deep down the intrinsic motivation is a highly personal process for each and every tourist.

References

Cohen, E. (1972) Towards a sociology of international tourism. *Social Research*, 39: 164–82.

Cohen, E. (1974) Who is a tourist? A conceptual clarification. *Sociological Review*, 22: 527–55.

Cooper, C. P., Fletcher, J., Gilbert, D.G. and Wanhill, S. (1993) *Tourism: Principles and Practice*. London: Pitman.

Crompton, J. (1979) An assessment of the image of Mexico as a vacation destination. *Journal of Travel Research*, 17 (fall): 18–23.

Dann, G. (1981) Tourist motivation: An appraisal. *Annals of Tourism Research*, 8 (2): 187–219.

Goodall, B. (1991) Understanding holiday choice. In C. Cooper (ed.) *Progress in Tourism, Recreation and Hospitality Management, Volume 3*. London: Belhaven.

Maslow, A. (1954) *Motivation and Personality*. New York: Harper and Row.

Mathesion, A. and Wall, G. (1982) *Tourism: Economic, Physical and Social Impacts*. Harlow: Longman

McIntosh, R. W. and Goeldner, C. (1990) *Tourism: Principles, Practices and Philosophies*. New York: Wiley.

Mountinho, L. (1987) Consumer behaviour in tourism. *European Journal of Marketing*, 21 (10): 3–44.

Pearce, D. G. (1995) *Tourism Today: A Geographical Analysis*, 2nd edn. Harlow: Longman.

Pearce, P. (1993) The fundamentals of tourist motivation. In D. Pearce and R. Butler (eds) *Tourism Research: Critique and Challenges*. London: Routledge.

Pearce, P. (2005) *Tourist Behaviour*. Clevedon: Channel View.

Plog, S. (1974) Why destination areas rise and fall in popularity. *The Cornell Hotel and Restaurant Administration Quarterly*, 15 (November): 13–16.

Ryan, C. (1991) *Recreational Tourism: A Social Science Perspective*. London: Routledge.

Uysal, M. (1998) The determinants of tourism demand: A theoretical perspective. In D. Ioannides and K. Debbage (eds) *The Economic Geography of the Tourist Industry: A Supply-side Analysis*. London: Routledge.

Further reading

The best studies to explore in this complex area are:

Argyle, M. (1996) *The Social Psychology of Leisure*. Harmondsworth: Penguin.

Pearce, P. (1982) *The Social Psychology of Tourist Behaviour*. Oxford: Pergamon.
Pearce, P. (1993) The fundamentals of tourist motivation. In D. Pearce and R. Butler (eds) *Tourism Research: Critique and Challenges*. London: Routledge.

Questions

1 Why is tourist motivation important for tourism managers to understand?
2 What is the role of consumer behaviour in understanding what tourists want to purchase? Do consumers always follow rational decision-making approaches when purchasing products such as holidays?
3 Should the consumer be the starting point for the analysis of tourism demand?
4 How useful is Maslow's model in understanding tourist motivation? Has it been made redundant and superseded by specific social psychology studies of tourism, or is it still the basis for all analyses of tourist motivation?

4

The supply of tourism

Learning outcomes

This chapter examines the way in which tourism supply is assembled by the tourism industry. On completion of the chapter, you should be able to understand:

- how individual businesses approach supply
- how supply issues are affected by macro-economic issues
- the significance of the tourism supply chain in conceptualizing how tourism businesses meet demand
- the interconnections between different elements of tourism (accommodation, transport, attractions and tourism agencies/services/facilities).

Introduction

In Chapter 3, some of the reasons why people choose to go on holiday and explanations of the diverse motivations associated with the demand for tourism services and products were discussed. Yet in any purchasing decision by potential tourists, there has to be a provision of a service, product or experience by a business, organization or destination to meet the visitors' need or demand. This provision is known as tourism supply or, as was explained in Chapter 1, as a form of production. In any analysis of supply, there are a number of basic questions which tourism businesses have to consider:

- *What should we produce as a business to meet a certain form of tourism demand?* (i.e. should we produce an upmarket high-cost holiday package for ecotourists using tailor-made packages or aim for mass market, low-cost package holidays?)
- *How should it be produced?* (i.e. should we contract in supplies to provide each element of the package product to reduce costs or should we produce each element to ensure quality control and consistency in product delivery?)
- *When, where and how should we produce the tourism product?* (i.e. do we produce an all-year round or seasonal tourism product?)
- *What destinations/places should be featured in the tourism experience?*
- *What form of business or businesses do we need to produce the tourism services and products so that we meet demand?*

These are all real questions that tourism businesses need to address as their long-term viability and success or failure will depend upon the management of their organizations' resources to meet demand in an efficient and profitable manner. To many people, the concept of tourism supply and the day-to-day operation and management of tourism businesses supplying tourists' needs may seem distant, unconnected and rather unreal. Yet it is the concept of supply which helps us to understand how the wide range of tourism businesses and organizations (and quite often businesses which do not see themselves as servicing tourists' needs such as taxi companies) combine to link the tourist with the services, experiences and products they seek in a destination.

This chapter seeks to provide an overview of tourism supply issues by explaining how to view the concept of supply, particularly the idea of a supply chain and the wide range of industry elements which characterize what is termed the 'tourism industry'. There is one underlying characteristic of the tourism industry that distinguishes it from other services and this is the way in which tourism is consumed by a mobile population who visit destination areas to consume a product, service or experience while, in contrast, the supply elements are often fixed geographically at certain places (i.e. a hotel, restaurant or visitor attraction). This means that businesses are required to sink considerable capital costs into different forms of tourism services and centres of production, in the expectation that the destination will appeal to visitors and assist in the promotion of their individual products and services. Therein lies the complexity of tourism supply – that the appeal of the product and influences on the consumption of specific elements of supply is a more complicated proposition than buying other consumer goods or services. Sessa (1983) categorized the supply of tourism services by businesses as follows:

- *tourism resources*, comprising both the natural and human resources of an area
- *general and tourism infrastructure*, which includes the transport and telecommunications infrastructure
- *receptive facilities*, which receive visitors, including accommodation, food and beverage establishments and apartments/condominiums
- *entertainment and sports facilities*, which provide a focus for tourists' activities
- *tourism reception services*, including travel agencies, tourist offices, car hire companies, guides, interpreters and visitor managers.

These 'elements of tourism' highlight the scope of tourism supply, but a number of less tangible elements of supply (i.e. image) also need to be considered.

As explained in Chapter 3, images of places have a powerful influence in the tourist's search process for a destination to go on holiday, and businesses need to be aware of this when entering the tourist market for the first time, or when introducing new products. What this means is that the wider tourism industry and agencies responsible for tourism in a destination (e.g. the tourist board) need to pull in the same direction, to work towards common goals and to promote the attributes of the destination in a positive manner so that the images of the area, place or destination are enhanced or maintained. For example, Iceland's appeal is marketed in terms of its attributes as a clean, green and environmentally responsible destination, with its beautiful lava landscapes, wilderness, vistas and views, its Viking heritage and its diversity of activities for visitors, from winter sports through to health-based tourism (thermal resorts). This image was developed and promoted so that the tourism destination and its products could be structured around a number of key elements which the visitor identifies with Iceland.

Influences on tourism supply issues: The business environment

Aside from issues of image, the business environment in which businesses operate can also have a major bearing on tourism supply. For example, in most countries tourism operates within a free market economy, and individual businesses operate in open competition. However, in some countries certain sectors of the tourism industry receive assistance from government through infrastructure provision, marketing and promotional support from tourist boards and other agencies. It is also apparent that when governments decide to promote inbound tourism to destinations such as Bali, supply needs to be able to meet demand. In many cases, demand poses severe pressures on destinations where supply is often a step behind demand. The case of Bali's demand growth illustrates this: in the 1930s, around 3000 visitors a year visited Bali. By 1970 this had grown to 23 000 rising sharply in 1981 to 158 000 and to over 1 246 000 in 1998. This massive expansion in demand requires that supply in all sectors of the industry keep pace, especially as the beach-resort nature of the destination was actively promoted in the 1980s and 1990s. This also raises the importance of marketing and promotion in developing a demand to fill the available supply. For example, in 2005, the national tourism organization for Scotland, VisitScotland, had a budget of £40 million to assist in promoting Destination Scotland domestically and internationally. Companies such as British Airways also spend in excess of £60 million a year on advertising to communicate with its customers.

There are few industries that gain a degree of leverage from government taxes to promote their activities. Given the level of state support and assistance, tourism does not operate in many countries in conditions of perfect competition. Yet, as Chapter 11 shows, intervention is justified to develop a tourism destination image and promote the attributes of tourism supply in the form of holidays, although supply is more complex than just holidays. What does concern individual businesses is the competition they face on a day-to-day basis and the degree of government regulation and intervention, which impacts upon their business activities. For example, in the UK there has been a significant growth in low-cost or budget airlines, which have been licensed to operate from regional and London bases. In each case, setting up a new airline operation involves high capital costs (even where aircraft are leased rather than purchased), so the number of companies able to enter this market are limited by the entry costs and government regulations. Low-cost airlines have challenged existing market conditions, where individual operators had a monopoly on certain routes and could charge a premium (high) price. The effect has been to reduce fares, generate new forms of demand (i.e. leisure travellers) and severely reduce the monopoly operators' ability to charge premium prices and maintain route profitability. easyJet was formed in 1995 and carried 30 000 passengers in its first year of operation. By 2003, it carried twenty million passengers and in 2005 it was carrying over two million passengers a month. Much of this growth has been new traffic which is price sensitive. In the USA, deregulation of the airline business in the late 1970s saw monopolies (and duopolies, where two companies controlled routes) challenged, new market conditions emerge and a major reorganization, restructuring and new environment develop for air travel. A similar example in the UK in the late 1990s was the privatization of British Rail and the end of its monopoly on rail travel. In each of these examples, the competitive environment which affects tourism businesses and their operation needs to be considered in relation to a number of underlying economic issues:

- What competitive market conditions exist for a specific sector of tourism (i.e. the airline sector, hotel sector or attraction sector)? Do conditions of monopoly, oligopoly (i.e. where a limited number of suppliers control supply) or other market conditions exist?
- How many businesses are involved in these markets? What size are they? Are they able to respond quickly to new competitive pressures, or are they characterized by complacency and an inability to redefine their operations in the light of aggressive competition?
- Do the businesses involved in tourism display patterns of market concentration, where a limited number of businesses dominate all aspects of production (i.e. from retailing through to supply of services and products in the destination such as in the UK tour operator market)?
- What are the capital costs of entering a tourism market? Are there high entry and exit barriers? As previously mentioned, starting an airline has high entry and exit costs, requires a high level of technical know-how and large capital investment and ongoing finance to service the business. Buying a guest house, on the other hand, has low entry costs and no barriers to entry in terms of technical

competencies to be able to run and manage it and host visitors. In contrast, the airline business requires a high degree of technical competencies.

- What types of products already exist in the market? Is there scope for innovation (see Chapter 10 for more detail on innovation) to develop new products without the risk of 'ambush marketing' by competitors who copy the idea and undercut the competition by loss-leaders to regain market share? Aggressive marketing and a limited number of loss-leaders have characterized the low-cost airlines and privatized railways in the UK in an attempt by their owners to capture price-sensitive leisure travellers. In other words, is there scope for price discrimination in the market to differentiate a whole range of products?

What these factors indicate is that the market conditions and business environment in which tourism operates is far from static. They are constantly changing, requiring businesses to adapt and to develop strategies to retain their market presence. Unlike many other goods and services, fashions, tastes, preferences and evolving consumer trends quickly translate into opportunities or problems in tourism supply as shown in the case study in Box 4.1. This traces the growth, changing corporate strategy and tactics used to diversify a company dependent upon brewing (e.g. Bass) into one of the world's largest hotel companies in 15 years.

Box 4.1 Case study: Corporate strategy and change in the hotel sector: The evolution of the Intercontinental Hotels Group

The Intercontinental Hotels Group can be traced back as far as 1777 when William Bass first established a brewery at Burton on Trent in the UK, and in the subsequent growth the company acquired other brewing concerns in the twentieth century. It merged in 1967 with Charringtons, making it one of the largest brewers in the UK. Following UK government legislation in 1989 (the Beer Order legislation) to reduce vertical integration and the number of tied public houses owned by breweries, Bass withdrew from many public house outlets and invested cash flow from its public house business into an international hotel business. The company already had a small hotel chain, acquired in 1987, but its major entry into the market was marked with its purchase of Holiday Inns International in 1988 and the North American Holiday Inn in 1990.

In 1990 Holiday Inn was reputed to be the world's leading mid-scale (mid-range) hotel brand, founded in 1952 by Kemmons Wilson in Memphis. In 1991, the company launched its Holiday Inn Express brand, a limited service brand aimed at the leisure and business market. By 2005, some 150 Holiday Inn Expresses were in existence in the UK and Europe, illustrating the scale and growth of this popular product. In 1994, the company also launched its luxury upscale brand – Crowne Plaza. In 1997 the company sold its mid-scale properties in the USA, retaining the brand through franchise agreements. Other non-core business was disposed of in the late 1990s, including Gala Bingo, Coral Bookmakers and additional public houses. Bass also moved into the eating-out business in 1995, with its acquisition of Harvester and other smaller businesses. The company continued to build its luxury business portfolio, launching its Staybridge Suites brand. In 1998 the company also acquired the Intercontinental hotel chain (originally founded in 1946 by Pan Am airlines) initially in Latin America and then across the world in places served by the airline (including its 40 000 aircrew as customers). Intercontinental operated in the mid-scale and upscale segments with a reputation for attention to detail.

In 2000, Bass purchased the Southern Pacific Hotel Corporation (SPHC) in Australia to make it Asia's leading hotel company with 59 hotels using the Park Royal and Centra brand. This was followed by the acquisition of Bristol Hotels and Resorts in the USA, a management company with 112 hotels. In June 2000, the Bass brewing division was sold to a Belgian brewer for £2.3 billion, and the company was finally repositioned, having moved from a domestic brewer to an international hospitality business. Bass then sold 988 pubs in 2001 to Six Continents Retail Brands and acquired the UK Posthouse chain for £810 million, as locations of strategic value for conversion to Holiday Inns. The company also purchased the Intercontinental Hong Kong for £241 million and, in October 2002, it separated its hotels business from its hospitality retailing division, creating Intercontinental Hotels Group plc.

In July 2003, Intercontinental Hotels Group decided to sell its Staybridge Suites hotels, entering into a 20-year management agreement with the purchaser, Hospitality Properties Trust. In December 2003, the company added Candlewood Suites to its portfolio, increasing its US presence to 109 hotels. In 2004, the company introduced Hotel Indigo, an alternative lodging experience. By 2004, the company had a global presence, as one of the world's largest hotel groups, owning, leasing, franchising or managing properties and operating over 3500 hotels worldwide with 537 000 guest rooms in 100 countries.

Bass had properties in a number of market segments including:

- economy
- mid-scale, limited service
- upscale – high-quality service for leisure travellers
- upper upscale – luxury brands for business travellers and international tourists.

In 2005, the company was divesting itself of many of its lower tier properties, franchising them or managing them, since its current strategy is to focus on its strengths in branding, managing and franchising as well as brand innovation. It has preferred to concentrate on the market segment with greater profit margins, the mid- and upscale segments. Therefore, it reduced its capacity by selling the majority of its hotels, to focus on what it excels at – managing hotels – thereby simplifying its asset ownership and concentrating on the skills of its employees. This example of one company's corporate strategy in the period since 1989 reveals its evolution into a global hotel chain and the process of constantly reviewing its strategic direction to assess how best to achieve its commercial potential.

Managing tourism supply issues

For tourism businesses, recognizing these evolving patterns, new trends and the need for innovation to address market conditions re-emphasizes the importance of managerial skills in the supply of tourism products and services – as discussed in the Bass case study in Box 4.1, where the creation of new brands led to the growth of new business. This also highlights what Mintzberg (1973) identified as the nature of managerial work in organizations – short-term coping, disparate activities and more concerned with brevity, variety and increasing fragmentation. Tourism managers and businesses are no exception to this and Mintzberg's research has an important bearing on how managers performed certain roles (see Table 4.1) labelled as interpersonal, informational and decisional roles. The ten managerial work roles which Mintzberg identified illustrates the scope of activities which operating and managing a tourism business require, as well as some of the complexities of how the individual business interacts with the wider body of interests conveniently labelled the 'tourism industry'. It also suggests how important prevailing market conditions are when they impact upon how a business operates, manages and responds to

Table 4.1 Mintzberg's ten managerial roles (source: Reproduced from *Tourism Management*, vol. 25, S. Charaupunsirikul and R. Wood, Mintzberg, managers and methodology, 551–6, © 2002, with permission from Elsevier)

Interpersonal roles:

Figurehead	Symbolic head: obliged to perform a number of routine duties of legal and social nature
Leader	Responsible for the motivation of subordinates; responsible for staffing and training
Liaison	Maintaining self-developed network of outside contacts/informers who provide information and favours

Information roles:

Monitor	Through seeking and receiving a variety of special information, develops through understanding of organization and environment
Disseminator	Transmits information received from outsiders and subordinates to members of the organization
Spokesperson	Transmits information to outsiders on organization's plans, serves as expert on organization's industry

Decisional roles:

Entrepreneurial	Searches organization and its environment for opportunities to bring about change
Resource allocater	Responsible for the allocation of organizational resources of all kinds
Negotiator	Responsible for representing the organization at major negotiations

opportunities, threats and shortcomings in its own organization. Yet to do this, a business needs also to understand its relationship to other tourism businesses. A convenient way to explain this is by using the tourism supply chain concept.

The tourism supply chain

Throughout the earlier chapters, the role of tourism as an amalgam of different interests, activities, stakeholders and businesses have been discussed. This section examines how these different interests are functionally linked together to form a distinct supply chain. The supply chain concept originates in economics and has been used to explain how different businesses enter into contractual relationships to supply services, products and goods, and how these goods are assembled into

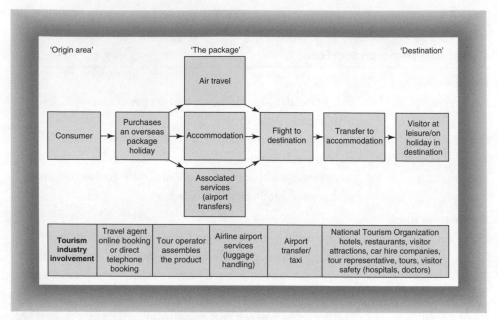

Figure 4.1   A typical tourism supply chain

products at different points in the supply chain. Tourism is well suited to the concept of the supply chain because the product, service or experience that is consumed is assembled, and comprises a wide range of suppliers. All too often our knowledge of the supply chain is quite restrictive, since a wide range of components are consumed in tourism including the use of bars, restaurants, handicrafts, food, infrastructure and related services. A schematic diagram of a typical tourism supply chain is shown in Figure 4.1. This shows that once the consumer has chosen a destination and product (as explained in Chapter 3), the decision to purchase involves contacting a tourism retailer (e.g. a retail agent, a direct selling company or an internet-based seller such as www.expedia.co.uk). Having chosen a booking medium and selected a package from a tour operator, the package is then assembled.

The tour operator enters into contractual relationships with tourism suppliers such as airlines (although larger tour operators may also own their own charter or schedule airline), hotel operators and suppliers of associated services such as airport transfers. These suppliers, in turn, contract suppliers who service their business needs: in-flight caterers, airline leasing companies, airport terminal services (i.e. check-in services, baggage handling, flight controllers, customer service agents for visitors and those with special needs, such as the disabled). The labour dispute in 2005 between Gateway Gourmet and its staff at Heathrow Airport illustrates how a disruption in one element of the supply chain can cause the system to collapse: British Airways was forced to cease flights for a number of days and incurred losses of £1 million a day. At the destination, ground services are also contracted. An example is the employment of tour representatives to meet guests at the airport, welcome them into their accommodation and utilize the opportunities for retail sales of additional services such as tours and events. This not only yields additional revenue for the tour operator, with representatives paid a commission based on sales targets, but also trades on the visitor's *naïveté* regarding the destination and cost of services, as well as the welcoming image that reassures the uninitiated. In some hotels, similar kickbacks and commissions are paid to the concierge for each sale of a particular company's product and the display of leaflets and brochures in some hotels in destinations such as Los Angeles are contingent upon the company's commission rate. Typically this will range from below 5 per cent to 10 per cent, thereby artificially inflating the price paid by visitors compared to the local population. Such practices may be culturally acceptable for tourism businesses in the locality, along with blatant and aggressive/ intimidatory behaviour by tour guides/drivers demanding gratuities with statements such as 'It is customary to give me 10 per cent of your ticket price for being your guide today' or threatening substantial abuse if the visitor leaves the tour. This may have very negative images for visitors from countries where tipping is not a cultural practice, and certainly promotes the image of tourists as targets to be ripped off by unscrupulous operators; this is why some destinations have instigated customer care hotlines to address such issues. What these examples also show is that where tourism services are provided, these are not only formal contracts and relationships, but also alliances between recommenders (i.e. tour representatives and hotel concierges) and providers at each stage. Thus a business opportunity presents itself, with each agent in the process taking a percentage of the proceeds or using the opportunity to generate additional revenue through indirect means (i.e. goods or service) or by blatant, aggressive and intimidatory behaviour. Whilst thankfully the latter behaviour is not widespread, it does illustrate the value of tourism spending in the destination (or in the home area where services and tours are pre-paid to the tour operator who also take a commission).

With so many organizations involved in the supply chain in relation to tourist spending and activity, it is clear that these are critical break or pressure points where the service provision could potentially fall down. What this also suggests is that failings with the destination may be attributed back to the tour operator who is liable under EU law for the well-being and experience of the holidaymaker. This returns us to the theme of Chapter 3 – that the tourism industry needs to be organized and managed in the destination so the visitor's experience is not adversely affected by the actions or events of service providers in that destination. For this reason, we now turn our attention to the principal elements of the tourism industry: accommodation establishments, attractions, transportation, public and private sector organizations and associated services.

Accommodation

Accommodation performs a vital role in many countries' tourism sector: in addition to providing the basic infrastructure to accommodate visitors as tourists and business travellers, it is a focus for meetings, conferences and entertainment. For many resort areas, accommodation comprises the key element in attracting the visitor for a holiday for a week or longer. Accommodation is also the focal point of short-break holidays and is often packaged as part of an experience of a place. Accommodation ranges in type from the upmarket, luxury five-star establishment with hundreds of bedspaces that charge a premium price to their guests through to the small bed-and-breakfast operator who may have only six bedspaces and open solely during the tourist season. This wide range of accommodation types will be examined in more detail in Chapter 7 on accommodation, but it is important to recognize here that it is a capital-intensive sector of the tourism industry. Yet it is not just the size or scale of the accommodation sector which is significant: it is the significance of hotels in the rise of resorts which may be a planned leisure environment that becomes the containing context for the holiday. For example, on many Pacific islands, hotel chains and individual companies have built resort complexes, with the hotel/accommodation complex as the key element, around which a beach, leisure facilities, restaurants/hospitality services, activities and events are structured. The result is that visitors can visit the resort and never leave or experience other areas on the island. Such developments can dominate the tourism industry on small islands. Conversely, accommodation in towns and cities is a significant sector of the tourism industry due to the employment it generates, as well as its ability to host large number of visitors.

At a global scale, the scale of rooms in the hotel sector is estimated to be 17 million worldwide, growing at nearly 3 per cent a year. Europe dominates the market with 6.3 million rooms, with 6.1 million in the USA and 4.1 million in Asia. Independent operators own the majority of these rooms, in small owner-managed units. At the same time, a number of trends have affected accommodation in Europe and many other countries globally, including:

- increasing change and competition among accommodation businesses
- a growth in the financial power of major hotel chains and multinational companies
- more discerning customers (particularly those using technology such as the internet)
- new trends, such as the rise of budget hotel chains and their brands.

In North America, 70 per cent of hotel stock is a recognizable brand (e.g. Radisson, Holiday Inn and Marriot) whereas, with the exception of Nordic countries, chain domination is only around 20 per cent in Europe. The pattern of European accommodation is shown in Table 4.2, which illustrates the variations between the principal destination areas (France, Spain, the UK, Greece, Germany, Italy). Within each country there are also great variations in the location of accommodation, which is located in the gateway cities (e.g. London, Paris, Berlin, Amsterdam and Dublin), business capitals (e.g. Frankfurt, Brussels and Geneva) and resort areas in coastal and other locations (e.g. ski resorts).

Therefore the accommodation sector is a vital element in the supply of services and products for visitors, a feature which is as old as tourism itself (as discussed in Chapter 2). However, what has transformed the accommodation sector in the long-term is the demise of staging-post accommodation on tourist transit routes as transport technology has removed the need for inns and hotels to be located along routes. Whilst tourists still use accommodation when touring, such as in the USA and Canada when using recreational vehicles (motor homes) or cars, accommodation has tended to cluster at principal destinations such as cities and resort areas. Yet not all tourists use accommodation: VFR traffic may stay with family/friends and not be visible in the accommodation sector. This is the case in Auckland, New Zealand, where up to 50 per cent of visitors may seek this type of holiday. However, regardless of where the visitor stays, they are in all probability likely to use the attractions of the area they are visiting.

Visitor attractions and activities

During any visit to a destination, tourists engage in activities and events which provide a focal point for the use of their leisure time. Attractions and activities are

Table 4.2 The number of hotels and accommodation establishments in Europe in 1999 and 2004 (source: Based on Eurostat, © European Commission)

	Number in 1999	Number in 2004 (unless stated)
Austria	15 378	14 435
Belgium	2015	1957 (*2003*)
Denmark	464	480
Finland	1004	961
France	19 379	18 217 (*2003*)
Germany	38 914	36 884
Greece	7946	8889
Iceland	253	303
Ireland	5460	4821 (*2003*)
Italy	33 379	33 480 (*2003*)
Luxembourg	325	297
Netherlands	2826	3129
Norway	1176	1079
Portugal	1754	1934 (*2003*)
Spain	16 229	17 402
Sweden	1898	1833
Switzerland	5890	5643 (*2002*)
UK	51 300	44 126 (*2003*)
EU 15		189 024 (*2003*)
EU 25		200 219 (*2003*)

a fundamental element of any tourist's itinerary, and in some cases the attraction, event or activity may be the *raison d'être* for the visit. Attractions have been divided into numerous categories or listings by tourism researchers to try to understand how they impact upon, interact with and shape tourists' activities. The conventional ways in which attractions are viewed are in terms of:

● *Natural resources*: Resources that are naturally occurring and used by visitors as places to consume tourism (e.g. a beach environment) or as resources during a visit to a destination (e.g. a visit to a scenic area). The history of tourism is based on the discovery, recognition of the potential and exploitation of natural resources as tourist attractions, most notably the exploitation of spa waters. In a similar vein, development in the nineteenth century was based on the recognition of the attraction of a landscape and resource (the sea and coastline) as an attraction. Yet even in these areas the tourism industry has developed the other category of attraction – man-made resources.

● *Man-made resources*: These are attractions that have emerged as a response to the developing tourism market in a locality, and often build upon the natural attractions. However, in the post-war period, the rise of mass tourism and of demand for leisure environments saw the development of purpose-built resources to exploit the opportunity of rising visitor spending. The development of environments by entrepreneurs (such as Walt Disney's creation of Disneyland in California at Annaheim) and the subsequent growth of theme parks has highlighted the leisure potential of man-made environments. This was evident in 2005 with the opening of a Disneyland in Hong Kong. At the same time, visitors utilize man-made resources that were not specifically designed for a tourism audience (e.g. cathedrals, churches, castles, historic gardens and archaeological sites). The diverse range of attractions available to the tourist is continually evolving as the industry seeks to appeal to specific niche markets (consider, for example, the educational potential of developing science centres such as Living Earth in Edinburgh and the Glasgow Science Centre) by exploiting the educational and entertainment motivations (the so-called 'edutainment' market).

Aside from attractions *per se*, visitors are also attracted to destinations and areas by special events, such as festivals or sporting events such as the Soccer World Cup in Germany in 2006, the America's Cup sailing regatta in 2007 and the Olympic Games. VisitLondon announced in 2006 that it will be hosting the Tour de France in 2007, the first time the event has ever been hosted in the capital. It is reputed to be the largest sporting event in the world, attracting up to one million spectators, and is expected to generate £56 million for the tourism economy. The event is expectedto attract a spectator audience of around 12–15 million and it will be transmitted across the world by 78 television channels giving the destination hosting it massive media coverage. Indeed, sports tourism – which can be defined as spectators travelling to destinations to watch their football or rugby team compete in a game or competition – is beginning to be recognized as a major growth area of the tourism industry. Complementing the sport spectators are the smaller number of sporting participants – amateur or professional sportspeople (e.g. golfers) – who travel to destinations to compete in sporting events such as the Ryder Cup or Scottish Open. For example, in 2005 the Lions Rugby tour of New Zealand was estimated to have generated NZ$130 million in foreign exchange earnings from sports tourists (an extra 20 400 visitor arrivals staying 43 000 visitor nights) to follow the tour. According to the evaluation of the event for the New Zealand Ministry of Tourism, 15 per cent of visitors were from the UK, 14 per cent from Ireland, 10 per cent from Wales and 10 per cent from Australia. The event was spread across New Zealand and so the impacts were geographically distributed according to where the matches were played. The impact evaluation noted that visitor arrivals rose sharply before a test match with the All Blacks and the event led to the following amounts being spent:

- NZ$25 million on food and beverages
- NZ$24 million on accommodation
- NZ$20.1 million on match-related expenses
- NZ$12.5 million on air fares
- NZ$9 million on domestic travel
- NZ$10.8 million on retail shopping
- NZ$10.9 million on attractions and entertainment.

This highlights the wide-ranging impacts such events can have on the local and national economy. But probably one of the most visible examples is the Olympic Games as discussed in the case study in Box 4.2.

Box 4.2 Case study: The impacts of sporting events: Hosting the 2012 London Olympic Games

In July 2005, the International Olympic Committee (IOC) announced that London had been chosen as the successful candidate city to host the 2012 Games, some 54 years since it last hosted the event. One of the underlying arguments for hosting the Games was to harness the project's potential to regenerate one of East London's most deprived boroughs – the London Borough of Newham. The Games would be hosted in an Olympic park built in the Lower Lea Valley, 13 km east of central London. It was argued by the proponents of the bid that hosting the Games would enable the transformation of 200 ha of degraded land into a new park, stretching north to the Lee Valley Regional Park. It would also lead to the creation of new sporting infrastructure (e.g. a new 25 000-seater Olympic stadium, an aquatics centre, a velopark for cycling, a hockey centre and an indoor sports centre) and an Olympic village to host 17 800 athletes and officials. These would be a lasting legacy for the community. A funding package from the government and Greater London Development Authority of US$3.8 billion (£2.375 billion) was agreed upon to underpin the project, and the London hotel sector and London universities guaranteed they would make 40 000 guestrooms available for the event.

It is estimated that this development will create 12 000 new jobs as well as 7000 construction jobs while accelerating investment in major infrastructure projects such as the £1.25 billion East London tube line extension south to Crystal Palace and West Croydon and north to Hackney, connecting the area with the Channel Tunnel rail link at Stratford. Some analysts forecast this could boost tourism by £2 billion, with the example of the Sydney Olympics cited as a case of how the Games can increase tourism. Sydney saw a £5 billion boost to tourism in the five years after the Games, while the benefits to 'Brand Australia' are estimated at AU$6.1 billion (see Chapter 10 for more discussion of branding).

However, critics of hosting the Games in London point to the UK public sector's history of failing to manage large infrastructure projects to budget (e.g. the Millennium Dome) and to consider the long-term viability of mega-projects (as discussed in Chapter 9 in relation to Millennium-funded visitor attractions that subsequently failed as businesses). Critics point to the prospect of £1.5 billion of the total revenue coming from lottery tickets and £551 million from London council tax revenue – if the project stays on budget. Apart from the Los Angeles Olympics, no Games has ever made a profit, and in the case of Sydney the projects are estimated to have cost twice the initial prices set out in the bid document. Similar overruns also occurred in Athens when it hosted the Games.

There is also considerable scepticism among researchers that investing these large sums of money in physical projects as part of a regeneration strategy run contrary to stated government policy on regeneration. If government objectives are to strengthen community cohesion and community pride, it will also breach its own government guidelines on how lottery funds should be used. Likewise, some estimates predict that if the funding overruns occur the London council taxpayers could be footing a bill of £1300 for each household. The view that the Games would create 4000 new affordable homes on the Games site for local people is a costly legacy, even if local people will be able to afford them. Newham has a high proportion of council-tenanted accommodation and high levels of long-term unemployment despite the efforts of other regeneration schemes. If one looks to the impact of the Millennium Dome and its impact on social, economic and cultural regeneration, it is clear that few long-term benefits have accrued to the area. Even in the case of the Manchester Commonwealth Games, the government had to provide an additional £105 million for the project to be completed.

While the hosting of any mega event like the Olympic Games will bring a short-term tourism benefit (and even a lasting benefit, as has happened for Sydney according to the claims to have added to its brand values), it comes at a massive public cost. We should also not lose sight of who benefits from the economic boost – primarily businesses and corporations. East London remains an area with major pockets of deprivation. Under a simple cost-benefit analysis, the forecasts of benefits always look hopeful, but to include a social rationale for hosting the event to regenerate local communities is to run counter to the experience of previous hosts of the Olympic Games. In some cases, social dislocation has occurred to make way for redevelopment. If £2.3 billion is available to regenerate East London, then the investment in iconic projects such as sports stadia and a new city park may not necessarily be the best use of public resources. Only time will tell if the 2012 Games and the forecast impacts trickle down to local people and provide much-needed local employment. Hosting the Olympic Games is more about London raising its profile internationally as a world city and an attraction for inward investment and business – part of the desire to compete as a major destination – rather than about the lasting economic benefits that may accrue if the Games are a financial success.

Where sport or event tourism exists, the motivation to travel is the attraction of the activity, festival or special event. Structured around the sporting dimension are a wider range of tourism functions that might include an extended holiday after the event. In each case, such events or activities have profound economic impacts on the locality or area in which they are hosted due to the demand for accommodation, food and beverages, attendance of the event and other ancillary services as well as associated tourism activities such as sightseeing or touring. One further area of growth in the new millennium, which linked together activities and tourism, is the rise of adventure travel.

Activities as a focus of tourism: Adventure travel and tourism

Adventure tourism has been variously defined as a leisure activity which is undertaken in unusual, exotic, remote or unconventional destinations. The defining characteristic of adventure tourism is the heavy emphasis on outdoor pursuits, usually encompassing high levels of risk, adrenaline rushes, excitement and personal challenge. Adventure tourism is normally viewed as a continuum (as shown in

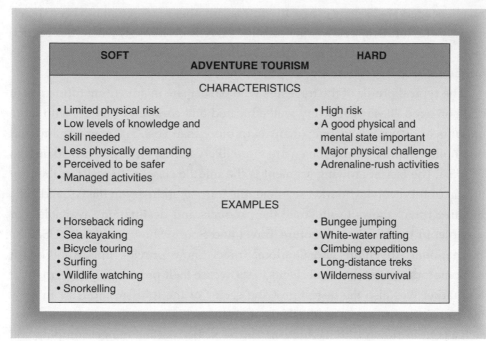

SOFT	ADVENTURE TOURISM	HARD
CHARACTERISTICS		

• Limited physical risk
• Low levels of knowledge and
  skill needed
• Less physically demanding
• Perceived to be safer
• Managed activities
		• High risk
		• A good physical and
		  mental state important
		• Major physical challenge
		• Adrenaline-rush activities

EXAMPLES		
• Horseback riding • Sea kayaking • Bicycle touring • Surfing • Wildlife watching • Snorkelling		• Bungee jumping • White-water rafting • Climbing expeditions • Long-distance treks • Wilderness survival

Figure 4.2   The characteristics of adventure tourism

Figure 4.2) that ranges from 'soft' experiences such as snorkelling to 'hard' experiences such as climbing Mount Everest.

The size of the adventure tourism market, comprising travellers who have booked a package from an adventure tour operator, is estimated to be four to five million trips a year, or 1 per cent of the international outbound tourism market. The major generating market is North America with two to three million trips a year, with one million from Europe and one million from other parts of the world. The potential market for such travel experiences is probably ten times that size, offering major growth prospects based on World Tourism Organization (UN-WTO) estimates. In the USA alone, in 1997 a Travel Industry Association of America survey indicated that half of the US population (98 million) had participated in adventure activities in the period 1992–1997. The market for adventure travel has also evolved in recent years with the growth of 'charity challenges', where travellers gain sponsorship for a trip. They typically pay the costs of the air fare and undertake to raise a minimum amount for the charity who have devised the trip. Research indicates that these travellers are ethically inclined, and may have participated in the UK in Raleigh International community and environmental expeditions for young travellers aged 17–25 years of age. In contrast, another market that has been developed by the tourism sector is the prestige adventure market, where the participants want to see something unusual, unique and exclusive to them (e.g. an individual ascent of Mount Everest) that offers an adrenaline rush.

The typical profile of the travellers who participate in adventure tourism is of a person aged 40–45 years, very well educated and computer literate, with large amounts of disposable income (many earn more than US$75 000 per annum) and long holiday entitlement. Women are more likely than men to be participants. In the USA, the fastest-growing segment is the middle classes. To assist in the promotion of this evolving market segment, the tourism industry in the UK and USA organize travel shows to illustrate the products and destinations available. For example, in the UK the Adventure Travel and Sports Show and in the USA the International Adventure and Outdoor Travel Show provide opportunities for the operators to meet potential clients to showcase their products. This segment of the market was also the fastest-growing sector of the tourism industry in New Zealand in the 1990s, as it established a number of adventure tourism destinations such as Queenstown with its *Awesome Threesome* (jetboating, bungee jumping and white-water rafting experiences). These patterns of growth encourage more tour operators to expand their product offerings to meet demand. However, the collapse of HIH Insurance in Australia in 2002 resulted in some adventure activities being suspended since participants lost their insurance cover and had to wait while new insurers and underwriters examined the risk of covering such operators. Despite events like this, and the negative publicity associated with adventure tourism accidents, the demand for these products and experiences continues to grow. Indeed, some operators have established adventure-themed hotels, emphasizing the activities as the major attractor rather than the natural attractions (i.e. scenery and location) and destination.

Critics of adventure tourism have pointed to the environmental costs of increasing numbers of travellers seeking remote locations to experience and undertake their activities, especially in National Parks and wilderness areas. Furthermore, relatively affluent visitors travelling to less developed countries to take part in adventure tourism has increased the potential for crime, abductions and attacks. Nevertheless, with growing accessibility to tourist destinations, the number of undeveloped, remote and unknown locations are fast running out. To reach these destinations, the tourism industry is dependent upon another critical element of supply – transport.

Transport

Transport is the most critical element in the promotion of the growth of domestic and international tourism. At a simple level, transport links the tourist from the origin area with the destination area. It enables the tourist (the holidaymaker, business traveller and other categories of traveller) to consume the products and experiences they have purchased, because it links the supply chain together. Figure 4.3 illustrates the all-embracing role of transport to:

- facilitate the tourist trip to the destination
- enable tourist travel within the destination.

In addition, transport may be an attraction in its own right (e.g. a cruise ship or a trip on the Orient Express). Tourists who 'tour' by road may use public transport or private transport (e.g. the car) to experience a variety of destinations. Increasingly, the transport sector is entering into strategic alliances (i.e. formal business partnerships)

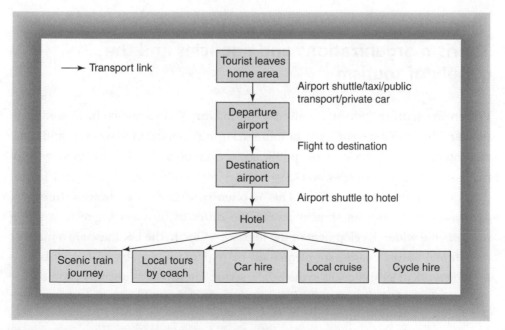

Figure 4.3   The role of transport in tourist travel

where different operators will seek to offer seamless transport experience for travellers, recognizing the selling opportunity. For example, if the tour operator can sell not only a holiday but also airport transfers, car hire and tours from approved partners with whom they have entered into a strategic alliance, then their profitability is increased. This can be achieved through commissions from selling partners' products and is evident in much of the web-based marketing by low-cost airlines as well as through airlines co-operating rather than competing. Figure 4.4 summarizes the complex range of issues which airlines face when deciding whether to enter into strategic alliances or other forms of collaboration. It shows that the airline has to examine its own motivation for entering into an alliance (strategic analysis) followed by the different options available for an alliance (i.e. joint development or merger/acquisition). This then leads to a review of possible collaboration partners. Then the alliance is reviewed against a range of operational issues associated with the alliance structure. This illustrates the increasing integration within the tourism sector, with different business interests linking together in the supply chain: a feature that will be discussed later in the chapter. The tourism industry and its growing complexity has seen the growth of organizations and agencies which have been developed to manage the supply of tourism.

Tourism organizations and agencies and the supply of tourism

Within the tourism industry, a number of 'institutional elements' have sought to manage the growing complexity of tourism supply in relation to services and business operations. At one level, the public sector has sought to plan and manage supply issues within countries and destinations to establish an orderly and logical direction for the tourism sector. This is often described as a strategic direction, expressed as a 'tourism strategy', with the different business interests working towards the wider development of the tourism sector. In the UK these are a number of national tourist boards, supplemented by regional or area-based tourist boards and the work of local councils in the public sector. These boards not only promote the region for which they are responsible but attempt to foster the continued economic development of tourism as well as encouraging members of the tourism sector to work together to enhance the quality of provision (see Chapter 11 for more detail).

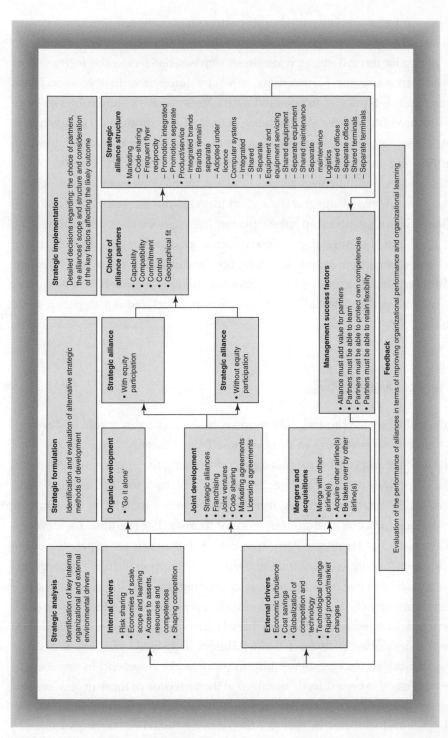

Figure 4.4 Conceptualization of the collaborative strategy process for international airlines (reprinted from *Strategic Management for Travel and Tourism*, N. Evans, D. Campbell and G. Stonehouse, 253, © 2003 with permission from Elsevier)

This has led to a growing number of partnerships between tourism industry partners (stakeholders), the local industry and the destination area. For example, in Western Australia the growth in wine-based tourism has led to the formation of public and private sector partnerships, whereby tourism industry associations have been created. Similarly, in Scotland's first National Park similar bodies have emerged to promote specific destinations or individual products (i.e. adventure tourism). These partnerships not only market the local products but also, through collaboration and partnership working, seek to raise the profile and number of visitors to the area by building on synergies between the businesses to increase visitor spending. These lobby groups receive a grant from the public sector and raise additional finance from membership subscriptions. Trade associations also operate at a national level, such as specialist industry sector groups (e.g. the Association of Scottish Visitor Attractions based in Stirling, Scotland). There are also much higher-profile industry lobby groups such as the Association of British Travel Agents (ABTA), which represents travel agents and tour operators and is a corporate trade association.

Tourist services and facilities

Whilst the public sector can facilitate tourism, it also has a direct role in developing the tourism infrastructure in destinations. This is usually vested in the local authority, who are responsible for managing/overseeing the appropriate provision of water, sewerage, roading and facilities that will be used by residents and tourists alike. At a national level, governments become involved in the strategic decision-making for infrastructure provision for tourism. For example, the development of Terminal 5 at Heathrow Airport in the UK has meant the expansion of the country's leading tourist gateway and infrastructure to support its future growth and development. In this instance, the state is approving the development that a private sector company (British Airports Authority) will implement in the long-term public interest. In other cases, the state directly invests in infrastructure provision (such as the development of the Channel Tunnel high-speed rail link project) to encourage private sector investment to pump-prime development. In some countries, the state has also been directly involved in the provision of tourism services and facilities, an example being the state-owned Tourist Hotel Corporation in New Zealand up until the 1990s. In Albania, the state controlled all aspects of tourism supply – the airline, hotel provision, tour guides and transport in the destination – though this is much less common in countries in the new millennium.

The private sector is also responsible for tourist services and facilities of course, and dominates the restaurant sector as well as provision of services used by tourists and non-tourists alike, such as retailing. In Europe, much of the activity in the restaurant sector is dominated by small businesses, many being family-run and employing fewer than ten people. In contrast, retailing is often dominated by chains and retail multiples in major tourist cities. In China, retail growth of 14 per cent occurred in 2004, much of which is attributed to 'leisure shopping'. In 2003, China had 236 shopping malls and by 2004 this reached 400, illustrating the scale of this growth and demand. Shanghai, which is preparing for the 2010 Expo (expected to attract 70 million visitors), is developing a multilingual digital map to link shopping and tourism together; this illustrates the synergy that exists between each activity. The infrastructure development for the Expo is expected to cost US$3 billion but is expected to lever US$6 billion in revenue. There is similar investment in retail infrastructure. Hong Kong International Airport's new terminal is an example of this, demonstrating the scale of leisure spending by the 85 000 travellers who use the facility each day (as well as the 36 000 meeters/greeters welcoming visitors and returning travellers). On average, departing international visitors spend three hours in the terminal ('dwell time') creating many opportunities for retailing. This illustrates the potential of linking tourism with business activity and the implications for managing the supply of tourism.

Managing the supply of tourism in the new millennium

Within the European tourism sector, a number of important economic changes have impacted upon the structure and organization of tourism. This has been described as consolidation, meaning that a large number of nationally based private firms have been sold, acquired and merged to create fewer, larger transnational tourism businesses. A transnational business operates across country boundaries. The EU and national government monopoly authorities are the main obstacle to continued consolidation.

Many businesses are vertically integrated, meaning that tour operator A has taken over hotel or transport operator B to make its business larger and to expand its range and market share of the available business through a diversified product base. In Europe, a steel and engineering firm, Preussag, acquired the leading travel companies in Germany (TUI) and the UK (Thomson) by developing a travel business. The consolidation strategy has enabled many travel companies to emerge as large national companies. For example, in Germany, the third largest travel retailer Rewe built its position by:

- acquiring a mass market tour operator ITS in the 1990s
- purchasing the DER Group from the Deutsche Bahn Group in 1999
- purchasing the tour operator LTU in 2000.

By purchasing stakes in different parts of the businesses, Rewe has acquired three long-haul and short-haul operations.

With the growth in travel retailing in direct sales via the phone and the world-wide web, it is not surprising that many of the acquisitions and mergers of larger travel businesses have led to investment in expanding the channels for distributing products and services. Yet such activities require large sums of capital investment. Preussag paid £1.8 billion for Thomson and has continued to invest in the hotels and airlines it owns as part of a vertically integrated tourism business. Similarly, Thomson has expected to invest £100 million in information technology systems and e-commerce.

Consolidation trends have seen some operators such as Preussag (now TUI) wanting to have a presence in most major outbound markets. This has made Preussag the leading operator in the UK, Germany, the Netherlands and Austria. It is the second largest in Scandinavia and Belgium and ranked third in Switzerland. In contrast, Airtours was ranked second in the UK, first in Scandinavia and fifth in Germany.

These trends in the travel industry reflect the highly competitive and constantly changing nature of this business. For many businesses operating in slow-growth or stagnating markets, such as the UK and Germany, cost control is vital. Spiralling costs were one of the reasons for to the collapse of Clarkson's in the UK in the 1970s. Thomson announced cost reductions in the late 1990s after poor financial results, seeking to save £50 million in cost savings 2000–2002. Streamlining internal business processes through the use of new technology to avoid duplication of business activities is one way in which large travel firms can achieve cost savings after undergoing mergers and takeovers.

The business strategies, that travel companies can pursue to develop their supply of tourism services and products include:

- Focusing on core business (i.e. a holiday company focusing on selling holidays rather than being vertically integrated and operating its own airline and hotels).
- Seeking to diversify its products. The leading French holiday company Club Méditerranée (Club Med), which traditionally sold packages to its 120 holiday resorts, has used this strategy. Since 1999 and its acquisition of Jet Tours (France's fourth ranked tour operator, which operated to 113 summer and 81 winter locations) it has diversified its operations to sell non-Club Med packages. Rewe in Germany has pursued a similar diversification strategy with its acquisition of a wider range of tour operating businesses in the long- and short-haul market.
- Choosing to operate in all segments of the tourism market. Preussag has adopted this tactic and others such as Kuoni are moving towards that goal.
- Non-holiday companies may choose to enter the market: easyJet planned to enter the cruise holiday business in 2005.

To implement these business strategies, companies in the tourism industry have adopted marketing-related concepts such as branding to differentiate their products in an increasingly competitive marketplace. For example, Club Med relaunched its worldwide image to re-emphasize its famous name and association with consumers, and particularly its dominant position in the French market. Thomas Cook, now owned by the German company C&N Touriste, has used its global image and historic association with pioneering tourism to continue its expansion throughout Europe. Norwegian Coastal Voyage has introduced a new brand – Natural Horizons – targeting upmarket wildlife travellers: prices start at £3935 for an 11-day cruise to Alaska from the UK. Tour operators have to consider the potential for retaining different brands for different markets in the various countries they operate in, or to move towards pan-European brands.

Changes in the supply of tourism products through a vertically integrated distribution chain (i.e. travel agents or direct sales) has begun to limit consumers' choice in terms of some of the larger conglomerates. For example, in 1998 Thomson's retail chain, Lunn Poly, sold 31 per cent of the company's holiday capacity. This translated into 47 per cent of Lunn Poly's sales as Thomson products reflected in other countries, where similar trends exist. Many of the larger travel companies are also investing heavily in direct selling by phone or on the worldwide web. In 2000 for example,

Airtours acquired a US internet company – Travel Services International – as a vehicle for its £100 million investment in e-commerce under the brand mytravelco. This mirrored trends by other tour operators such as Thomson. At the same time, many e-travel agencies have been established globally (e.g. Expedia) which are challenging the existing patterns of consumer purchasing.

What many travel suppliers are recognizing is the growth in e-commerce is necessary to respond to changes in demand over the next five years, which will include:

- a gradual reduction in the length of main holidays
- a rise in the number of additional (second and third holidays)
- increasing demand for activity holidays
- greater flexibility among consumers willing to book last-minute holidays, seat-only sales and more short breaks
- the rise of self-packaging of products online ('dynamic packaging').

These trends in consumer demand illustrate that the supply of tourism products and services requires highly refined management tools within the tourism sector if its members are to respond to changes and opportunities.

Summary

Within the larger travel companies, pressures on cost reduction and increased numbers of acquisitions and mergers have caused a considerable degree of change in the operating environment, which reinforces the need for leadership and many of the skills observed by Mintzberg. Tourism supply needs to be customer focused and, therefore, many tourism businesses not only have to think, work and act strategically (i.e. look to the future and the best way to operate), but also be cognizant of immediate operational and management issues so that profitability (the bottom line) is maintained. Being able to respond to the market increasingly requires the sophisticated use of information technology, innovative advertising and recognizable brands so that consumers will buy what is on offer. In the supply of tourism products and services, the culmination of transport, accommodation, attractions, associated services and the institutional elements need to co-exist so that destinations continue to attract the visitor. Managing the supply chain, to ensure tourism services are delivered in a coherent manner according to the specification sold to the visitor, requires a great many managerial skills on a day-to-day basis. When some-thing goes wrong and causes inconvenience to travellers, it is frequently picked up by the media. This means that companies need a fluid business strategy to be able to respond rapidly to changes in the operating environment. A global understand-ing of tourism trends, innovation in product development and how to adapt to adverse elements in the marketplace, as well as the opportunities that arise, is also required of managers.

References

Mintzberg, H. (1973) *The Nature of Managerial Work*. New York: Harper and Row.
Sessa, A. (1983) *Elements of Tourism*. Rome: Catal.

Further reading

The best sources to consult on tourism supply issues are:
Charaupunsirikul, S. and Wood, R. (2002) Mintzberg, managers and methodology: Some observations from a study of hotel general managers. *Tourism Management*, 23 (5): 551–6.
Ioannides, D. and K. Debbage (eds) (1998) *The Economic Geography of the Tourist Industry: A Supply-Side Analysis*. London: Routledge.
Witt, S., Brooke, M. and Buckley, P. (1991) *The Management of International Tourism*. London: Routledge.

Questions

1 Why is tourism supply important to the production of the tourist experience?
2 How do economic market conditions affect the competitive environment for tourism businesses?
3 Why does the supply chain concept help to explain the way tourism products are assembled?
4 What future factors will impact upon the management of supply issues for the tourism industry?

5

Transporting the tourist I: Surface transport

Learning outcomes

Transport forms the vital link between tourists and destinations. It also provides the focus for many tourist activities such as sightseeing and cruising. After reading this chapter, you should be able to understand:

- the relationship between transport and tourism
- the significance of different modes of surface transport and their contribution to tourism
- the role of operational issues in developing competitive modes of tourist transport.

Introduction

The pursuit of tourism through the ages has stimulated a steady growth in the range of destinations visited and has been characterized by a growing impact upon different countries and places. This is directly related to changes in transport technology and its affordability, or diffusion of tourism from a travelling elite initially to a wider mass market. In the nineteenth century the building of railways and cheap fares (combined with increases in leisure time) permitted a mass market development of seaside trips in many European countries, initially as day trips and later as holidays, as this form of tourism became more widely available. This is illustrated in Figure 5.1, which shows how the innovation of rail travel and its decreasing costs led to growing numbers of people travelling as tourists as previous modes of transport (e.g. the paddle steamer) were replaced by mass forms of transport. What this example also shows is that transport is a vital facilitator of tourism: it enables the tourist to travel from their home area (origin) to their

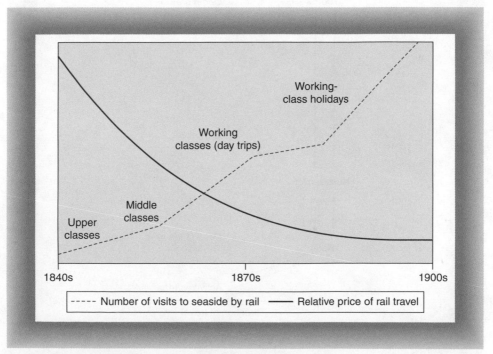

Figure 5.1 Hypothetical example of the impact of railway technology on the growth of coastal tourism in Victorian and Edwardian England

destination and to return. This tourist trip has a reciprocal or two-way element: the tourist travels out on a mode of transport and then returns at a set period of time later. These simple principles of tourist travel were introduced in Chapter 4 and are reiterated here so that they can be used as a basis to differentiate different forms of tourist travel.

In the example shown in Figure 5.2, the tourist travels on a number of different forms of transport from the origin to destination area. Conventionally, each element of travel has been viewed as a passive element, as a means to an end (reaching the destination area). However, this is now very outdated. In the case of package holidays, service interruptions (especially flight delays) can severely impact upon the tourist's enjoyment of their holiday and so, like accommodation, transport should actually be seen as an integral element upon which the tourist experience is built. For example, when I worked for a coach operator, the major complaints clients made were about how their holiday had been ruined or affected when they were

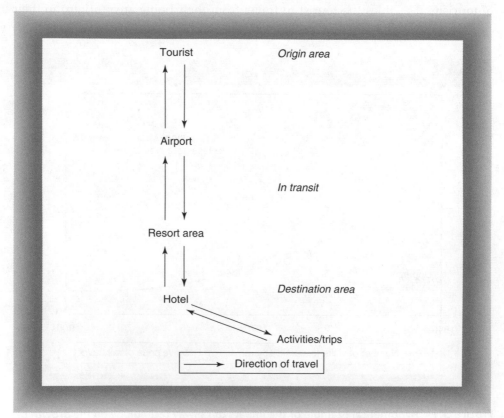

Figure 5.2   Tourist travel from origin to destination area and return

left behind at a pick-up point, there was a service breakdown or delays occurred that caused inconvenience, stress and tarnished their holiday experience. It was not just the holiday but also the transport that impacted upon the customer's satisfaction. In fact travellers often have unrealistic expectations of transport providers, especially budget travellers who expect the standards of provision and customer care offered by full-price well-known airline brands when delays or operational problems occur. This is emphasized in the following extract:

> the purchaser of the tourism product (*the tourist*) must experience the trip to access the product, the quality of the transportation experience becomes an important aspect of the tourist experience and, therefore a key criterion that enters into destination choice. Poor service, scheduling problems, and/or long delays associated with a transportation service, for example, can seriously affect a traveller's perceptions and levels of enjoyment with respect to a trip. Tourists require safe, comfortable, affordable, and efficient intermodal transportation networks that enable precious vacation periods to be enjoyed to their maximum potential. (Lamb and Davidson, 1996: 264–5)

It also illustrates the interrelationships between transport and tourism where four main elements exist:

1 the tourist
2 the relationship between transport and the tourist experience
3 the effect of transport problems on the tourist's perception
4 the tourist's requirement for safe, reliable and efficient modes of transport.

Transport, tourism and the tour

The mode of transport by which tourists seek to travel may be the main motivation for a holiday or the containing context of a holiday, and this is the case with a cruise or coach tour. In these examples, the basic element of tourism, the tour (which takes in a number of destinations on an itinerary, as discussed in Chapter 2 with regard to the Grand Tour), is followed. The basic principle of a tour is shown in Figure 5.3: the tourist travels to the point of departure, then boards the mode of transport (a coach or cruise ship) and engages in the tour, which follows a set route over a

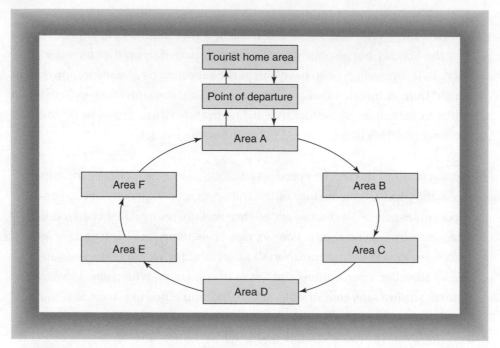

Figure 5.3   A tour with an itinerary, visiting different areas

period of time. At each point of call (Areas A to D), the mode of transport may require an overnight stay on the mode of transport (the cruise ship) or in serviced accommodation, and time is made available for visiting attractions and for sightseeing. The coach or cruise then travels to the next area. Eventually the tour returns back to the point of departure and the tour is completed. In recent years, cruise companies have introduced the concept of fly-cruises to offer more compact, time-efficient cruises. Passengers fly to a point of departure when they undertake a cruise or part of a cruise before returning by ship or aircraft. At a less organized level, the principles of touring are inherent in the activities of holidaymakers who undertake domestic driving holidays or tours in their destination area. Therefore, transporting the tourist, the tour and travel in general are fundamental elements of the dynamic phenomenon known as tourism.

The movement of people, often in large volumes, requires specific managerial skills and an understanding of logistics – particularly of how the transport system and its different elements are managed. For the transport sector, managing the supply of transport so it meets demand and operates in an efficient, timely and convenient manner is an underlying feature for transporting tourists. For this reason, this chapter and Chapter 6 examine the transport sector and the principal modes of transport by land, water and air. In each case the management issues involving tourists will be highlighted and key concepts associated with each mode of transport. However, prior to discussing land-based transport it is useful to examine a number of concepts that are used in understanding how tourist transport is shaped by government.

Policy issues in tourist transport

Much of the provision of transport which tourists use is a direct response of private-sector firms' desire to provide a service which is a profitable enterprise in its own right. Yet the provision of transport does not occur in an unconstrained market with no controls or regulation. Whilst tourists may wish to travel and transport operators want to provide a service, governments develop policies and regulatory frameworks to facilitate, sometimes constrain, and manage transport provision. Governments may pursue policies that promote a high level of regulation or policies that promote total deregulation. For example, in a highly regulated environment, the government may operate its own airline (a 'flag carrier'), to promote tourism development in a country. In contrast, in a highly deregulated environment, the government may adopt a 'hands-off' approach, wanting competition and the market to determine what services are provided. Whilst policy objectives may set the direction the government wants to pursue, governments also have responsibility for the provision of infrastructure given the high capital costs of airports, ports and railways, roads, bridges and waterways. However, in recent years, governments have tried to defray these high capital costs by encouraging private-sector investment and leasing the asset to the developer for 20–25 years so they recoup the cost plus a profit, then the asset returns to the state. These changing approaches to transport policy have followed distinct phases in countries such as the UK, where Button and Gillingwater (1983) identified four eras, each of which had a clear impact on tourism development and provision. A fifth era that has developed since the 1990s can also be discerned:

1 *The Railway Age*, from the 1840s onwards, during which private-sector investment was employed to develop land-based transport (except during the First World War when state control was exercised).

2 *The Age of Protection*, which dominated the 1920s and 1930s when road transport emerged and unplanned car and coach travel developed. Governments intervened to prevent excessive competition, which in the USA led to the 1935 Motor Carriage Act that protected the Greyhound Bus Operators by giving this one operator a monopoly on inter-urban bus travel.

3 *The Age of Administrative Planning* followed the Second World War, with the weaknesses exposed in railway companies leading to nationalization and a national passenger network to ensure national efficiency. The financial costs of large-scale nationalization led to major subsidies, which were restructured in the 1960s after the Beeching Report (the network was cut back considerably). In 1968, the Transport Act in the UK led to further reorganization of public transport with the creation of the National Bus Company (NBC).

4 *The Age of Contestability* characterized the USA in the 1970s and the UK in the 1980s. It was based on the principles of deregulation to achieve greater efficiency and to reduce public subsidies. In the UK, it led to the sale of state-owned assets (e.g. the sale of the NBC) and the establishment of private transport providers such as British Airways, Sealink Ferries and Stena, and, in the early 1990s, to the privatization of British Rail.

5 *The Age of Public–Private Partnerships* has emerged in the UK since the Labour government entered power in the late 1990s. It has seen continuity with previous policies of privatization and a greater emphasis on private-sector expertise to manage transport infrastructure. Concerns for efficiency and renewed investment in infrastructure have led to complex solutions to harness public–private partnerships in redeveloping aged infrastructure like the London Underground. Where the private sector assesses the risk of investment as not justified in terms of likely returns, the state has had to reinvest using taxpayers' funds. Where competition is seen as beneficial, it is promoted, particularly in air travel.

One additional level of policy measure that is important in Europe is the role of the European Union and its attempt to develop pan-European policies towards transport provision. EU states have been slow to engage in rail competition following EU Directive 91/440 in 1991 that sought to separate infrastructure from operations. Sweden initially separated its operations from infrastructure, followed by the UK and Germany in 1994 (see Figure 5.4 which depicts the UK railway industry post-privatization). France established the RRF infrastructure authority in 1997 (although most of its responsibilities are delegated to SNCF) while the Netherlands implemented similar changes in July 2001, but poor management led to virtual re-nationalization.

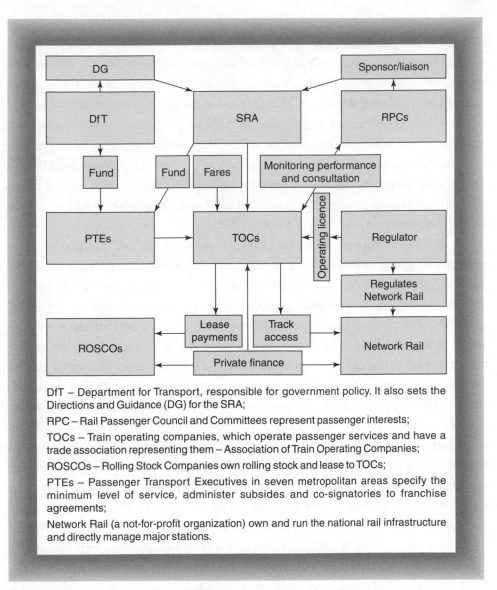

DfT – Department for Transport, responsible for government policy. It also sets the Directions and Guidance (DG) for the SRA;

RPC – Rail Passenger Council and Committees represent passenger interests;

TOCs – Train operating companies, which operate passenger services and have a trade association representing them – Association of Train Operating Companies;

ROSCOs – Rolling Stock Companies own rolling stock and lease to TOCs;

PTEs – Passenger Transport Executives in seven metropolitan areas specify the minimum level of service, administer subsides and co-signatories to franchise agreements;

Network Rail (a not-for-profit organization) own and run the national rail infrastructure and directly manage major stations.

Figure 5.4   The UK rail passenger industry structure (source: Page, 2002; © Mintel)

To compete with air-based traffic and to address European air congestion, the EU proposed plans for a trans-European network (TENS) of high-speed road and rail links in Europe. The EU identified nine rail projects totalling 35 000 km of high-speed lines after 1994 (15 000 km of existing railway to be upgraded and 20 000 km of new routes), for completion in 2009. A 1994 study by the EC/Union of

International Railway Companies (UIC) forecast that with a TENS network in operation, rail may account for 23.5 per cent of the estimated 1.5 billion passenger kilometres which would be travelled in western Europe by 2010. This would require passengers to switch their mode of travel so that the car would account for 60.2 per cent of traffic flows, rail 23.5 per cent and air 16.5 per cent. Whilst the EU pointed to success in new high-speed operations (e.g. Spain's AVE route from Madrid to Seville saw the share of air traffic drop from 40 per cent to 13 per cent and the Paris–Brussels THALY service led to a 15 per cent drop in car usage), these are the exception rather than the norm. These flagship projects are frequently used to justify additional investment, given that road and air congestion add 6 per cent to EU fuel consumption.

In 2003, the UK Department for Transport issued a White Paper (a discussion paper) setting out its proposed policy for airport development in the UK to 2033. This recognized that air travel had increased fivefold during 1970–2002, from 32 million passengers to 189 million passengers. Their forecasts were for between 350 and 460 million passengers travelling; these forecasts are based on half the population flying each year, and 70 per cent of these flights being to overseas destinations. Strong industrial lobby groups such as the British Airport Authority, airlines and freight companies argued for the major economic benefits of air transport to the UK economy and the importance of expansion. However, the White Paper did not consider promoting rail travel for domestic trips as an alternative to air transport when much of the recent growth in UK airport usage has been promoted by low-cost airlines. Consequently, whilst the EU is avidly promoting rail travel as an option to road and air travel in the EU, the UK government has favoured air travel, although airlines are not required to pay for the full economic and environmental impact of their activities, since aviation fuel is exempt from excise duty. Therefore, even within the EU, member states are pursuing their own ideological stance towards transport policies affecting tourism, in spite of other policy objectives aimed towards sustainable economic activity.

This discussion of policy issues illustrates that government policy can directly affect the supply of transport services in its use of regulation–deregulation measures. Notable entrepreneurs in the transport sector have responded to the opportunities afforded by transport policy changes (e.g. the deregulation of the bus industry and railway system after 1985) as the rise of Stagecoach as a global transport operator in the UK has shown (also see the case study later in Box 5.1 on megabus.com). The rise of Virgin and easyJet as transport brands has also followed a similar pattern.

Policy changes such as deregulation have also altered the shape and nature of transport provision for tourists (as the discussion of air transport in Chapter 6 shows). In some cases deregulation has increased choice; in other instances an initial increase in choice has been followed by consolidation that has actually reduced choice. Recognizing the linkages between transport and tourism can also yield invaluable business opportunities (consider, for example, the growth in airport shuttle companies). In some cases, airport authorities have taken the lead, such as the British Airport Authority in the UK, with the construction of the Heathrow Express, a fast rail link from Paddington in central London to Heathrow. With these issues in mind, attention now turns to land-based transport.

Land-based transport

Land-based transport is often neglected in discussions of transport and tourism, and yet it forms the dominant mode of travel for many domestic tourist trips. Air travel normally attracts more attention due to the scale and pace of development in this market since the early 1970s. However, land-based transport has a long history and covers a number of distinct forms: the car, the cycle, bus and coach travel and rail travel.

The car and tourist travel

In the post-war period, the growth of car ownership has made tourist travel more flexible but it has also induced overuse at accessible sites. Ease of access, fuelled by a growth in road building and the upgrading of minor roads in many developed countries, has been a self-reinforcing process, leading to overuse and a greater dominance of passive recreational activities. Car ownership expanded rapidly in most countries in the 1970s and 1980s, adding pressure to the road network especially at holiday times (e.g. the August holiday exodus from Paris to holiday destinations). Among the key factors which affect the use of roads by tourists are access, the quality of the infrastructure, grades of road and signage to steer tourists to tour areas, which may be off the beaten track. In New Zealand Destination Northland's Twin Coast Highway has started an initiative to encourage tourists to travel on a circuit, spreading the distribution of visitors by encouraging them to explore heritage sites, wineries and golf courses via less-used roads. Intermodal connections (i.e. connections between different modes of transport) between airports, ports and rail termini and tourist areas are also important. There is also recognition that tourist areas need to develop new linear land and water corridors that integrate various forms of transport to explore scenic regions.

Regions and countries should consider the concept of seamless transport systems for tourists. This means that the individual transport networks that exist for each mode of tourist transport need to be planned and integrated into a holistic framework. This will ensure that the tourist's experience of transport is a continuous one which is not characterized by major gaps in provision and a lack of integration (e.g. airports need to be linked to tourist districts so that visitors transfer from one mode of transport to another with relative ease).

Probably the most influential study of car usage among recreationalists was Wall's (1971) study of Kingston-upon-Hull in the UK. It highlighted the importance of seasonality and timing of pleasure trips by car and the dominance of the car as a mode of transport for urban dwellers. It also considered the role of the journey by car as a form of recreation in itself; the car is more than just a means of transport. Wall also found that the majority of pleasure trips were day trips less than 100 km away from Hull, being concentrated in a limited number of resorts along the Yorkshire coast and southerly part of the region.

Eaton and Holding (1996) identified the growing scale of such visits to the countryside by visitors in cars. In 1991, 103 million visits were made to National Parks in the UK (Countryside Commission 1992), the most popular being the Lake District and Peak District Parks. It was estimated in 1992 that car traffic would grow by 267 per cent by the year 2025. Rising car usage has coincided with the decline in public transport usage for tourist and recreational trips. Yet many National Parks seem unlikely to be able to cope with the levels of usage predicted by 2025, given their urban catchments and the relative accessibility by motorway and A roads in the UK. Eaton and Holding (1996) reviewed the absence of effective policies to meet the practical problems of congestion facing many sites in the countryside in Britain. This situation is little different a decade later, with many National Parks besieged by cars in the peak season – which seems to be at odds with the conservation goals intended when National Parks were initially conceived. This problem is worse when concentrated at 'honey pots' (locations which attract large numbers in a confined area) in National Parks. Research by Connell (2005) reaffirmed many of these issues in Scotland's first National Park, created in 2001, the Loch Lomond and Trossachs National Park.

The UK Tourism Society's response to the government taskforce on tourism and the environment (English Tourist Board/Employment Department 1991) highlighted the impact of the car by commenting that:

> no analysis of the relationship between tourism and the environment can ignore transportation. Tourism is inconceivable without it. Throughout Europe some 40 per cent of leisure time away from home is spent travelling, and the vast majority of this is by car … Approaching 30 per cent of the UK's energy requirements go on transportation … [and] … the impact of traffic congestion, noise and air pollution … [will] … diminish the quality of the experience for visitors.

A number of sensitive areas, including Yosemite National Park in the USA, have had to develop management plans to control the impact of the car. Yosemite had allowed access by car since 1917, but by the 1920s it was handling one million vehicle movements a year. The 1980 and 2000 Final Yosemite Valley Plan introduced out-of-park car parks and a shuttle bus for peak periods as management tools.

One additional area that is worthy of discussion in terms of road transport is the car hire industry. This is neglected in many studies of tourism and transport, and yet it is a major driver of car-based activity. The car hire business can be divided into three distinct segments:

1 Airport rentals, which often command a 15 per cent premium charge over and above other rentals due to the charges imposed by airport authorities. These are based on the principle that this is a captive market which is able to pay the price demanded. This may be the case for corporate travel, where such prices have been discounted on the basis of volume business and leisure travellers pay premium prices.
2 Downtown rental locations.
3 Replacement vehicles for corporates and individuals whose cars are off the road being repaired or serviced.

In Europe the car hire business is dominated by the main brands, which also dominate the US market: Avis, Budget, National (formed from Eurodollar and Alamo) and Hertz. The scale of the industry is illustrated by two of the market leaders: Avis, which employs 4600 staff in Europe and has a fleet of 80 000 vehicles, and Hertz, with 7000 rental locations worldwide. The traditional ownership patterns in which car manufacturers were key stakeholders have changed as manufacturers have reduced their involvement. Many car hire companies have looked at leasing vehicles rather than purchasing now that second-hand car values have dropped in Europe due to oversupply of new vehicles. The cost of car hire for tourists varies considerably by country, reflecting tax regimes and other local factors. In Europe, Finland is the most expensive, being 48 per cent dearer than the cheapest rental costs in Belgium and Luxembourg. In the USA, the car rental market is worth in excess of US$16.5 billion. The market sustains varying pricing strategies, a feature observed by the American Automobile Association in 2002 when they noted that hire car rates in the same city could vary between 18 and 190 per cent for the same product. Typically, rates varied around 77 per cent, with the greatest variations in key tourist destinations in states such as California and Nevada. Unsurprisingly a common complaint amongst car hirers is that hidden charges and a lack of transparency dominate the retailing of this product. Overall the most lucrative markets for car rental are France, Germany, Italy, Spain and the UK, which reflects the domestic, and international tourism markets in each country, which dominate patterns of tourism in Europe.

Cycling

Bicycles are used by tourists either occasionally by those visiting a destination, who may hire a cycle for a day, or for long-distance cycling holidays undertaken by the more determined. Lumsdon (1996: 5) defines cycle tourism as cycling that is 'part of or the primary activity of, a holiday trip … it falls within a categorisation of activity holidays'. The UK Department of Transport statistics suggest that up to 40 per cent of cycle journeys are for leisure purposes, as Lumsdon (1997: 115) shows:

> Leisure cycling has great potential for growth, it can be a stimulus to tourism, it is a high-quality way to enjoy the countryside and a good way to introduce people to cycling for their everyday transport needs. To encourage leisure cycling there needs to be small scale improvements, especially near where people live, followed by better signposting, marketing and information. Flagship leisure routes, using quiet roads or disused railway paths, can increase the profile and boost leisure cycling in town and countryside. (Department of Transport, 1996: 13, cited in Lumsdon, 1997: 115)

But who are the typical cycle tourists and what motivates them to use this form of transport? The Scottish Tourist Board's (1991) innovative study on the *Tourism Potential of Cycling and Cycle Routes in Scotland* indicated that cycling had grown in popularity as a recreational activity in the 1970s and 1980s, with the Cyclists Tourist Club having 40 000 members in the UK. A later study by the Countryside Commission (1995), *The Market for Recreational Cycling in the Countryside*, identified some of the main motivations for cycling, including:

- keeping fit
- having fun
- getting some fresh air
- accessing the countryside.

In a tourism context, Lumsdon's (1996) study simplifies the market segments involved in cycle tourism to include:

- *Holiday cyclists*, comprising couples, families or friends who seek a holiday where they can enjoy opportunities to cycle but not necessarily every day. They seek traffic-free routes and are independent travellers who are not interested in a package holiday. While they are likely to take their own bikes on holiday, a proportion of them will hire bikes. They are likely to cycle 25–40 km each day that they travel by bike.
- *Short-break cyclists*, who seek to escape and select packages that will provide local knowledge (with or without cycle hire) and comfortable accommodation. They are likely to travel in groups and to cycle 25–40 km a day.
- *Day excursionists*, who are casual cyclists who undertake leisurely circular rides of 15–25 km. They are not prepared to travel long distances to visit attractions or facilities but prefer to seek quiet country lanes, which are signposted. They tend to comprise 25–30 per cent of the market for cycling and are increasingly using their own bikes rather than hiring them.

The Royal Commission on Environmental Pollution (HMSO, 1994) identified the role of cycling as a mode of personal transport that is sustainable and has minimal pollution and effects on others. It recommended that cycle trips should be quadrupled to 10 per cent of all journeys in the UK by 2005, highlighting the need for further infrastructure to achieve such growth targets. By 2004 SUSTRANS, the National

Cycle Network (NCN) that has promoted cycle routes, found that 201 million trips a year were being made on the NCN and that 60 million of these were on traffic-free components of the NCN. One of the important findings of the Royal Commission was that local authorities in the UK should have a control role in meeting the 2005 targets and in infrastructure provision. This was to be achieved through the existing planning mechanism – the local authority's annual Transport Policies and Programme Submissions (TPPs). While the purpose was to improve the level of cycle use, it has implications for tourism, which can utilize any infrastructure put in place for residents and leisure users in local areas. A number of UK local authorities appointed cycling officers, who have developed strategy documents for local use, but one of the principal catalysts for facilitating the development of a national cycle network in the UK is SUSTRANS.

The UK's national cycle network

SUSTRANS is a national sustainable transport and construction company operating as a charity that designs and builds routes. One of its early aims was to develop a 2000-mile national cycle network to link all the main urban centres in the UK, using a combination of traffic-calmed roads, cycle paths, disused railway lines and river/canal paths. This aim was realized in 1996 via a grant of £43.5 million from the Millennium Commission (comprising 20 per cent of the total cost) to form a 10 400-km route on the basis of its original vision. This was the UK's National Cycle Network. By 2005 it had achieved its ambitious target to expand to 16 000 km. In 2000, over 23.5 million cycling trips were made on the network and rising to 77 million in 2004. Estimates seem to indicate that the network has the potential to generate 750 million cycling and walking trips per annum by 2015. SUSTRANS (2002) argues that the network generates £635 million from cycle tourism, with the following economic impacts:

- £146 per domestic trip (based on expenditure of £30–£35 a night)
- £300 per overseas cycling holiday trip
- £9 per trip for each cycling day trip
- £4 per local leisure cycling trip.

Indeed the UK Leisure Day Visits Survey in the UK recognized that the average cycle day trip comprises 62.9 km in length, 3.6 hours in duration and with a party size of 4.6.

The market segments for cycle tourism trips identified by SUSTRANS (2002) comprised:

- infrequent leisure cyclists
- occasional leisure cyclists
- frequent leisure cyclists
- cycling enthusiasts.

Each of these has specific product requirements as Table 5.1 shows.

The C2C cycle route is indicative of the generative effect it may have. The C2C route is a 270-km coast-to-coast route in northern England which attracts over 10 000 cycle tourists to an economically marginal area (West Cumbria and the North Pennines). This has generated an annual expenditure of £100 per person and £1.1 million for the local tourism economy.

There is also a European Cycle Route Network and some of the principal routes are:

- the 5000-km Atlantis route (Isle of Skye, Scotland, to Cadiz, Spain)
- the 470-km Noordzee route (Den Helder in the Netherlands to Boulogne-sur-Mer in France).

According to Lumsdon (1996: 10–12), there are three ways that the National Cycle Network may contribute to sustainable tourism (i.e. tourism which does not further damage or harm the resource base upon which it depends):

1 By encouraging tourists to switch from cars to cycles at their destination, although it needs a cycle-friendly culture to implement such changes in tourist attitudes. This could reduce recreational car journeys at the destination by 20–30 per cent.
2 By reducing car-based day excursions, particularly at honey pot attractions or sites near to resorts and urban areas. The National Cycle Network may offer 'escape routes' to allow tourists to get off the beaten track.
3 By encouraging growth in cycle-based holidays, in both the short-break and longer duration categories, among UK residents and overseas visitors.

Cycle tourism is certainly beginning to assume a much higher profile in the UK and if their use for leisure encourages people to become more avid cyclists and

Table 5.1 Cycle tourism market segments and product requirements (source: SUSTRANS, 2002: 7, reproduced with permission from SUSTRANS, www.sustrans.org.uk)

Market segment	Types of activity required	Product requirements
Infrequent leisure cyclists	Traffic-free cycling Packaged cycle touring holidays	Traffic-free cycle paths Cycle hire Packaged cycling holidays
Occasional leisure cyclists	Day cycle rides (20–25 miles on quiet country roads and traffic-free paths) Centre-based cycling short breaks Access to countryside from town and home	Circular day cycle routes with maps and information Safe places to leave the car while cycling Ideas for cycling short breaks Cycle parking and storage Cycle repair/rescue
Frequent leisure cyclists	Day cycle rides (30–35 miles on quiet country roads and traffic-free paths) Centre-based cycling short breaks Access to countryside from town and home	Circular day cycle routes with maps Safe places to leave the car while cycling Cycle access by train (for some) Ideas for cycling short breaks and cycle touring holidays Cycle friendly accommodation Cycle parking and storage Cycle repair/rescue
Cycling enthusiasts	Day cycle rides (up to 40–50 miles primarily on quiet country roads) Independent cycle touring holidays and short breaks Access to countryside from town and home	Ideas for day cycle rides – cycling enthusiasts tend to plan their own rides, using cycle route leaflets for ideas and information Cycle access by train (generally more important for cycling enthusiasts than for other market segments) Cycle friendly accommodation Cycle parking and storage Cycle repair

to reduce car usage, it will certainly make a valid contribution to local authority Agenda 21 objectives to achieve more sustainable development in transport and tourism.

Coach and bus travel

Bus and coach travel assumed a growing significance in the 1930s in most countries (see Chapter 2). There is a tendency to interchange the terms 'bus' and 'coach' which may create confusion and complexity. Bus travel usually refers to a specific form of urban and rural passenger transport which tourists may use at the destination they are staying at. In the UK, a bus trip is defined as a 24-km or less trip, with coach travel replacing that travel over 24 km. In other European countries, specific terms (such as the Autocar in France) distinguish coach travel from bus travel. However, such a definition does not distinguish between the market for international and domestic coach services. The European Conference of Ministers of Transport (1987) classify the international coach travel market in terms of three categories of service (scheduled; shuttle and occasional services):

- *Scheduled services* (Lines). These services transport passengers at specified times, often based on a timetable, over specified routes. They involve the picking up and setting down of passengers at established stops. Such services are provided under a licence for a prescribed period for which the service is offered. Timetables, tariffs and the vehicles to be used are also specified and particular conditions are attached to the service provided, such as the pan-European Eurolines service. These services are sometimes called 'express coach services' and are operated by consortia of companies or individual operators.
- *Shuttle services*. These consist of trips transporting groups of tourists or individuals from the same point of departure to the same destination. Later the traveller will be transported back to the original departure point and the service usually involves accommodation for the group at the destination. The service must comply with the conditions of an itinerary and length of stay, and no passengers are carried on the last outward or first inward journey. These services are often referred to 'holiday shuttles'.

- *Occasional services*. These include a range of different services such as:
  - closed-door tours (one vehicle is used throughout the journey for the same group and the tour returns to the original point of departure), often referred to as 'continental coach holidays' or 'continental coach tours'
  - services with the return trip unladen
  - all other services.

  These international services are complemented by domestic tourism and day trip markets where a variety of market segments exist for:
  - day excursions
  - extended tours (coach holidays) including the newly merged Shearings and Wallace Arnold who sell 500 000 holidays a year and aim to increase this to one million
  - private hire (including the market for group travel, which typically involves travel by coach for social reasons such as a group outing and educational trips)
  - airport shuttle services
  - urban excursions, such as the all-day ticket tours in London: tourists purchase a day ticket and can board and get off the bus as many times as they wish in order to tour and attend visitor attractions.

In the UK, the coach tourism holiday market is estimated to be worth £2–4 billion a year, with 11 million holidays sold. Shearings has a 14 per cent share of the market. The majority of these holidays are still sold through travel agents.

The market segments to which coach travel appeals is far from homogenous, and ranges from the 'youth travel market' for express domestic and continental services to the elderly markets which dominate coach tours. In 2005, Shearings' in-house research found that 89 per cent of its clients booked six or more holidays a year, which illustrates the significance of the elderly market. Coach travel has an image that appeals to low-income groups and of being a slow mode of surface transport. In recent years, a number of new trends have come to dominate coach travel including the rise of the multimodal operator such as Stagecoach, which has global coach and bus operations (it acquired the long-distance CoachUSA in 1999) and operates over 28 000 vehicles (also see the case study in Box 5.1). The coach and bus sector employs a large workforce with 196 000 employees in Germany, 155 000 in the UK, 126 000 in France and 32 000 in the Netherlands.

There is a tendency to underplay the role of local bus services and urban services in the tourism industry; tourists may use these when staying in a destination.

Box 5.1 Case study: Innovation in coach travel – Stagecoach's megabus.com

In August 2003, the UK's Stagecoach bus company launched a low-cost internet-booking coach service based on trips between the UK's main cities (see Plate 5.1). Its dark blue vehicles proudly boasted single fares for £1.00 plus a booking fee. By 2005 the megabus network had developed a network of services (Figure 5.5) covering 40 UK cities since 2004, with around 1.5 million passengers a year, and two-hourly services on major trunk routes (e.g. London–Birmingham) and lesser frequencies on longer distance routes (e.g. London–Aberdeen). This was the first major competition of any significance for the UK's National Express inter-city coach service which operates to 1200 possible pick-up/drop-off locations in the UK. The service is modelled on the low-cost airline model of ticketless travel, with seats being yield managed and cheaper fares for travellers the longer in advance they book. Fares are from £1 for a single ticket plus a 50 pence booking fee.

Interestingly, post-nationalization, around 80 per cent of National Express services are operated by contracted-out services and this is effectively a monopoly on long-distance coach travel (with a few notable exceptions). It was over 20 years ago that the National Express monopoly over long-distance coach travel was challenged by the ill-fated British Coachways Consortium of private operators. This group ran competing services on trunk routes between major cities, but lost considerable sums of money when National Express reduced its prices to undercut them (it was effectively being subsidized by the National Bus Company parent organization at the time). Since that time, there has been little national competition on the National Express network, with the exception of the impact of the low-cost airline market in seeking to attract price-sensitive travellers.

In contrast to British Coachways, megabus.com has introduced sophisticated yield management systems like those used by airlines and railway companies with a strong brand and web presence (Plates 5.2 and 5.3). This allows the operator to price each seat according to demand and supply, increasing the prices where demand is highest. Some of the lead-in fares of £1 have closely mirrored the promotional tools used by the low-cost airlines (Chapter 6). Online sales have also been complemented by a call centre for telephone bookings. The company has invested £6.6 million in a fleet of luxury double-deckers to increase the comfort level on longer-distance routes with coaches serving other routes. Since its inception in 2003, 2.6 million people have travelled on the new megabus services. Business was helped in September 2005, following the London ter-rorist attack, by the provision of 100 000 free seats (booking fee only) to and from London, which was intended to boost leisure travel and to stimulate demand which was

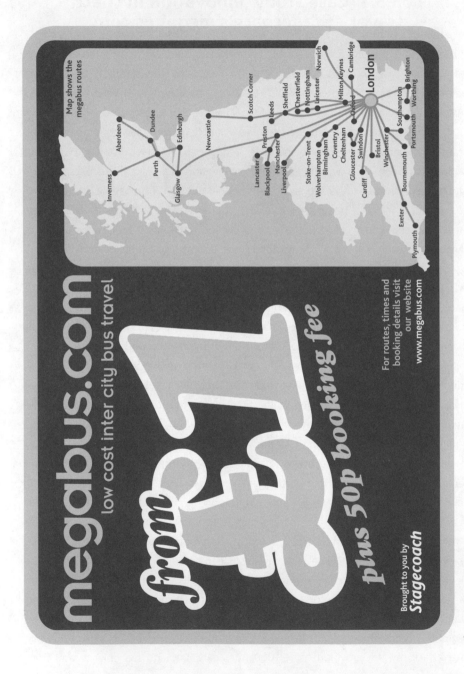

Plate 5.1   Advertisements for the MegaBus

Plate 5.1 Continued

Figure 5.5   Map showing the Megabus routes

affected adversely by the terrorist event. Other transport providers such as GNER with its east coast rail franchise also provided major incentives for travel to London to stimulate demand. Megabus has won innovation awards such as Transport Innovation of the Year at the UK's National Transport Awards and Scottish Transport Awards.

The Stagecoach parent company has acquired a 35 per cent share in its main Scottish rival – Citylink (the National Express equivalent) which carries around three million passengers a year to 200 destinations. This joint venture is expected to generate

Plate 5.2 A MegaBus vehicle

annual revenue of £18 million in the Scottish coach market. The existing 65 per cent share of Scottish Citylink will be retained by the parent company Comfort Delgro, which operates the Metroline bus services for Transport for London; Dublin's rail services (Aerdart), Comcab (a computerized taxi service in London with 3700 vehicles), SBS Transit in Singapore (a rail-bus operator) and Citylink coach services in Eire. The impact of megabus.com has led other long-distance coach operators such as National Express to offer a similar priced product for travellers who book in advance – its Fun Fares – as a response to the competition. Fares are £1 to £10, with no booking fee on many routes. easyBus has also begun to operate a limited number of services from north London (Hendon) to Milton Keynes for £1 to £5 fares and there are plans for easyBus to begin to expand its operations on the M1 motorway corridor, initially from London to Luton airport and further afield in the future.

These developments in the coach market illustrate the importance of large transport integrated operators and new entrants with the investment power to add value to travel products through innovation and high specification vehicles. This is reflected in Stagecoach's announcement in October 2005 that they would replicate the low-cost coach product with a trial of the low-cost train product – megatrain.com. This, however, is more problematic for the company as there are numerous regulatory obstacles which

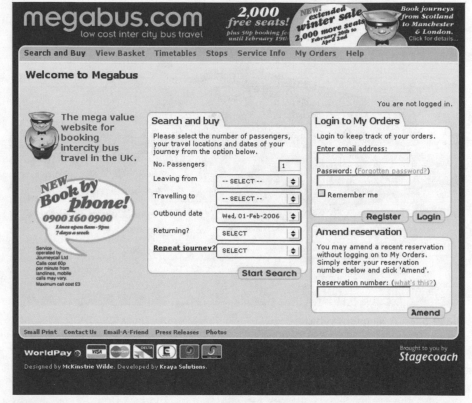

Plate 5.3   Booking online for MegaBus

the company will have to overcome if megatrain is to become a regular feature. The company introduced the lead-in £1 fares on its South West Trains franchise between London, Portsmouth and Southampton. It will offer 3000 off-peak seats a week (40 per departure) on the services provided on the new state-of-the-art Desiro trains. If such a scheme can overcome any government regulations (in the Ticketing and Settlement Agreement), after the 34-week trial period, it will certainly stimulate a low-cost revolution on the rail franchises it holds, thereby filling off-peak capacity and improving revenue generation. These new initiatives not only mirror some of the trends in the low-cost airlines market, they also mark a major step forward in terms of innovation in generating demand for land-based travel at a time when concerns about the environmental costs of low-cost air travel are growing. Stagecoach has been heralded as a major operator seeking also to move passengers from car-based travel to public transport modes with improved marketing, information and initiatives encouraging a reduction in car use.

In the UK, the bus industry is largely controlled (post-deregulation in 1985, when the National Bus Company was sold off as 70 units for £1 billion), by five major organizations that have a turnover of £3.3 billion. In 1990, these groups had 5 per cent of the market and this grew to 66.5 per cent in 2002 as a process of consolidation occurred. The ownership pattern was dominated by First Group (22 per cent); Stagecoach (16 per cent); Arriva (14.5 per cent); Go-ahead (8.3 per cent); National Express (5.7 per cent); the rest of the market was accounted for by small operators (14.5 per cent) and the public sector (3.5 per cent); management buy-out accounted for 9.1 per cent. The pattern of bus use has declined from 42 per cent of all journeys in 1952 to less than 6 per cent today whilst car use has grown from 27 per cent in 1952 to over 85 per cent now. Public transport on buses in the UK is supported by a central government bus subsidy of over £1.6 billion a year in a sector with a £4.6 billion turnover a year. This covers a 29 per cent partial rebate for fuel duty and 45 per cent of the cost of concessionary fares (for the old, young and disabled) as well as services that are not commercially viable.

In Europe, patterns of bus and coach travel based on express services tend to be point to point (i.e. city to city) or city to city via non-urban areas. They tend to use major transport corridors (i.e. motorways) wherever possible to gain economies in travel time so that they are price and time competitive with rail travel. In contrast, coach tours, particularly packaged tours, have a tendency to follow what are called 'milk runs': they follow a set itinerary to showcase the main attractions, sometimes even replicating the Grand Tour in Europe (see Chapter 2). In the UK, milk runs with a strong heritage appeal might typically depart from London, visit Oxford, Stratford-upon-Avon, Bath, Chester, the Lake District and Scotland, and return on the east coast via York and Cambridge to London, depending on the length of the tour.

Coach tourism in the UK generated £153 million for the UK economy (an average of £219 per trip and £57 per night). Of this, £28 million was contributed by overseas coach trips to the UK (with an average of £280 per trip and £47 per night) and comprised 4 per cent of all overseas expenditure in the UK. The majority of these trips are holidays, as part of a tour with the majority on a four- to seven-night tour staying in hotels or guesthouses. A study undertaken for the Confederation of Passenger Transport noted that:

- UK tourists undertook 4.2 million coach tours, staying 15.8 million nights away and spending £643 million
- UK residents undertook 36.2 million day trips on coach tours and spent £844 million

- the UK coach tour industry generated £1883 million and generated over 79 000 jobs (full and part time) equivalent to 59 000 full-time equivalent jobs.

In Scotland, the 100 000 overseas visitors on coach tours generated £28 million. The majority travelled from Germany (40 000 tourists) and were responsible for £12 million in expenditure. The majority of overseas coach tours (54 per cent) arrived through the north-east coast of the UK (typically Hull or Newcastle with lesser numbers on the new Rossyth–Zeebrugge service) although 28 per cent came via Dover with 11 per cent using the Channel Tunnel and a further 5 per cent travelling from the Irish Republic, using Irish Seas crossings. Key markets for overseas coach tourism in Scotland are the Highlands of Scotland and the urban gateways and major destinations of Glasgow and Edinburgh. The major differences between the domestic and overseas patterns of visitation are:

- the domestic visitors tend to be focused on a limited range of destinations, particularly the Highlands, Stirling, Edinburgh and, to a lesser degree, Glasgow
- the overseas visitors tend to follow a more dispersed pattern of visits, reflecting the tendency to tour and also to visit a wider range of destinations; they focus on the Glasgow–Edinburgh gateways followed by the Highlands as part of a circuit. The circuit has a tendency to include only smaller city destinations on more extended tours.

The structure, organization and management of coach and bus operations in each country is specifically shaped by the history, regulations and policies towards transport, and by a strong tradition of visiting established destinations – except where a major draw such as the Eden Project in Cornwall or new attractions in cities act as a hub for day excursions or visits. In most countries (excluding the UK), protection of the rail network has meant bus and coach travel has not competed on an even basis, although there is evidence that this is changing. More recently, the liberalization of European coach travel allowing operators to operate in different countries and the rise of new markets, such as the shuttle and long-distance markets opened up by the Channel Tunnel, have directly impacted on the further growth and expansion of coach travel.

Rail travel

Globally, railways are a major mode of moving tourists and leisure trippers around countries and between countries. In the USA, rail travel has the smallest proportion of passengers carried on any mode of transport (0.3 per cent), since the car dominates (with 85 per cent of passenger kilometres) followed by air travel (10 per cent) and coach (3.1 per cent). In Europe, rail travel has a 6.2 per cent share of passenger trips, higher than air travel, although passenger cars account for nearly 79 per cent of trips followed by bus and coach travel (8.3 per cent). In Europe, railways are a major business with a 75 billion euro turnover per annum, employing one million people and investing 250 million euros per annum in research and development. The role of rail in European passenger traffic has slipped from its 10 per cent share of traffic in 1970 to around 6 per cent in 2002. At the same time, state subsidies for rail have grown, with the EU railway system costing taxpayers over 35 billion euros annually in grants for infrastructure projects and support.

With increasing congestion on many of the developed countries' road and air networks, rail travel has a number of natural advantages over competing modes of transport. The convenience of rail travel for short- to long-distance trips from one city centre to another remains. In a European context, rail travel fulfils a wide range of functions for travellers as it is convenient for daily commuting needs, business trips and recreational travel. Three specific types of recreational rail user can be discerned within Europe: day-trippers, domestic tourists and international tourists who use rail travel as part of their itinerary to visit visitor destinations

Much of the growth in European rail travel has been in the high-speed rail services but they only carry 13 per cent of all European rail passengers. The use of rail in relation to tourism and leisure travel occurs under a number of journey types, with a combination of types in the typical tourism and leisure journey:

- The use of dedicated rail corridors which connect major gateways (airports and ports) of a country to the final destination, or as a mode of transit to the tourist accommodation in the nearby city.
- The use of rapid transit systems and metros to travel within urban areas.
- The use of high-speed and non-high-speed intercity rail corridors to facilitate movement as part of an itinerary or city-to-city journey, typically for business and leisure travel. These journeys may cross country borders, forming international networks.
- The use of local rail services outside urban areas, often used in peak hours by commuters to journey to/from mainline/intercity rail terminals en route to other destinations.
- The use of rail services in peripheral tourist destinations (e.g. the Caledonian Sleeper which serves the London to the Highlands of Scotland market) which

sometimes have a scenic value as tourist journeys in their own right (e.g. the Central Otago, New Zealand, Taireri Gorge half-day rail tour).

- Purpose-built rail excursions/holidays on historic services such as the Orient Express.

It is clear that rail travel, aside from commuting, offers a wide range of options for tourist and leisure travel. In Europe rail continues to have a slow rate of overall growth compared to other modes of transport: at a pan-European level, rail travel is constantly outperformed by the increase in air and car-related travel of around 2–4 per cent per annum in the volume of passenger kilometres travelled.

Despite the declining importance of rail (excluding high-speed services), a wide range of issues have been suggested as important in trying to attract more tourists to use rail as a mode of travel. These include improved marketing to raise awareness of new services, better ticketing options such as through tickets and more seamless travel across rail networks, e-commerce (see the case study in Box 5.1), frequent traveller schemes and greater attention to service quality issues. In addition, a wide range of business issues was highlighted for railway companies including broadening their distribution channels (e.g. in 2002, the Caledonian Sleeper adopted e-ticketing and paperless check-ins in line with innovations from the airline sector). Attempts to improve customer usability of rail services (e.g. simplification of ticketing systems to remove confusion over tickets and prices) have been proven to generate a substantial volume of business in their first year of operation. It is also notable that rail operators are slowly recognizing the link between transport and tourism, with value-for-money fares for leisure travel stimulated in Europe by the onset of the low-cost airlines. Physical improvements to the travel environment have also illustrated the need to invest in a better travelling environment for tourists with new rolling stock and state-of-the-art travel facilities. Virgin Trains' new service enhancements on trunk routes and cross-country services which include music channels, laptop sockets and the segregation of mobile phone users have now been mirrored in innovations by other rail companies. Developments in e-commerce such as the Trainline.com (in which Stagecoach has a controlling interest) have been important in making rail a more accessible option for travellers. Partnerships and collaborations have also been developed; for example the Midland Mainline railway company and the short-break operator Supabreak online in the UK have expanded the seamless approach to integrated tourist travel with packages harmonized and more accessible.

Water-based transport

The potential of water- or sea-based transport has been greatly overlooked in most analyses of tourism, largely because much attention has been given to the growth in tourism by air since 1945. Yet prior to the development of rail and air travel, sea-based travel was of major importance in crossing water (e.g. ferries), for pleasure on inland waterways (e.g. canal boats) or as a mode of tourist travel (e.g. cruising) (see Plate 5.4).

Cruises

Many modern-day shipping companies such as P&O developed water-based transport as a means of travelling between continents, linking the UK with its empire in India and the Far East during the nineteenth century. In 1842, the P&O passenger ship Hindustan undertook its inaugural trip, stimulated by the company's contract to carry mail from Southampton to Calcutta. By 1844, P&O had also begun deep-sea cruises in the Mediterranean and in the late 1880s other companies (it was later to acquire) began cruises. For example, in 1886 the North of Scotland and Orkney and Shetland Company began cruises to the Norwegian fjords at a cost of £10, while in 1889 the Orient Line began cruises to Norway and the Mediterranean. By 1890, the P&O line had developed a global network of direct and connecting services for passenger services (as shown in Figure 5.6) which remained largely unaltered (with the exception of the withdrawal of Indian services after that country's independence) up until the 1960s when air services began to challenge passenger liners. What is apparent from Figure 5.6 is the demand for business travel between the UK and its Imperial territories. P&O became a global brand in the nineteenth century, much earlier than many of the marketing debates on the internationalization of the tourism industry in the 1960s, although monopoly contracts on mail services did help to support its expansion of the passenger routes. The company reconfigured its business activities after the development of passenger airliners. For example, in the 1970s P&O invested in its North American market and the growing demand for cruises as passenger liner business declined. In fact the company has a history of adapting to new business environments. For example, it adapted a ship no longer needed for mail services in 1904 for the cruise line Vectis: this was the first time it had developed a dedicated cruise liner that carried 160 first-class passengers

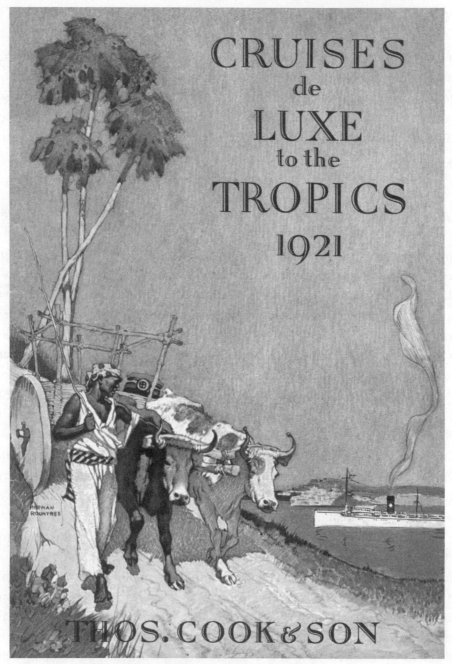

Plate 5.4 1920s cruise of the tropics organized by Thomas Cook

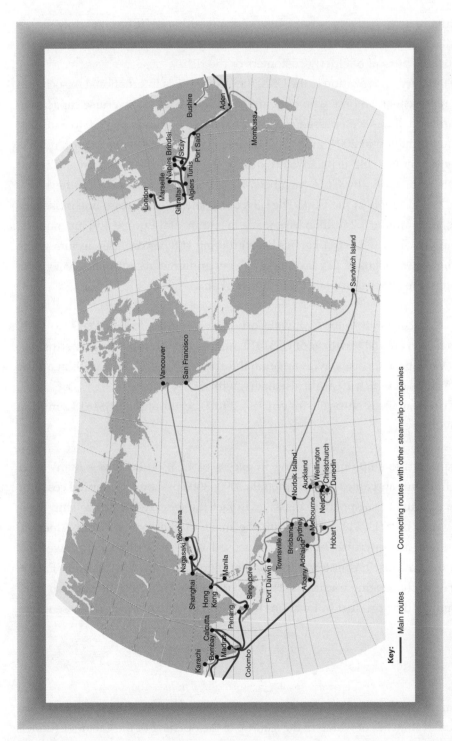

Figure 5.6 Schematic diagram of the steamer routes operated by the Peninsular and Orient (P&O) Steam Navigation Company in 1890 (redrawn and redesigned from Horwath and Horwath, 1986, *The Story of P&O: The Peninsular and Oriental Steam Navigation Company*. London: Widenfield and Nicolson)

in absolute luxury. Cruising is not a new concept, although it has certainly seen a revival at a global scale since the 1990s and has become a more popular activity, no longer just the pursuit of elderly customers or the rich.

The industry organization in the USA, the Cruise Lines International Association (CLIA), represents members who offer around 95 per cent of the cruise capacity in North America. It has seen passenger sales rise from 3.6 million in 1990 to 5 million in 1997 to 8.8 million in 2004, more than doubling in 14 years. This, in part, reflects the growth in cruise ship capacity since during the period 2000–2005 an additional 68 vessels were added by CLIA members. Most bookings are made via the 17 000 affiliated travel agents in the USA. The USA dominates world cruise line passenger volumes, with around 1.2 million trips made in continental Europe and just under a million in the UK. The US market has been growing at 8 per cent per annum while Europe has shown signs of 12 per cent growth per annum in recent years. At a global scale, three companies dominate the cruise market:

- Carnival (incorporating the Carnival Corporation and the former P&O Cruises), which has an annual turnover of US$1410 million and 20 ships, 30 000 berths
- Royal Caribbean Cruises, with an annual turnover of US$3784.2 million a year and 29 ships of which 19 are cruise liners, with 41 994 berths
- Star Cruises, with 20 ships (18 for cruises), 29 000 berths and a US$1618.2 million turnover a year.

With many cruise ships now costing in excess of US$300 million – many over US$400 million – and able to accommodate 2000–3000 passengers, capital costs for this area of tourist transport are massive. In fact the worldwide cruise ship business is worth over US$14 billion, with the main market being North America. Whilst much of the cruise business is focused on the Caribbean followed by Europe, the Far East has entered the market together with Australasian/Pacific island cruises challenging traditional patterns of cruises. The cruise line industry has been dominated by product innovations to attract a growing variety of passengers.

Ferries

Ferries are more functional modes of tourist transport than cruise ships and are used to cross stretches of water. In the lead-up to the opening of the Channel Tunnel, many ferry operators attempted to market the UK's short-sea ferry crossing as cruises. In reality, ferries offer travellers a different element in their holiday, trip or excursion and a time for rest, relaxation and a break from their main form of transport. One of the most frequently crossed waterways is the English Channel. The construction of the Channel Tunnel offered an all-weather mode of crossing this stretch of water yet, despite the concerns over the Channel Tunnel's impact on UK ferry services, passenger volumes through the Port of Dover have risen from 11 million in 1994 to 16.2 million in 2005. One consequence of the increased competition from the Channel Tunnel and low-cost airlines was the merger of the two Dover–France ferry companies, Stena Line and P&O Ferries. The major blow for the ferry companies was the loss of duty-free sales on board ferries in 1999, which had accounted for 65 per cent of profits from short-sea ferry routes. This gave an estimated loss of revenue of £350 million for UK–European services and led to price rises on fares of up to 40 per cent, which, together with rises in fuel costs, resulted in a drop in passenger volumes of between 16 and 20 per cent. However, ferry companies see this as a temporary problem even when the impact of low-cost airlines on ferry business is taken into account. Estimates of UK–Europe travel to France, Holland, Germany and Belgium found:

- 68.6 per cent flew
- 31.4 per cent went above or under the English Channel, of whom:
  - the ferries carried 18.2 per cent
  - the Channel Tunnel carried 13.3 per cent.

The majority of travellers travelling by ferry from the UK used short-sea routes across the English Channel (66 per cent), the Western Channel in southern/south western England/Irish Sea (25.8 per cent) and the North Sea (7.6 per cent) (see Figure 5.7). In the short-sea sector, a number of smaller, peripheral ferry services from Sheerness, Folkestone and Ramsgate have been cut as the industry has focused operations in Dover. In addition, the company Hoverspeed withdrew its Hovercraft services in September 2000 after 32 years of operation and then its catamaran service in 2005. The rapidly changing competitive environment has meant that tourism managers have had to carefully set out future strategies to ensure the viability of their business, and in some cases, operations were closed, rationalized, merged or sold. In 2004, P&O Stena Line further rationalized its UK fleet, operating 25 vessels to counter the drop in patronage due to low-cost airlines, and then closing 4 of its

Figure 5.7   Travel by ferry from the UK

13 routes after full-year losses of £40 million. Businesses have had to keep sight of their existing and future passengers via more active marketing campaigns to extol the virtues of cross-channel ferry travel now Eurotunnel and low-cost airlines have became well established. A comparison of the route network of ferry operations in 2000 and 2006 indicates that the ferry companies have relocated surplus capacity away from the competitive short-sea crossing of Dover–France to other short-sea crossings which have more revenue generation potential. The port in Dover has diversified and expanded the cruise business, with 37 cruises departing in 2006 from the port.

A rapid period of change in the holiday market and turmoil in the operating environment highlights the importance of being proactive in managing the tourism business. In each case, operators have sought to add value to the services they provide by upgrading onboard facilities, particularly food and beverages, children's lounges and business lounges, and increasing the size of ferries so they can carry over 2000 passengers in some cases. For some locations, such as the Highlands and Islands of Scotland and the Greek islands (with up to 60 000 ferry departures in the peak months), ferries provide the vital link between the mainland tourism market and the destination.

Inland waterways

Inland waterways are another a relatively neglected area of study in tourism research. They are seen as the product of a bygone era, linked to industrialization from the late eighteenth century onwards when canals and waterways were developed in many European countries to transport products from source areas to market. Yet many towns and cities with waterways and river networks have seen a renaissance in their regeneration for tourism purposes in the late twentieth century, with Birmingham, UK, a case in point. It is the junction of many of the UK's canals and waterways, with a well-developed riverboat and canal-based holiday market. Much of this regeneration activity has been a successful partnership of waterway agencies such as the British Waterways Board (BWB) and local authorities, often supported in the UK by grants from the Lottery and Millennium funds. BWB manages 3220 km of canals and rivers in the UK with a budget of almost £200 million, part of which has been spent on re-opening old canals for leisure and in creating a new focus for tourism such as the Millennium Wheel in Falkirk, Scotland. In other contexts, such as the Norfolk Broads, a major holiday and boating industry exists which is based on inland waterways (see Box 5.2).

Managing land- and surface-based tourist transport

The various modes of transport examined in this chapter have highlighted the diversity and wide range of uses which tourists, make of transport, from linking the home to the nearest departure point through to using transport as a holiday context (e.g. a cruise). Integrating the transport modes to ensure a seamless travel experience

Box 5.2 Boating on the Norfolk Broads: A tourism resource?

The Norfolk Broads (hereafter the Broads) is a wetland region in East Anglia, created in the medieval period through a series of flooded peat diggings. The region comprises a wetland area focused on a number of rivers such as the Bure, the Yare and Waveney and their tributaries in the eastern part of Norfolk and northern part of Suffolk, with 200 km of lock-free waters to explore by boat. In 1989 the area was accorded virtual National Park status when the Broads Authority was established by the 1988 Norfolk and Suffolk Broads Act and the area now receives in excess of a million visitors a year. The Act granted the Broads Authority the same autonomy as a National Park in terms of finance, policy and administration and thus it receives a 75 per cent grant from central government.

Boating for pleasure dates back to the 1870s when the early wherries (local sailing vessels which carried cargo) began to carry passengers. In the 1880s, John Loyne pioneered the hire boat industry and in 1908 the present-day H. Blake and Co. was established to rent purpose-built vessels to visitors who travelled to the area by rail. Thus, the use of transport for recreational day use and for much longer holiday use led to the development of a form of water-based tourism which is transport dependent. In 1995, boat companies owned 1481 motor cruisers and launches, which were hired to approximately 200 000 visitors a year. The industry is dominated by the two main holiday companies – Hoseseasons and Blakes Holidays. There are also a further four independent boatyards, fifty-one day-hire yards and a further six yards operating tours. The sailing and yachting activity in the Broads is reflected in the 3261 sailing craft registered in the area. Overall, the area has 13 104 craft registered to use the Broads, of which 3475 are motor boats and 1753 are registered as hire boats.

Very heavy usage occurs at weekends in the northern parts of the river system (e.g. the Thurne Mouth and the middle reaches of the river Bure at Horning and Wroxham/Hoveton). For example, a Broads Authority boat movement census highlighted that on one peak Sunday in August, there were 6296 craft movements recorded at 14 census points. In contrast, the upper reaches of many rivers are protected by their relative inaccessibility and, in a few cases, by low bridges.

The hire boat industry is estimated to contribute £25 million to the local economy, with boating employing over 1622 people: 884 full time, 148 part time and 590 on a seasonal basis. Furthermore, recreational and tourist spending indirectly contributes to 5000–5500 jobs in the hospitality sector and local tourist attractions as well as in the local marine industry. Therefore, what the example of Broads shows is that even inland waterways offers a major resource for transporting tourists and as an attraction and holiday in their own right. This popularity is not without its environmental impacts: motorcraft can create boat wash, which causes bankside erosion, and excessive use can cause congestion and impact upon the visitor's experience of the Broads. The demand for one-day hires and the need to manage over 13 000 vessels poses a challenge for the Broads Authority.

without major service interruptions is a major challenge for the tourism industry, since transport functions are often contracted out to suppliers who may not have a tourism ethos (e.g. coach operators or taxis). In each case, transport providers interface with tourists, and so ensuring they are good ambassadors for tourism has become a priority for many destination areas as has ensuring those people who interface with tourists recognize the service standards which travellers now experience in other areas of the service economy. The transport sector has been very slow to embrace these ideas since it have been operationally led and focused on operating vehicles, plant and capital investment rather than looking at the tourist as a customer. This issue permeates most forms of surface-based transport, as tourism and service provision in the air transport sector have been more innovative.

Much of the planning and integration of surface transport has been achieved in many European capitals by innovative and forward-looking planning in the post-war period and purpose-building new infrastructure; in some older European capitals existing infrastructure still has gaps in the provision of terminals, with visitors often having to travel from central areas to airports on systems that are not integrated and are complicated to use. Transport provision needs champions within each destination area so that the tourist can be easily connected with terminals, attractions, accommodation and gateways, such as ports and airports – a theme which will be returned to in Chapter 6. Airports are the most obvious example of where the private sector takes the lead in integrating transport and tourism. The work of BAA in the UK illustrates this, with each airport having a surface transport strategy, working within the UK government's encouragement of the use of public transport for more journeys. A third of passengers travel to BAA's three London airports by public transport and it is seeking to expand that to 50 per cent. Specific initiatives include the development of the Heathrow Express, the St Pancras Express, the M4 spur road bus lane, discounted London Underground travelcards being issued to airline staff, public–private sector partnerships to improve railway stations, enhancements to bus services (including a subsidy to the Glasgow Airport link) and environmental levies on car parking to support public transport initiatives. Given the significance of these, it is useful to turn in the next chapter to the important role of airports as transport terminals as receiving and sending areas for air travellers.

References

Button, K.J. and Gillingwater K. (eds) (1983) *Future Transport Policy*. London: Routledge.

Connell, J. (2005) Analysing coach tourism in Scotland: trends and patterns. In S. J. Page *Transport and Tourism: Global Perspectives*. Harlow: Prentice Hall.

Countryside Commission (1992) *Trends in Transport and the Countryside*. Cheltenham: Countryside Commission.

Countryside Commission (1995) *The Market for Recreational Cycling in the Countryside*. Cheltenham: Countryside Commission.

Eaton, B. and Holding, D. (1996) The evaluation of public transport alternatives to the car in British National Parks. *Journal of Transport Geography*, 4(1): 55–65.

English Tourist Board/Employment Department (1991) *Tourism and the Environment: Maintaining the Balance*. London: English Tourist Board.

European Conference of Ministers of Transport (1987) cited in S. Page (1994) The European coach travel marker. *Travel and Tourism Analyst*, 1: 19–39.

HMSO (1994) *Royal Commission on Environmental Pollution*. Eighteenth Report, Transport and the Environment, Cmmd. 2674. London: HMSO.

Lamb, B. and Davidson, S. (1996) Tourism and transportation in Ontario, Canada. In L. Harrison and W. Husbands (eds) *Practising Responsible Tourism: International Case Studies in Tourism Planning, Policy and Development*. Chichester: Wiley.

Lumsdon, L. (1996) Future for cycle tourism in Britain. *INSIGHTS*, A27–A32.

Lumsdon, L. (1997) Recreational cycling: Is this the way to stimulate interest in everyday urban cycling? In R. Tolley (ed.) *The Greening of Urban Transport Planning for Walking and Cycling in Western Cities*, 2nd edn. Chichester: Wiley.

Scottish Tourist Board (1991) *Tourism Potential of Cycling and Cycle Routes in Scotland*. Edinburgh: Scottish Tourist Board.

SUSTRANS (2002) *Cycle Tourism: Information Pack TT21*. SUSTRANS online www.sustrans.org.uk, accessed 11 October 2002.

Wall, G. (1971) Car owners and holiday activities. In P. Lavery (ed.) *Recreational Geography*. Newton Abbot: David and Charles.

Further reading

Lumsdon, L. and Page, S. J. (eds) (2004) *Tourism and Transport: Issues and Agenda in the New Millennium*. Oxford: Elsevier.

The most comprehensive book on transport and tourism is:
Page, S. J. (2005) *Transport and Tourism: Global Perspectives*. Second edition. Harlow: Prentice Hall.

Questions

1 How would you develop a model of tourist transport and its relationship to tourist activity?

2 Why is the car so important to tourist activity patterns? What advantages and disadvantages does it have compared with other modes of surface travel?

3 What role does transport play as a focus for tourist activities?

4 How important is the integration of different forms of transport to achieve a seamless tourism experience?

Chapter **6**

Transporting the tourist II: The aviation sector

Learning outcomes

This chapter examines the role of the aviation industry in tourism as a global phenomenon which is responsible for enabling people to travel to destinations worldwide. On completion of the chapter, you should be able to understand:

- the structure and organization of the aviation sector and the role of airports in the handling of tourists as travellers
- key trends in the airline sector and the importance of the low-cost airlines as a new business sector in Europe
- the way in which airlines market their businesses to travellers.

Introduction

In Chapter 5, the role of surface transport highlighted the fundamental link between tourism and transport in a number of different contexts. One of the underlying themes was how the link between transport (the industry) is linked to the tourist (the consumer) which in simple terms raises a fundamental question: how are these two elements managed so that consumer needs are met? This returns to many of the issues initially developed in Chapter 1 on the role of tourism management and who should manage such issues. This chapter addresses these issues by focusing on the aviation sector, since it has seen the greatest volume growth in passengers of all forms of transport (excluding car usage and owner-ship). It is focused on a complex transport system upon which the tourist experi-ences directly impact. This is shaped from the point they enter an airport through to the point they get off their aircraft at the destination, a process that is repeated on the return journey. In other words, the management of the tourist by the airline industry reveals an integrated transport system, which can largely be defined as:

> the process whereby individual (and groups of) airlines seek to organize, direct and harness their resources, personnel and their business activities to meet the needs of their organization and customers in an effective and effi-cient manner. (Page 2002: 209)

This also involves the close working relationship of the airlines with airports to ensure the smooth, safe and reliable processing and transfer of tourists through the system with the minimum of disruption and inconvenience. This is crucial as the airline industry carries a large volume of passengers and the airport system has to be able to process the volume of travellers in an efficient manner so that the system continues to have the capacity to allow the flow of travellers through the system. Therefore, this chapter commences with a discussion of the role of the airport as a terminal facility that links the tourist with the supply of transport – air transport. It offers a seamless travel process from departure to arrival in principle, although sometimes service interruptions and unavoidable delays may cause problems in the airline transport system. This is followed with a discussion of air travel, emphasizing its growth and significance as a mode of tourist transport, how it is regulated, the role of airlines' operations and the significance of recent develop-ments in the airline market, including the rise of low-cost airlines and future prospects for global air travel.

The role of the airport as a tourist terminal facility

For tourists, airports must be one of the most highly developed and complex envir-onments that they will experience. Airports operate as well-developed systems, where a wide range of tourist interactions occur. At a simple level the airport is the point of processing for travel to a destination through to a highly developed shopping and retail environment. Other analogies of airports as postmodern citadels of tourism and consumption have led commentators to examine the architecture, subtle design features and careful management measures devised to encourage consumers to spend their money, with layouts designed to nurture a captive audi-ence. Airports are more than just transport termini where tourists transfer from a ground-based form of transport to air-based forms of transport. In larger capital cities, airports are major integrated transport hubs, with a wide range of feeder routes by public transport and road (including other air travellers in transit) who are sorted, sifted, channelled and directed towards departing flights as part of their tourism experience. Airports have changed out of all recognition from their early 1930s origins where they were simple buildings that provided a waiting area for flights. Today they are multi-million-pound businesses, with vast capital invest-ment in transport infrastructure to facilitate the air travel function, as well as a large number of other functions – including retailing, support services, car hire, onward travel by other modes of transport and large car parking facilities, as well as a cargo function.

The scale of these activities in terms of passenger movements through airports is illustrated in Table 6.1, which shows the volume of passengers passing through the busiest 20 airports in the world in 2001 and 2004. Nearly 76 million people trav-elled through Atlanta (the busiest world airport) in 2001 and almost 84 million in 2004. Table 6.1 also shows the relative growth of other airport markets, especially Asia. The scale of the numbers using these terminal areas reinforces the size of the management challenge for airport operators in ensuring that business activities run smoothly. The Airport International Council (www.aic.org), which represents 550 airport operators worldwide with 1441 airports in 165 countries, identified the

Table 6.1 Top 20 world airports in 2001 and 2004 (source: Airport Council International)

2004 Ranking	2001 Ranking	Airport	Passenger flow 2001	Passenger flow 2004
1	1	Atlanta, GA (ATL)	75 849 375	83 606 583
2	2	Chicago, IL (ORD)	67 448 064	75 533 822
3	5	Los Angeles, CA (LAX)	61 606 204	60 688 609
4	3	London, GB (LHR)	60 743 084	67 344 054
5	4	Tokyo, JP (HND)	58 692 688	62 291 405
6	6	Dallas/Ft Worth Airport, TX (DFW)	55 150 693	59 412 217
7	8	Frankfurt, DE (FRA)	48 559 980	51 098 000
8	7	Paris, FR (CDG)	47 996 529	51 260 363
9	9	Amsterdam, NL (AMS)	39 531 123	42 541 180
10	10	Denver, CO (DEN)	36 092 806	42 393 766
11	11	Phoenix, AZ (PHX)	35 439 031	39 504 898
12	12	Las Vegas, NV (LAS)	35 180 960	41 441 531
13	15	Minneapolis/St Paul, MN (MSP)	34 308 389	36 713 173
14	13	Houston, TX (IAH)	34 803 580	36 506 116
	14	San Francisco, CA (SFO)	34 632 474	
15	16	Madrid, ES (MAD)	34 047 931	38 704 731
16	17	Hong Kong, CN (HKG)	32 546 029	36 711 926
17	18	Detroit, MI (DTW)	32 294 121	35 187 517
	19	Miami, FL (MIA)	31 668 450	
	20	London, GB (LGW)	31 182 361	
18	21	Bangkok	30 623 366	37 960 169
19	23	New York (JFK)	29 349 000	37 518 143
20	20	Beijing (PEK)		34 883 190

following key issues as challenges for airports in ensuring the visitor experience is maintained:

- The need to cope with larger aircraft size, as 600-seat aircraft are likely to be introduced on long-haul routes.
- The need to embrace technological change such as new navigation systems so that the capacity at individual airports can be increased to cope with demand. This is important given the Boeing Commercial Airplane Group (2004) *Current*

Market Outlook 2004 indication that the future demand will lead to a greater use of medium-haul aircraft, increasing the number and frequency of aircraft wishing to take off and land at airports worldwide. This prediction runs counter to the forecasts of Airbus, which has replaced the jumbo jet with the new A380, able to carry in excess of 550 passengers on trunk routes.

- The recognition that air travel has now begun to reach a mass market rather than the elite group it served in the 1950s and early 1960s.
- A need to speed up the passenger flows at airports, including the removal of bottlenecks and delays with baggage handling, by introducing new technology and smart technology to track travellers and their personal belongings.
- Addressing security issues at airports, which are seen as one of the weakest links, as well as enhancing safety matters for travellers.

In each case, the AIC recognize the importance of investing in the airport system and its constituent parts so that the interface with the traveller is enhanced. Perhaps one of the greatest challenges for the airport sector is in recognizing and acknowledging the fact that:

> The airport cavalcade can baffle or startle the inexperienced passenger … Laden with suitcases and packages, calm and rational people grow uptight, defensive with aggression, fail to allow themselves time to familiarise themselves with the layout or study the free guides to terminals. (Barlay 1995: 48)

This quotation illustrates the importance of designing passenger-friendly environments that are welcoming, have a relaxed feel (such as London Stansted's terminal building designed by Sir Norman Foster) and provide opportunities for travellers to reduce the stress, anxiety and uncertainty associated with air travel.

For the airport sector, various issues affect how the traveller perceives the terminal including:

- speed of check-in
- efficiency of passport control and customs clearance
- luggage retrieval
- availability of shops, duty-free and associated services
- a spacious and relaxed environment to wait prior to boarding the aircraft.

Source: Developed from Barlay (1995: 49) cited in Page (2005)

This identifies the themes that airport managers need to address as they become more customer oriented, and investment in new terminals and redevelopments integrate the latest thinking on passenger-friendly environments. This is somewhat of a culture change for airports as traditionally (i.e. since the 1950s) they were largely operationally focused and only paid lip service to the needs of travellers. The airport manager's focus has changed out of all recognition since the impact of privatization and the need for a greater consumer orientation in order to generate profits for shareholders and other investors.

The greater commercialization in airport operations has been coupled with the development of global airport companies (such as BAA plc and Amsterdam Schipol) and non-airport transport companies that have entered airport management (e.g. FirstGroup and Stagecoach in the UK). As a result, airports have become part of the wider globalization of transport and tourism activities. Such companies recognize that managing airports is not just about providing some of the services and facilities which travellers need; it is also about coordinating, planning, leading and communicating between the airport and the diverse range of ancillary services such as handling agents, concessionaires (i.e. businesses which operate under licence or franchise on airport premises, such as retailers), government bodies (e.g. the Federal Aviation Authority in the USA) and industry bodies (e.g. AIC) as well as the airlines. Airport operations have certainly seen a greater emphasis on business skills and communication such as marketing than on its traditional, operationally led focus since the wave of commercialization has swept through the airport sector. This is also reflected in the evolution of airports as business entities that recognize their different revenue streams.

What is an airport and how is it operated?

In physical terms, Doganis (1992) defines an airport as:

> Essentially one or more runways for aircraft together with associated buildings or terminals where passengers … are processed … the majority of airport authorities own and operate their runways, terminals and associated facilities, such as taxiways or aprons. (Doganis 1992: 7)

The historical evolution of airports in many countries has followed a complex pattern based on historical, legal and other factors (i.e. changing government policy and the different roles of public- and private-sector involvement). Explaining airport development in many instances has been associated with opportunities for the expansion of gateway airport terminals and the post-war reuse of former military bases and available sites, as well as new-build projects. Airport development in part mirrors the expansion of tourism in the post-war period, but the lead times for airport development due to the capital intensive nature of their sunk costs means that development horizons are at least ten years for new runways and terminals and associated infrastructure (i.e. expanding new road infrastructure to cope with demand).

However, Doganis (1992: 7) distinguishes between the three principal activities of airports:

- essential operational services and facilities
- traffic-handling services
- commercial activities.

Whilst the dominant activity to be considered for the safe and efficient management of the airport as a terminal area are its passenger flows, it is clear that the airport houses a complex system in which a wide range of interrelated activities take place.

The scope of activities broadly encompasses the following:

- ground handling
- baggage handling
- passenger terminal operations
- airport security
- cargo operations
- airport technical services
- air traffic control
- aircraft scheduling (take-off/landing slot allocation)
- airport and aircraft emergency services
- airport access.

After Page (2005)

The way in which airports are managed is also partly determined by their pattern of ownership. New forms of ownership have emerged as the demand for air travel has grown and state involvement in airport provision has been reduced, allowing owners to pursue commercial strategies so they can invest and grow their capacity and ability to respond more quickly to the market. There are four main types of ownership:

1 *State ownership with direct government control*, characterized by a single government department (e.g. a Civil Aviation Department) which operates the country's airports. The alternative to a centralized government pattern of control and management is localized ownership, such as municipal ownership.
2 *Public ownership through an airport authority*, usually as a limited liability or private company.
3 *Mixed public and private ownership* is an organizational model that has been adopted at larger Italian airports, where a company manages the airport, with public and private shareholders.
4 *Private ownership* was a model of limited appeal prior to the wave of privatization in the 1980s; an example is the UK government's privatization of BAA in 1987.

Privatization is seen as a politically sensitive issue, since it involves the transfer of state assets accumulated from taxpayers' revenue in major capital assets that may give the private sector significant commercial opportunities.

However, the most fundamental issues that are involved in any airport development are:

- costs
- the economic features of airports
- sources of revenue
- methods of charging and pricing airport aeronautical services
- the type of commercial strategy to adopt
- potential sources of commercial revenue
- the most appropriate management structure for an airport as a commercial/ non-commercial organization
- financial performance indicators.

(*Source*: Based on Doganis 1992 and Ashford, Stanton and Moore 1991)

Aside from revenue issues, managers of airport facilities need to understand the costs and economic characteristics of airports so as to recognize both the commercial potential and where fixed costs exist. By far the largest cost, as one would expect since tourism is a people industry, is staffing costs. These are often in excess of 40 per cent of the operational costs, though these are closely followed by ongoing capital charges (i.e. interest payments on loans and the cost of depreciation on the capital assets). Other operational costs (e.g. electricity, water and supplies) typically comprise 11 per cent of costs while maintenance and administrative costs can account for the remaining costs. In contrast to costs, revenue can be divided into two categories:

1 Operating revenues, which are generated by directly running and operating the airport (e.g. the terminal area, leased areas and grounds).
2 Non-operating revenues, which include income from activities not associated with the airport core business which airport analysts divide into aeronautic or traffic revenues and non-aeronautical or commercial revenues.

For the airport there is a range of possible revenue sources (though not all airports necessarily collect or use the revenue in a set way):

- landing fees (which the AIC have suggested do not exceed 4 per cent of airlines' operating costs)
- airport air traffic control charges
- aircraft parking
- passenger charges
- freight charges
- aircraft handling services.

In terms of non-aeronautical revenue, Doganis (1992) outlines the following sources:

- rents or lease income from airport tenants
- recharges to tenants for utilities and services provided
- concession income (e.g. from duty-free and tax-free shops)
- direct sales in shops operated by the airport authority
- revenue from car parking where it is airport operated

- miscellaneous items
- non-airport related income (e.g. through land development or hotel development).

Within a European context, Doganis noted that aeronautical revenue accounted for 56 per cent of revenue and non-aeronautical revenue for 44 per cent of income. In the USA, airports generated more revenue from commercial sources (e.g. concessions, 33 per cent; rents, 23 per cent; car parking, 4 per cent; other non-aeronautical sources, 17 per cent and aeronautical fees 23 per cent). In terms of non-airport revenue, airports need to understand the scope of airport users, who comprise:

- passengers (departing, arriving and transferring between flights)
- the airlines, which are major consumers of space for storage, maintenance, staff and catering
- airport employees
- airline crews
- meeters and greeters (i.e. those who are accompanying or meeting friends and relatives departing or arriving by air)
- visitors to airports, particularly where airports market their shopping facilities and opportunities to observe aircraft activity in purpose-built viewing areas
- local residents
- the local business community.

Based on Doganis (1992: 115)

Among some of the more contentious issues which airport management has to deal with are passenger safety and security, and environmental issues.

Future airport management issues: Safety, security and environmental concerns

Safety and security are firmly in the travelling public's minds following the 11 September incidents across the USA. A number of agencies within and outside of airports are responsible for passenger safety on the ground and in the air. At the airport, the principal concerns are associated with ensuring the integrity of the perimeter fence and that intruders do not penetrate the security cordon. Prevention of terrorism has become an issue and security has been enhanced in recent years with the introduction and greater use of closed circuit television cameras (CCTV). New technology such as biometrics (the use of technology that recognizes passengers' unique physiological characteristics: the fingerprint or iris patterns) are being trialled along with passenger profiling by crime detection agencies, enhanced baggage screening (such as Munich's double baggage screen) and greater collaboration between airline agencies to deter would-be terrorists.

Among the major constraints facing airports in the future are community objections to noise and pollution emissions. These are increasingly being documented by airports (see BAA's reports for each airport it operates at www.baa.co.uk and these consider the mitigating measures they are taking to address these concerns). As a major land user and consumer of space, and being the focal point of transport activity, it is inevitable that airports will be the focus of attention concerning transport-related pollution; this has been illustrated by the inquiry into the development and expansion of Heathrow's Terminal Five. The debate has been re-examined following the announcement in July 2002 by the UK government's national consultation regarding the future airports policy for the UK (www.dftgov.uk). This preceded the new Airports Policy White Paper in 2003 which heralds the largest airport expansion programme in the UK since the privatization of BAA, with new runways and airports across the UK to accommodate forecast growth in demand. The environmental effects of such development are summarized as:

- affecting those people who live close to airports or under flight paths
- emissions that affect the built and natural environment
- increased land-take from new development, especially where green belt land or ecologically sensitive areas are affected: one plan was for a new airport site in south-east England on a wildlife site in Cliffe, Kent (subsequently abandoned)
- additional congestion as a result of additional passengers travelling to the airports.

Much of the initial discussion focuses on statistics that suggest up to 50 per cent of the UK population travel by air once a year whilst the economy has been expanding. Yet interestingly the UK government made no mention of demand management measures such as realistic pricing policies to reduce demand from low-cost airlines, who have generated large volumes of price-sensitive business. In addition, the discussion paper does not examine the implications of hidden subsidies such as aviation fuel, which is exempt from tax under international agreements. As a result, the full costs of pollution are not charged to the users and suppliers. It is estimated that this may subsidize the UK aviation industry by £7 billion a year and give it unfair advantages over other forms of transport, although research shows that substituting air travel for rail is only successful where journey times are up to three hours in length. Whatever the case, airports have been in a very enviable position in terms of their growth prospects as a result of future air travel, and this seems set to continue. The environmental consequences of such development are likely to be controversial at a time when demand for air travel continues to out-grow the rate of expansion of national economies.

At a local level, the national consultation highlights the need for a new runway in Scotland and a new integrated transport infrastructure at either Glasgow or Edinburgh airport since low-cost air travel has led to growth rates of up to 12 per cent per annum in air travel at Edinburgh airport. Airport development is likely to have a national impact since future development is being directly linked to eco-nomic growth in the UK, with large lobby groups including the aviation industry making a case for continuing prosperity based around the air transport sector.

The international airline industry

> The airline industry developed as a commercial enterprise during the 1930s as technological advances in aviation enabled companies to develop regular passenger services, cross-subsidized by the provision of freight and air postal services. In the post-war period, modern-day air transport emerged as an international business, providing services and products for a diverse group of users including scheduled and non-scheduled (charter) transporta-tion for air travellers and cargo transportation for businesses. (Page 2002: 209)

The airline industry is truly a global business, and the effects of 11 September and the ensuing financial problems experienced by many airlines only led to a slight drop in international tourist arrivals to 689 million in 2001, from 697 million in 2000. It is clear that the pace of change in the aviation sector is rapid and under-standing the nature of underlying and current trends is important from a tourism management perspective so managers and the industry can understand how to respond to such issues.

Trends in the airline industry in the new millennium

The airline industry in its broadest form, as shown in Figure 6.1, is a complex amal-gam of transport-related sectors and interest groups which operate, regulate and interact with the aviation sector. The previous section reviewed one of these sectors – the airport – and in this section the focus is on the trends and patterns of development of the airline sector: passenger airlines. These can be divided into two distinct groups:

1 *Scheduled services*, which operate between destinations to a predetermined timetable and take the form of two types of services, one operated by domestic airlines and one by international airlines. There are over 650 airlines which pro-vide scheduled services internationally. Quite often, a country may run a state-owned airline (known as a flag carrier) that safeguards the tourism market for the destination and air access. Other airlines can be part publicly and part privately owned or wholly privately owned. Where airlines operate on high-volume routes between major destinations, these are termed 'trunk routes', which are fed by feeder or regional airlines. This, the hub and spoke operation, is illus-trated in Figure 6.2. Yet one recent innovation noted by Boeing Commercial Airplane Group (2002) is the rise in point-to-point, or city pair flights, using medium-sized aircraft that remove the hub-and-spoke pattern of development; this may be observed in Figure 6.3. These point-to-point flights are also illus-trated later with reference to the low-cost carriers that have pioneered this con-cept, often using secondary, lesser-known airports at a distance from the major tourist destination, with lower landing costs.

2 *Charter airlines*, which do not operate to published timetables, being chartered to tour operators (travel intermediaries) who then sell the seats. In recent years, char-ter aircraft have also pioneered the sale of seat-only sales, which account for up to 20 per cent of their sales, particularly on Mediterranean holidays. Charters have, therefore, been associated with leisure travel (see Chapter 2) and one example of their large-scale use is for the Hajj pilgrimage to Mecca, during which up to a million visitors travel for a religious event each year. Many scheduled carriers or tour oper-ators also have their own charter airlines as part of an integrated tourism business.

Globally, the airline industry carried 1600 million passengers in 1998 on 18 000 air-craft operating to and from 10 000 airports. In Europe, the total demand for air traffic in 1998 was 541 million passengers, and this is expected to rise to 1101 million in

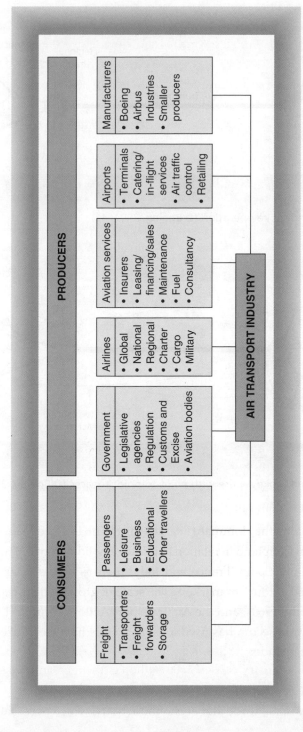

Figure 6.1   The structure of the air transport sector: its constituent parts, producers and consumers (source: developed from ATAG (2000) *The Economic Benefits of Air Transport*)

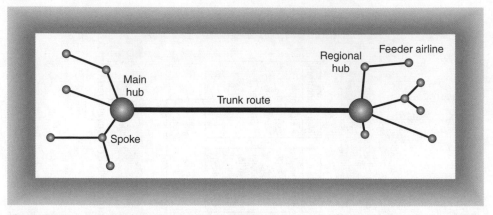

Figure 6.2   Hub and spoke operation (© Boeing, 2001: 41)

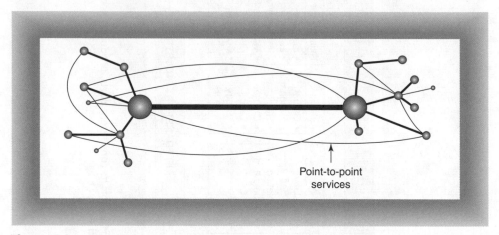

Figure 6.3   Hub and spoke service with point-to-point services (© Boeing, 2001: 41)

2015. The UK remains the dominant market for traffic in European air travel, as discussed further in Chapter 8 in relation to package holiday travel. The next largest markets are Germany, Spain, France and Italy; there is thus a clear relationship with the key European tourism markets. The scale of growth in air travel has been phenomenal since the 1960s, and the Air Transport Action Group (ATAG), a lobby group for the aviation sector, has used a list of factors have been used to explain this growth. These include:

● falling real cost of air travel
● increased international trade and economic activity, which necessitates travel

- rising disposable incomes
- political stability
- a gradual relaxation of travel restrictions in many countries (i.e. South Korea and China allowed greater outbound travel in the 1990s; China allowed greater inbound travel in the 1990s)
- greater leisure time and tourism promotion
- rising air transport liberalization
- new countries with low levels of air transport activity expanding their traffic volumes (e.g. East Asia-Pacific).

These factors are reflected in a series of trends in air travel since the 1970s, which Doganis (2001) explains in terms of the following:

- The effects of increasing liberalization (at the same time as airports were being privatized to accommodate changes in demand), which have removed many of the existing controls on air route capacity and frequency of services, where monopoly, duopoly or collusion prevented fair and open competition.
- The relatively low price of aviation fuel since the mid-1980s, which typically accounts for 30–33 per cent of airline operating costs (but rose sharply in the new millennium).
- Actual declines in the growth rate of air travel from growth rates of up to 12 per cent in the 1960s and 7.8 per cent growth per annum prior to 1987, to 4.8 per cent per annum between 1987 and 1997. ATAG predicts growth rates of 4–5 per cent in the 2001–2010 period; this is a global slowdown, but the rate of growth is still in excess of growth of many countries' GDP, which is often seen as a driver of air traffic. Even so, some regions such as Asia-Pacific will certainly outperform these rates.
- Major restructuring in the nature of supply and market demand for air travel since the 1970s. Doganis (2001) found that in 1972 the USA and Europe were dominant, with 66 per cent of all international air travel. In the 1990s, this had dropped to 50 per cent as Asian airlines with lower cost bases (i.e. greater flexibility in staff utilization and lower salary and operating costs) reconfigured the nature of air transport supply as demand from Asia-Pacific also expanded.
- The yields (the actual profitability of an airline seat or flight) dropped in the 1990s, reflected in lower revenue per passenger kilometre, due to increased capacity on many flights/routes and lower prices. Doganis (2001) found that the percentage of passengers travelling on promotional fares (i.e. discounted rates)

rose from 51 per cent to 71 per cent in the early to late 1990s. To address the falling yields, airlines have had to reduce the unit costs of operation (i.e. the cost of each individual input which goes into a flight including in-flight service, staffing and associated costs). Where airlines failed to reduce costs quicker than drops in yields, they have been forced to raise the number of passengers they carry (loadings) or face financial problems.

- The growth in globalization and international ownership of airlines, as governments sell interests or whole airlines off to reduce their liability and need for investment – in much the same way as the airports were privatized in the 1980s and 1990s. The most notable privatization in the 1980s was British Airways. Accompanying these changes are greater involvement in collaboration and partnerships (e.g. airline alliances), greater concentration of airlines in a large number of global carriers and increased numbers of mergers and agreements for working together.
- A constant decline in fare levels has forced a response by the airline industry: to bypass travel agents and their commissions, which have been as high as 12 per cent of operating costs. This is known as 'disintermediation', and involves selling direct to the customer and using paperless tickets, both of which remove the role of a travel agent.
- Infrastructure constraints, induced by liberalization and more airlines seeking take-off and landing slots at congested gateway or hub airports, as well as pressure on airlines to be more environmentally responsible and reduce noise emissions.

ATAG estimates that, by 2010, the global airline industry will generate 28 million jobs and account for an economic impact of US$1800, with 2.3 billion passengers travelling.

Managing the airline industry

From the previous discussion, it is evident that the aviation sector has experienced and continues to undergo rapid change. Adapting to such change is a key challenge for management so that it can ensure profitability. Many airlines began life as state-owned enterprises, and this indicates the need for massive investment since the airline industry is very capital intensive, requiring a steady and predictable long-term stream of revenue to absorb the high capital and operating costs. For example, a Boeing 737 can cost US$30 million new and that excludes some of the fit-out costs: deploying such resources to their optimum use is critical. The airlines of many smaller countries are still subsidized and maintained for political reasons especially in Asia-Pacific and South America.

Airline management requires airlines balancing those issues they have to deal with on a day-to-day basis (operational issues) and longer-term basis (strategic issues) together with their marketing. In reality, the management process for airline companies is an ongoing activity that requires a predetermined structure within the organization to ensure that all the business activities are adequately integrated to meet the needs of its internal customers (those within the organization) and the external business needs (the customer or purchaser of services and products). This involves overseeing the activities of airline operations (domestic and international airline business) and diverse activities that affect the organization's main business (e.g. ground handling, planning, human resource management and reservations). To streamline and ensure different parts of an airline work efficiently, many larger companies have been organized into functional business units and in some cases have outsourced, franchised or disposed of elements of the business that are not profitable or central to core activity. This is most noticeable in low-cost airlines, which have stripped out all but the basic elements needed for the business to function. Yet:

> airline managers are not free agents. Their actions are circumscribed by a host of national and international regulations. These are both economic and non-economic in character and may well place severe limitations on airlines' freedom of action. (Doganis 1991: 24)

As a result regulation is a major factor affecting the business environment for aviation and this is a very complex area involving politics, decision-making, governments, airlines and changing international pressure for greater liberalization.

Regulating international air transport

Many countries' airlines have seen growing pressure over the last 20 years for the state to be less involved in the protection of national flag carriers and to allow other airlines to fly between countries and compete for traffic. Within many sectors of the tourism industry, there is a great debate on why certain activities need to be regulated. In the case of air travel, regulation is needed for a number of reasons. Appropriate international regulation and supervision of the industry ensures airlines do not operate in an unsafe manner. Regulations set minimum standards for operating aircraft, and non-economic regulations are designed to cover the safety and operational guidelines for airline services. There are regulations concerning, for example,

- the airworthiness of aircraft, their maintenance and overhaul and the training of engineers who undertake this work
- the numbers and type of flight crew and cabin staff required on specific types of flight together with their qualifications and training
- the aviation infrastructure such as airports, meteorological services, en route navigational facilities and safety standards.

Technical and safety standards are developed and policed by civil aviation bodies in each country (for example, the Civil Aviation Authority in the UK). Technical standards and safety procedures are incumbent upon airline managers, and adhering to high standards of technical expertise and safety is now seen as essential to maintaining a competitive advantage. Other forms of regulation include environmental regulations associated with the noise and emissions that airlines create and the effects in and around airports and their local population. As mentioned above, many airports have begun to develop stringent environmental conditions that airlines must meet if they operate from their airports – otherwise they may be fined or banned.

The economic regulation of airlines can be traced back to the Paris Convention (1919) which established the principle that states have sovereign rights over their territory (i.e. their airspace). This led to the eventual development of bilateral agreements between countries to allow airlines rights to overfly their airspace and the right to operate into and out of other countries. In 1944, the Chicago Convention led to multilateral agreement on the:

- exchange of air traffic rights, or 'freedom of the air' (see Table 6.2)
- control of fares and freight tariffs
- control of frequencies and capacity.

Table 6.2 Air rights (redrawn from Figure G.1: Air transport freedom rights, which first appeared in *Asia Pacific Air Transport: Challenges and Policy Reforms* edited by Christopher Findlay, Chia Lin Sien and Karmjit Singh, p. 193, with the kind permission of the publisher, Institute of Southeast Asian Studies, Singapore, http.//bookshop.iseas.edu.sg)

Aviation rights

First freedom rights grant a foreign carrier the right to fly over the home country without landing.

Second freedom rights grant a foreign carrier the right to land at specified points in the home country, for purposes of refuelling and maintenance, but not to pick up or disembark traffic (passengers, cargo, or mail).

Third freedom rights allow for traffic that was picked up by a foreign carrier outside the home country to be disembarked at specified destinations in the home country.

Fourth freedom rights allow a foreign carrier to pick up originating traffic in the home country, for transport to the foreign country in which the carrier is based.

Fifth freedom rights (also called beyond rights) permit the foreign carrier to pick up or disembark traffic en route.

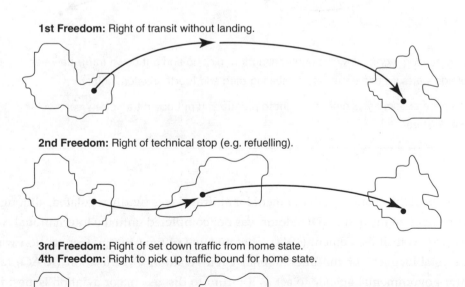

1st Freedom: Right of transit without landing.

2nd Freedom: Right of technical stop (e.g. refuelling).

3rd Freedom: Right of set down traffic from home state.
4th Freedom: Right to pick up traffic bound for home state.

(Continued)

Table 6.2 (*Continued*)

5th Freedom: Right to pick up and put down traffic between two foreign states as an extension of routes to/from home state.

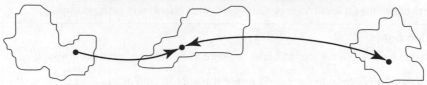

6th Freedom: Unofficial right to pick up and put down traffic between foreign states via home state (by combining 3rd and 4th Freedom rights).

7th Freedom: Right to pick up and put down traffic between two foreign states

Sixth freedom rights allow the unofficial right to pick up and put down traffic between foreign states via home state (by combining third and fourth freedom rights).

Seventh freedom rights grant the right to pick up and put down traffic between two foreign states.

As a result the operating environment for air travel was rigidly regulated, although agreement on the first two freedoms was not completed until the International Air Services Transit Agreement (1944). The outcome of the Chicago Convention was the establishment of the International Civil Aviation Organization (ICAO), an inter-governmental agency to act as a forum to discuss major aviation issues. In addition, the International Air Transport Association (IATA) was established as a rival to ICAO in 1945, to represent the interests of airline companies. IATA's primary purpose remains coordination and standardization of airline operations, representing airlines in a diverse range of negotiations with airport authorities, ICAO, governments and even hijackers. It also operates the clearing house for inter-air-line debts arising from inter-airline traffic (carriage of airline passengers or freight on a service holding tickets issued by other airlines).

Airlines also use bilateral agreements, based on the principle of reciprocity (a fair and equal exchange of rights) while pooling agreements exist (except in the USA where US antitrust legislation prohibits such agreements which are viewed as being anti-competitive). Pooling agreements have been used in duopolistic situations to share the market between two airlines. Where business may not be sufficient to justify a two-airline operation, a revenue cost pool may be used where one airline operates the service on behalf of the pool partners. Airlines may also enter into inter-airline royalty agreements where airlines wish to pick up 'fifth freedom' traffic (see Table 6.2) where they do not have such rights. By making royalty payments to the airline of the country involved, it may gain such rights. Such a range of regulatory measures ensures that the management of airlines is a complex process when dealing with the international aviation market. A further change to this regulatory environment was the decision of the US government in 1978 to deregulate its domestic airline industry. A more recent development is the evolution of 'open skies' policies since 1992. These have emerged because of:

- increasing concentration in the US airline market following deregulation, with former domestic airlines emerging as major international carriers
- international airlines searching for marketing benefits from mergers in their home country and minority share purchases/strategic alliances to operate in other markets (which are discussed further below)
- the growing trend towards privatization of national flag carriers.

Open skies policies involve bilateral air service agreements where market access and price controls are removed. According to Boeing Commercial Airplane Group (2004) 50 per cent of the world's airline traffic is now based on open skies agreements, illustrating the scale of change in just over a decade.

Deregulation in the USA aimed to achieve greater competition, and resulted in a 62 per cent increase in domestic passenger traffic between 1978 and 1990 followed by greater integration and concentration within the industry. It led to a new business environment where airline companies reorganized their activities to achieve cost reductions, least-cost solutions and network maximization with the intention of making operations more cost effective. Hub and spoke operations (see Figure 6.2) allowed airlines to develop a network to serve a large number of people over a wide area, with the hub acting as a switching point for passengers travelling on feeder routes along the spokes which cannot sustain a trunk route. This has resulted in the geographical concentration of hubs in major US cities and the six largest US airlines developing four major hub cities – Atlanta, Chicago, Dallas and Denver. The more competitive and unregulated the market, the greater the degree of planning and adjustment needed to match supply and demand. This is normally undertaken under the auspices of the marketing process.

Airline marketing: Its role and recent innovations

Growing global competition in the air travel market has meant that the 1990s were the decade of the air traveller as a consumer, usually seeking enhanced service quality. This has gone a stage further in the new millennium as the price-sensitive customer is a dominant element, especially in domestic air travel, and concerned with a minimum standard of service. Airlines have been forced not only to reduce operating costs and compete aggressively for business, but also to focus on the needs of their customers. Airline marketing is now more complex as it is vital to the management process of deciding what to produce and how it should be sold. Thus, 'the role of airline marketing is to bring together the supply of air services, which each airline can largely control, with the demand, which it can influence but not control, and to do this in a way which is both profitable and meets the airline's corporate objectives' (Doganis 1991: 202). BA explained its financial turnaround from a loss of £544 million in 1981–1982 to a profit of £272 million in 1983–1984 in terms of a more focused marketing orientation involving recognizing customers' needs and setting about satisfying them. This has now come full circle, with a re-evaluation of the company's core business and marketing focus as its business has been significantly affected by the rise of low-cost carriers on short-haul domestic and European routes. BA has had not only had to align its fare structure with what customers are prepared to pay, but also to rationalize its operations. For example, until July 2002 BA had reduced fares on 71 routes and removed restrictions on lower priced tickets to stimulate demand. This was a result of the company's poor financial performance for the financial year ended 30 March 2002, where a £200 million loss before tax compared to a £150 million profit in 2000. In February 2002, the company announced its 'Future Size and Shape' study which began a process of realigning the company to demand, by removing unprofitable sections of its business through capacity and overhead reduction. One notable outcome was the decision to reposition its short-haul routes to compete with the low-cost airlines. This strategy has moved a stage further since 2005, with the realignment of its ailing regional airline – Citiexpress (rebranded BA Connect), which carries 3.5 million passengers a year. The airline is reported to have a two-year timeline for the turnaround or closure of the subsidiary, with targets of 10 per cent growth per annum combined with cost savings.

How airlines use marketing functions

The role of marketing in the management of airline services can be summarized as a four-stage process:

1 Identify markets and market segments using research methods and existing data sources and traffic forecasts.
2 Use the market analysis to assess which products to offer, known as product planning. At this stage, price becomes a critical factor. Therefore product planning is related to:
   (a) market needs identified from market research;
   (b) the current and future product features of competing airlines and the cost of different product features;
   (c) assessing what price the customers can be expected to pay for the product.
3 Develop a marketing plan to plan and organize the selling of the products. Sales and distribution outlets need to be considered together with a detailed programme of advertising and promotion, such as the impact and effect which adverts on the side of taxis may have for the travelling public.
4 Monitor and review the airline's ability to meet service standards, assessed through sales figures, customer surveys, analysis of complaints and long-term planning to develop new service and product features.
After Page (2002)

The role of marketing, particularly advertising, has also assumed an increasingly important role in the evolution of the low-cost carrier market.

The low-cost carriers: Aligning service provision to demand

Airlines have traditionally targeted service quality in the business travel and luxury market for first-class travel. This is because it is the most profitable segment of the market for scheduled airlines, with premium pricing and high profit margins per seat; the yields of economy class are lower and profitability is attained by achieving high load factors. However, this traditional strategy has been significantly challenged in many markets that have allowed liberalization of services – in the USA in the 1980s, Europe in the 1990s and elsewhere in the new millennium – allowing new entrants to compete for business – notably low-cost carriers since more travellers now seek budget fares (see Box 6.1). What makes the low-cost model interesting is the way the carriers start up new routes, offer massive incentives to build the market and then create long-term demand, often developing lesser-known airports and destinations.

These innovations in low-cost flying have been translated into the low-cost revolution that has permeated the UK and mainland Europe since the last wave of deregulation after 1997. Companies in Australasia (e.g. Virgin Blue, OzJet, JetStar) and Asia (Air Asia, JetStar Asia, Valuair) are following this pattern. There are also examples of low-cost entrants in Brazil (Gol) though none rival the most cost-competitive model of Air Asia, based in Malaysia, which has generated a great deal of first-time fliers. It has the enviable reputation of having the lowest production costs of any low-cost airline globally. However, the most visible impact has been the massive expansion of low-cost carriers in Europe.

Low-cost carriers in Europe

The evolution of low-cost carriers in the UK is shown in Table 6.4, which highlights the dominant players: Ryanair, easyJet, and a number of other competitors such as BMIbaby that are shown in Table 6.5. The full-cost carrier British Airways cut 15 per cent off its costs 2001–2003, since it has low-cost competition on 70 per cent of its routes now; its yields are double those of the revenue per flight of Ryanair and 45 per cent higher than easyJet's. These companies share certain factors with the model of low-cost airline operations outlined in Box 6.1, and they are summarized in Table 6.6. The scale and significance of low-cost airlines in the UK

Box 6.1 Case study: The low-cost carrier: The SouthWest phenomenon

Low-cost air travel, often termed no-frills or budget airline travel, is a relatively new phenomenon in Europe – despite the ill-fated attempt in the 1970s by Freddie Laker and his Skytrain concept, which sought to compete on the North Atlantic market. In fact some analysts point to the establishment in 1949 of Pacific South West Airlines as the pioneer low-cost airline. Yet low-cost air travel was well established in the USA long before deregulation, with certain airlines specializing in this niche market. Indeed, the growth of SouthWest airlines in the USA since 1971 epitomizes the traits of the low-cost carrier and established many of the basic business principles of streamlined airline operations (see Table 6.3 for key data on SouthWest).

SouthWest entered new markets at a low price, using lesser-known secondary airports, and demand outstripped supply. Following deregulation in 1978, SouthWest expanded across the USA in a cautious manner as many other carriers went bankrupt or were taken over. It avoided head-on competition with the major carriers, though when it had to face such competition (such as when United launched its shuttle services in California) it initially saw market share drop; business then recovered (as United could not operate services viably) to the point where SouthWest was the dominant intra-state carrier in California. *So how does SouthWest manage to operate a viable business where competitors fail?*

In terms of the economics of airline operation (see Figure 6.4 for an illustration of the main costs in airline operation), it manages to operate at a cost structure well below its revenue. This means it can operate at a cost base that is often 25–40 per cent below that of its competitors where unrestricted fares are low. In 2003, the airline cut all commission for travel agent bookings, following on from a decision by Delta Airlines in March 2002. Many of SouthWest's flight sectors are short and so revenue per kilometre flown is relatively high; the company has a simple fare structure, high levels of punctuality and correspondingly high levels of customer satisfaction. SouthWest usually attracted a good mix of business and leisure travellers, despite being no-frills high-density one-class seating. There is no seat allocation and to keep costs down only snacks are offered to passengers. Pilots entered into a ten-year agreement on remuneration levels, which are key element of operation for the airline, in return for share options to help stabilize costs. By standardizing its fleet type with only Boeing 737s, SouthWest keeps maintenance and staff training costs low. Using fifteen- to twenty-minute turnaround times at terminals can increase the number of flight sectors an aircraft can fly in a day: on

Table 6.3 Key facts on SouthWest Airline operations (Based on data provided on www.southwest.com)

- In 2002, the airline served 58 cities in 30 US states, with a fleet of 366 Boeing 737s
- It had a net income of US$5111.1 in 2001
- In 2001 it carried 64.4 million passengers with an average load factor of 68.1 per cent
- In 2002, its average fare was US$82.84 for a one-way trip on an average flight length of 715 miles
- In 2001, SouthWest booked 7.2 million passengers monthly
- It provides 90 per cent of all discount air travel in the USA
- In May 2002, the *Wall Street Journal* ranked the airline first for customer service based on the American Customer Satisfaction Index
- The airline was ranked among the top 4 US airlines for National Airline Quality Ratings of 11 airlines in April 2002, based on punctuality, baggage handling, overbooking and customer complaints
- SouthWest was the first airline company to establish a home page on the internet (www.southwest.com)
- The airline's booking costs are $1 for an internet booking and $6–8 for a travel agent booking
- According to search engines such as Lycos, SouthWest is one of the most commonly searched airlines on the web
- It has 2800 departures a day
- The year 2001 marked 29 consecutive years of profit
- The company employs 35 000 staff

average eight per day and twelve hours' flying time. The company is also rated as one of the most successful airline companies internationally, flying 70 million passengers a year, with a US$1 billion turnover, flights to 60 US cities and 3000 departures a day. Part of its corporate success is attributed to its team-based approach to management, high level of supervisory staff to teams and corporate ethos, with few internal barriers to its operations. As a result, the airline has around 30 per cent of the USA's low-cost airline capacity, which is estimated to be around 25–30 per cent of the domestic market. Low-cost carriers are estimated to compete on 70 per cent of US domestic air routes. Interestingly, four of the eleven largest US carriers in 2004 were low-cost airlines (SouthWest, America West, Jet Blue and Air Tran).

This model has not been universally successful in North America, with examples of new entrants (Independence Air and Frontier Airlines) having ongoing financial problems. In 2004 America West merged with the full-cost carrier US Airways, which was bankrupt.

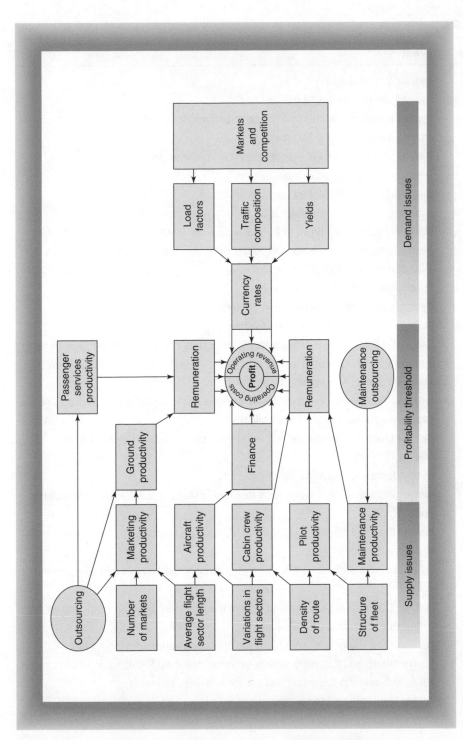

Figure 6.4 The main costs in operating an airline (source: modified from Page 2005; reprinted from *Journal of Air Transport Management*, 3, Seristö and Vepsäläinen, Airline Cost Drivers, 11–22, © 1997 with permission from Elsevier)

Table 6.4 A brief history of low-cost airline development in the UK

Date	Event
1985	Ryanair is established
1991	Ryanair's losses reach £18 million
1992	Ryanair moves its UK hub from Luton to London Stansted. It makes a pre-tax profit
1995	easyJet is established in October
	Ryanair begins a new UK domestic service from Prestwick Airport, Ayr, Scotland
1996	Debonair is established in June
1997	Virgin Express is established
1997	Ryanair is floated on the stock market
	Ryanair has a pre-tax profit of US$53 million for 1997–1998
	Ryanair adds four new European routes to its UK–Ireland flights
1998	Ryanair adds seven new European routes
	British Airways establishes GO in May
1999	Debonair goes into receivership in September
2000	BUZZ, a subsidiary of KLM, is established
	GO is sold off by British Airways to venture capitalists 3i for £100 million through a management buy-out after losses of £20 million in each year of operation
	Jersey European Airways rebrands itself Flybe
2001	British Midland establishes its BMIbaby low-cost carrier based at East Midlands Airport
2002	easyJet purchases GO for £400 million
	Ryanair places the largest aircraft order ever for a low-cost carrier: 100 new Boeing 737s
	Flybe adopts a low-cost model of operation
2003	easyJet introduces new technology to allow customers to view/amend bookings online
2003	In April Ryanair acquires BUZZ from KLM, opening up new French regional airports and routes
2003	EU Jet, based in Ireland with Kent International Airport as a hub, begins operation in May
2003	In June, Duo Airways Ltd, formed from a management buy-out from Maersk Air, begins operation from Birmingham
2004	TUI launches Thomsonfly.com, with regional departures from Doncaster, Bournemouth and Coventry initially, with summer-only flights from 11 airports in 2006. The airline is the rebranded company airline, Britannia
2004	In May Duo Airways Ltd collapses

(Continued)

Table 6.4 (*Continued*)

Date	Event
2004	Ryanair.com is named by Google as the most searched travel website in Europe. The airline carried 24 million passengers in 2004
2005	Ryanair places an additional order of 70 firm and 70 options on Boeing aircraft, taking it to a total of 225 firm orders and 200 options for delivery 2005–2012, as older aircraft are retired. This reflects the company's ambition to carry 70 million passengers a year by 2012, based on average growth of 27 per cent per annum in passenger numbers 1995–2005
2005	Ryanair and easyJet, followed by Air Berlin, are established as Europe's largest low-cost carriers
2005	Virgin Express and SN Brussels merge
2005	Flybe is carrying 5.5 million passengers a year; Ryanair is carrying 33 million passengers a year and easyJet is carrying 29.5 million passengers a year
2005	EU Jet (Eire-based) ceases trading, leaving passengers stranded

Table 6.5 Selected scheduled low-cost airlines operating in the United Kingdom

Aer Arann	Jetz
Air Berlin	Monarch
Air Scotland	Ryanair
Air South West	Sky Europe
BMIbaby	Thomsonfly
easyJet	Transavia
Excel Airways	Virgin Express
Flybe	Wizz Air
Globespan	

is reflected in over 20 per cent of the market dominated by this sector and can be illustrated by the history of Ryanair and its subsequent development.

Figure 6.5 illustrates the competitive nature of the airline market in Europe and the ongoing impact of the low-cost phenomenon with its lower staffing costs, lower handling costs, lower operational costs and ability to provide a simple product the consumer understands. In marketing terms, the full-cost carriers have

Table 6.6 Key characteristics of low-cost carriers which make them more competitive than other carriers

- Some carriers have introduced single/one-way fares not requiring stopovers or Saturday night stays to get advanced purchase (APEX) prices
- No complimentary in-flight service (no frills) often reduces operating costs 6–7 per cent.
- One-class cabins (in most cases)
- No pre-assigned seating (in most cases)
- Ticketless travel – up to 98 per cent of bookings (i.e. Ryanair in 2005) made online at travellers' convenience
- High-frequency routes to compete with other airlines for popular destinations and up to three flights a day on low-density routes
- Short turnarounds that are often less than half an hour, with higher aircraft rotations (i.e. the level of utilization is higher than other airlines) and less time charged on the airport apron and runway
- The use of secondary airports where feasible (including the provision of public transport where none exists)
- Point-to-point flights
- Lower staffing costs, with fewer cabin crew (since there is no complimentary in-flight service; having no food service and thus no cleaning also reduces turnaround times)
- Flexibility in staff rostering, no overnight stays for staff at non-base locations and streamlined operations (e.g. on some airlines toilets on domestic flights are only emptied at cabin crew request and not at each turnaround, thus reducing costs)
- Many of the aircraft are leased, reducing the level of depreciation and standardizing costs
- Many airline functions, such as ground staff and check-in, are outsourced, reducing overhead costs by 11–15 per cent
- Standardized aircraft types (i.e. Boeing 737s) reduce maintenance costs and the range of spare parts which need to be held for repairs
- Limited office space at the airports
- Heavy emphasis on advertising, especially billboards, to offset the declining use of travel agents as the main source of bookings
- Heavy dependence upon the internet and telephone for bookings
- Small administrative staff, with many sales-related staff (as well as pilots in some cases) on commission to improve performance
- Narrower seating on Boeing 737s (148 seats on Ryanair's 737s as opposed to the standard 126 configuration on full-cost carrier configurations)
- Multi-skilled staff (can handle check-in and departure gate)
- Innovation (e.g. New-York-based Jet Blue has introduced live television on board to add greater perceived value to the product, shifting the attention away from competition just on price; in 2005, Air Asia moved into more flexible mobile technology for expanding its distribution channels, introducing a mobile phone booking service for tickets)

(Continued)

Table 6.6 (*Continued*)

- Higher yield per passenger and innovative means of securing additional passenger revenue (e.g. in 2003, Ryanair derived 16 per cent of revenue from non-passenger sources other than tickets: 28 million euros from car hire; 23 million euros from in-flight sales; 12 million euros from internet revenue; 35 million euros from non-flight revenue). It aims to increase non-flight revenue from commission on accommodation bookings and areas of activity. The company aims to increase its proportion of free seats (taxes only) from 20 per cent in 2004 to 50 per cent by 2009
- Ongoing cost cutting, with Ryanair considering taking out window shades, seatback pockets and seat reclines
- Diversification into full-cost carrier markets (e.g. German Wings has 40 per cent of its market as business travellers with 500 company accounts) and Air Berlin offers hot meals on flights over 3.5 hours
- Ryanair introducing web check-in to reduce queues at airports and for passengers to only pay for the luggage services they use

Box 6.2 Case Study: The history and development of Ryanair

Ryanair is the airline founded in Ireland in 1985 by the Guinness Peat Aviation aircraft-leasing company. The airline's traffic grew from 80 000 passengers in 1986 to 600 000 in 1989, when it introduced aged jets – BAC-111s – on its flights to expand capacity. In the first four years of operation, until 1989, Ryanair lost £20 million. By 1994 it was transporting 1.5 million passengers a year after reconfiguring its operations, replicating the success of SouthWest by standardizing its fleet, and purchasing used Boeing 737s from Britannia and Lufthansa. By 2000 it had managed to achieve the same rate of growth per annum as SouthWest reaching seven million passengers in 2002 and almost twenty-five million passengers in 2004. As a result it has set a growth rate that other low-cost carriers seek to emulate – particularly easyJet, which carried almost thirty million passengers for the year ending October 2005. The majority of its flights are booked on the internet, and the scale of growth in low-cost carriers in the UK has led to the development of new markets, often with loss-leading fares initially to develop a market presence. Its methods have also been termed 'ambush marketing' – taking the market from the larger established carriers with greater overheads and less flexibility. This illustrates how volatile and changeable the airline market is, particularly regarding the scale and pace of change, where dominant market players can be severely affected by new trends such as the low-cost airline phenomenon.

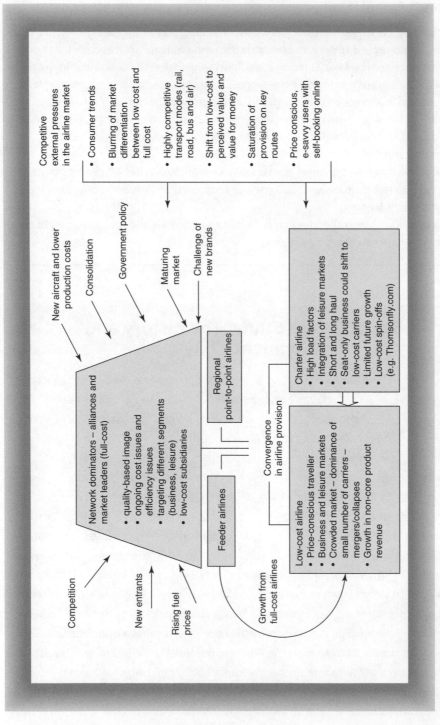

Figure 6.5   The competitive environment for airlines in Europe to 2010

seen head-to-head competition on price, responding with enhanced frequency of flights, loyalty campaigns, direct marketing and, in some cases, spin-off low-cost carriers to compete (using the same principles but applying it to their product). Globally, full-cost carriers have been reluctant to brand their spin-off low-cost carriers with the full-service image, so as to protect their brand image and market position. In some extreme cases, full-cost carriers have withdrawn from over-competitive markets and reallocated their resources to other parts of their business or network. Already, analysts are warning of over-capacity in Europe on trunk routes (e.g. Dublin and Brussels) since 78 of 115 of Europe's air routes have low-cost competitors, with easyJet opening one new route pair a week to grow capacity and demand. This situation is only likely to increase (unless the low-cost carriers can keep generating new demand by opening new routes). With estimates of over 300 firm orders and 350 options for new aircraft for 2012 by low-cost carriers, and analysts' consideration that 250 000 passengers are needed to fill an aircraft to break even, a growth of passenger numbers by 75 million in Europe by 2012 is required. Full-cost carriers in Europe have only 30 planes on order. The low-cost phenomenon has redefined the business environment for air travel but full-cost carriers on long-haul routes have also responded through innovative approaches using airline marketing techniques.

Airline marketing and developing client relationships: Frequent flyer programmes and alliances

To continually build and develop the market for air travel, whilst competing with low-cost carriers, full-cost airlines have begun to recognize the benefits of collaboration and joint working in terms of alliances to address the competition. The concept of frequent flyer programmes (FFPs) is one example of building good client relationships to encourage customer loyalty as part of customer relationship management. These programmes were originally developed in the USA in May 1981 by American Airlines (AA). FFPs were developed to attract business following deregulation. AA used its database of passengers to identify frequent flyers who were enrolled into a Very Important Travellers Club. The reward for loyalty was free air travel on a route that consistently had a high ratio of unsold seats – Hawaii. AA's Advantage FFP aimed to maximize revenue yield and its load factor, it helped to develop Dallas as a logical hub and it captured business from AA's competitors' airlines. Other companies (e.g. United, TWA and Delta) soon launched similar schemes. To broaden the marketing appeal of FFPs, non-airline travel services (car rental companies, tour operators and hotel chains), airline-affiliated credit card purchases (mileage credits added according to the volume of spending) and other services now attract FFP points. It is a basic element of airline marketing strategy in the USA, and European and other global carriers have also introduced it.

British Airways was added to the AA FFP to give it an international dimension; soon Qantas joined. This became the Oneworld global alliance, which now comprises Aer Lingus, Qantas, British Airways, Cathay Pacific, Iberia, Lan Chile and Finnair, with Royal Jordanian joining in late 2006. Malév in Hungary and JAL are also seeking to join. The Oneworld alliance operates to 550 destinations in 130 countries. The Star Alliance is a major airline alliance was formed in the Asia-Pacific region to challenge the Oneworld alliance. It is a combination of 18 airlines including Air New Zealand, United, Lufthansa, Thai Airways International, SAS, Varig, ANA, Asian Airlines, BMI (British Midland), LOT Polish Airlines, Singapore Airlines, Spanair, TAP Air Portugal, US Airways, Austrian Airlines, Blue1 Air and Air Canada; it offers services to over 795 destinations in 139 countries (with their capacity linked together by the StarNet computer to allow them to talk to each other). There is also a smaller alliance, Skyteam, comprising Aeromexico, Air France, Alitalia, Continental Airlines, CZA Czech Airlines, Delta, KLM, Korean Air and Northwest Airlines. Over half of the world airline capacity is linked to airline marketing alliances and this reflects a growing consolidation in the market. Alliances allow partner airlines to grow their network; achieve economies of scale in ticketing, maintenance and purchasing; and provide the consumer with seamless travel.

Doganis (2001) identified two types of airline alliance in existence:

1 commercial alliances, which are operationally driven and focused on the early stages of alliance development
2 strategic alliances, leading towards full merger of airlines.

This is reflected in the three stages to alliance development. The first phase is revenue generation, where partners can enter and exit easily, and involves a series of code shares, joint FFPs, network coordination, joint sales, shared business lounges and an alliance logo. In the second phase, the alliance is cemented together in order to make cost savings for its members from common ground handling, joint maintenance, sales and call centres, purchasing and fleet harmonization. Exit is difficult at this stage. In the last phase, a joint venture situation, exit is almost impossible as it involves franchising, joint product development, sharing aircraft and crews and a single alliance brand. The emergence of alliances reflects a more sophisticated business approach to airline development, although some airlines still seek to differentiate themselves on the basis of unique selling features or propositions – especially in the luxury market, through in-flight food provision.

In-flight catering: A marketing opportunity?

Food provision is estimated to account for 5–10 per cent of the total cost of the fare and some airlines recognize that it is an important element of the in-flight experience, particularly in business and first class where customer expectations are high as a result of advertising campaigns. In contrast, economy travellers often view in-flight food as a sign of value for money although food critics have questioned the need for food as a sign of service quality. With the growth of low-cost airlines, many have decided to remove this element of their cost structures and to charge for in-flight catering. However, airline managers have universally endorsed the role of food as a vital element in airline marketing as recent advertising campaigns have attempted to differentiate airline service. For example, British Airways champions high-quality culinary experiences on board its aircraft as promoted on BA.com:

> British Airways seeks to take the best of world cuisine, finding inspiration from culinary circles, trends, fashion and art and then adapting these for delivery and presentation in an aircraft environment. The British Airways 'Signature Style' offers a clear directional message for our in-flight food strategy. It illustrates our commitment, passion and dedication to creating new standards in an exciting, challenging and continually progressive industry. (BA.com, accessed 23 December 2005)

To steer this strategy, BA has a range of leading chefs and advisers as part of its Culinary Council, to advise, inspire and lead their 'Signature Dishes' (unique dishes that are associated with an individual chef or restaurant). This is a completely different approach to that of the low-cost airlines, which have downgraded food provision, in many cases, to snacks which are free or to be purchased.

Some airlines perceive food provision as more than a simple element of their product or service and it may explain why customers focus on it as a source of dissatisfaction when their expectations are not met. Yet catering at 30 000 feet is not easy since the tastebuds of passengers change due to pressurization, and their digestive systems become sluggish due to humidity levels and dehydration. Airline meals often come in for very bad press for their poor flavour, although in business and first class meals are often of a gourmet standard to add value to the in-flight experience. Airline meals are often prepared on the ground and frozen then reheated prior to take-off, and this can affect its quality; changes to our tastebuds in the air compound complaints that airline food can sometimes seem very bland. Whilst many short-haul budget airlines do not offer in-flight meals to save costs of £5–6 per passenger (passengers can purchase snacks and sandwiches), food provision on long-haul flights is seen as a way of occupying the travellers' time to create the illusion that the flight is shorter than it actually is. In the USA, in 2005 Northwest Airlines replaced its domestic in-flight food provision with a range of snacks for US$3 (a smartsnack snack box) and a US$5 breakfast or lunch/dinner. The airline estimated that this would save it US$20–30 million a year, at a time it was seeking to cut costs.

The growth in contract catering (for example, Lufthansa's LSG Sky Chefs in Europe) has removed the problem of food provision from the immediate remit of airline managers and has created a new business activity for large companies able to meet the exacting requirements of airlines (for example, on a Boeing 747 50 000 catering items are required per flight). Despite the logistical and technical problems of providing quality food on board aircraft, it remains essential in the expectations of consumers on full-cost carriers, and continues to assist airline managers in the perceived differentiation of their products and services, especially in the premium sector of the market (i.e. full economy fares, business and first class). Major advertising campaigns have been designed around these very attributes in an attempt to nurture the high-value business traveller.

The food service sector for the airline industry is estimated to be worth US$15 billion a year globally. LSG Sky Chefs' market share is around 30 per cent, with a turnover of 2.3 billion euros a year. The scale of these catering operations are reflected in LSG Sky Chefs' provision of around 362 million airline meals a year for 270 airlines in 48 countries. Individual markets, such as India, are estimated to worth US$50 million a year and companies such as Gate Gourmet offer services to 200 airlines worldwide. Much of the growth in this sector of the industry is due to the outsourcing of the airline meals provision as airlines sell off these operations in a bid to reduce costs. In the UK, analysts have indicated that around half of the companies servicing the airline catering market are not operating in profit, highlighting the cost pressures which are being placed on their operations by airlines in terms of the service they require and the prices they are prepared to pay.

Future trends

Airlines are a complex industry to understand, especially as they are working in a constant state of flux and change. As Page (2005) indicated, the main challenges for airline managers in the new millennium are:

- technical change (that is, the greater use of technology such as computer reservation systems (CRS) and global distribution systems which are more complex and all-embracing than the former CRS)
- regional change, where new trading blocs (for example, the Association of Southeast Asian Nations or ASEAN) are posing new challenges for patterns of trade and business travel.

For the traveller, air travel poses ongoing health risks, especially highlighted by the recent concern over deep vein thrombosis (DVT) on long-haul flights where cramped conditions and a lack of movement by passengers in flight can aggravate the situation. Research by the Aviation Health Institute (www.aviation-health.com) examined 447 examples of DVT, of which 67 led to death. The profile of deaths were:

- one third male; two thirds female
- just under half were aged 20 to 49 years of age
- 83 per cent occurred on long-haul flights, the bulk of which were in economy class (12.5 per cent in business class)
- the onset of DVT is after the flight.

In addition, there has been a worrying growth in disruptive behaviour on board flights known more commonly as 'air rage'. In the UK, it is estimated that over 1200 incidents of air rage occur each year. This was estimated to be growing at

10 per cent a year. Some of the explanations of the causes of air rage offered by travel medicine research included:

- a lack of oxygen on board; if airlines reduce fuel costs by using recirculated rather than fresh air passenger belligerence is increased and compliant behaviour reduced
- lack of training for staff to deal with difficult travellers as low-cost travel is not accompanied by reduced expectations.

The Civil Aviation Authority (CAA) in the UK indicate that whilst this is not a widespread problem, violence occurred in 10 per cent of cases, with alcohol involved in a further 45 per cent of cases, and smoking (which is banned on most European flights) in toilets also being a problem. Although air rage is downplayed by airlines and the CAA, it is nonetheless very disruptive and potentially dangerous; this is exacerbated when drunk passengers are carried by airlines despite guidelines that are supposed to prevent them from boarding. The majority of such offences are committed by males (77 per cent of cases), largely 20 to 40 years of years of age, with only 5 per cent of cases occurring in first or business class. Typical problems included disruptive passengers using verbal abuse and being unruly because they were offended by airline regulations. Only a small number of incidents led to physical restraints being used or an aircraft being diverted. The likelihood of an offence occurring in UK airspace or on an UK outbound/inbound flight was 1:22 000 for a serious incident on a flight. Greater risks were encountered in the quality of recirculated cabin air provided to passengers in flight and the ongoing debates over the problems of dehydration due to dry air.

Conclusion

The future global aviation industry is likely to contain a limited number of global mega-carriers, with smaller airlines integrated into their operations by strategic alliances and other devices (for example, part ownership by the larger carriers). The major constraint on this rapidly evolving business activity for airline managers will be the availability of uncongested airspace and airports with sufficient capacity, a feature which the low-cost carriers have addressed through the use of secondary airports. This is already affecting air travel in Europe and the USA, while the environmental lobby regularly opposes airport expansion near to major urban centres. These managerial issues have to be addressed and accommodated within the day-to-day operation and longer-term planning by airline managers so that passengers are not adversely affected by delays, congestion and inadequate planning.

References

Ashford, H, Stanton, H. and Moore, C. (1991) *Airport Operations*. London: Pitman.

Barlay, S. (1995) *Cleared for Take-off: Behind the Scenes of Air Travel*. London: Kyle Cathie Limited.

Boeing Commercial Airplane Group (2002) *2002 Current Market Outlook*. Seattle: Boeing Commercial Airplane Group.

Boeing Commercial Airplane Group (2004) *Current Market Outlook* 2004. Seattle: Boeing Commercial Airplane Group.

Doganis, R. (1991) *Flying Off Course: The Economics of International Airlines*. London: Routledge.

Doganis, R. (1992) *The Airport Business*. London: Routledge.

Doganis, R. (2001) *The Airline Business in the Twenty-First Century*. London: Routledge.

Page, S. J. (2002) Airline management. In M. Warner (ed.) *Encyclopaedia of Business and Management*, *Vol. 1*, 2nd edn. London: Thomson Learning (online version).

Page, S. J. (2005) *Transport and Tourism: Global Perspectives*, 2nd edn. Harlow: Pearson Education.

Further reading

The following are very good sources and accessible as well as easy to read:

Doganis, R. (1992) *The Airport Business*. London: Routledge.

Doganis, R. (2001) *The Airline Business in the Twenty-First Century*. London: Routledge.

Graham, A. (2003) *Managing Airports*, 2nd edn. Oxford: Butterworth Heinemann.

Hanlon, P. (1999) *Global Airlines: Competition in a Transnational Industry*, 2nd edn. Oxford: Butterworth Heinemann.

Page, S. J. (2005) *Transport and Tourism: Global Perspectives*, 2nd edn. Harlow: Pearson Education.

Questions

1 Why are airports so important as staging points for international travel?

2 What range of issues would you have to deal with as an airport manager?

3 Why is the US airline industry facing a crisis?

4 How have the low-cost carriers affected the business of leisure travel?

7

Accommodation and hospitality services

Learning outcomes

This chapter examines the significance of the tourist accommodation product and hospitality services consumed by tourists. The chapter will outline the diversity of accommodation types and a number of current trends in the accommodation sector. On completion of the chapter, you should be able to understand:

- the scope and nature of tourist accommodation
- the range of operational issues affecting the accommodation sector
- the differences between serviced and non-serviced accommodation
- the importance of environmental issues in the management of hotels.

Introduction

Accommodation provides the base from which tourists can engage in the process of staying at a destination. It is an element of the wider hospitality sector that is used by tourists. Accommodation has emerged as the focal point for the hosting of guests and visitors through the ages: a guest pays a fee in return for a specified service and grade of accommodation, and associated services such as food and beverages. The accommodation establishment as a commercial venture, especially the evolution of the commercial hotel in the Victorian period, has dominated the literature on accommodation, as entrepreneurs responded to the demand for serviced accommodation of a high standard. The development of accommodation has normally accompanied the growth of resorts, areas of tourism activity and the demand to visit specific areas. Like the tourist, accommodation assumes many forms, and not all of them fit the conventional image of the hotel. Indeed, recent trends in accommodation have seen great changes in the form and nature of accommodation provision.

This chapter examines the scope and nature of accommodation, the impact of globalization and the operational issues that affect the accommodation sector. To understand the wider context of accommodation as a hospitality service, the hospitality industry is examined. The characteristics of the accommodation sector are also considered through a case study of German hotels. The discussion then turns to the growing differentiation of accommodation in the serviced and non-serviced sector. The accommodation sector is part of the capital-intensive infrastructure that tourists utilize, and is very labour intensive in servicing visitors' needs.

The hospitality sector

Hospitality is the very essence of tourism, involving the consumption of food, drink and accommodation in an environment away from the normal home base. The very nature of hospitality involves hosting and hospitality, provided by a host and involving a guest. Historically, hospitality was not necessarily a commercial endeavour, as you might host someone with the expectation they might host you at a later stage (as is the case with visiting friends and relatives). In modern-day society (although not necessarily in traditional societies) hospitality has become a commercialized experience, where the guest pays for the services/goods they consume via a bill. This commercialized transaction has its historical roots in the ale houses of medieval times, which were followed by the emergence of coaching inns on long-distance journeys and public houses. It was not until the mid-seventeenth century that the idea of a hotel developed in Paris, and this subsequently continued in eighteenth-century London. Much of the subsequent growth in Victorian and Edwardian times saw hotels developed at major transport nodes, such as railway termini in cities, and around commercial districts to cater for business travellers. Certain districts of cities also began to develop different reputations for tourist accommodation at this time, as high-class establishments aimed at the luxury market were developed (e.g. in London's West End) whilst other districts developed a reputation for lower grades of accommodation.

Accommodation is only one component of the hospitality sector, as the following typology of establishments providing hospitality services suggests:

- hotels
- restaurants
- cafes and catering places
- night clubs and licensed clubs
- take-away food bars
- public houses
- canteens
- camping and caravanning sites
- holiday camps
- short-stay tourist accommodation
- university and higher-education accommodation provision
- catering services to educational establishments
- contract caterers (e.g. Compass Catering and Brake Brothers in the UK).

In the UK, an indication of the scale of the hospitality sector can be gauged from the following statistics – there are over:

- 27 700 hotels
- 122 000 restaurants
- 110 000 public houses, clubs and bars
- 25 000 contract catering companies.

These employ over 1.6 million people in main jobs and over 111 000 people in second jobs. But it is the accommodation sector which tends to attract a great deal of interest due to its role in housing tourists during their stay at a destination.

The accommodation sector

It is the scope and significance of the accommodation sector which is of interest to tourism analysts, not least because it often comprises the largest element of tourist expenditure during a trip (excluding visiting friends and relatives). More specifically, hotels provide a base for business travel, meetings and conferences and these are also lucrative, high-yielding business (i.e. they attract high profit margins due to the expenditure by business travellers and delegates), with rooms being hired for meetings, and functions being provided along with entertainment. Both business travellers and leisure travellers staying in hotel accommodation have a higher propensity to spend whilst they are away than when they are at home. Therefore, hotels not only meet the visitor's basic requirement – of shelter for the night – but also add value to the experience by providing ancillary services and products. Hotels also have the advantage that hosting guests has the potential to generate additional revenue from food and beverage services.

The accommodation sector as a global phenomenon and operational issues

In Chapter 1, the growing globalization of the tourism sector was briefly introduced, with global companies responding to consumer trends. Globalization has resulted in various forms of company that operate in a globalized or transnational manner. These comprise:

- global corporations which operate throughout the world, such as the Holiday Inn which franchises its brand across the world
- multinational corporations, with operations in countries outside their main base or headquarters
- smaller multinationals, which operate in a limited number of countries.

Following on from the issues discussed at the end of Chapter 4, a company can adopt transnational strategies by:

- franchising its operation to other businesses in other countries
- licensing other companies or premises to operate using its brand, logo or trademark
- entering into non-investment management agreements
- acquiring overseas properties and interests
- pursuing mergers to integrate business interests horizontally to operate in a number of countries.

These provide businesses with a number of options when deciding on the best mode of entering a market in another country (known as entry mode).

These changes have led to nearly 30 per cent of all of the world's accommodation stock being chain controlled (chains in this case are international businesses operating globally). Chain hotels often expatriate profits back to the country in which the hotel chain is based. In addition, many of the chains have highly developed distribution channels, being affiliated to major global distribution systems that distribute the product electronically to travel agents. The Horwarth and Horwarth Worldwide Hotel Industry report predicted that by 2050 up to 60 per cent of hotels will be affiliated to global chains, continuing the consolidation trend discussed in Chapter 4.

According to the World Tourism Organization (UN-WTO), global hotel rooms have increased from 14 million rooms in 1997 to over 17 million in 2005 and this growth has been pivotal to countries increasing their capacity to accommodate continued growth in domestic and international tourism. The majority of investment has arisen from private-sector finance, although some governments provide incentives to hotel developers (e.g. tax breaks and tax holidays) to encourage investment in this sector. With hotel room construction costs now in excess of £100 000 in London, one can see the enormous capital costs of development. Add to this the cost of land, and one immediately sees why some modest London hotels command resale values in excess of £100 million.

Growth in chain-owned hotels is a fast-changing area of activity in tourism, as groups acquire, takeover and divest themselves of properties (as the example of IHC in Chapter 4 indicated). The major areas of activity are often in the key tourist locations (e.g. resorts and cities), which is evident from a brief analysis of VisitLondon's monitor of hotel activity. Much of the UK activity has occurred in and around London as the country's main tourist gateway and business centre.

A lack of development land and restriction on new projects in the West End of London has pushed development to the east, south and north of London's traditional central tourist district in the boroughs of Kensington and Chelsea, Hammersmith, Camden and Westminster. Whilst the main tourist market (i.e. domestic and international tourists undertaking leisure travel) provide a base for the accommodation sector, Horwarth and Horwarth also highlighted a number of other markets for hotel accommodation including:

• airline crews on layovers in between flight schedules, resting before continuing their duties
• conference delegates
• tour groups
• government officials
• other categories of travellers.

The business traveller remains the premium market for hotels, since they stay shorter periods than leisure travellers, but spend higher sums per visit. The Horwarth and Horwarth study also found that the balance of domestic:international visitors in chain hotels were 48:52 per cent compared to 51:49 per cent in independent hotels. In this respect, the Horwarth and Horwarth study highlights the diversity of markets which hotels serve, although some accommodation may specialize in certain markets as we will see in the discussion of boutique hotels later in this chapter. In a European context, private accommodation still remains the most important for certain markets such as Greece, Spain, Italy, Portugal, Finland, Sweden and the UK. In contrast, Danes, Germans, Irish, Austrians and visitors from Luxembourg have a propensity to use hotels for domestic and international travel. This highlights the divergence among different countries and illustrates the appeal of different elements in the accommodation industry.

The characteristics of the accommodation industry

Accommodation has been conceptualized by some researchers as a product and this is illustrated in Figure 7.1 which depicts the principal factors that can impact upon the way the product is constructed, portrayed and sold to customers. For example, large luxury hotels will emphasize facilities, service and image to certain market segments, such as business travellers, to secure business. In contrast, economy

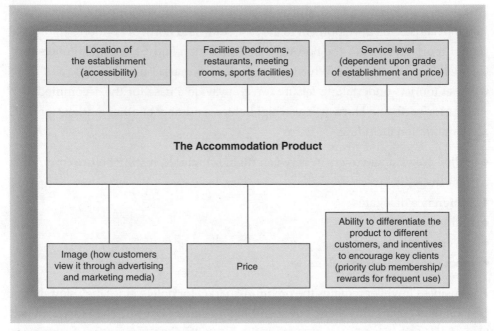

Figure 7.1 Accommodation as a product

hotels will ultimately emphasize price as the key determinant of the product formulation. In each case, the accommodation product is a complex amalgam of factors that combine to provide the tourist with something they wish to consume. Tourist accommodation is also characterized by a number of features described in Table 7.1. To illustrate the different characteristics of accommodation and the importance of each of these, Box 7.1 contains a short case study of the German hotel sector.

Types of tourist accommodation

The accommodation sector, like the tourism industry, has undergone profound changes since 1945, as the sector has been characterized by constant innovation, evolution and diversification of the product range (see Table 7.3). The pre-1945 pattern of tourist accommodation was dominated by serviced accommodation, with a rapid growth in non-serviced types of accommodation after 1945. Yet even the distinction between serviced and non-serviced accommodation is blurring, with the growth of apartment hotels which permit self-catering but also have arrangements so that

Table 7.1 Forms of tourist accommodation

| | Usage | |
	Business	Leisure
Serviced accommodation		
Hotels	X	X
Resort hotels		X
Educational establishments	X	X
Airport hotels	X	X
Motels	X	X
Inns	X	X
State-run hotels	X	X
Bed and breakfast		X
Apartment hotels	X	X
Non-serviced accommodation		
Holiday villages/centres/camps		X
Caravans		X
Camp sites		X
Gîtes		X
Holiday cottages		X
Villas		X
Youth hostels		X
Backpacker hostels		X
Recreational vehicles		X
Other		
Staying with friends/relatives	X	X
House swaps		X

guests can enjoy food and beverage services at local restaurants and have them charged back to their account. However, the two sectors will be considered separately here.

Serviced accommodation sector: Hotels

Throughout this chapter, much of the discussion has been on the most recognizable element of the serviced accommodation sector – the hotel. Yet even though it

Box 7.1 Case study: The German hotel industry

The German hotel sector is an interesting example to use to illustrate the operation and nature of tourist accommodation because it has a very decentralized distribution of properties, since it is not dominated by one capital city – as is the case in many other European countries. Berlin, Hamburg, Munich, Cologne and Frankfurt am Main are the principal cities that dominate patterns of hotel supply. Although Germany had a problem of oversupply, tourism demand is expanding to fill surplus capacity following reunification. Much of the market for German hotels consists of domestic visitors but it is the largest country in the world for trade fairs, festivals and special events such as the Munich Oktoberfest (beer festival) which attracts six million visitors annually. In 2004, there were 293 395 000 overnight stays by domestic travellers and 41 746 000 by international travellers in Germany. Of these, 158 416 000 overnight stays were by domestic travellers in a hotel/guesthouse and 36 631 000 were by international travellers.

The capacity of the German accommodation sector in 2004 is shown in Table 7.2. There is a wide range of accommodation types, with hotels forming less than a quarter of the available stock. Serviced accommodation still forms the dominant element of Germany's stock, but the non-serviced sector (e.g. second homes, holiday apartments and cottages) provides a major component of the market for visitor's overnight stays. The patronage of this accommodation is heavily skewed towards a seasonal usage in the months of June to October, although, as already mentioned, among overseas visitors the preference is for hotel accommodation (57 per cent), followed by bed-and-breakfast establishments (16 per cent), inns (5 per cent) and guesthouses (2 per cent); other establishments (including campsites) account for 20 per cent of the market share. Figure 7.2 illustrates the geographical distribution of these overnight stays, which are dominated by Bavaria (17 per cent), Lower Saxony (12 per cent), Baden-Wuerttenburg (11 per cent) and Rhineland-Palatinate (11 per cent); these four states account for 51 per cent of all visits. The year 2006 will prove to be interesting: Germany is hosting the FIFA World Cup and urban accommodation usage may intensify. In 2004, overnight stays by overseas visitors were dominated by ten major cities (Berlin, Munich, Frankfurt, Cologne, Hamburg, Düsseldorf, Stuttgart, Nuremberg, Dresden and Heidelberg) which accounted for 43 per cent of all overnight stays spent in Germany. This pattern of urban tourism is in part attributed to Germany's global role as the leading destination for trade fairs, with six large exhibition venues in Hanover, Frankfurt, Cologne, Düsseldorf, Munich and Berlin. This is complemented by a significant conference market, with Germany ranked third in Europe. The average overseas stay linked to conferences in 2004 was 1.8 days in length.

Table 7.2 Capacities in Germany by type of accommodation (source: Federal Statistical Office, 2005: 4, cited in German National Tourist Board, 2005, *Incoming Tourism to Germany: Facts and Figures 2004*: 20)

Type of accommodation	Accommodation capacity	
	Establishments in operation (as of July 2004)	**Share in per cent**
Hotels	13 078	24.7
Bed-and-breakfast hotels	8 687	16.4
Inns	9 901	18.7
Guesthouses	5 244	9.9
Traditional accommodation providers	**36 910**	**69.7**
Leisure, recreational and training centres	2 631	5.0
Holiday centres	87	0.2
Holiday homes or apartments	10 638	20.1
Holiday cottages, youth hostels	1 617	3.1
Preventative medical clinics and rehabilitation clinics	1 044	2.0
All accommodation types	52 967*	100.0

*including 40 boarding houses (recorded for the first time in 2004)

The overseas market for business travel to Germany in 2004 comprised traditional business trips (58 per cent), trade fairs and exhibitions (21 per cent), conferences (19 per cent) and incentive travel (2 per cent), which accounted for 8.2 million trips.

Significant market differences exist in German cities. Frankfurt, which has the second largest European airport and is a key business centre, focuses on the international hotel guest market; in contrast Hamburg is predominantly a domestic market, while Berlin is somewhere in between these two extremes as it re-establishes itself as an international location for visitors.

In 2000, a city survey by the consulting firm Parnell Kerr Foster (PKF) provided a breakdown of the business mix in upscale city hotels in Europe and Germany. In Europe,

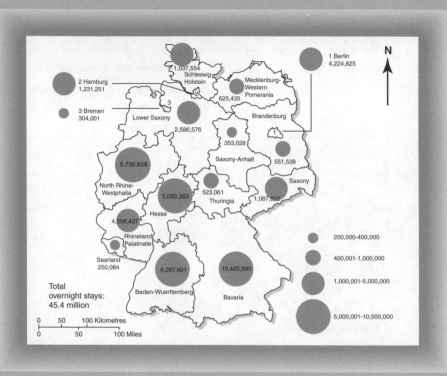

Figure 7.2 Overnight stays in Germany by foreign visitors in 2004 by federal state (data reproduced with permission from Deutsche Zentrale für Tourismus)

it found the following segments based on their 1999 survey data:

- full rate (11.1 per cent)
- corporate discount rate (34.5 per cent)
- tour operator/group rate (15 per cent)
- leisure break (13.3 per cent)
- conference/incentive travel (13.5 per cent)
- airline crew (8.2 per cent)
- other (4.4 per cent).

In the case of Frankfurt, among the 19 hotels surveyed, PKF found:

- 16.6 per cent paying the full rate
- 19.9 per cent were aircrew
- 13.6 per cent were conference/incentive business

- 31.8 per cent enjoyed a corporate discount rate
- 8.1 per cent were on a tour operator or group discounted rate
- 8.5 per cent were taking a leisure break.

Studies such as Deloitte's (a global consulting firm) Hotel Benchmark survey of international hotels place Germany's leading destinations in a global context. For example, in 2003 Berlin had an average hotel occupancy rate of 64.1 per cent, charging an average room rate of US$86, with a revenue per available room rate of US$55 per room (this being the amount of revenue derived after the cost of supplying the room is deducted). Berlin performed consistently worse than other equivalent European cities on each measure although occupancy rates had improved marginally (1.7 per cent on 2002). Yet analysts also point out that German hotels in major cities outperform those in non-urban areas and small towns, with the most profitable locations being the airport hotels. Even so, profitability varies by city, with some studies pointing to higher profits in some cities such as Frankfurt due to additional revenue from non-room revenue. Arthur Andersen, the global consulting firm, noted the importance of understanding the costs of hotel operation (staffing, administration, marketing, maintenance and energy costs), which also distinguish between different features of the accommodation sector (see Table 7.3).

This case study has highlighted a number of key issues in the accommodation sector including seasonality and the importance of location, with the major cities performing well compared to the German average, as well as the significance of conferences and trade fairs. It has also shown that hotels are complex business ventures and demonstrated the importance of certain costs which can affect profitability.

was argued above that the greatest changes have occurred in the non-serviced sector, hotels have not been immune to change. A hotel is not simply a premises with rooms, food and beverage services, but a business oriented towards a constantly changing clientele. In some countries, there has been a rapid expansion of hotels into the fast-growing health resort market (e.g. Iceland and Estonia). In other cases, the business of hotels has become highly competitive and independent. Small hotels of fewer than fifty rooms of one- to three-star status have become much more prone to insolvency (i.e. likely to run into financial difficulty), typically due to cash-flow problems, where inadequate revenue cannot cover fixed costs. Owners need to plan for regular refurbishment and investment to remain competitive, and such costs are often deferred due to poor financial performance. Some luxury hotels will

Table 7.3 Characteristics of tourist accommodation

- Seasonality – periods of demand are typically buoyant in the peak season (i.e. the summer season) with a drop in the low season, usually winter (except for accommodation located in ski resorts).
- Occupancy levels – demand for rooms is spread across seasons, but more precisely according to weeks and days. Accommodation seeks to sell its rooms; they are a perishable product that cannot be stored or sold at a later stage.
- Location, which often determines the appeal and accessibility of properties. Typically, a distance-decay principle exists in accommodation locations, with the luxury properties located in the prime in-town sites with greater access to attractions and facilities. Similar micro-locational factors also operate at airports, with the most accessible and prestigious properties in easy reach of the airport.
- Different grading systems exist, which may be statutory or voluntary, using a star rating to denote the quality of the establishment.
- Properties can range from complex business ventures at the luxury end of the market through to basic hostel accommodation. Accommodation has a high capital asset value relative to the prices charged to customers, with yield per client relatively modest in relation to cost structures.
- Accommodation has high fixed costs to service and owners/managers seek to optimize occupancy levels to cover costs.
- Accommodation provision is subject to numerous regulatory codes and laws in terms of the fixed plant (i.e. health and safety legislation) as well as specialist laws governing food safety where food is served. Larger premises require a wide range of skilled staff to operate key departments such as front office functions, food and beverage services, housekeeping services, and concierge and portering staff. In some cases, unskilled staff are employed in menial roles, but skilled staff are needed to operate and manage each department.

refurbish their properties every five to ten years. Hotel managers need to understand how the operation of their establishment(s) generates revenue, and the scale of costs. Some of these costs were outlined in the German hotel case study in Box 7.1 but it is important to understand other causes of low profitability: employee costs, the cost of staff per room, restaurant costs, supply costs and costs of debt that have to be serviced. How the hotels generate their business is also significant for the hotel manager, particularly when underlying issues of seasonality are considered. Hotels located in city areas suffer less seasonality in occupancy levels than those located in mountain areas where unreliable weather may impact upon the levels of business they can generate.

One important consideration for hotel managers is the global demand and the resources and marketing efforts needed to generate business. The location of the hotel and its size are important determinants of profitability, and affiliation to distribution channels can offer global booking systems (e.g. global distribution systems) as well as a website. These affiliations help to generate business that is supported by promotions, loyalty programmes, links to other tourism businesses and services as part of the distribution system. Two basic types of affiliations exist for hotels:

1 *voluntary chain associations*, which have limited marketing activities for members with low fees and shorter member contracts; they are aimed at smaller independent hotels
2 *franchised products* run by the larger integrated hotel chains, with complex purchasing facilities, but higher fees for members. The participating companies often have ten- to fifteen-year contracts.

Among the voluntary chain associations, the most well known is Best Western which has a non-profit approach, being American-based but organized on a country-by-country basis. It has a global brand recognition and charges an initial entrance fee to members. It then charges a yearly flat fee, plus a fee per room booked. Up to 10 per cent of its business is generated by company reservation systems and Best Western charges a reservation fee from call-centre bookings. Other voluntary associations tend to operate in a country or across a number of countries (e.g. Alpine Classic, which operates in Austria, France, Germany, Switzerland and Italy). In contrast, franchise chains are more global. Notable examples include Holiday Inn, which is the largest global hotel brand based on room capacity, and the Comfort Inn chain owned by Choice in the USA, which is the second largest. The Holiday Inn chain charges an initial fee based on the number of rooms in an establishment then a number of other charges including:

- a 5 per cent royalty based on an establishment's gross room revenue
- a 2.5 per cent royalty based on gross room revenue to cover marketing costs
- a reservation charge per room per month.

Joining a chain not only generates business from reservation systems; the image of the chain is important, as well as client relationships, because Holiday Inn has global agreements with fifty-five multinational companies and four operators. As a recognizable brand it also receives a large proportion of bookings by telephone and email as well as in person, known as 'walk-ins'. Even so, the internet is estimated to generate around 5 per cent of hotel bookings and this is expected to grow rapidly in future years.

To develop profitability, larger hotels have also adopted revenue or yield management strategies, pioneered in the airline industry. By identifying peaks and troughs in hotel bookings from previous years, hotels can provide a predicted pattern of demand based on experience. Using such models, hotels can then charge prices based on likely demand future room capacity and seek to balance supply with demand to maximize occupancy. The hotel monitors the booking rate and can adjust prices according to future demand, flexibly responding to market conditions. This will take into account the expected business mix, as outlined in the German hotel case study in Box 7.1, and the profitability of each segment, since filling a hotel with low-yielding business such as air crews is unviable – this sort of business needs to be mixed with full-price and discounted business. Investment in yield management computer systems (as well as the training and know-how) may not have been attractive to smaller hotels but these systems can now be accessed by non-chain hotels via the internet for a monthly fee. Yield management has been widely used in the larger urban-based and resort hotels.

Trends in hotel development have indicated that mega-hotels with over 5000 rooms have also been constructed (examples are the MGM Grand Hotel and Casino in Las Vegas). Yet estimates by tourism authorities in Las Vegas indicated that each new 1000 rooms opened need an additional 275 000 tourists a year to fill them. This in turn needs significant investment in transportation to allow visitors to access Las Vegas, and increased marketing efforts to attract the visitor. Therefore, the hotel manager, hotel chain and developer must be aware of existing levels of supply so that markets do not become saturated and occupancy does not drop, impacting upon profitability. In some New Zealand resorts such as Queenstown, a distinct cycle of development in hotel and motel development from the 1970s can be discerned: demand led to a growth in supply to fill shortages. This was followed by oversupply, given the lead-time in approval and construction of hotels. Then supply was filled by demand and then the cycle began again. Such patterns can be discerned in other destinations as the tourism market does not operate in an ideal competitive environment owing the development process, which can lead to shortages in capacity then oversupply. Much of the discussion of hotels and trends has indicated that larger chain properties are the future direction for profitability, given the process of consolidation. But one interesting new trend that has challenged this is the growth of boutique hotels.

The boutique hotel

Boutique hotels are a new category of property in the hotel sector which have been described as townhouses or small style-led properties that are fashion-conscious and are modelled on the concept of a 1960s clothing boutique, based on unique products and goods. Such properties defy conventional star ratings, their attraction being the consumer who seeks a unique experience, different to that provided by the conventional chain hotel. In this respect, the boutique hotel is a lifestyle product, with unique architectural or style features. In the USA, the operators in this market are Ian Schrager, Kimpton, Joie de Vivre, Starwood and the South Beach Group. Such operators have styled their properties as fashionable properties to stay in, and they are associated with consumers who are trendsetters in the music, media and film industry. In some boutique hotels (such as the Malmaison chain in the UK, which has five properties) there is no room service and few frills in the eating establishments. Some owners have even reduced the fitting-out costs of hotels by adopting a minimalist strategy. In the USA, occupancy levels in boutique properties have grown steadily from 69 per cent in 1995 to 71 per cent in 2000 – a good performance. In some instances, boutique hotels have reduced costs by reducing service levels, compensating for this with their style features and their marketing of the limited services as positive elements. For example, the property owned by Firmdale in Knightsbridge, London, does not have a restaurant and so has marketed itself as an exclusive bed-and-breakfast hotel. Many boutique operators are also responding to the market more flexibly than are larger chain hotels, through a process of continuous improvement. A number of factors that are promoting a continued growth in boutique hotels include:

- the internet, making it simpler for customers to access this new form of hotel
- a number of larger hotel chains are entering this market, such as the Hilton Group and Marriott International.

The entry of chains to the boutique market may be a contradiction in that the individuality of each hotel could be compromised by the homogeneity of chain principles (i.e. the experience should be uniform in each property regardless of location). However, the principles of boutique hotels are being embodied to emphasize the individuality of the property. In Europe, a recent report in 2002 by Pricewater-houseCoopers consultants forecast that this sector would grow by 85 per cent over the period to 2007. The study identified operators who stated they were planning to build up to 6800 new bedrooms by 2007 in addition to over 8000 already in existence. The number of boutique properties had grown to 92 properties in the previous 5 years, raising the key challenge: how could these unique properties continue to expand without becoming ubiquitous like the chain-owned hotels?

There are also properties that are small and family run with fewer than 12 rooms; they dominate the bed-and-breakfast/small hotel sector. This form of serviced accommodation has also been developed into the home-stay concept (the visitor stays on the farm or in the home of a family who act as hosts and allow the visitor to experience the local way of life) in countries such as New Zealand where it enables rural farmers to supplement their income. At the other extreme are the resort hotel complexes popularized by Club Med, where all tourist-services are included and paid for at the time the holiday is purchased. At the same time, a trend towards luxury travel has caused a rise in luxury accommodation as a significant growth market, as the case study in Box 7.2 shows.

These developments in the luxury market, however, have also been overshadowed by one further trend – the rise of the budget accommodation market.

Box 7.2 Case study: Luxury travel and the accommodation sector

Luxury tourism, defined as the consumption of an expensive and high-quality experience, was the norm among the travelling elite in the eighteenth, nineteenth and early twentieth century. It included the Grand Tour, travel on luxury cruise liners and travel on the early commercial airlines. As these products and experiences have become more widely available, tourism businesses have sought to push back the boundaries of luxury travel to cater for the increasing demand for such experiences. Luxury experiences may involve travel to exclusive tourist resorts, tailor-made packages, including private jets, and an emphasis on comfort, service, relaxation, sumptuous quality, attention to detail and exacting standards. Some analysts have argued that the consumption of luxury is about emotion, the key factor being the experience rather than the nature of the product. In surveys of luxury, the elements of travel and tourism are often rated as amongst the highest elements on people's wish lists; this illustrates the importance of luxury in terms of perception and consumption in relation to travel and tourism.

Luxury travel is controversial because it emphasizes the very basis of tourism: inequality between those with the means to consume such experiences and those unable to consume them. In addition, when one begins to consider the wider global inequalities that exist between the rich Westernized tourists who consume experiences in less developed areas where the population may subsist on less than a dollar (45 p) a day, this form of extravagant conspicuous consumption acts as a reminder of how exploitative tourism can be. It may also accentuate the social and cultural impact of the tourist upon the host, where the differences in wealth and lifestyle cause behaviour change among the host population (see Chapter 12 for more detail).

The scale of luxury travel has been documented by Bakker (2005) using the Merrill Lynch and Capgemini Global Wealth Report. This identified that there are 8.3 million people with at least US$1 million in financial assets, and the scale of such wealth has been expanding due to continued rises in GDP. As a result, there has been major growth in the demand for luxury tourism in North America and Asia-Pacific. The luxury holiday is a very profitable market segment for the tourism sector, due to the high margins on luxury products where price is not the sole discriminatory factor. More important are the wider value-added elements, the exclusivity of the experience and, above all, the uniqueness for the consumer. Even with growth in the general tourism market, there is growing evidence, according to Bakker (2005) of consumers being prepared to 'trade up' (i.e. upgrade the quality of their experience) to a luxury experience whilst economizing in other areas of household spending. This has been seen in the package holiday market where some holiday companies and their charter airline have offered travellers an opportunity to 'start the holiday in luxury', 'by treating yourself' to the equivalent of premium or business-class seating and service.

An interesting finding of Bakker's research is that luxury tourism experiences are not necessarily associated with expensive brands or those deemed fashionable. Whilst some benchmarks exist (e.g. the Orient Express) as quality tourism experiences, these are experiences rather than trend-led brands that exist in other areas of consumer purchases. In the luxury market, a tailored experience with a high degree of customization is about turning a dream into reality. Interestingly, the scale of demand according to Bakker (2005) is evident from 3 per cent of travellers spending 20 per cent of global tourism expenditure: in excess of US$25 000 a year. Bakker identified the UK market for luxury travel as being around 500 000 bookings a year where expenditure was at least £10 000 a booking. This is far from a homogenous market, although with accommodation a key element of the overall cost of a holiday, it is certainly an area that bears further examination.

Bakker (2005) segmented the market for luxury travel into:

- those wealthy travellers who choose luxury as a norm
- corporate travellers (e.g. business or first-class air travel and luxury hotels) who are high-ranked employees in companies
- lifestyle travellers who look for unique features in their trip
- the one-off, once-in-a-lifetime traveller (e.g. honeymooners, retirees or those prepared to pay a premium for travel).

In the accommodation sector, hotels such as Dubai's Burj Al-Arab (see Box 9.1) have set new standards of luxury.

One trend has been for hotel developers in the luxury sector to form partnerships with leading brand names (e.g. Armani has created Armani Hotels and Resorts in Dubai). In luxury hotels, the uniqueness of each experience and each property is valued as opposed to the standardized provision of the ubiquitous and homogenous global brand. Some hotels in this market have looked to the past, creating hotels with an Art Deco theme or focusing on the unique features of the destination area to create a special experience. The byword of the luxury market is exclusivity, individuality, personal care and a memorable experience that is not available elsewhere, usually involving a high degree of personal customization of the product.

Budget accommodation and hotels

The North American market, with its large car-based domestic tourism traffic, saw the motel evolve as a cheaper, more flexible form of accommodation. Normally located on principal routeways and roads, motels evolved as a cost-effective way to accommodate a range of budget-conscious travellers who did not want to pay hotel prices. Motels have developed outside North America, particularly in Australia and New Zealand, and have become a ubiquitous feature of the accommodation sector in these countries, filling a niche for budget serviced accommodation. Motels often provide catering facilities for travellers. They are typically smaller than the average 50-room hotel, being run or managed as family businesses, although some may be affiliated to chains such as Best Western.

In Europe, other forms of budget accommodation exist such as youth hostels. In the UK, youth hostels began in 1931. They now operate at 230 locations in

England and Wales, and there are 4500 globally. There has also been investment in new forms of youth-oriented hostel accommodation in the form of backpacker hostels. For example, in late 2005, SmartCity Hostels in Edinburgh's old town area announced the development of a £10 million 620-bedspace hostel with en-suite accommodation. This is set to be the first in a series of chain hostels in key UK locations, and, to help off-set the problems caused by seasonality, the University of Edinburgh will lease a pro-portion of the bedspaces during the academic year which will be turned over to tourist use in the peak summer season, especially during the Edinburgh Festival and for Hogmanay at the end of the old year. This shows that the traditional market for budget accommodation has been challenged in recent years by the rise of the budget hostels, but most notably by the expansion of budget hotels.

The budget hotel market is most highly developed in France, where two com-panies – Accor and Group Envergure – run two thirds of Europe's branded budget hotel rooms. Accor own the largest European brand – Ibis, which has 45 per cent of its rooms located in 17 countries aside from France. In contrast, Group Envergure's eight budget brands are almost entirely based in France. The UK is emerging as the second-largest budget hotel market in Europe. In 2000, there were over 47 000 beds in the UK in budget hotels, and in 2005 this was in excess of 57 000 rooms. Hotel chains have entered this market in Europe, with major brands such as Travelodge and Express by Holiday Inn complemented by new entrants such as the Cendant Corporation with the Days Inn brand. The budget operators are typically leisure- and hospitality-integrated companies, with Whitbread owning the Travel Inn chain and Compass (the world's leading contract catering business) operating the Travelodge brand, who control 53 per cent of the budget market in the UK. Other prominent brands are Express by Holiday Inn. The third-largest budget hotel market in Europe is Germany, dominated by Accor's brands (Ibis and Etap).

At a pan-European scale, the top budget hotel management companies are as follows:

- Accor, based in France (with its three leading brands – Ibis, Etap and Formule 1) with 1082 hotels and 91 758 rooms
- Group Envergure, based in France (with its leading brands – Campanile, Premiere Classe and Kyriad) with 870 hotels and 52 294 rooms
- Choice, based in the USA, with its Comfort Inn brand, 239 hotels and 14 643 rooms
- Whitbread, based in the UK, with its Travel Inn brand comprising 266 hotels and 14 000 rooms
- Compass, based in the UK, with its Travelodge brand, 208 hotels and 10 825 rooms.

The hotel-chain domination of the European budget sector reflects its profitability, with low staffing requirements (i.e. a full-time staff of 20 can operate a 100-room hotel) and the costs of construction are modest: modular construction techniques allow prefabricated rooms to be built and fitted out relatively cheaply and thus in the UK costs per room may be only £40 000 for new-build properties – a fraction of the cost of building an in-town luxury hotel. Many new-build budget hotels are located at out-of-town sites, or adjacent to motorway junctions to meet the needs of car-borne traffic. Major city budget hotels have often converted older properties, with low fit-out costs per room of typically £5000 in the UK, since the accommodation offered is of a basic standard. This expanding segment is taking business away from existing budget providers such as the Youth Hostel market and from the mid-range hotels (three-star hotels) since prices are competitively priced per room (i.e. £39–45), mirroring the North American and Australasian motel sector. The success in Europe of the budget hotel market can be related to the guarantee of quality and minimum standards through the involvement of credible consumer brands, convenience of car parking and location (adjacent to intersections or out-of-town sites) and value for money. Budget hotels also attract mid-week business travellers, leisure travellers and weekend breaks to keep occupancy levels high.

Another trend is towards the unique and more authentic 'hip' budget hotel market. According to Ypma (2001), what makes a hip hotel is fantasy, originality, location, style and authenticity. Table 7.4 is a list of outstanding hip hotels compiled from Ypma's *Hip Hotels: Budget* (2001), which outlines the characteristics of some of these trendy locations and unusual properties.

The non-serviced accommodation sector

Whilst the budget market has experienced considerable growth in recent years, the non-serviced sector has also seen major changes. In the Victorian and Edwardian period, coastal seaside resorts grew and so did commercial accommodation such as hotels, guesthouses and boarding houses. The seaside landlady, with her rules and conventions for guests (i.e. set mealtimes and the need to vacate the room each day) heralded an age when regimentation and rigid social rules dominated. In the post-war period, these accommodation forms began to be replaced by innovations in the non-serviced sector. In the inter-war period, holiday homes developed in many countries throughout the world as the new middle classes developed leisure

Table 7.4 International examples of 'hip' budget hotels (source: adapted and developed from Ypma, 2001)

Name of hotel	Location	Distinctive features
Kirketon Hotel	Sydney, Australia	• small architecturally designed hotel • outstanding restaurant • elegant interior
Prairie Hotel	Flinder Range, Parachilna, South Australia	• hotel in which *Holy Smoke* was filmed • recycled objects as art • rooms built below ground level for temperature control • unusual menu (e.g. emu omelettes; minced skippy on a bun) • stark landscape • eco-modern design and outback vernacular architecture (e.g. corrugated roof, wooden veranda)
Waka Ganga	Bali	• Balinese traditional architecture blended with contemporary living • eco-friendly privacy (thatched guest bungalow) • nature-based retreat
T Sandt (The Sand)	Antwerp, Belgium	• historic building around 600 years old • restaurant decorated in Belgian beer bottles • blend of historic detailing in some rooms and loft-type bedrooms in other parts of the hotel
Caron de Beaumarchais	Paris, France	• Louis XVI style décor • the clockmaker heritage of Caron de Beaumarchais is retained

(Continued)

Table 7.4 (*continued*)

Name of hotel	Location	Distinctive features
The Penzance Art Club	Cornwall, UK	• intimate scale • major attention to detail • practical living for guests • building is a Georgian mansion that was once the Portuguese embassy • floor of the basement restaurant has sand on the floor • entrance hall is used as a gallery • bohemian chic presentation
Samode Haveli (converted into a hotel in 1985)	Jaipur, Rajastan, India	• spacious and colourful house • former maharajah's townhouse (one of 150 converted to hotels in India) • Mughal architecture (Muslim and Hindu cultures blended together) • frescoed alcove in dining room • complex geometric patterns used to create light entering guest rooms • authentic Indian experience

habits. Yet in the post-war period, a new genre of accommodation developed from caravan parks to self-catering villages and, more recently, to holiday parks (e.g. Center Parcs which is now owned by its former competitor, Oasis, in the UK). Since the 1970s, Mediterranean apartments in Spain and other destinations have been developed for self-catering holidays, along with timeshare developments as a new form of limited-ownership 'second home'. *Gîte* holidays are a time-honoured tradition for urban French workers in southern France, and novels such as Peter Mayle's *A Year in Provence* have portrayed the virtues of such holidays.

In each category of non-serviced accommodation, specialist operators have nurtured this niche (examples being Eurocamps' sited tents and caravans and Hoseasons' boating holidays on canals and waterways). What is also notable is that major capital investment and large corporations have also entered this market. Each leisure company has other tourism interests: the Rank Group operates holiday camps/villages using their original brand names (Butlins, Haven and Warner) in the UK. Haven and its sister company, British Holidays, operates 40 sites as Holiday Parks in the UK. A further development in the non-serviced sector is the rise in the use of university campuses in holiday letting in addition to their well-developed conference businesses. The University of Stirling in Scotland has over 3000 bedspaces which it lets to holidaymakers as well as conference guests, and its economic impact as a specialist accommodation provider in the Stirling region is estimated at £12 million.

One sector that has seen substantial growth in recent years is the caravan sector. In the UK, Caravan Club membership in 2005 was over 800 000 and these people use the 7000 or more campsites in the UK. Yet an increasing number are using caravans that cost anything from £8000 to £30 000 to purchase new. The image of caravanning as being low-status and low-quality holiday market business has been rectified by the higher standards of comfort now provided by fixed and touring caravans. They are very popular among young families and the retired. Since the first caravan the Wanderer, was built in 1885 in Bristol, the use of caravans has developed into a substantial element of the European holiday industry. In the UK, this generates around £2.5 billion as an industry through retail sales, products and holidays, employing 90 000 people (many on a seasonal basis). The major expansion of sites since the 1930s pre-dates many planning restrictions and the sites are often near to or in coastal areas as well as in forest and valley areas. Some of the fixed caravans – known as holiday homes – are located in the UK's 2200 holiday parks.

Registrations of motorhomes, which are dominant in the USA and Australia, have increased from 3539 in 1988 to 4798 in 2000 in the UK. This is part of the wider growth in caravans, motorhomes and holiday homes in the UK from a total stock of 710 000 units in 1975 to 1 054 000 units in 2000; growth continued until 2004 and then began to slow down. As a result, some 62.5 million nights were spent in such accommodation in the UK in 2000, making it the most popular form of accommodation after VFR. It accounts for around 17 per cent (around £1.6 billion) of holiday spend in the UK, the majority of nights being spent in England and Wales. Some features of Wales' caravan tourism sector are shown in Table 7.5. In Europe, there are approximately 4 275 000 tourism caravans and 920 000 motorhomes in use, being most popular in Germany, the Netherlands, France, Italy and Finland. Many analysts tend to overlook this sector even though it has seen a massive re-imaging

Table 7.5 Key features of domestic caravan tourism[1] in Wales (source: adapted from Wales Tourist Board 2005, Domestic (UK) Caravan Tourism to Wales, www.wtbonline.gov.uk, accessed on 8 December 2005)

Wales has around 1600 caravan sites and 90 000 pitches (i.e. a place where you pitch your caravan overnight). Caravanning in Wales has the following characteristics:

- It generates 2.5 million domestic tourism visits.
- It generates £276 million, equivalent to 25 per cent of all domestic tourism spending in Wales.
- Almost half of all caravan trips occur in north Wales, with around 33 per cent of these trips generated by visitors from the major urban conurbations of north-west England and Merseyside. A further 27 per cent of visitors are also from the West Midlands conurbation and 25 per cent are residents of Wales.
- Around 66 per cent of caravan trips are to coastal locations.
- Caravan tourism is highly seasonal, with 50 per cent of trips occurring July–September.
- The average spend per trip is very low at around £30.
- Families are a dominant element of this market, comprising over 50 per cent of the total.
- In terms of social class, the lower socio-economic groupings (D and E) are a dominant element in this market, accounting for around 33 per cent of all trips.
- Caravan-based tourists have a higher propensity to engage in activity-based tourism than other holidaymakers.

Note
[1] The Wales Tourist Board defines a caravan trip as 'stays in touring vans, static (owned) vans and static (rented) vans'

and development since the 1970s, with flexibility and less need for planning cited as key reasons for using such accommodation.

Other issues for the accommodation sector

Whilst accommodation establishments provide the focus for hosting and hospitality for guests, not all accommodation premises/sites have hospitality services. These are often provided by restaurants, fast-food establishments, cafes, bars, clubs and canteens. Some parts of the fast-food sector have a very long history of provision for tourism and leisure markets (e.g. the fish and chip shop at coastal resorts in the UK). Recently some chains such as Harry Ramsden's have entered this market. The fast-food market uses contract catering and portion-control techniques to keep their prices down and their delivery is fast to increase the volume of sales; this poses a challenge to independent cafes and restaurants. As in the hotel sector, trends towards consolidation can be observed in the hospitality sector with the rise of contract caterers (e.g. Compass Catering in the UK) and franchises in the fast-food market (McDonald's, KFC, Burger King, Wendy's and Pizza Hut). These outlets pose a threat to conventional food retailing. For example, in the UK in 2004, there were 1235 branches of McDonald's, 700 of Burger King, 578 of Pizza Hut, 41 of TGI (the latter two restaurants both owned by Whitbread), 300 of Wimpy and 170 of Harry Ramsden's fish and chips outlets (owned by Compass), plus numerous other small chains such as Pizza Express. Restaurants and cafes have had to respond with innovative marketing. Formula-style cafes such as Starbucks have emphasized the pleasures of quality coffee consumption and relaxation in contrast to the fast-food experience. In 2004, Starbucks had over 360 outlets, Costa over 300, Caffè Nero 175 and Coffee Republic over 50 outlets, reflecting the massive expansion in coffee/cafes in the UK market by chains.

In more innovative forms of marketing of cities, regions and districts, food consumption has been heralded as the main attraction or theme for the tourism sector. For example, regional food and wine festivals have been used to pump-prime the tourism sector, yielding business for the accommodation sector, and promoting and showcasing local products. In Perth, Scotland, an annual food festival is used to promote the district's tourism industry; this is supported by VisitScotland's area office and public-sector funds as a means of encouraging visitor activity. Rolling events, such as the French market it hosts which tours different UK locations, have had a similar impact on Perth as an attraction for visitors. This follows the highly visible and distinctive growth of farmers' markets in many small towns and similar locations in Europe which have acted as a nucleus for visitor activity. In Wales Abergavenny, a small town north of Cardiff, has an annual food festival funded by the Welsh Development Agency, Welsh Assembly, Wales Tourist Board and Monmouthshire County Council. This attracts around 25 000 visitors a year, with 67 per cent of visitors from Wales and 38 per cent from the UK, to a little-known tourist destination. Interestingly, two thirds of the visitors state that the food festival is the main reason for visiting, yet this has raised the town's profile and led to repeat visits. Thus we see that hospitality services can in fact be developed as the prime attraction for a region when they are carefully developed around a unique theme, utilizing local produce, famous chefs and celebrities, as well as high-quality public relations and media coverage. This was certainly the case for Abergavenny, which was featured on the BBC's Rick Stein's *Food Heroes* series and in the accompanying book.

An interesting example of this approach contributing to a destination becoming over-popular is the small harbour town of Padstow in north Cornwall, which is still a working port. It is the location for many of the celebrity chef Rick Stein's ventures. His success has led to this small town becoming so saturated in the peak season that it is no longer pleasurable to visit. The boom in visiting (including a growth in second-home ownership and massive increases in property prices) followed the filming of Stein's first BBC television series which featured his Padstow seafood restaurant and provided the main stimulus to the destination's redevelopment. Increased visitor volumes have been added to by the success of the Camel Trail, a cycle route in north Cornwall which follows the estuary to Padstow in a highly scenic and attractive area. However, the town's historic form is small and it needs drastically to restrict tourist access by car to deal with the major problems of congestion in the peak season: a problem faced by many small historic cities in Europe. Measures such as those discussed in Box 12.1 in Venice are needed to manage the major influx of day trippers to Padstow. Nearby resorts such as Newquay in north Cornwall routinely have visitor numbers in excess of 31 times the resident population in a county where tourism is now estimated to comprise 24 per cent of GDP. The combination of economic generation by the successful repositioning of a locality such as Padstow, combined with the investment by North Cornwall District Council to stimulate economic development around tourism and marine activities, now needs to be accompanied by measures of visitor management due to the major success it has achieved (see Chapter 12 for more detail on this issue).

Environmental issues

Many accommodation providers have also had to respond to global concerns associated with environmental issues. Some hotels have embraced the principles of sustainable development to mirror customer concerns with the energy consumed by their stay. For example, recycling, and re-using linen and towels, are minor measures that hotels have introduced. Much more major measures have been undertaken by small hotels, which have run environmental audits to assess the environmental costs of their activities in relation to:

- energy consumption
- transport

- waste
- purchasing
- health
- the local environment.

In 1991 the Inter-Continental Hotels Group developed an environmental Reference Manual to guide staff on environmental management measures. In 1992, the International Hotels Environment Initiative developed *Environmental Management for Hotels: The Industry Guide to Best Practice*. In Scotland, the Green Tourism Business Scheme, operated on behalf of VisitScotland, has embraced the hotel sector and other accommodation providers, as part of VisitScotland's Quality Assurance Scheme. To join the scheme, a business needs to undergo voluntary accreditation based on an assessment by an independent environmental assessor. The scheme is based upon the implementation measures a business applies and can help raise market appeal for the business's products. Some examples cited by the scheme include making savings of up to £3000 in large hotels through using a compactor for waste disposal, and saving £300 a year in family-run hotels by installing low energy candle bulbs in chandeliers. It is estimated that businesses can save between 10 per cent and 20 per cent of operating costs by using such measures (see www.greenbusiness.org.uk).

Human resource issues have also assumed a growing significance for the hotel and hospitality sector, which has a poor image as an employer. This poor image is partly linked to pay and financial rewards but also highlights cultural issues – where images of servility are conveyed by perceptions of what hotel work involves. Problems in training, shortages of skilled senior and technical staff as well as managerial concerns over service and product quality dominate the ongoing debates over the continued problems this sector faces. Recruiting and retaining good staff remains a perennial problem for the global accommodation sector, in a business where high levels of staff-to-guest interaction not only determine the levels of the guest's satisfaction with the accommodation product, but can impact upon their images of the product and the levels of repeat visitation.

A recent study on the cost of recruitment of staff in the hospitality sector estimated an average cost to a company of £500–£1 200 per employee. This does not include the cost of retention in a sector which has notoriously high rates of staff turnover. Add to this the difficulty of recruiting staff to work in the hospitality sector, and it is not surprising to find major hotels in the UK recruiting workers from the former Eastern Europe after those countries acceded to the EU. Poland, Latvia, the

Czech Republic, Estonia, Hungary and other new EU member states are providing a much-needed workforce for the hospitality sector. These employees are proving to be a more stable workforce than the traditional antipodean recruits (i.e. those from Australia/New Zealand) who were typically visiting on an overseas experience and would work for six months and then move on. The major difference in income levels (take-home wages of £150–£250 a month more in the UK than in Poland) versus the earning potential in the UK hospitality sector has proved to be a key attractor of migrant workers. The addition of ten new member states to the EU in 2005 expanded the EU population to 450 million, a 20 per cent increase, opening up new labour markets.

Conclusion

The accommodation sector is a central element of the tourist experience of a place. Indeed it is often purchased in a package holiday and is one of the most frequent areas of disquiet when consumer complaints are made. Yet the international growth in chain activity in the accommodation sector highlights the potential profitability in this market when the product mix, visitor mix and supply–demand interactions are well managed. Accommodation provides a containing context for the visitor and one where tourism managerial skills need to be harnessed at two levels:

1 Within the organization, so that operational issues are addressed to maintain profitability. The accommodation manager needs a good understanding of business issues (i.e. hotel operations, finance, accounting, food and beverage issues and marketing).
2 In a customer-focused role so that the guest is satisfied with their visit and can be a good ambassador for the hotel product.

Increasingly, accommodation managers need to be aware of competitive pressures in a rapidly evolving marketplace, as reflected in the case of budget and boutique hotels. Customer attitudes and needs are also important, and the growth of environmental awareness among hotel chains – some of which have recognized the cost savings which greater environmental responsibility can confer – reflects this. One thing is certain in the accommodation sector – the consumer's tastes and needs are constantly evolving, and this is reflected in recent trends and developments. Managers and property owners unable to respond to change will find that they will be passed by, as innovations, market changes and price competition redefine the business environment for accommodation providers.

References

Bakker, M. (2005) Luxury travel. *Travel and Tourism Analyst*.

Wales Tourist Board (2005) Domestic (UK) Caravan tourism to Wales. www.webonline.gov.uk, accessed 1 January 2006.

Ypma, A. (2001) *Hip Hotels: Budget*. London: Thames and Hudson.

Further reading

The most accessible source on this topic is:

Verginis, C. and Wood, R. (eds) (1999) *Accommodation Management: Perspectives for the International Hotel Industry*. London: Thomson Learning.

Yu, L. (1999) *The International Hospitality Business: Management and Operations*. New York: Haworth Press.

Questions

1 Why does hotel accommodation play such an important role in the business travel market?

2 What is the wide range of forms of serviced accommodation?

3 How has the non-serviced accommodation sector developed since 1945? What are the main explanations for growth in certain sections of this market?

4 What is the future for boutique hotels?

8

Tour operating and travel retailing

Learning outcomes

This chapter examines the way in which tourism products and services are sold to the consumer. The role of the tour operator and the travel agent are evaluated in terms of their respective roles in the supply chain. On completion of this chapter, you should be able to understand:

- how the distribution chain operates in tourism
- how tour operators package holidays
- the role of travel agents in retail operations
- the use of information communication technology (ICT) in travel retailing
- the managerial skills needed to manage a travel agency and to present holiday products to consumers.

Introduction

For tourism to occur, consumers need to purchase, arrange or acquire the means by which they can travel from their home area and (origin area) to a destination. One element in this process is tour operators and travel retailers. Tour operating and retailing tourism products to consumers are key parts in the production, selling and distribution of tourism services. The organizations that do this link the supply to the source of demand. Yet tourism is not like many other products or services. It is intangible; it is often an experience or product that cannot be stored, tried or tested before purchase, and so the consumer often buys as an act of faith, in the belief that what the tourism industry supplies is in line with their expectations and needs. This is epitomized in the following quotation:

> The travel industry, according to everybody outside it, is run by cowboys. Despite the abundance of professionally run companies, both big and small, the perception is still that holiday firms rip off unsuspecting customers … ABTA fights gamely to defend the industry, but it's like pushing water uphill. Even though a lot of criticism is unfair, you can't help thinking that the industry has brought a lot on itself … But the biggest problem is that operators are often selling a product where the gap between perception and reality is huge. Mass-market holidays are often sold as a dream vacation when they are often anything but. (Source: www.travelmole.com, Issue 226, 17 September 2002: Comment)

One of the main ways in which the tourism industry communicates, trades and interacts with the tourist is through the distribution chain (i.e. the way in which the product is sold to the consumer) using intermediaries – agents that sell products for the industry. Historically, tourism products were retailed through travel agents who offered products from tour operators, known as 'principals'. In a European context, the official EU statistical agency Eurostat estimated that the greatest concentration of activity by tour operators and travel agents is in Germany (9033 businesses with a €5925 million turnover per annum), Italy (6350 businesses and a €6481 million turnover), France (2279 businesses and a €6866 million turnover) and the UK (6050 businesses and a €14 710 million turnover). Across the EU different distribution forms of travel products are used. Belgian, Danish, German, Greek and Austrian tourists prefer to book direct with operators; in other countries, travel agents are a preferred form of booking, usually for package holidays. The exception is Spain, where travel agents are also used to book domestic travel, especially for late booking.

These traditional patterns of purchasing have been challenged by trends such as direct selling. Portland Holidays was one of the companies that began to change the relationship between the tourism sector and the public in the 1980s, by selling direct to the customer and cutting out the travel agent. More recently, this relationship has changed again with the impact of information communication technologies (ICT) such as the worldwide web, and ease of communication by email, to create a new form of distribution – a virtual distribution channel. The last five years

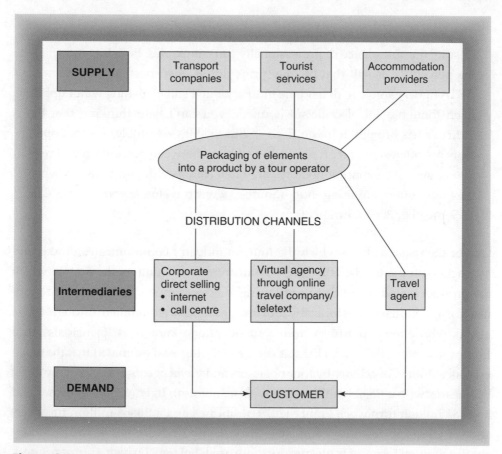

Figure 8.1 How tour operators link the elements of a holiday together to produce, assemble and distribute the package to the consumer

have seen dramatic changes in the tourism sector as technological advances have revolutionized the way in which the tourism industry communicates and interacts with its consumers. Chapter 6 illustrated the significance of technology as one element in the growth strategy and expansion of low-cost airlines. Selling online holidays and the rise of e-travel agents, as well as direct selling to bypass existing distribution channels, have created a high degree of change and uncertainty within the tourism sector. For example, in February 2006 Travelsupermarket.com in the UK launched a package holiday price check site, where holidays from 120 travel websites can be compared to provide the most competitive prices. The site was expected to receive around two million hits a month and was positioned to attract those people who do not want to self-package online: instead, it will direct clients to the best options. This comes at a time when new technological advances, such as dynamic packaging (the availability of software that allows a client to organize and purchase the elements of a holiday online), have made major inroads. In the UK, it is estimated that a significant proportion of travellers have used such software to avoid visiting travel agents. These changes have provided major challenges to the way the travel agent and tour operator distribute their products through various distribution channels (see Figure 8.1). However, as Figure 8.1 shows, the travel agent and tour operator still have a role to play, as this chapter will show.

The tour operator

Defining the tour operator is a far from easy process because their role, activities and form have changed dramatically from the early days when Thomas Cook first organized a package trip by rail in the 1840s. One useful approach is to identify what a tour operator does as a means of establishing their characteristics and form. In simple terms a tour operator will organize, package together different elements of the tourism experience (as shown in Figure 8.1) and offer them for sale to the public either through the medium of a brochure, leaflet or advertisement, or using ICT. If a tour operator is to offer a package, also known as an inclusive tour, it will normally have to include at least two elements that are offered for sale at the inclusive sale price, and will involve a stay of more than 24 hours in overnight accommodation. These elements normally include transport, accommodation and other tourist services (see Table 8.1).

Table 8.1 Elements of an inclusive tour (a package)

Basic elements:
- Aircraft seat
- Accommodation at destination
- Return transfer from airport to accommodation
- Services of a tour operator representative
- Insurance

Optional add-ins:
- Car hire
- Excursions

Alternative forms:
- Multi-destination packages that visit more than one destination/country
- Optional extensions to the package to extend the itinerary
- Linear tours by coach operators

The type and range of packages sold by the tourism industry can normally be divided into two types: those using the traditional charter flight and those using scheduled flights, where it is uneconomic for the tour operator to purchase charter flights.

The type of packages are often segmented according to:

- Mode of travel, such as ferry or coach holiday (typified in the UK by Shearings). It may also be based on twin-transport packages such as fly–drive, which are very popular with inbound tourists in the USA.
- Mode of accommodation, where hotel chains become tour operators by packaging their surplus capacity to offer weekend or short breaks in business-oriented hotels, selling rail or air transport and visits to attractions as an all-inclusive package.
- Whether they are international or domestic packages.
- Length of holiday (whether a short break, i.e. fewer than four nights away, or a along holiday, i.e. more than four nights, is offered).
- Distance, where the market is divided into short-haul and long-haul; over 90 per cent of UK outbound packages are short haul.
- Destination type (e.g. city breaks, beach holidays, adventure holidays).

These tours may be organized by small independent tour operators, who special-ize in certain segments (e.g. youth operators such as PGL in the UK); larger operators, such as TUI, which have trans-European; or global operations, such as MyTravel Group. In addition, there are over 300 tour operators who organize the itineraries, activities and logistics of inbound visitors to countries such as the UK and who are represented by their trade organization – the British of Incoming Tour Operators Association (BITOA). But why do tour operators exist, and why do people use them? The answers lie in the way they operate and the economic benefits that they provide to the customer.

Economics of tour operation: Managing for profit

Tour operators have the ability to purchase services and elements of the tourism experience from other principals or suppliers at significant discounts by buying in bulk. They fulfil a major role in the tourism sector as they allow the different tourism sectors in Figure 8.1 to sell their capacity in advance – often a long time in advance as contracts are drawn up a year prior to tourists using accommodation or services. This obviates the need for smaller, specialized businesses to market and distribute their product to a wide range of potential retailers, hoping that cus-tomers will choose their product or service over and above others. The bulk purchase agreements in large resorts areas mean that, in the summer season, the complete capacity of hotels, self-catering and other forms of accommodation may be block booked, leaving the business free to develop its own expertise in running or man-aging its business. Similarly, the tour operator connects together with all the ancil-lary services to negotiate contracts and deals that will allow a holiday to be sold and be delivered on the ground.

So, as Chapters 5 and 6 showed in terms of transport, the tour operator will bulk purchase airline seats, airport transfer services from coach operators, and taxis in the destination area, as well as a whole host of local entertainment and visitor attraction opportunities to be sold to clients at the booking stage or in the destination. The result is that tour operators traditionally provided a guaranteed level of sales which allowed principals to fix their costs in advance and allow the operators to achieve economies of scale by gaining heavily discounted rates on their purchases. The out-come is a business opportunity for the tour operator, which creates a package, prod-uct or experience through assembling the elements together, advertising and selling

	January	April	June	September	December
Year 1	Research ▬▬▬▬ Research ▬▬▬▬				
Research and planing			• Package holiday prospects • Destination selection	• Analysis of competing choice of destination	
Year 2	Select destination ▪ Brochure production ▪ Printing of brochure proofs (Design, development, printing contracts agreed)				
Negotiation	• Hotel capacity determined • Departure dates identified • Brochure production decisions	• Negotiate with airlines for charter seats, transfers and hotel rooms	• Contracts concluded		
Administration			• Determine exchange rates • Estimate selling prices • Proofs of brochures from printers • Recruit booking staff	• Final tour prices added to brochure • Printing of brochure	
Marketing				• Brochure distributed to agents and launched • Publicize to press and media	
Year 3	January	April	May	September	December
	Peak advertising ▬▬ Recruitment and training of holiday reps ▬▬ First tour departs ▬▬				

Figure 8.2 Planning horizon for a tour operator's summer programme (modified from Holloway, 2001)

them, and using third-party agents to deliver each element on the ground. It is obvious that tourists may experience dissatisfaction, if there are service interruptions or breakdowns in the delivery, and the seamless experience does not occur. Therefore, managing the tourist experience to ensure the holiday experience is an enjoyable and rewarding one is a key element of customer care for tour operators. The tour operator will often add a mark-up on the product they are selling by calculating all the input costs and their overheads and adding a profit margin to produce a price.

The process of establishing a tour through from the initial idea to its sale and delivery to the client is shown in Figure 8.2, a schematic illustration using a time line to highlight the long time frames involved in researching, planning, developing, administering and implementing a tour programme. Figure 8.2 also illustrates the vast range of risks that the tour operator takes in planning a holiday, including:

- estimating the likely market
- competing with long-established tour operators in a destination with a recognizable brand
- investing heavily in human resources and infrastructure to set up a destination.

Given these major risks, it is important for tour operators to recognize how important it is to set up and operate their business in a competitive and sustainable manner so that the investment pays a dividend over and above the costs of operation.

Tour operating business performance

Tour operating business performance is determined by the skill of the company in buying its product components (e.g. aircraft seats, accommodation and transfers) at a competitive price, and reselling at a price that is lower than that for which a consumer could assemble the same product. One consequence is that tour operators standardize packages (which differ little between destinations) to keep prices low.

Tour operators may keep their prices low by:

- negotiating low prices from supplier
- reducing profit margins
- cutting their cost structures.

Those tour operators that have become integrated tourism companies and operate aircraft can reduce the prices for air travel through heavy usage of an aircraft (i.e. increasing the number of flights it can achieve each day). This will typically involve flying from a base in the UK to another destination, bringing a plane-load of passengers back to a return destination in the UK, and then flying to the same destination again and then back again to the original base; this is known as a W pattern (see Figure 8.3). This flight scheduling is very efficient until flight delays (e.g. due to air traffic control) occur; these throw the entire schedule back and cause knock-on effects for passengers on other flights.

To achieve cost reductions, charter flights must have high load factors to break even, typically 80–90 per cent, compared to 50–70 per cent for scheduled flights (this depends on the cost base of the carrier). Any unsold seats therefore may be

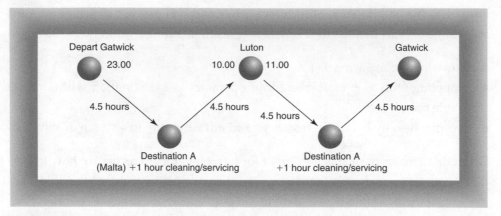

Figure 8.3   A hypothetical W flight pattern for a charter aircraft

unloaded onto the market at cost or less to fill the aircraft, either as seat-only sales/ cheap holidays or for purchase through consolidators (air-brokers). Consolidators purchase surplus capacity and have the responsibility for marketing and selling such seats. For the airline/tour operator, additional passengers may yield extra revenue from on-board duty-free sales or through purchasing the company's holiday package even if a loss is made on the flight.

Costing charter operators' prices is a complex process, as 'dead legs' at the beginning and end of a season have to be incorporated. At the beginning of a season, an aircraft on a W pattern will fly out with tourists but return empty and vice versa at the end of the season. To extend the season, operators may provide inducements such as low-cost accommodation to attract low-season business to fill capacity. One such example is the winter flows of elderly people from northern Europe wintering in the Mediterranean. Hotels discount their rates hoping guests will spend money in their premises to compensate for discounts given. Yet, as was suggested in Chapter 6, the future growth in the package holiday market in the UK is likely to limit the scope for further development of the charter airline and the use of seat-only sales, as the low-cost airline companies have begun to challenge this sector's cost competitiveness. The response is likely to be continued innovation by tour operators and principals to adapt tour supply to the needs of ever-changing customers. This is why companies such as Thomson Holidays have introduced the concept of dynamic packaging for clients as well as rebranding its charter airline from Britannia to Thomsonfly.com, with an associated low-cost airline element. Businesses have to constantly adapt and respond to changes in the market and the most adept and strategic businesses often anticipate or shape consumer tastes in the holiday market through their product offerings.

Regulating tour operating

Like any other form of business, tour operating is regulated in many countries. Since the 1960s, the UK has seen a number of massive tour operator collapses, and this led ABTA, the Association of British Travel Agents, to set up its bonding scheme in the 1970s. In 1975, the government made it compulsory for operators to contribute 2 per cent of their turnover to ABTA's bonding scheme. This is to safeguard tourists from company insolvencies and being stranded overseas – as happened in the 1990s with the collapse of the International Leisure Group, which severely depleted ABTA's fund. This situation has persisted with a number of notable collapses in 2005, partly due to the small profit margins which companies often work on. The collapse of low-cost airline EU Jet in 2005 sparked a parliamentary inquiry on consumer protection for travellers, since low-cost airlines are not covered by the ATOL bonding scheme (this is a scheme whereby any company wishing to run packages overseas must obtain an Air Travel Organiser's Licence from the Civil Aviation Authority (CAA) so that if the company goes bankrupt any stranded customers are brought home by the ATOL fund). During the inquiry, a £1 passenger levy was proposed to provide protection in the event of a low-cost airline collapse. Low-cost airlines vehemently opposed this additional cost to its fares, arguing that it might encourage poor management performance and make their flights less competitive; initial plans were to extend this levy to all scheduled flights. In November 2005 the UK government directed the CAA to review the ATOL bonding scheme to provide a less burdensome and complex administrative scheme to cover customer refund and repatriation requirements (i.e. if an ATOL-bonded tour operator collapses while you are overseas on holiday, the scheme will cover the costs of bringing you home). The CAA are aiming to reduce some of the costs to ATOL members, moving towards a system that is not bond focused, but is a per customer levy to reinvigorate the Air Travel Trust Fund which covers repatriation costs. A licensing scheme that the CAA operates in the UK requires tour operators wishing to operate specific programmes to obtain an Air Travel Organisers' Licence (ATOL). ATOL's data are very useful as they identify some of the dimensions of this market, as the discussion will show.

The European holiday market

The European market is one of the most highly developed and complex areas of activity globally in relation to the development of tour operators. It has seen a great deal of activity, as Chapter 4 highlighted, particularly in terms of investment, acquisitions and mergers. This is reflected in the scale of tourism activity. Since the expansion of the EU from 15 to 25 member states, domestic tourism has been the main driver of tourism demand. In terms of inbound tourism to EU countries, 74 per cent of the accommodation nights spent by non-residents (i.e. tourists) in hotels and similar establishments was by travellers from within the EU. This illustrates the importance of intra-regional tourist flows (i.e. travel within the region) in the EU. For the majority of EU countries, either Germany or the UK is their main holiday market. For example:

- in the Czech Republic, Greece, Italy, Latvia, Lithuania, Hungary, Austria and Poland, German tourists are the most important source market
- in Belgium, Spain, France, Ireland, Cyprus, the Netherlands and Portugal, British tourists are the most important source market.

In addition to the UK and Germany, Scandinavia has been a major driver of demand in the package holiday market. Much of the traffic from these source countries has been destined for coastal locations in Mediterranean Europe. Yet this does not provide the complete picture. Figure 8.4 provides an illustration of the main air traffic flows between major hubs expressed as city-to-city points (including leisure and business travel) and acts as a counterbalance to the notion that all tourist travel is to coastal destinations. The city-pairs data in Figure 8.4 imply that the principal destinations of EU travellers have traditionally been no more than three hours' flying time. Even so, many of the coastal Mediterranean flows emerge in addition to the city-to-city flows.

The demand for package holidays and outbound travel is examined in Box 8.1, the case study of one country as a generating market. Norway is a lesser-known market. It is distinctive as Norwegians have a high propensity for holiday-taking. The case study also helps to explain the dynamics of holiday traffic emanating from one country, and which is the choice of destination influenced by what tour operators offer.

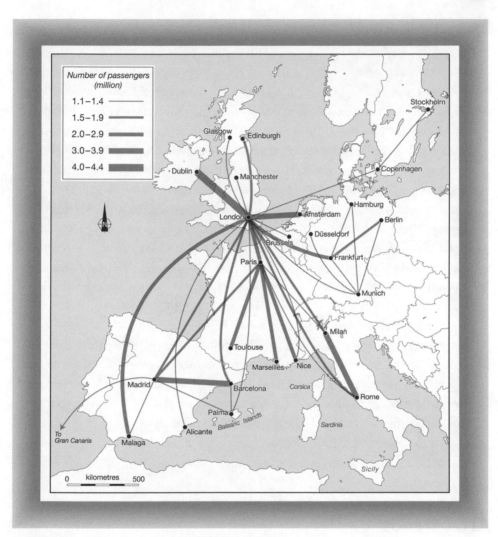

Figure 8.4   Main traffic flows between major hubs

Box 8.1 Case study: Holidaymaking in Norway

Norway, which is not an EU member country, is an interesting example because it con-
tradicts the widely accepted notion that in many developed countries up to 50 per cent
of the population do not take a holiday in a given year. In Norway, historically levels of
holidaytaking have been high, rising from 61 per cent in 1970 to 75 per cent in 1978. In

subsequent years the percentage taking a holiday has stayed relatively stable at over 70 per cent. Norway has the highest levels of holidaytaking in Europe, followed by Germany (74 per cent) and the Netherlands (under 70 per cent). In a given year, Norwegians take 1.5 holiday trips, typically of 15 or 16 days in length. The length of time spent on holiday has risen in recent years due to a growth in weekend trips (especially short breaks to cities) for two or three nights. Travel is relatively expensive in Norway with its high cost of living, so only 50 per cent of those with incomes less than NOK100 000 (NOK 1 = 0.084 euros) went on holiday. In contrast, 90 per cent of those with incomes over NOK500 000, took a holiday. The elderly and low-income households are those less likely to take holidays. Changes in the Norwegian holiday market also highlight the ways in which tour operators have had to adapt and develop holiday products. For example, in 1990 around a third of Norwegian outbound travel was to non-Nordic countries (i.e. those outside Scandinavia). By 2003 over 40 per cent of travel was to non-Nordic countries, as travellers ventured further afield. In fact 47 per cent of all Norwegian tourism is outbound although this is not as high as among German, Danish and Dutch tourists, who typically choose overseas destinations for 60–70 per cent of their holiday trips.

Spain was the most popular destination for the Norwegian outbound market, with in excess of 500 000 trips a year. This is followed by Denmark, Greece and Sweden, accounting for almost two thirds of outbound travel. Lower down the list of preferred destinations, changes have occurred in recent years, as France replaced the UK and Germany as popular destinations, and Italy has also become a desirable destination to visit. As a result, tour operators have had to shift the emphasis of their supply to cater to these changing trends.

ATOL trends

In a UK context, a range of detailed data exists, as documented in the ATOL data. Table 8.2 shows the total passengers carried on ATOL-protected air holidays and flights. In terms of trends, in the period 2000–2005, the number of passengers carried in the summer season rose to a peak of 18.8 million in 2001 but has hovered around 17.5–17.7 million in subsequent years, as self-packaging has grown along with seat-only sales. The revenue earned from these ATOL-bonded summer holidays has seen some initial growth followed by a decline and a recovery after 2003. What is perhaps more important for the tour operating businesses is the average cost of a summer package, which has shown consistent increases of around under

Table 8.2 Passengers carried and revenue earned under all ATOL licences in the UK 2000–2005 (source: Developed from CAA (2002), *ATOL Business*, Issue 20; CAA (2005), ATOL Business, Issue 26; © CAA)

	Number of passengers (million)	£ billion revenue earned	% change over last year in revenue earned	£ average cost per ATOL-bonded holiday
Summer season				
(April–September)				
2000	17.9	7.8	13.1	437
2001	18.8	8.3	6.0	441
2002	17.7	7.9	−4.7	449
2003	17.5	7.9	−0.8	449
2004	17.7	8.3	5.9	469
Winter season				
(October–March)				
2000/01	10.4	4.7	12.2	456
2001/02	10.2	4.8	2.1	470
2002/03	10.0	4.9	1.8	489
2003/04	10.3	5.3	8.0	510
2004/05	10.5	5.7	9.2	545
Year to March				
2000	26.2	11.2	5.7	426
2001	28.3	12.6	12.8	444
2002	29.0	13.1	4.1	451
2003	27.6	12.8	−2.3	463
2004	27.8	13.1	2.5	471
2005	28.3	14.1	7.2	498

10 per cent in the period 2000–2004, from £437 to £469, which is broadly in line with inflation. A notable trend, when comparing the summer and winter seasons, is the continued percentage growth in revenue in the winter market. Most important is the very significant increasing cost of winter packages (in contrast to summer packages) of almost 20 per cent during 2000–2005. For operators, this is an interesting trend: the average cost is considerably higher in the winter market than the summer market, being £76 more expensive in 2004/2005 compared to £19 more in 2000.

Aggregated figures for both winter and summer packages (for the year ended March) in Table 8.2 show that the overall volume of passengers has risen back to the 2001 level but revenue has increased significantly, clearly as a result of the cost of winter holidays. In overall terms, the increased cost of winter holidays has led to the rise in the average cost of an ATOL-bonded holiday which is now just under £500. These trends not only illustrate the recent evolution of ATOL-bonded holidays but also the fluctuation in the volume of passengers, revenue earned and increasing cost of holidays. However, as the CAA observe, while the number of ATOL-protected sales of holidays has increased since 2000, as a proportion of all air travel they have decreased. In 2005, the proportion of ATOL-protected air travel was 56 per cent, but as more consumers are booking direct than through ATOL-bonded travel organizations, the 14 per cent decline 2001–2005 in ATOL protected air travel is predicted to fall even further.

Table 8.3 provides a more detailed insight into the volume of business licensed by ATOL in 2002 and 2005. A comparison of the top thirty largest ATOL-licensed operators shows that, in three years, online specialists (e.g. Expedia Inc, The Destination Group Ltd, Flightbookers and Travelocity.co.uk Ltd) have entered the top forty rankings in 2005. In 2002, no online specialists were prominent in the rankings. This confirms the rapid rise of the online operators in the UK, which saw a 92 per cent increase in passenger volumes in 2004–2005 alone. The four major licensees (TUI UK Ltd, First Choice, Thomas Cook and MyTravel) retained their position as volume-driven businesses 2002–2005, despite some movement in their respective rankings. The dominance of individual brands and companies, however, does not highlight the underlying growth in large integrated tourism companies. Table 8.4 shows that in 2005, three of the top ten rankings of companies were now dominated by online businesses owned by large groups and companies. In some cases (e.g. Cendant Corporation), this position in the market has been achieved through acquisitions of other companies to grow their capacity. Yet the indisputable fact is that in 2005, ten companies controlled 62 per cent of the ATOL-licensed holidays, and four controlled 46 per cent. In addition, in 2004–2005, the capacity for the top ten groups increased by 2 per cent at the expense of the top four groups. The result is that new medium-sized corporations have made major inroads to the market, while the smaller ATOL holders have reduced their market share by 10 per cent. In other words, the competitive behaviour of organizations such as Cendant Corporation has reallocated capacity whilst placing pressure on the smaller companies. Competition from medium and large corporations

Table 8.3 Passengers carried under the top 30 largest Air Travel Organizers' Licences 2002 and 2005 (source: modified from CAA, 2002, *ATOL Business*, Issue 20; CAA, 2005, *ATOL Business*, Issue 26; © CAA)

Twelve months to March	2002	Twelve months to March	2005
1 TUI UK Ltd	3 925 198	1 TUI UK Ltd	4 747 955
2 MyTravel Group plc	3 784 811	2 First Choice Holidays & Flights Ltd	2 685 989
3 Thomas Cook Tour Operations Ltd	2 834 895	3 Thomas Cook Tour Operations Ltd	2 497 778
4 First Choice Holidays and Flights Ltd	1 918 424	4 MyTravel Tour Operators Ltd	2 351 818
5 Unijet Travel Ltd	996 107	5 Expedia Inc	582 457
6 Avro plc	689 534	6 Direct Holidays plc	580 590
7 Direct Holidays plc	650 259	7 Gold Medal Travel Group plc	518 990
8 Trailfinders Ltd	606 786	8 Trailfinders Ltd	498 729
9 Gold Medal Travel Group plc	481 430	9 Avro plc	416 503
10 Cosmosair plc	457 094	10 Lotus International Ltd	414 808
11 Virgin Holidays Ltd	449 065	11 Panorama Holiday Group Ltd	395 055
12 Panorama Holiday Group Ltd	425 972	12 Travelworld Vacations Ltd	387 859
13 Thomas Cook Retail Ltd	410 285	13 The Globespan Group plc	370 015
14 Libra Holidays Ltd	336 535	14 Virgin Holidays Ltd	367 259
15 Lotus International Ltd	310 595	15 Cosmosair plc	343 099

(Continued)

Table 8.3 (Continued)

Twelve months to March	2002	Twelve months to March	2005
16 Specialist Holidays Ltd	309 227	16 Thomas Cook Retail Ltd	324 810
17 Accoladia Ltd	308 622	17 Freedom Flights Ltd	299 267
18 Kuoni Travel Ltd	290 181	18 Kuoni Travel Ltd	283 317
19 Kosmar Villa Holidays Ltd	250 851	19 Libra Holidays Ltd	264 312
20 Travelworld Vacations Ltd	235 651	20 Kosmar Villa Holidays plc	238 954
21 HCCT (Holidays) Ltd	219 025	21 Travelbag Ltd	235 985
22 Travel 2 Ltd	210 654	22 Travel 2 Ltd	218 269
23 Golden Sun Holidays Ltd	205 462	23 The Destination Group Ltd	217 565
24 Lunn Poly Ltd	183 324	24 The Really Great Holiday Company plc	204 929
25 The Really Great Holiday Company plc	179 187	25 Flight Centre (UK) Ltd	196 564
26 Travelbag plc	169 109	26 Carnival PLC[1]	195 740
27 Cresta Holidays Ltd	168 952	27 Hotelplan Ltd	193 886
28 Hotelplan Ltd	168 313	28 HCCT (Holidays) Ltd	179 171
29 Air Miles Travel Promotions Ltd	167 134	29 Air Miles Travel Promotions Ltd	164 906
30 Saga Holidays Ltd	159 447	30 Saga Holidays Ltd	148 315

[1]The 2004 figures for Carnival PLC include P&O Princess Cruises International Ltd, after its business was transferred in October 2004

Table 8.4 Passengers licensed to the top ten groups and companies (source: CAA 2005, *ATOL Business*, Issue 26; © CAA)

Group and licence holders	Passengers licensed for current year	% Total	Passengers licensed for previous year	% Total	% Change
1 TUI Group Total (TUI UK Ltd; The International Academy Ltd)	4 762 111	16	4 826 943	16	−1
2 Thomas Cook Group Total (Thomas Cook Retail Ltd; Thomas Cook Tour Operations Ltd; Thomas Cook Signature Ltd; Style Holidays Ltd)	3 157 789	10	3 173 596	10	(0)
3 MyTravel Group Total (MyTravel Tour Operations Ltd; BCT Travel Group Ltd; Direct Holidays plc; Panorama Holiday Group Ltd)	3 109 601	10	4 157 754	13	(25)
4 First Choice Holidays Group Total (First Choice Holidays and Flights Ltd; SkiBound Ltd; Exodus Travels Ltd; Meon Travel Ltd; Sunsail Ltd; Hayes and Jarvis (Travel) Ltd; Waymark Holidays Ltd; Citalia Holidays Ltd; Crown Travel Ltd; Trips Worldwide Ltd; Adventures Worldwide Ltd; Trek America Ltd; Trina Tours Ltd; Magic of the Orient; Sunshine Cruises Ltd)	2 861 468	9	2 610 099	8	10
5 Cosmos Group Total (Cosmosair plc; Cosmos Coach Tours Ltd; Avro plc; Archers Tours Ltd; The Charter Warehouse Ltd)	1 082 249	4	1 183 730	4	(9)

(Continued)

Table 8.4 (*Continued*)

Group and licence holders	Passengers licensed for current year	% Total	Passengers licensed for previous year	% Total	% Change
6 InterActive Corporation Group Total (Expedia Inc; Expedia Corporate Travel UK Ltd; Interval Travel Ltd; Travelscape Inc)	850 988	3	536 605	2	59
7 Cendant Corporation Group Total (RCI Europe; Travel 2 Ltd; Holiday Cottages Group Ltd; International Life Leisure Ltd; Bridge the World Travel Service Ltd; Flightbookers; Individual Travellers Company; Travelbag)	809 484	3	312 075	1	159
8 Excel Airways Group Total (Freedom Flights Ltd; Excel Holidays Ltd; The Really Great Holiday Company Ltd)	772 792	3	251 455	1	207
9 Gold Medal Travel Group plc	675 000	2	654 848	2	3
10 Lastminute Group Total (Last Minute Network Ltd; The Destination Group Ltd; Globepost Ltd; Travelcoast Ltd; Travelbargains Ltd; Joint Ventures Travel plc)	602 466	2	546 902	2	10
Total passengers licensed to the top ten groups and companies	18 683 948	62	18 254 007	59	2
Total passengers licensed to the top four groups	13 890 969	46	14 768 392	48	(6)
Passengers licensed to all ATOL holders	30 212 492	100	31 037 351	100	(3)

combined with the challenge of dynamic packaging and low-cost airlines has begun to redefine the business environment and profit levels for the smaller ATOL businesses.

Due to the high level of mergers and takeovers in the UK tour operating sector in 2000 the Department of Trade and Industry Foreign Package Holiday Order stated that travel agents owned by a tour operator controlling more than 5 per cent of the package market should identify their links with suppliers in brochures and shop interiors so as not to encourage anti-competitive behaviour by only recommending company products at the expense of competitors (this is known as 'directional selling'). With continued consolidation in the tour operator sector in the UK and Europe (such as TUI's growth as the largest integrated tourism company), it is interesting to consider how the larger transnational and smaller businesses compete.

How do these companies compete for business?

In June 2002, MyTravel initiated a price war over its 2003 summer holiday brochure by claiming its prices in its first edition brochure were lower (306 were priced lower) than its rivals (i.e. Thomson and First Choice). This is a very characteristic action from the tour operator sector, especially the larger companies, for the following reasons:

- they seek to expand their market share, market dominance and position in consumers' minds
- they seek to convert domestic holidaytaking to outbound travel by conveying images of low-cost holidays
- they acquire smaller or equivalent businesses in competing businesses and expand into new areas
- they drive down the cost from suppliers and by repackaging the product, so that no-frills packages (i.e. no airport transfers, no holiday representative or in-flight meals) are provided in the market appealing to the lower end of the consumer spectrum
- they drive out the smaller operators in the long-term, to consolidate further their market dominance
- they have recently started to establish online direct selling or purchase an online company/enter into a strategic alliance with an online distribution channel.

In some cases, such predatory behaviour has not effected dramatic change. For example, following the collapse of the ILG group, other companies were formed to fill market niches, as business opportunities emerged. In addition, more complex economic forces such as currency fluctuations and changing consumer behaviour have led to companies rethinking how they operate and compete. An example is the practice of most tour operators of issuing holiday brochures in multiple editions. In the 1970s and 1980s, consumers were encouraged to book early for discounts and price guarantees. In the late 1980s, the traditional booking period was in late December (after Christmas), when much of the tour operators' advertising on television and in the press is mobilized to stimulate consumer activity (as the AIDA model in Chapter 3 indicated). This provided operators with client funds from early in the year until bills were due from suppliers, often as late as September, providing up to nine months' interest-bearing income. With increased ICT, clients recognized the value of late bookings as supply normally exceeded demand in most years for outbound inclusive tours from the UK and many European countries. Most notable in the last five years has been the switch to massive investment in online technology by the four leading ATOL groups in the UK, as competition has intensified.

Tour operators responded to the loss of investment income from banking clients' money prior to their paying suppliers for the holiday and services by introducing fluid pricing. Larger discounts for early booking and price increases were provided in later brochure reissues; a second edition relaunch for its summer 2003 programme cost MyTravel an estimated £5 million in 2002. Other strategies have been to develop new markets, such as long-haul markets (which now exceed 20 per cent of outbound UK business). Seat-only sales on charter flights have also seen some operators expand their business. More common strategies are to seek new, cheaper destinations as the European industry did in the 1980s with Greece then Turkey, as sun, sea and sand packages remain popular. This was replicated in the period since 2000 with the opening up of Eastern Europe's holiday potential as the new Mediterranean for package holidays. With over 50 per cent of UK holidaymakers choosing packages when travelling overseas abroad at some time, it is evident that operators have had to switch attention from first-time, novice travellers (i.e. the 1950s and 1960s) to repeat travellers. The result has been product diversification to grow the range of possible holiday options, including:

● city breaks and additional short breaks as secondary airports open up new potential destinations (such as Iceland Air's service to Reykjavik)

- long-haul and adventure travel such as ecotourism and nature holidays
- greater flexibility and tailoring of the packages to the client's needs, and new pick-and-mix technology such as dynamic packaging.

Increased competition is likely to lead to further consolidation in the marketplace among tour operators, especially as virtual tour operators sell more capacity on the worldwide web as part of a growing e-business strategy. But the tour operating sector is not simply characterized by constant growth and profitability among the businesses working within the sector. For example, in 2001, 23 ATOL-licensed companies went bankrupt and £3 million in compensation was awarded to travellers. In the period 1985–2001, £159 million was paid from the bond ATOL retains from tour operators to 190 000 people for 300 ATOL operators failing. The CAA pays any shortfalls in compensation from the bond from its Air Travel Trust Fund, which in 2002 was reportedly £8 million in debt, highlighting the need to re-evaluate the role of bonds and tour operators' solvency in 2005. In 2005, Experian in the UK reported that 492 businesses in the leisure and hotel sector (including caravan parks) went bankrupt out of a total of 18 122 companies while 581 in the transport sector also endured the same fate.

However, much of the activity in the further integration and consolidation is likely to focus upon:

- expansion via acquisitions (e.g. Cendant Corporation's Strategy in 2004–2005)
- integration of air and hotel businesses (e.g. low-cost airlines and hotel companies)
- further widening of distribution channels (e.g. online; possible new mobile phone booking technology)
- widening geographical coverage of markets and tour operators merge/enter into strategic alliances
- the impact of the Euro, which may allow operators to buy capacity cheaper from weaker currencies providing lower-priced holidays (e.g. UK purchasing of cheap Eastern European capacity)
- a gradual levelling of package holiday prices across the EU
- greater cost controls and more sophisticated yield management systems to derive revenue according to demand
- new business strategies towards products (i.e. focus on core business versus diversification)
- a greater alignment of business activity towards changing consumer behaviour, as markets for products become more specialized, tailored and tourist focused.

Consumer trends affecting the future of tour operating

For the travel retailer, one of the principal changes observed over the last decade has been a diversification away from the preoccupation with mass tourism as the market (i.e. the demand) for tourism products has changed. Industry commentators such as Auliana Poon has described this as a transition with tourism retailing from 'old' to 'new' forms of tourism and many industry analysts believe we are in an age where the combined impact of consumer tastes, technology and the influence of the media is rapidly changing the nature of tourism trends and behaviour. The globalized media now provides 24-hour coverage of world affairs and the instant nature of broadcasting, the internet and other media sources plays an important role in portraying global tourism and its development in different destinations.

Old tourism was best described as driven by consumers who were inexperienced travellers satisfied with homogenous tourism products (i.e. similar mass-produced packages) which were predictable and based on sun-based destinations (i.e. the Mediterranean resorts) seeking escape from the routine of everyday life, especially work. In contrast, 'new' tourism is characterized by more experienced travellers who have a growing concern about the environmental impact of their holidays on the places they visit. Yet interestingly, an industry report in 2005 by Thomson Holidays found that 30 per cent of UK tourists were uninterested in sustainable tourism and their impact on the environment, implying that 'old' forms of tourism remain the cornerstone of the package holiday market. In contrast, the 'new' tourist seeks more individualized products rather than the mass products that are less predictable, full of surprise, discovery and a memorable experience rather than simply a repetition of last year's beach holiday. The 'new' tourist is looking for something different; the holiday is an extension of their life rather than simple escape. In contrast to 'old' tourism, which was very much supply driven, as the history of mass package holidays has shown, the 'new' tourist is seeking to define what they want. Whilst 'old' and 'new' tourism coexist, 'new' tourism offers the tourism industry many growth opportunities, given that tourism businesses can react to the demand for increased flexibility through greater use of information technology. In particular, marketing techniques (e.g. market segmentation to break demand up into discrete components) can be applied to create a move towards niche products.

Demographic factors

One very visible factor characterizing most Western countries is the ageing population, with a growth in the segment of the population aged 50 to 70 years of age.
This is often labelled the rise of the 'senior' or 'grey' market. Many of these people
now enjoy a higher standard of health care, are less sedentary and have experience
of travel. What is also notable about this section of the travelling population is
that they tend to spend up to 30 per cent more on travel than other age groups,
given their greater disposable income. Many people in these age groups are
described by marketers as 'empty nesters': their children have grown up and left
home, and many are taking early retirement, are mortgage free and have more free
time translating into a greater propensity to travel. In many Western countries with
well-funded state and private pension schemes, this has been a key element of
growth, although concerns over the sustainability of pensions funded by a declining pool of people of working age raises many questions over how this will translate into long-term growth. In France, senior travellers comprise approximately
30 per cent of the population; this is 28 per cent in Canada, 27 per cent in Japan,
27 per cent in the USA and 20 per cent in Germany. In many countries, tour operators, visitor attractions and accommodation providers have experienced continued
increases in the mature market. Indeed, some tour operators who direct-sell specialize in this market (such as Saga in the UK and Elderhost in the USA). In the USA
alone, the forecasts of the growth of the mature market aged between 55 and 74
years of age will increase from around 40 million in 2001 to 74 million in 2031. The
implications for tourism managers are that not only will the market for mature
tourists only continue to grow, but that they will potentially be tourists for much
longer due to increases in longevity. The conventional view among the tourism
industry is that this age group is less technologically able, and so more prepared to
rely on travel agents as holiday organizers. However, there is growing evidence in
consumer surveys of e-preparedness and technological use that these groups are
embracing the internet.

Consumer issues in tour operating

With the growing expansion of the holiday market, reduced costs and the continued growth in the package market a number of trends have become evident. The

growing variety of destinations has meant that competition between countries has intensified cost pressures. For example, in 2002 Spain experienced a 20 per cent drop in visitor arrivals up to July, the first decline since its growth in 1960s; this is attributed to cost and wider issues such as image and the availability of cheaper alternatives such as Morocco, Bulgaria, Croatia, Turkey and Tunisia. But by 2004, growth had resumed, and in 2005, the 6 per cent growth in visitor arrivals was attributed to a 31 per cent increase in low-cost airline arrivals in Spain. At the same time, reduced prices and increased numbers of people taking budget holidays has been accompanied by growing numbers of complaints. According to ABTA, in 2000 almost 5 per cent of the UK's 20 million package holidaytakers were fairly or very dissatisfied with their holidays. This reflected a growth in dissatisfaction with the quality of accommodation, perceived safety standards of overseas chartered aircraft, surcharges and failure to provide what was advertised. The actual official complaints made to ABTA are relatively low, at around 19 000 in 1999, although legal recourse and litigation is growing in popularity as a small minority seek legal redress; an example is the deep vein thrombosis claims against airlines in recent years.

In the EU, the 1993 EC Directive on Package Travel has brought a greater degree of precision into the roles and responsibilities of the tour operator. The response of the Department for Trade and Industry (DTI) led to the following measures being implemented:

- all tours must be licensed
- a greater degree of honesty is required in holiday brochure descriptions
- an obligation has been placed on travel agents to take responsibility for the information contained in brochures they stock and to ensure adequate advice to clients on:
  - health
  - passport and visa requirements
  - insurance needs.

In addition, the tour operator is liable for losses resulting from misleading information or where suppliers do not provide the services paid for and contracted. The growing litigation towards tour operators by holidaymakers has continued apace, as the EC Directive encourages a greater duty of care for visitors.

This also highlights the greater onus on the tour operator in terms of the provision of support staff in the destination, namely the holiday representative ('the rep'). Reps are useful trouble-shooters who can often remedy problems or complaints *in situ*. The job is very demanding and involves being the public relations agent of the company, often on call twenty-four hours a day, seven days a week in the peak season. Reps typically intersperse a number of roles including:

- meeting and greeting incoming and departing passengers at the airport to ensure airport transfers drop the right passengers at the correct accommodation
- handling a wide range of destination-specific enquiries and requests and providing social events
- publicizing company-endorsed tours and services for which a commission is received by the company
- dealing with special requests (i.e. arrangements for disabled guests) and acting as a go-betweens for the tourist and hotel, local police, medical services and other agencies when required.

Typical roles in terms of safeguarding tourists' well-being include locating lost baggage, calling doctors when clients get ill, or (on rare occasions) die and in extreme cases liaising with police and authorities, as well as rebooking flights when emergencies arise. At airports, when flight delays occur holiday reps may have to deal with disgruntled passengers and offer company refreshment vouchers. They also address complaints about the accommodation. A recognizable human face in a strange environment, able to offer tourists local advice on health and safety issues, is paramount in ensuring their well-being. Whilst the role, character and ability of the holiday rep will be critical in undertaking this key client liaison role, training and excellent interpersonal skills (i.e. the ability to empathize with people and their problems) is essential as the tourist experience and client satisfaction are critical in gaining repeat business. In the UK, Thomson Holidays has an enviable reputation for generating repeat business as its in-flight customer satisfaction scores frequently show. Yet the demand for budget, cost-conscious holidays has led some tour operators to remove holiday reps, replacing them with a 24 hour call centre to provide advice and help to tourists.

A recent European Court of Justice ruling in January 2006 has also upheld EC legislation that provides compensation for passengers delayed on airlines who may have purchased seat-only sales (these seats are a growing trend on low-cost airlines). The ruling meant that passengers could have to be compensated £172 for delays outside the airline's control and this may impact on airlines such as Ryanair and easyJet where average fares paid are around £42. This further extension of consumer protection for travel in the EU provides support for the argument that travel is now being more heavily regulated.

Marketing and planning the holiday: The holiday brochure

Traditionally the printed holiday brochure has been the tour operator's most powerful marketing tool, since the intangible nature of tourism makes it imperative that the potential customer can read about what they may want to purchase. This has been accompanied by online brochures, websites and virtual tours of destinations, making the places accessible to potential visitors. It is not uncommon for up to 50 per cent of tour operators' marketing budgets to be spent on brochure production although web-based materials have now become a key element of investment. This has to be viewed in the wider context of planning, organizing and implementing a tour programme. In the hypothetical example shown in Figure 8.2 the tour operator has to undertake a series of stages of work including:

- research and planning
- negotiation with suppliers
- administration
- marketing.

With the exception of the initial research stage, the holiday brochure is an integral part of the planning and marketing process. Figure 8.5 highlights the time frames involved in brochure production and distribution, with many holiday brochures costing as much as £1 a copy and print runs of millions for large operators as MyTravel. Yet brochures have high wastage rates and are disposed of in large numbers. Of 120 million printed in the UK, nearly 48 million were never used according to data provided by Green Flag International (Holloway 2001). It is estimated that this adds up to £20 to the average cost of a package holiday.

The printed holiday brochure currently in vogue among tour operators has evolved from its modern-day predecessor, introduced in 1953 by Thomas Cook. It

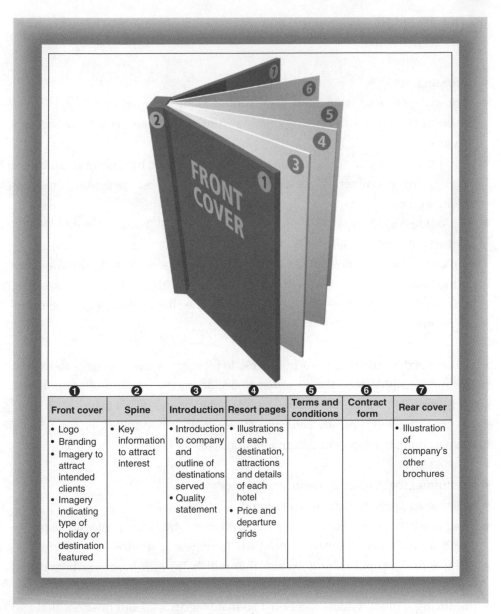

① Front cover	**②** Spine	**③** Introduction	**④** Resort pages	**⑤** Terms and conditions	**⑥** Contract form	**⑦** Rear cover
• Logo • Branding • Imagery to attract intended clients • Imagery indicating type of holiday or destination featured	• Key information to attract interest	• Introduction to company and outline of destinations served • Quality statement	• Illustrations of each destination, attractions and details of each hotel • Price and departure grids			• Illustration of company's other brochures

Figure 8.5 Structure of inclusive holiday brochures (© Eric Laws, 1997; redrawn and reproduced with the author's permission)

adopted a similar format to that of women's magazines, reflecting the important role of women as holiday decision-makers. The 1960s saw holiday brochures become glossier, packed with information, and its role has gradually changed to its present one of holiday catalogue.

Holiday brochures distributed through travel agents seek to achieve a number of objectives:

- to obtain sales
- to provide information to assist in decision-making by purchasers in relation to the destination, product offerings, timing (summer/winter), price and ancillary services
- to afford cost-effective distribution for the tour operator, by having an attractive cover, being prominently racked in travel agents and generating business among agents
- to provide an effective tool to allow agents to sell holidays with detailed products/booking codes
- to allow a contract to be agreed between the tour operator and customer, providing information on procedures for changing the booking, complaints, refunds, the details of the product purchased, the client's details and the insurance premium paid.

In the case of direct mail, the brochure seeks to fill some of the objectives above, but places more emphasis on the customer to decide on the product offering. It also seeks to appeal to the market segment it is targeted at and needs to be easy to use.

A brochure will typically comprise the elements embodied in Figure 8.5 and involve a complex process of design including:

- identifying the market audience and product
- utilizing an appropriate company brand
- designing a mock-up, using a computer, with illustrations and professional photographs of the hotel, destination, product offerings and services
- using a desktop publishing system that will help with brochure layout and design
- producing a proof, which is checked so that inaccuracies can be identified and rectified prior to printing.

With increasing consumer regulation in most countries, holiday brochures must get potential tourists to book a holiday, advertising dreams or images of their ideal holiday, but must also be honest, truthful and accurate. Above all they must not make false statements that can be prosecuted in many countries under trade descriptions legislation. This is now a more stringent requirement since the EU Directive on Package Travel has made it easier for the tourist to litigate against the tour operator who is responsible for the supplier abroad. The need for truth and honesty is endorsed by ABTA in its Code of Conduct for Tour Operators, making the brochure a legal document to which complaints may refer in future claims for compensation.

To meet the obligations of a tour operator's licence, Holloway (2001) identifies the following information, as being required in a holiday brochure:

- the name of the firm responsible for the inclusive tour
- the means of transport used, including, in the case of air transport, the name of the carrier(s), type and class of aircraft used and whether scheduled or charter aircraft are operated
- full details of destinations, itinerary and times of travel
- the duration of each tour (number of days/nights)
- a full description of the location and type of accommodation provided, including any meals
- whether services or a representative are available abroad
- a clear indication of the price for each tour, including any taxes
- exact details of special arrangements (e.g. if there is a games room in the hotel, whether this is available at all times and whether any charges are made for the use of this equipment)
- full conditions of booking, including details of cancellation conditions
- details of any insurance coverage (clients should have the right to choose their own insurance, providing this offers equivalent coverage)
- details of documentation required for travel to the destinations featured, and any health hazards or inoculations recommended.

Source: Holloway (2001: 253–4)

Brochures are normally distributed to travel agents, and operators need to build in wastage costs – operators typically have to distribute twenty brochures to gain one booking even though this may be for a group of two or three people. Many agents operate different policies on distribution including:

- having brochures available on display with open access
- displaying one copy only – consumers need to ask for a copy.

Even these policies are not a guarantee of success. Operators can classify agents in terms of performance, with high-performing agents selling 100 plus holidays a year and low performers selling fewer than 5 a year. This appears to hold true for mass package holidays, although the significance of the number of sales obviously depends on the value of each holiday.

Once a client has decided to make a booking the tour operator will retail the product through a computer reservation system (CRS), direct to the public or via the internet. Whilst a significant proportion of package bookings are still made via travel agents – who use call centres for manual bookings or the company CRS system where a tour operator link is made direct to the travel agent – the internet has become more commonplace as the rise of online companies highlighted earlier. In the USA, online bookings now account for around 30 per cent of travel bookings.

As consolidation continues to affect the European holiday market, it is no surprise to find 80 per cent of inclusive tours sold through 20 per cent of agents, with commissions paid to agents, plus an override (1–5 per cent) in addition to the basic 10 per cent for high performance. However, in 1998 Thomson cut commissions to a three-tier level, ranging from 7 per cent to 12 per cent. This has fuelled a lowering of commission levels in 2005 by the leading groups (Thomson and First Choice). The evolution of the worldwide web is placing additional pressure on selling through conventional means. This debate re-emerged in 2005 and 2006 when a number of leading tour operators cut commissions to 7 per cent for agents.

Travel agents

Distributing tourism products is intended to entice customers to purchase an offering, linking the supply with demand. In technical terms, the distribution is a system that links various tourism organizations (e.g. operators and agents) together with the objective of describing, explaining and confirming the travel arrangements to the consumer. Explaining the tourism offering to the consumer requires retailers (and operators through their brochures) to recognize, identify and incorporate the following elements of tourism:

- Tourism is intangible, meaning it is a speculative investment and an expensive purchase where the product is usually conveyed to the customer via a brochure.

- Tourism is perishable, and so can only be sold for the period it is available (it cannot be stored). This highlights the importance of last minute bookings to sell surplus capacity.
- Tourism is dynamic, meaning that it is forever in a state of flux; a product whose prices can rise and fall
- Tourism is heterogenous, meaning it is not a standardized product that is produced and delivered in a homogenous manner. It varies, and interactions can enhance or adversely affect it, since it is dependent upon people and many unknown factors.
- Tourism is inseparable, meaning that in the consumer's mind, it is purchased and consumed as an overall experience and so communicating what is being offered, its value and scope is important. Since the consumer is transported to the product, it is an unusual form of distribution, where there is a need for timely information on all of the elements as outlined in the brochure.

The traditional package holiday has normally been retailed through agents who have recognized and sold holidays with the above factors in mind. Travel agents remain a key intermediary in the distribution chain, and are characterized by many features. Some have argued that, given the impact of online retailing and home-working (people working flexibly from home to be available to clients outside the usual 9 am to 5 pm shop-based travel retailing times). The travel agent is under threat and this is discussed more fully in Chapter 10.

The evolution of travel agents

When Thomas Cook organized the first tour package by rail from Leicester to Loughborough, the age of travel retailing emerged. Travel agents were mainly independent agents, with the exception of the growing Thomas Cook outlets. Their primary role was in acting as agents selling travel tickets for rail, sea and land-based services as well as accommodation. Even in the inter-war years, travel agents retained this brokerage role, receiving a commission on each sale. The 1940s saw the emergence of air-based travel but agents had not reached a mass market. Their travel products were still oriented towards a small section of the international travelling public. The 1960s heralded the greatest changes in travel agencies, with commissions, licensing and greater airline–agency relations, particularly the sale of group travel. By developing increased levels of information, service and specialized products, agents began to become more involved in the tour operation side of travel by organizing tours and selling cruises from block allocations. During the 1970s, these changes saw many travel agents expand with the growth of package travel, basing their business on volume sales. In the 1980s and 1990s, many agencies entered into tour operating, with growing numbers of mergers and acquisitions, and consolidation. Grouping into formal alliances or consortia enabled agencies to seek greater commissions, using increased levels of technology to assist in distribution, while the high street has seen large chains emerge. Many of these changes are documented in Table 8.5, which highlights the relationship between the trading environment in the post-war period and the style of travel retailing which evolved to characterize each era.

Characteristics of travel agents

In the UK, there are around 7000 travel agency branches and 1890 travel agents, although recent closures/sales and acquisitions means that this figure is often in a state of flux. These are affiliated to their industry body ABTA, the Association of British Travel Agents. The structure of travel agents has changed over the last 20 years: consolidation has led to greater pressure on independent agents and less choice for the consumer, as multiples dominate the retailing of products. Travel agents as businesses carry no stock and act on behalf of the tour operators, so they have little financial risk and do not purchase products themselves. They receive a commission for each sale and, as agents, do not become part of the contract of sale, which is between the tour operator and the customer.

Their role is based upon the products they sell and they can be either generalist agencies selling a wide variety of products or specialist agencies selling a certain type of product. Some agencies, by virtue of their geographical location or appeal, can be low-cost, low-revenue businesses (selling low-cost packages) whilst others located in more prosperous areas can be high volume, selling high-value cruises and similar products. Other specialist agents, like Austravel, only sell long-haul travel and so are niche agents.

High street agents do not specialize in business and corporate travel, although the market for specialist agents is worth over £10.5 billion a year in the UK. One very controversial area of debate in travel agents is the process of racking: agents

Table 8.5 Changes in travel retailing (© Eric Laws, 1997: 122; Reproduced with the author's permission)

Period	Trading environment	Type of travel retailing
1950s	Limited demand for holidays or other travel Reconstruction of war-damaged city centres	Full-service travel specialists located in major urban and business centres Limited competition
1960s	Gradual increase in city centre travel retailers with the development of demand for leisure travel	Coach and other domestic holidays sold by small coach companies and through newsagents
1970s	Rapid expansion in demand for holidays	Successful retailers expand the number of outlets – proliferation of high street retailers
1980s	Development of out-of-town shopping malls and large-scale town centres Many high streets suffer from shop closures and temporary tenants	First computerized reservations system for inclusive holidays Larger travel agency chains grow by acquiring smaller 'miniples', consolidating ownership and putting pressure on independents Development of specialized holiday shops and decline of full-service travel agencies
1990s	Increasing financial pressure on travel retailers, increasing rate of acquisition and mergers	Increasingly selective racking policies Technological developments enable customers to create their own holiday packages by booking direct from home

emphasize/display certain businesses' products (perhaps their own company's in the case of integrated businesses) to favour them because of the promise of higher commissions. This perceived favouritism, often described as 'directional selling', has led the independent travel agents in the UK to launch their Campaign for Real Travel Agents, to counter this. They claim their 300 members will offer impartial, objective advice and promote smaller, independent operators' products. In contrast, the dominance of the top three groups (TUI, Thomas Cook and Going Places) highlights their control of UK travel retailing.

Ultimately, the travel agency is a physical location that offers a convenient place to purchase travel products. It provides a source of information as well as a point of sale, via booking agents. Agents' perceived expert product knowledge (often gained from training and educational trips to the destinations on sale) is seen as offering a competitive advantage, although this is becoming more problematic given the low salaries and young age profile of travel agents as well as the growing product range now available to consumers.

It is evident that travel agents cannot offer a limitless product range, since research indicates that, beyond a certain point, trying to offer too many products erodes agency profitability. As a result, specializing in a limited range of tour operators allows agents to develop product knowledge, tailor them to the markets they serve and recognize their own limitations. With the endless possibilities and knowledge available on the worldwide web, it is apparent that agents are having to compete by developing specialist knowledge and advice to maintain their competitive edge.

The organization of travel agents

Whilst the businesses in this sector can be broadly split into the independent travel agencies and the multiples who are owned and operated by tour operators and other tourism concerns, two basic principles characterize success in each: good quality customer service and management. In terms of management, controlling costs, ensuring highly motivated staff are employed and building upon a customer base through word of mouth are all critical. The independent agencies, which are manager-owned and typically employ fewer than five staff, contrast with the larger chain agencies, located in prominent high street or shopping mall locations, which have high passer-by traffic.

Travel agents typically deal with a diverse range of tasks including:

- making reservations
- planning itineraries (including complex round-the-world travel)
- calculating fares and charges
- producing tickets

- advising clients on destinations, resorts, airline companies and a wide range of travel products
- communicating with clients verbally and in writing
- maintaining accurate records on reservations
- ensuring racks are stocked well or supplies are kept in-house
- acting as intermediaries where customer complaints occur.

Not only do travel agency staff need technical skills in reading timetables, calculating fares and an ability to write tickets, they also need good interpersonal skills in closing a sale and in being able to use technology (e.g. CRS). Agents also need to be able to explain the growing complexity of air fares and the conditions attached to them in simple, plain English. An agency manager will have to be able to manage a group of staff and will also be engaged in the financial management of accounts and cash flow, the invoicing of clients and the controlling of expenditure in running the business.

Above all, it is critical to ensure all staff provide a high level of customer service so as to make sales and build the client base. To do this:

- customers must be greeted warmly, typically with a smile
- staff must ensure high standards of dress, appearance and personal grooming as customers are influenced by first impressions; their personal posture, manner and body language are also important as being alert, attentive and willing to empathize and match client needs with available products is key
- all staff must be polite and able to express themselves clearly, while always maintaining eye contact
- telephones must be answered promptly and courteously.

In selling a product, a set sequence is usually adhered to, as in Figure 8.6. This illustrates the consumer psychology of a holiday purchase, where an agent will need to gradually understand what the consumer wants, how to fulfil that demand and the type of interaction that is sought. In particular, a process of search, evaluation and re-evaluation goes on in the agency or on a return visit if the client takes away brochures to assess product offerings. The agent has a critical role to play, not necessarily in providing definitive answers, but in guiding the consumer, presenting options (and in managing their dismissal) until a suitable product is located. It is clear that this is a time-intensive undertaking and, therefore, it is apparent why

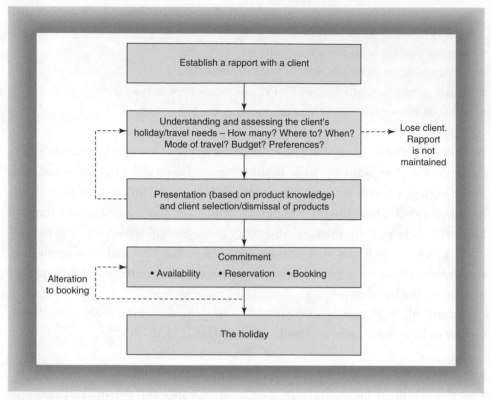

Figure 8.6   The travel agent–client purchase process

many consumers will go through this process using technology such as the world-wide web as well as using a travel agency.

Business travel

The process is somewhat different in the case of business travel, where agencies offer this service. Here the client will be looking for time savings, be less price sensitive (traditionally) and will be very demanding of time and service. Bookings are often made at short notice, sometimes outside office hours, and special help with visas and other documents will be sought. Those agents who offer a business travel service have found this a highly competitive market, and tied arrangements with companies exist. In return for agreements on a certain volume of business, a travel agency may provide a set rate of discount or charge a set management fee for all the business it handles for a company. The latter is proving to be very popular with large companies to reduce business travel costs. Contracts can be constructed in a number of ways, but above all seek to provide companies with greater cost controls on corporate travel and to reduce costs.

The Guild of Business Travel Agents, with 40 members represents, 75–80 per cent of all business air travel in the UK, which is dominated by the multiples. The key players are American Express, Carlson Wagonlit and The Travel Company. These multiples can provide substantial discounts by purchasing bulk volumes of air travel. If companies employ travel managers instead of agents, agencies are excluded. This trend is reflected in the growth of a UK professional body, the Institute of Travel Management, and further impacts on the business of travel agents. Direct links between larger businesses and airlines in global alliances are possible; so that discounted travel occurs through volume rebates. In the USA, Topaz International found business travel agents were the best source for finding cheaper airline fares, typically 19 per cent lower than internet fares. Even so, internet-based Expedia has purchased US business travel management firm Metropolitan Travel as a new IT solution for business travel. Even low-cost airlines such as easyJet have entered into agreements with business travel organizations to grow the business travel market.

Travel agents and information communication technology

In terms of information communication technology (ICT), there are a number of key elements that impact upon travel agents. ICT is designed to allow agents to access the principal's supply of products and services, process bookings and manage corporate performance, but a number of issues are evident:

- CRS are expensive for small and medium agencies to maintain, so internet bookings may be a more cost-effective medium
- CRS do not necessarily provide agents with improved business levels unless used to their full
- there is inherent bias in CRS, with airlines having to pay fees to have a presence
- new forms of technology are overtaking CRS in some market segments, such as the development of electronic agencies (e-travel agencies), the worldwide web,

direct-selling operators (known as business to consumer) and a number of operators selling discounted travel (i.e. Expedia, e-bookers and the low-cost airlines
online).

E-ticketing has emerged as a new force in global travel markets and this has the
potential to bypass the travel agent and the airlines' global distribution systems
(GDS). In Europe, Lufthansa led the way by introducing this mode of ticketless travel
with ETIX, a concept now adopted by many airlines worldwide. By 2007, all airline
tickets will be paperless. The system enables passengers with only hand luggage to
bypass long check-in counters at airports and allows consumers to buy tickets over
the internet without paper coupons. Many of the low-cost airlines adopted paperless
e-tickets to reduce administrative costs and this innovation has now permeated
global air travel. The GDS company Sabre estimated that almost 70 per cent of
its North American tickets are now issued this way, while in the UK, Galileo
(the European GDS) reported that in 2001 e-ticketing represented 10 per cent of its
business. Yet Galileo also estimate that 70 per cent of UK e-tickets are still issued
through travel agents. One response from travel agents according to Sabre is to desire
tools that will allow them to access the growing demand for online travel.

Online travel continues to grow in significance and many companies are now
expecting to see this as a major driver of their business, which does pose problems
for the travel agent if tour operators and airlines now encourage direct booking.
This has even begun to hit the new generation of online travel agents created in the
late 1990s. British Airways, for example, wants to grow its bookings online from 22
per cent in 2005 to 50 per cent by 2007, which is backed up by major marketing campaigns that will cut out the travel agent and other online agents, steering customers
to the BA.com site. In fact, in late 2005, there was evidence to suggest that around
4.5 per cent of all internet traffic was travel-related, an illustration of the rapid
growth in this area of activity, and the concerns which the travel agent sector
face (also see Chapter 10 on how new forms of agents have developed – notably
home-workers).

The future of travel retailing

In Chapter 4, the theme of disintermediation was examined, which is the ability of
tourism suppliers to use ICT to communicate direct with consumers in their home.

Box 8.2 Case study: VisitScotland.com: Destination marketing and travel retailing

As part of the growing move towards promoting destinations and linking online promotion with retailing of travel products, VisitScotland initiated the development of VisitScotland.com set up in 2002 and based in Livingston. It was set up with £7.5 million public-sector funding and with £4.5 million from its then private-sector partner, Schlumberger Sema (which subsequently sold its share to Atos.Origin). VisitScotland.com was created so that it could provide a dynamic booking service. Investment by the two partners resulted in the linking of tourism supply as an online inventory for consumers to search and book online, with a view to becoming financially viable between 2007 and 2010. In 2005, it had a £1.9 million loss and accumulated losses of £5.6 million, due to the set-up and running costs, in line with many other e-tourism ventures in their early stages. The majority of VisitScotland advertising directs consumers to book on the VisitScotland.com site. In 2004, the VisitScotland.com site had 18.7 million hits, had 317 000 bookings and was estimated to comprise 0.45 per cent of the online market in the UK. As part of the wider development of VisitScotland.com, to encourage more small business engagement and to add more capacity to the web-based booking system, VisitScotland.com has proposed a new initiative to remove the costs for small businesses of web design for accommodation providers. The 'web in the box' concept means that small businesses will be able to use a template and tailor-made solution using a website content tool. The web in the box will comprise:

- a customer management system
- a booking engine
- a database
- a MyHotel element to compile the individual web page for the business.

The innovation in the scheme is in the no commission element, with the funding of the scheme via VisitScotland.com through the credit card fee. The importance of the web in the box is in the power it provides to the individual business to become e-enabled. For bookings made on the operators' websites, no commission is charged, while any bookings made via VisitScotland.com incur a 10 per cent commission. The scheme has enormous potential in allowing a large online provider (VisitScotland.com) to allow the consumer to package the supply chain. It also illustrates a growing area of activity for destination management-based businesses like VisitScotland.com. This represents a new form of collaboration, known as c-commerce (collaborative commerce). The result is a move away from accommodation providers relying upon their own online capacity and a shift towards self-development and limiting costs in reaching a wider market.

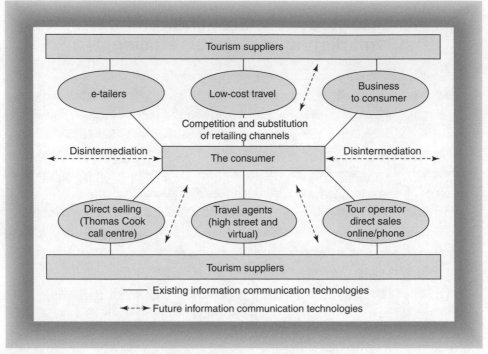

Figure 8.7   The future of travel retailing

The travel agent once had a virtual monopoly on the distribution of travel services, especially inclusive tours, but the future is still unclear. To completely eliminate the travel agent would require new ICTs to provide all of the social, economic and psychological benefits that agencies offer the travelling public. Nevertheless, they will still remain the public face of the tourism industry in a retail setting, as the range of ICT makes travel a more complex process since more options and products are available. Far from disintermediation leading to the demise of travel agencies (see Figure 8.7), it may lead to a resurgence in the holiday market as technology proves to offer too much choice, is time consuming for travellers and does not provide the psychological benefit of a brochure as a purchase. Figure 8.7 shows the existing and future forms of travel retailing, spurred on by the evolution of ICT in the reselling of travel products.

Conclusion

Travel agents will have to evaluate constantly how to protect commission levels and how to reach a highly fragmented travel market, as ICT establishes more niches. The pressure on independent travel agents in a highly competitive environment is set to continue, but new promotional tools and modes of distribution will see agents use marketing and advertising to maintain a presence. For example, rebranding holidays under agency names, such as Thomas Cook's initiative, or offering no deposit bookings; offering clients home-based sales visits; and using technology to retain face-to-face contact whilst improving ease of sales will certainly be a trend for the future. However, technology has certainly redefined the role of the agent and the tour operator with even the more traditional tour operator role in question, as dynamic packaging and low-cost airline accommodation sales challenging the traditional notion of a package holiday.

References

Holloway, J. C. (2001) *The Business of Tourism*, 6th edn. Harlow: Pearson.
Laws, E. (1997) *Managing Package Holidays*. London: Thomson Learning.

Further reading

The best sources are:
Holloway, J. C. (2006) *The Business of Tourism*, 7th edn. Harlow: Pearson.
Laws, E. (1997) *Managing Package Holidays*. London: Thomson Learning.

Questions

1 Why are tour operators important in the tourism industry? How is their role changing with the introduction of e-commerce?
2 What is a package holiday? How is it assembled and sold? What other services and support do tour operators offer their clients?
3 How do travel agents operate? What are their main roles and responsibilities? What types of services and products do they sell?
4 What is the future of the travel agent as a retailer? Will their traditional high street location be maintained?

Chapter **9**

Visitor attractions

Joanne Connell and Stephen J. Page

Learning outcomes

This chapter examines visitor attractions as a key element of both the tourist's activities and as a business activity which has specific management requirements. After reading this chapter you will understand:

- how to define and classify visitor attractions
- the marketing and management issues associated with visitor attraction development
- the importance of managing the visitor experience at attractions and future issues for tourism managers.

Introduction

Along with the transport and accommodation sector, attractions form one of the central components of tourism, providing a vital element in the visitor's enjoyment and experience. Attractions are a central element in terms of what tourists visit at destinations as well as being something they may visit en route to a destination. In many respects, they are the lifeblood of a destination, because they are part of the appeal, ambience and overall experience that visitors seek to consume in areas they visit. One of the major problems in identifying attractions is that they are patronized by tourists, but in terms of the scale and volume of visits, they are dominated by leisure and day trippers as well as local residents. In this respect the market for attractions is large and forms a vital part of the infrastructure of the destination area. Attractions provide a vital nucleus for visitor spending in destinations, and when they are linked to regeneration strategies such as that of Liverpool's European City of Culture, they can be harnessed to create a new image and help reposition the city as a place to visit. Thus, a successful attraction industry is vital for a healthy tourism sector so that visitors have sufficient opportunity to undertake visits and to spend during their stay.

Not surprisingly, attractions are also a major draw for many visitors, and urban regeneration strategies by public- and private-sector agencies have pinned future tourism development around such hubs of visitor attraction activity. The process by which attractions may be integrated into urban regeneration strategies is shown in Figure 9.1. This shows that when an area or destination has declined, intervention by the private sector and public-sector agencies can create a new focus, by pump-priming (i.e. stimulating redevelopment through incentives and through the development of infrastructure) to attract new investment. In principle this is not dissimilar to the resort lifecycle, discussed in Chapter 2, which is based on the marketing concept of the product lifecycle. In many successful urban regeneration schemes where tourism has been a key component (e.g. Cardiff Bay in Wales, which was Europe's largest urban regeneration scheme), visitor attractions and the creation of a visitor environment around these attractions has contributed to the success of the regeneration scheme. In the case of Cardiff, locating a number of major anchor projects (i.e. flagship projects of national and international significance) together with supporting tourist infrastructure (i.e. accommodation, transport, retailing and restaurants) has enabled a new visitor destination to emerge around the attractions. Yet one of the main problems in examining visitor attractions is in defining what comprises an attraction.

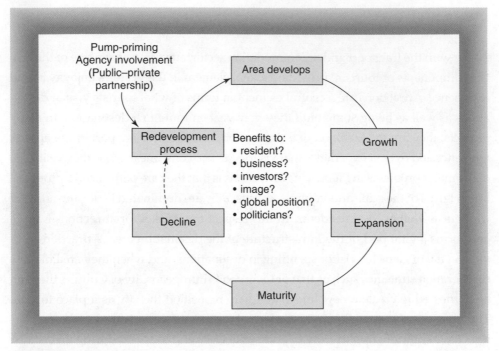

Figure 9.1 Tourism and regeneration

Classifying visitor attractions

Within tourism studies, the issue of defining visitor attractions has proved difficult due to the diversity of users (tourists, residents, day trippers) who provide a marker broader than just tourists. As a result many researchers acknowledge that this diverse client base makes the most appropriate term to use 'visitor attractions'. One useful definition used by the National Tourism Organizations in the UK outlines the scope of an attraction as:

> Where the main purpose is sightseeing. The attraction must be a permanent established excursion destination, a primary purpose of which is to allow access for entertainment, interest or education; rather than being primarily a retail outlet or a venue for sporting, theatrical or film performances. It must be open to the public, without prior booking, for published periods each year, and should be capable of attracting day visitors or tourists as well as local residents. In addition, the attraction must be a single business, under a

single management, so that it is capable of answering the economic questions on revenue, employment … (VisitScotland, 2004: 8)

The scope helps to show how the sector incorporates a diverse range of attractions that combine to cater for visitors. However, it is also a somewhat restrictive and narrow definition because it does not acknowledge the significance of other elements of attractions including:

- The role of shopping as a key activity and drawcard for tourists, especially the diverse elements of the retail experience (i.e. shopping malls, markets, farmers' markets) which are an attraction in their own right. As Table 9.1 shows, London has 42 markets, promoted by Transport for London and London Underground as a Real London Markets brand. This is reflected in the way the Real London Markets' brochure conveys the atmosphere, image and character of the locality:

  > there are so many reasons to visit, whether it's to savour the sights and smells of the Caribbean, the lure of finding that bargain antique or second-hand book or hearing the wit of a Cockney trader. When you've worked up a hunger from browsing and haggling, stop for a while to eat at an authentic pie and mash shop or snack on a falafel or crepe, before continuing your journey from stall to stall (Real London Markets, 2002: 2)

  In fact, the Gretna Green Outlet Village on the main tourist route between England and Scotland attracts over a million visitors a year, illustrating the scale of demand for a visitor retail experience.
- Events and festivals held on a periodic, non-permanent or one-off basis have an enormous potential to build the tourism capacity of a destination. They may also stimulate investment in tourism infrastructure to accommodate the short- or long-term impact of growth in demand. The most notable example is the Olympic Games, discussed in Box 4.2.
- The imagery created by using destinations as film or television locations can not only stimulate regional, national and global tourist interest, but also lead to a sudden influx of visitors. Some recent examples include filming the *Lord of the Rings* trilogy in New Zealand and *Harry Potter* in the UK, with some tourism

Table 9.1 Street markets as visitor attractions: London (developed from Transport for London and London Underground, 2002, *Real London Markets*. London: Transport for London)

Name of market	Speciality
Central London	
Covent Garden	Converted market with antiques and crafts and a piazza with performers and buskers
The Courtyard, St Martin in the Fields	Ceramics and arts
Gray's Antique Market	Antiques
Berwick Street, Soho	Food
Charing Cross Collectors' Fair	Flea market
London Silver Vaults	Silverware
North London	
Camden Market, Camden Lock	Clothing and all types of items
Camden Passage	Antiques
Chapel Market, Islington	Various
Nags Head, Seven Sisters	Various
Wembley	Clothing and various
Hampstead Community Market	Various
East London	
Petticoat Lane, Aldgate	Clothing
Spitalfields	Books, fabrics, clothing and food
Billingsgate Fish Market, Isle of Dogs	Fish
Columbia Road Flower Market	Flowers
Brick Lane (The Lane)	Various
Leadenhall Market	Food
Smithfield Market	Wholesale meat
Ridley Road Market (Dalston Market)	Various
Leather Lane	Various
Roman Road Market	Various
Whitechapel Market	Various
Hackney Stadium	Second-hand goods
Walthamstow Market	Various
Kingsland Waste (The Waste)	Second-hand goods
South London	
Borough Market	Food
Bermondsey Market	Antiques

(*Continued*)

Table 9.1 (*Continued*)

Name of market	Speciality
East Street Market	Caribbean foods
Brixton Market	Handicrafts
Greenwich Market	Clothing and jewellery
Gabriel's Wharf	Clothing
New Covent Garden Flower Market	Flowers
Merton Abbey Mills Market	Weekend market
Riverside Market	Second-hand books
West London	
Bayswater Road Market	Art laid out on pavement
Chelsea Antiques Market	Antiques
Portobello Market	Antiques, clothing and jewellery
Shepherd's Bush Market	Local ethnic market (Afro-Caribbean dimension)
London Farmers' Markets, Notting Hill Gate	Fresh food from farms within 100 miles of London
North End Road, Fulham	Food
Church Street and Bell Street	Various

Various – a variety of food, clothing and mixed retailing.
Note: There are also other famous London markets, some smaller and not easily accessible by London Underground, and some that are a major draw for leisure shopping, such as Romford market in Essex. The above table is illustrative rather than all-inclusive.

organizations harnessing these media images to create tourism associations with the area, its attractions and the film tourism potential. For example, in northern Scotland, the BBC series *Monarch of the Glen* led to the branding of an area as Monarch of the Glen Country.

- The geographical elements of a destination (termed 'GeoTourism') take the geological features of a region as the attraction and rationale for visiting. A unique landscape, such as lava flow (the Giant's Causeway in Ireland), effects of sand-based weathering of sandstone in western Australia (Bungle Bungle) or the white cliffs of Dover have powerful associations that create the attraction of the destination. Man-made elements in the region, such as local food and wine, crafts and vernacular (in the regional architectural style) buildings along with human elements such as the cultures of indigenous peoples also feature in defining the attraction of an area or destination.

Consequently, a broader definition of the term 'attraction' incorporates a wider range of locations as Pearce (1991: 46) suggests: 'A tourist attraction is a named site with a specific human or natural feature which is the focus of visitor and management attention.'

It is important to differentiate an attraction from a destination, since attractions are normally single units with a specific geographical focus. A destination may be based on a series of attractions, as the example of Cardiff Bay's regeneration illustrated earlier. However, there are exceptions to this, such as Walt Disney World, Orlando, that can be classified as a destination with an attraction and cluster of serviced accommodation. One of the perennial problems in studying visitor attractions is the global paucity of research data that measures visitor volumes at attractions. Even where data exist, they are rarely collected on a similar basis, making international comparisons problematic. One starting point in seeking to establish the basis of the scale and volume of visitor attractions in any destination or area is to seek to classify attractions.

There are three ways to consider the scope of attractions:

1 *Natural or man-made attractions,* such as a National Park (natural) or the Tower of London (man-made). Natural attractions may be further divided into whether they are managed or left in a natural state.
2 Holloway (2001) identifies attractions that can be *nodal or linear in character.* A nodal attraction may be a capital city, such as London, Rome or Paris, that is the focus of the visit and an attraction in its own right – a feature which many tourism organizations utilize in place-marketing strategies by using icons that reflect the place's image (e.g. the Eiffel Tower as representing Paris). The linear resource most widely used by visitors is the coastal resort. Linear resorts act as attractions in their own right (e.g. Blackpool's Illuminations, which attract visitors to the town in the shoulder season; £2 million is spent on promoting this attraction, which can be dated back to 1912). A number of other UK seaside resorts have also used similar schemes very successfully, such as Southend in the 1950s and 1960s.
3 The differentiation between *sites as locations, permanent attractions and special events.* Special events are temporary and short-term, and may be constructed or natural (see www.festivals.com for a global listing of festivals and events by category and a listing of the most unusual sporting events).

Many classifications and categorizations of attractions exist. One of the most interesting classifications is that developed by the English Tourism Council (now

VisitEngland) which identifies the following attraction types and is a commonly used system of classification:

- cathedral and churches
- country parks
- farms
- gardens
- historic houses and castles
- other historic properties
- leisure and theme parks
- museums and galleries
- steam railways
- visitor centres
- wildlife attractions and zoos.

The physical environment is also important, since attractions can be located in the:

- natural environment, such as forests, mountains and other natural settings
- built environment that has been adapted for visitor use (e.g. workplaces and historic houses)
- built environment that has been designed for visitors.

Walsh-Heron and Stevens (1990: 2) confirm and expand the function of a visitor attraction, defined as a place, venue or focus of activity. The elements of a visitor attraction are that it:

- sets out to attract visitors (day visitors from resident and tourist population) and is managed accordingly
- provides a pleasurable experience and an enjoyable way for customers to spend their leisure time
- is developed to achieve this goal
- is managed as an attraction, providing satisfaction to customers
- provides an appropriate level of facilities and services to meet and cater to the demands, needs and interests of its visitors
- may or may not charge an admission fee.

Points of particular interest from Walsh-Heron and Stevens's list are that attractions have a psychological element – they provide a pleasurable experience and give satisfaction to visitors – as well as an appropriate level of services. Walsh-Heron and Stevens (1990: 3) define further criteria relating to management that assist in defining whether an enterprise is an attraction. The criteria are that:

management must: perceive and recognise itself to be a tourist attraction; promote and market the attraction publicly; provide on-site management and staffing; and be recognised as a 'tourist attraction' by the visitor.

Visitor attractions in the UK: Recent trends and patterns

The UK has amongst the most accessible data on visitor attractions, and whilst it is not representative of all countries, we can use it to trace trends and patterns. A comparison of the UK data on paid attractions for 2001 and 2004 (Table 9.2 and Table 9.3) illustrates that, in almost every case, the volume of visits has increased marginally or declined 2001–2004. As *Visitor Attraction Trends: England 2004* reported, in 2004 the summer, traditionally the peak season for visitor attractions, was wet. This contributed to the fall in visits in the paid attraction sector. Overall, the larger attractions (i.e. those with over 20 000 visits a year) received a modest

Table 9.2 Top paid-admission attractions in the UK, 2001 (modified and developed from English Tourism Council, 2002)

Attraction	Visitor numbers
London Eye	3 850 000
Tower of London	2 019 210
Eden Project	1 700 000
Natural History Museum, London	1 696 176
Legoland	1 632 000
Victoria and Albert Museum	1 446 344
Science Museum, London	1 352 649
Flamingo Land Theme Park and Zoo	1 322 000
Windermere Lake Cruises	1 241 918
Canterbury Cathedral	1 151 099

growth of 2 per cent in visitor numbers 2003–2004. As Tables 9.2 and 9.3 show, London and south-east England dominate the list of top attractions which receive over a million visits a year; even so, some 45 per cent of attractions in England reported an increase in revenue 2003–2004 according to *Visitor Attraction Trends: England 2004*. The most notable change 2001–2004 is in the free admission category (Tables 9.4 and 9.5) after the UK Department for Media, Culture and Sport announced that admission to the national museums and galleries would be free (December 2001).

The philosophy underpinning this policy shift was informed by a desire to make these attractions more socially inclusive, to attract more visits from social groups D and E. In the period December 2001–June 2002, these attractions saw a 62 per cent increase in visitor numbers to seven million, a 2.7 million increase. Yet, as Martin (2003) argued, these additional visits have not materialized from the social classes D and E. The profile of museum and gallery visitors has remained fairly static, being dominated by social groups ABC, although in numerical terms more social groups D and E have visited such attractions. Social exclusion among groups D and E has not been addressed, the reasons for which are cost of travel to cultural attractions, traditional leisure habits, lack of awareness of free admission, and geographical proximity to the attractions, since visits are dominated by those living in London and the south-east.

Table 9.3 Top paid-admission attractions in the UK, 2004
(*adaped from Visitor Attraction Trends: England 2004*)

Attraction	Visitor numbers
London Eye	3 700 000
Tower of London	2 139 366
Pleasureland Theme Park	2 109 000
Pleasure Beach, Great Yarmouth	1 500 000
Flamingo Land Theme Park and Zoo	1 380 110
Legoland	1 369 308
Windermere Lake Cruises	1 289 866
New Metroland	1 250 000
Eden Project	1 223 959
Chester Zoo	1 161 684
Drayton Manor Family Theme Park	1 100 000

Table 9.4 Top free-admission attractions in the UK, 2001 (modified and developed from English Tourism Council, 2002)

Attraction	Visitor numbers
Blackpool Pleasure Beach	6 500 000
National Gallery	4 918 985
British Museum	4 800 000
Tate Modern	3 551 885
Pleasureland Theme Park	2 100 000
Clacton Pier	1 750 000
York Minster	1 600 000
Pleasure Beach, Great Yarmouth	1 500 000
National Portrait Gallery	1 269 819
Poole Pottery	1 063 499

Table 9.5 Top free-admission attractions in the UK, 2004 (adapted from *Visitor Attraction Trends: England 2004*)

Attraction	Visitor numbers
Blackpool Pleasure Beach	6 200 000
Albert Dock, Liverpool	5 000 000
National Gallery	4 959 946
British Museum	4 868 127
Tate Modern	4 441 225
Natural History Museum	3 240 344
Xscape Castelford	2 800 000
Science Museum	2 154 366
Victoria and Albert Museum	2 010 825
Eastbourne Pier	1 550 000

Visits to free attractions since 2001 have attracted a greater volume of visitors than paid attractions which in itself brings problems of management and planning for these sites. For example, in 2001–2002, the Victoria and Albert Museum experienced a 157 per cent increase in visitors after free admission was introduced although, as Martin (2003) observed, visitors gaining free admission were more likely to give a donation, buy a guidebook and spend money visiting a special exhibition. Even so, the Natural History Museum had noted that a large proportion of visitors were spending no more than when admission charges were in place. This may call into question the viability of such a scheme if central government funding penalizes those large attractions which successfully attract high visitor numbers yet this does not convert to a major increase in visitor spending.

The visitor attraction market 2001–2004 did not see massive growth in the attractions charging for admission, whilst the flagship free attractions that stopped charging (e.g. the Victoria and Albert Museum, Science Museum and Natural History Museum) have seen visitor numbers almost double in most cases, posing major visitor management dilemmas. In 2004, the top five visitor attractions in the UK in terms of visitor volumes and eight of the top eleven attractions all had free admission. Despite the problems of classifying attractions, Table 9.6 does provide data for a number of European comparisons. This highlights the diversity of the attraction classifications by country and problems of drawing parallels in each country, as well as the broad product basis of many European visitor attractions, to which attention now turns.

Visitor attractions: Product considerations

Visitor attractions offer both products and experiences. One of the main management issues for visitor attraction operators is matching the product to the benefits sought by the consumer. Kotler's (1994) view is that products consist of three levels (Figure 9.2), and Swarbrooke (2002) argued that this may be adapted to a visitor attraction setting. The core product is the central component and comprises the main benefits that will be identified by the visitor as a motivation for visiting. The second layer of a product is the tangible aspect, which visitors can purchase. The third aspect of a product is the augmented product, which includes the additional services a visitor receives and makes up the total product.

Gunn (1988) also conceptualized a tourist attraction in a way where the product basis can be considered. Gunn identified three zones in relation to the spatial layout of an attraction, the nuclei contains the core attraction and the zone of closure contains the ancillary services associated with the attraction, such as shops, car park and tea room. The inviolate belt is an area that protects the core product from the commercialized areas of the zone of closure (Figure 9.3). A more detailed

Table 9.6 Profile of visitor attractions in selected European countries (compiled from Scottish Enterprise and Highlands and Islands Enterprise *New Horizons: International Benchmarking and Best Practice for Visitor Attractions*, 2001, Scottish Enterprise, Glasgow and www.scotexchange.com, Know Your Market section)

Ireland

There are 397 visitor attractions, of which 297 are fee paying and 118 are free. Of the fee-paying attractions, 70 per cent have been developed since 1984, with 40 per cent (104) developed since 1989.

Much of the stimulus for development has been linked to government planning and EU structural funding from the Operational Programme for Tourism. This was designed to increase the competitive position of the tourism sector, and many of the projects have a strong cultural and historical linkage. Estimates are of IR£450 million of investment in tourist facilities, training and marketing in Ireland during 1989–1993.

The attractions are dominated by historic houses and castles which account for 35 per cent of visits, with 80 per cent of attractions providing craft and bookshop facilities. A further 60 per cent have food and beverage facilities. Up to 65 per cent of visitors to Ireland felt an attraction was a major reason for visiting the country.

The volume of visitor demand was 8.6 million visits in 1995, with 37 per cent of visitors from Europe, 14 per cent North America and 12 per cent UK. In terms of visitor numbers 5 per cent of attractions had 150 000 visitors or more; 4 per cent had 100 000–150 000; 10 per cent, 50 000–100 000; 31 per cent, 10 000–50 000; 50 per cent, up to 10 000.

Denmark

There are 100 attractions with over 50 000 visitors a year and approximately 200 attractions with over 20 000 visitors a year. Those with lower than 20 000 visitors are not recorded but the Danish Tourist Board estimate that there are about 500 such attractions. In total the visitor attraction sector receives 30 million visits a year.

The supply of visitor attractions comprises 75 art museums; 181 museums of cultural history; 58 zoos and wildlife parks; 41 amusement parks; 8 aqua domes; 118 golf courses; 81 castles and country houses. A further 1800 sq. km of conservation areas exist and 3000 km of cycle routes.

The majority of attractions are funded by the public sector, with 80 per cent of the top 100 attractions funded by the public sector. Entrance charges apply to the majority of museums but these are low.

(Continued)

Table 9.6 (*Continued*)

The government funded Labour Market Holiday Foundation has funded 30 new attractions, based on a 12.5 per cent tax on employee wages. It has equated to £44 million investment.

In the last five years a 10–12 per cent growth in attraction visitor numbers has occurred at the fifty largest attractions. The majority of visitation is from the domestic market, which accounts for 85–90 per cent of visitors.

The Netherlands

There are around 1150 attractions listed in the national museums guide as well as other visitor attractions, with the world's greatest concentration of museums per sq. metre. Amsterdam alone has 62 museums.

Museums are operated by the public sector and not for profit bodies, with 400 museums part of the Nederlandse Museumvereniging (Museums Association).

Many attractions are highly specialized and most open all year round. All attractions charge for admission.

The top seven attractions have over a million visitors a year. A 140 per cent growth in visitation occurred 1985–1995 according to the Dutch National Tourism Organization, driven by new attractions, events and some growth at existing sites. Much of this is urban-based, especially in the Randstadt (the ringed city urban agglomeration that includes Amsterdam, Rotterdam and The Hague).

France

There are 40 000 monuments, 4000 prestigious sites and 4000 museums.

France is the world's leading international tourism destination, so the diversity of attractions is not surprising. There is a strong linkage to national and regional tourism development plans. The operation of public–private sector partnerships underpins development together with state funding for high-risk innovative projects. All successful projects, with a few exceptions, are state funded and linked to economic regeneration.

French visitor attractions are classified in the state tourism agency guide into caves and caverns; villages of character; gardens; zoos and botanical gardens; rural museums; river tourism; and railway tourism. This is certainly different to the many other classifications.

The market for visitor attractions is largely domestic, since 80 per cent of French take their holidays within France.

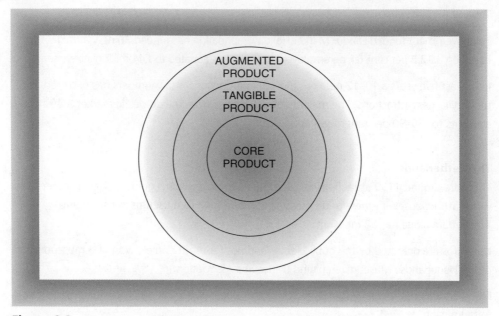

Figure 9.2   The three levels of a product (modified from Kotler, 1994)

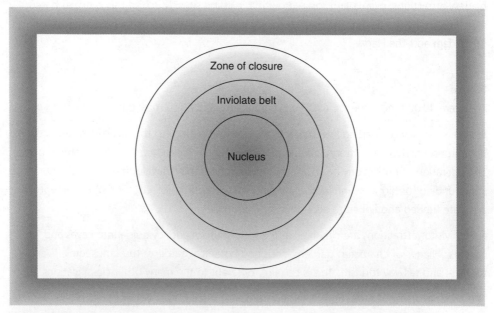

Figure 9.3   Gunn's model of a tourist attraction (based on Gunn, 1972, © 1972, *Tourism Planning*, C. Gunn. Reproduced by permission of Taylor & Francis, Inc., http://www.routledge-ny.com)

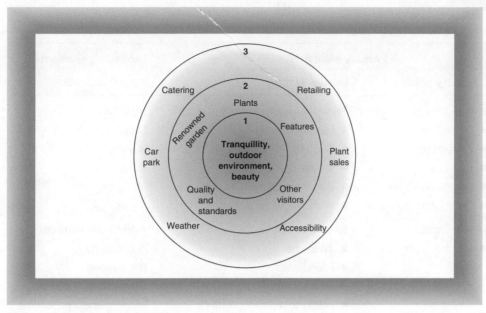

Figure 9.4 A garden as a visitor attraction product (© Jo Connell, reproduced with permission from the author)

model of attractions as products can be applied, as Figure 9.4 shows in the case of a historic garden such as Kew Gardens in London, where three levels of a garden visitor attraction product exist.

Attractions as a leisure product

Jansen-Verbeke (1986) developed a framework with which to analyse tourism visits to places and these ideas can be applied to attractions. Still focusing on the idea of a garden as a visitor attraction, the application of the leisure product idea is useful in helping to understand how the structure and presentation of visitor attractions can be analysed from a product perspective. As Table 9.7 shows, the facilities which gardens offer can be divided into primary elements, secondary elements and additional elements. While the range of elements available in gardens will vary, the framework identifies the scope of characteristics and facilities. This can also be applied to areas of cities such as London's West End where the leisure product can be constructed. However, such products will also have a life cycle.

Table 9.7 The categorization of the garden as a leisure product (source: © Jo Connell, reproduced with permission from the author)

Primary elements		Secondary elements
Activity place	**Leisure setting**	
Leisure interest facilities:	*Physical characteristics*:	Tea room
● Guided walks	● Design	Shop
● Exhibitions	● Planting	Nursery
● Routes	● Garden features	Seats
● Self-guided trails	● Garden buildings	
● Events and festivals	● Water features	
Physical features:	*Social features*:	**Additional elements:**
● Children's play area	● Welcome	Accessibility
	● Friendliness	Car parking
	● Helpfulness	Signposting
	● Ability to answer questions	Foreign language leaflets
	● Ambience	Information
	● Health and safety considerations	Plant labels

Visitor attractions and the product life cycle

Within marketing, there is a widely accepted notion that products will evolve through time and follow a specific product life cycle (see Figure 9.5) that was adapted from marketing and applied to tourism, as the discussion of the resort life cycle in Chapter 2 suggested. For purpose-designed visitor attractions, the life-cycle concept is quite relevant. However, for those attractions that were not originally designed for visitation, Swarbrooke (2002) believes that the model is of less relevance because it is difficult to identify the start of the introduction phase. Motivations for opening may be based on the need to derive extra revenue for maintenance or conservation work and the attraction market is not viewed as the core business. For example, the 'core business' of the National Trust in England and Wales is conservation and education, not running visitor attractions, but it needs visitors to fund its work. However, it is still pertinent for operators of such attractions to be aware of market changes as it becomes more difficult to attract visitors in a market characterized by oversupply of attractions.

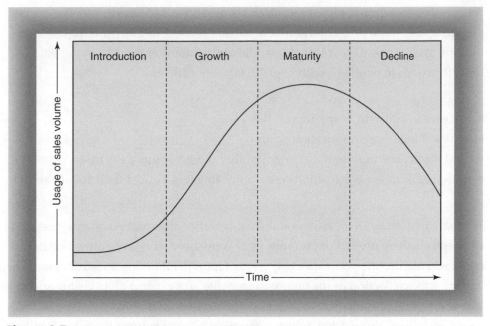

Figure 9.5   The product life cycle (reprinted from *The Development and Management of Visitor Attractions*, J. Swarbrooke, 51, © 2002 with permission from Elsevier)

In a Scottish context, research by Lennon (2001) noted that those attractions that had invested and diversified their product base through retail areas (e.g. merchandising), were receiving additional benefits in relation to visitor spending at attractions. In Scotland the average dwell time at an attraction was two hours and forty-two minutes, although this comprised eighty minutes at the attraction; twenty minutes' retailing; twenty-eight minutes at a catering outlet and thirty-four minutes at other elements of the operation. Therefore, by developing a broader product base attractions were seeking to expand the dwell time at their site. The significance of attractions is illustrated in that almost 6000 full-time employees work in Scottish visitor attractions, with almost 3000 unpaid volunteers helping at trusts and other sites. This illustrates the economic potential of broadening the product base in expanding employment opportunities.

A crucial fact to acknowledge in the management of visitor attractions is that the long-term quality of the product and the visitor experience can be adversely affected by external and internal threats. Consequently, a strategy to focus efforts in managing potential impacts from the internal environment (i.e. within the attraction itself) can assist a visitor attraction in striving towards a viable future.

As research by Lennon (2001) found, the competition for leisure spending across the attraction, retail and entertainment sectors has led to a distinct visitor attraction life cycle. Lennon found that the following pattern emerged among paid and free attractions in Scotland with over 10 000 visitors a year:

- in Years 1–2 growth is apparent
- in Year 3 a decline in visitation occurs
- paid attractions maintain a greater stability in visitor numbers up to Year 4
- non-paid admission attractions see decline in Years 3 and 4 then stabilization.

Yet a range of attraction operators and their operational activities and business strategy explains this pattern. For example, there were those who saw a attraction decline cycle, where a decline set in after two years of growth following initial opening. The decline was a reflection of the failure to innovate and expand their visitor offering, and was typical of many public-sector operations in Scotland. In contrast, a series of Year 4 revivalists also existed, which underwent a major refurbishment or reinvestment to nurture visitor interest again. A further attraction type was also discerned in terms of the constant innovators, where attractions constantly re-invest, seek to diversify their product offering, upgrade their facilities and pump-prime the attraction life-cycle model by intervening through ongoing reinvestment.

Stevens (1991: 110) notes that attractions provide a 'consumer product which is based upon the unique experience and immediate point of sale consumption', the implication of which is the need to emphasize visitor care. A clear understanding of the nature of the visitor experience and how it can be enhanced to achieve high levels of visitor satisfaction, according to the type of attraction and types of visitor, are variables over which owners/managers can have a greater degree of control in relation to the management of the attraction.

Visitor attractions and the visitor experience

Swarbrooke (2002) comments that the visitor attraction product is now usually viewed as an experience. The visitor experience is a somewhat nebulous concept because it is a complex amalgam of factors that shape the tourist's feelings and attitude towards his or her visit. The visitor experience is likely to be different for each individual visitor as it forms through a series of value judgements based on emotional and physical responses to a site, and resulting in satisfaction/dissatisfaction with one or more components of the site.

The visitor experience at attractions: Key influences

Yale (1997) states that the success of a tourist attraction lies in four critical areas:

1 accessibility
2 opening hours
3 on-site amenities, such as parking, visitor centre, signs and labels, shops, guides, refreshments, toilets, litter bins, seating and disabled provision
4 off-site amenities, such as signposting, local accommodation and local services.

Swarbrooke (2002) identified four key factors that influence the success of attractions:

1 the organization and its resources
2 the product
3 the market
4 the management of the attraction (see Table 9.8).

An intangible quality or '*magic*' is necessary, as well as highly professional management and innovative concepts.

Swarbrooke (2002) asserts that a range of elements affect the visitor experience on site beyond the core focus of the attraction. These elements include: the tangible elements of the product (such as retail outlets, cafes, toilet facilities and site cleanliness), the service delivery elements (including the appearance, attitudes, behaviour and competence of staff), the expectation, behaviour and attitude of the visitor and a number of factors that are largely outside the control of either the attraction or visitor, such as climatic conditions and the mix of people using the attraction at one time. The visitor experience is the combination and interrelationship of these factors and will be different for each individual visitor.

Design issues, such as signposting and seating provision, present an image of the attraction to the visitor that may or may not be favourable. Thus the contemporary management of an attraction can influence the visitor experience through design

Table 9.8 Factors influencing the success of tourist attractions (after Swarbrooke, 2002)

The organization and its resources	Experience of developing and managing attractions	Financial resources	Marketing – see the management of the attraction				
The product	Novel approach or new idea	Location	On-site attraction	High quality environment	Good customer service	Visitor facilities	Value for money
The market	Growth markets – targeting markets which are likely to expand						
The management of the attraction	Experienced professional managers	Adequate attention to market research	Realizing that marketing is not just about brochures and adverts	Long-term strategic view	Accepting importance of word-of-mouth	Planned marketing strategy with proper financing	Staff training

and resource issues. As important as the physical management of the site are customer care and the acknowledgement of the crucial relationship between the staff, the service and the needs of the visitor. Each element is important and a lack of care – whether it is in the signage, car parking, quality of catering or cleanliness of the toilets – can destroy the overall visitor experience.

Visitor responses to perceived levels of crowding and impacts on the resource base materialize in terms of dissatisfaction with the site or, indeed, displacement of the visitor. In reality, the tourist experience at an attraction is likely to be affected by a wide range of factors, some of which are inevitably not linked with the destination *per se* but hinge on the mood and personal circumstance of the visitor. The experience is also likely to be affected by the expectations and preconceived ideas that the visitor may possess prior to a visit, as well as the cultural origin of the visitor and prior socialization. The recognition of these individual factors reflects previous consumer product experience or expectations, which influence the satisfaction/dissatisfaction process. It is impossible to control all the factors relating to the visit experience and it should be recognized that, while a visitor may be completely satisfied with the core product and the tangible service elements, an external factor, such as the weather or transport infrastructure, might spoil the experience. In addition, it is also worth noting that success in attraction development, particularly within a defined tourism region, can be dependent upon how the various sites are linked together through marketing and information to visitors. Providing brochures and advertising that create an awareness of visit opportunities can help to spread visitors across a region, especially when there is major investment at an attraction to stimulate tourism development.

Creating clusters of attractions can be successful, as with the regeneration of Stirling's old town through the public- and private-sector Stirling Initiative over the last 20 years. This used the drawcard of Stirling Castle, and a number of other attractions were created to fit a heritage theme to add to the range of heritage experiences (e.g. the Old Town Jail, Argyll's Lodgings and newly opened Tolbooth Art Centre). Other large-scale projects such as the Falkirk Wheel certainly assist in spreading the visitor impact and spending away from the 80 per cent currently focused on the Stirling region as well as creating a new destination in this case in the Forth Valley area.

Attractions, when integrated into the product, can provide tangible economic impacts for the locality and tourism economy. Visitor spending at these attractions is often viewed as the basis of their contribution to the economy; for the visitor they may be the reason for visiting a destination. Bilbao's Guggenheim Museum has provided the catalyst for a growth in visitor activity and spending in a locality which did not historically have a highly developed tourism sector. Such iconic attractions can also create a 'must-visit' trend amongst certain segments of the tourism market (cultural tourists in the case of the Guggenheim). In Edinburgh, the location of the Royal Yacht Britannia at Leith combined with the development of Ocean Point retail complex has created a new nucleus for visitor activity and visitor spending in an area that has hitherto not been associated with tourism. Similarly, the economic impact of hosting events is often cited by developing organ-ization as a prime motive for progressing an attraction project. This is particularly apparent in one of the world's most ambitious attempts to develop an economy based on tourism: in Dubai, with unusual attractions requiring one of the largest injections of capital into attraction projects globally. For this reason, Box 9.1 outlines how Dubai has harnessed tourism and attractions to create a world-class tourism destination in a desert environment.

Box 9.1 Case study: Using visitor attractions to develop tourism: The case of Dubai

Dubai, part of the United Arab Emirates, has attracted worldwide attention for its ambi-tious plans to create itself as a future global city. It is not only home to one of the world's largest architectural experiments, but is also seeking to create a modern tourist destin-ation with iconic attractions. For example, in 1999, Dubai opened Burjun Al-Arab, a 56-storey hotel (the largest in the world) constructed from a soil-like material. Dubai is seeking to develop a future economy that will not be dependent upon oil revenue, and where inward investment and tourism will coexist. There is a current boom in second-home purchases and inward investment in real estate. The world project off the coast of Dubai, a waterfront environment in the desert, is creating the seemingly impossible – a tourist attraction in the hostile environment of the desert.

   At the heart of the destination's expansion from a transport perspective has been Emirates Airline, with its massive expansion plans, routing long-haul travel via Dubai and as a final destination. The country aims to attract 15 million tourists by 2010, and the US$15 billion expansion of Emirates Airline fleet and US$4 billion expansion of Dubai International Airport are part of the infrastructure to facilitate that growth. Currently tourism accounts for

12 per cent of Dubai's GDP, based on the 4.7 million visitors in 2002. Yet with 1.5 billion people in easy travelling distance, Dubai has set ambitious tourism growth targets. Currently, Arab visitors comprise 38 per cent of arrivals, although the greatest growth has been in European leisure travellers. Some of the existing growth has been due to sporting events and hotel capacity has risen from 167 hotels in 1993 to almost 300 in 2005. But to drive tourism growth, Dubai recognizes it needs world-class visitor attractions as part of its tourism capacity, and it has identified the need to develop capacity around the following themes:

- ecotourism
- shopping
- sport
- culture
- conferences and exhibitions.

The flagship project to drive this growth is a visitor experience – Dubailand, comprising 45 tourism, leisure and entertainment projects. Dubailand is a US$5 billion, 180 million square foot project that will appeal to a diverse range of visitors. The initial phase of development will last to 2010 and will be divided into six lands: Downtown, Ecotourism World, Retail World, Attractions World, Sports World and Leisure World.

Aside from the engineering challenges and willingness to build the unimaginable in the desert (similar to Las Vegas), the 145 million square foot of five theme parks makes this the largest visitor attraction development scheme in the world. The 1.5 billion people within two hours' flight of Dubai is seen as the prime market for these projects: Emirates Airline serves 145 destinations. These are 30 tax-free shopping malls, and the ongoing investment in Dubai, plus the fact it is a stopover location for Europe–Australasia flights, has made it a thriving tourist resort. It is a good example of a supply-led development, with the ambition both to have the 'wow' factor and to amaze visitors at the destination's achievements.

Managing the visitor experience: Potential and prospects

Two main factors underpin the need to ensure customers are satisfied with their visit experience. First, visitor satisfaction can encourage regular and repeat visits, and this is more cost effective than seeking new visitors. Second, positive word-of-mouth recommendations work in the favour of attraction operators since minimal marketing input is required to attract new visitors. Word of mouth can work inversely too and the communication of bad experiences to friends and family is likely to influence visit decision-making negatively. Managing the visitor experience is a vital, although complex requirement in the operation of a visitor attraction and it is essential for attraction owners/managers to recognize the significance of the visit/visitor experience in sustaining visitor satisfaction and, inevitably, visitor numbers (see Table 9.8). Understanding the visitor experience is a key factor in determining the success of a visitor attraction, and has wider implications for the public perception of specific attractions as day-trip destinations.

A number of models have been developed to evaluate quality and customer satisfaction in business operations, the most notable of which is SERVQUAL (Parasuraman, Zeithmal and Berry, 1985). Considered a seminal study in consumer behaviour, the basis of this evaluative framework is the difference between consumer expectation and perception of service, based on five generic service-quality dimensions necessary for customer satisfaction (see Table 9.9). Parasuraman *et al.* (1985) identified five gaps between service providers and consumers, but later work suggested that another gap existed – that between the customer's and the provider's perception of the experience. These issues form the basis for managing the visitor at attractions and have to be viewed alongside future trends and issues affecting visitor attractions (also see Chapter 10 for more detail on service provision and the management of tourism experiences).

The future for visitor attraction management

It is widely recognized that a range of factors impact upon the success or failure of visitor attractions to operate as tourism enterprises. This must be viewed against the visitor's growing expectations during their visit and the need for attractions to improve standards in many countries worldwide. It also involves the need for attractions to refresh their products in order to retain their market share. Even though some operate as trusts and are based in the not-for-profit sector, their future survival depends upon managing their assets and enterprise in an efficient and robust manner so that visitors are attracted and they remain viable in an increasingly competitive environment globally. Some of the key factors that

Table 9.9 Dimensions of service quality based on the SERVQUAL principle

Reliability	Ability to perform services dependably
Responsiveness	Willingness to assist customers and provide prompt service
Assurance	Courtesy, trustworthiness and knowledge of staff
Empathy	Display caring attitude to customers
Tangibles	Presentation of physical facilities

will shape visitor attractions in the future have been identified by Swarbrooke (2001) as:

- coping with the scale and diversity of competition, especially in the leisure market
- recruiting, rewarding and retaining staff
- staying ahead of developments in marketing
- recognizing the role of marketing consortia in achieving economies of cost in advertising
- satisfying consumers
- meeting the needs of special groups of visitors such as the disabled
- offering unique selling propositions and the 'wow' factor at attractions to appeal to visitors.

Many of these factors can be grouped into a number of categories of challenges for the future:

1 product development and innovation
2 marketing and promotion
3 revenue generation and funding
4 education and training
5 community and public-sector intervention.

Product development and innovation

This is vital if an attraction is to remain ahead of the competition and to take account of trends in the global and national marketplace. Chapter 10 examines innovation in more detail; here it is worth noting that most successful attractions seek to identify new concepts, business processes or techniques such as interpretation or technology to appeal to a sophisticated audience. One of the greatest developments for many attractions is in the use of film in interpretation and interactive technology to appeal to children, such as the Newseum in Washington DC: this cost US$50 million to develop and is a free admission museum of news and journalism. In its first nine months of operation it attracted 325 000 visitors – which is very interactive and mediaworthy! In a similar vein the Futurescope in Poitiers, France, which opened in 1987, incorporates film as the basis of the theme park's operation with IMAX and OMNIMAX, and also features roof projection and seat oscillation. Acting in much the same way as Lomond Shores in Scotland as a regeneration project led by the public sector, Futurescope has generated 1200 direct and 15 000 indirect jobs and received 2.8 million visitors in 1997 (largely domestic visitors). In the technology field, virtual reality attractions such as the New York Skyride and the Madame Tussaud Scenerama in Amsterdam offer simulated trips that also orientate the visitor to the destination.

Marketing and promotion

Whilst innovation is a key to success, ensuring that this is communicated to the potential customer through marketing and promotion is essential. Most attractions use limited budgets for public relations (PR) rather than media advertising, with many profile attractions having media kits, websites and virtual reality tours as well as targeting groups through promotional campaigns that are price driven. These seek to make the public aware of the role of attractions in leisure spending and that they are venues for fun and enjoyment, as well as being safe and interesting. In the USA, the Smithsonian Museum in Washington DC and the Museum of Modern Art in New York both have very sophisticated websites and these have also provided a conduit for electronic trading such as retailing, ticket purchases and corporate hospitality bookings. In some cases, attractions have entered into strategic alliances and partnerships to develop synergies across the attraction and tourism sector to develop their business interests. For example, the Singapore Tourist Board screens all copy produced by attractions and places it in guidebooks and at strategic points of interest for visitors, ensuring the style and image of the tourist board is consistent. In New York, the Convention and Visitor Bureau links attractions and other tourist services with discount schemes and includes all attractions on an

activities map. Other examples of partnership innovation include museums cooper-
ating in Boston to undertake joint marketing initiatives and ultimately to raise public
awareness. Other museums share best practice. Some attractions have introduced
initiatives to extend their life cycle such as adding new visitor features or in-built
regeneration strategies. One of the most interesting examples is Singapore Zoo's
development of a nocturnal tour. Others have sought to extend the season through
packaging the attraction with other products or services to create all-year-round
opening opportunities as well as differential pricing mechanisms. The Santa Claus
Land in Finland has developed products to appeal to overseas markets at different
times of the year and has created eight peak seasons.

Revenue generation and funding

By presenting attractions as a series of products, managers can expand the scope for
increasing the total spend per person while also appealing to the buoyant demand
for retailing that has produced opportunities for themed development and linkage
to the products and experiences offered by the attraction. Most successful attractions are heavily involved in hospitality, and have a prestigious cafe or restaurant
that creates a nice ambience as well as good spending opportunities. In fact the
Singapore Tourist Board has identified and themed food and hospitality into its
tourism strategy for the twenty-first century – Tourism 21. It uses the Singapore Food
Festival to add promotional opportunities and a means to promote the ethnic diversity and 'Asia-ness' of the destination. Other attractions also have well-developed
corporate hospitality functions, offering various places to host events and meetings
as well as product launches. Many of the London museums have embraced this
important source of funding, and also corporate membership. One of the principal
tasks of revenue generation from existing visitors is to find ways to extend the
dwell time on site, as discussed earlier in the case of Scotland. Greater division of
attractions into sections/segments and experiences encourage a greater on-site
time as well as increasing the range of retailing opportunities.

Education and training

The growth of awareness that many attractions now operate in what is called
'the cultural industries sector', and the growing need for education, training and

management development activities to recognize the changing nature of attractions as businesses. It is evident that a series of cultural industries exist within a tourism context, and Myerscough (1988) identified the cultural events, artefacts and resources that are of vital significance to the tourism industry. Attractions provide the key element of this system. In an urban context, the cultural industries comprised a diverse group of attractions including nightclubs, libraries, museums and art galleries. In the UK these activities employed over 68 500 people in the 1990s, which is reflected in the fact that many countries (e.g. Scotland), towns and cities now have cultural industries strategies to promote these activities. This is shown in the European bids each year for cities to become European City of Culture with the perceived focus on attractions as a key element of tourism development and the associated controversy on how this will assist the attraction sector in developing its education and training needs to improve service delivery. It is also evident in the work underway in Liverpool with its 2008 European City of Culture project, as reflected in the management of the event by Liverpool Culture Company and the budget required to manage the event (Table 9.10).

Table 9.10 Financing of Liverpool Culture Company 2005–2009 to deliver the European Capital of Culture Programme in 2008 (adapted from Liverpool Culture Company, 2005, *Strategic Business Plan 2005–2009*)

Objective	Total funding allocated 2005–2009 (£)
1 To create and present the best of local, national and international art and events in all genres	34 353 288
2 To build community enthusiasm, creativity and participation	11 223 935
3 To maintain, enhance and grow the cultural infrastructure of the city	26 331 620
4 To attract investment	5 943 841
5 To reposition Liverpool as a world-class city by 2008	12 046 301
6 To provide efficient and effective management of the European Capital of Culture Programme	5 044 014

The use of volunteers in many contexts provides many useful lessons for employed staff. Some countries (such as France) are exemplars of training in the visitor attraction sector since this is seen as gaining a competitive advantage. As Chapter 10 will show, certain tourism operators in the attraction sector such as Disney also lead the world in staff training and motivation to enhance guest care, the visitor experience and product development.

Community and public sector intervention

Visitor attractions are a vital element of any community and its tourism infrastructure and so local funding support for the low season is often seen as an essential element for success in cultural industry strategies. Off-season visits by local residents, who are also ambassadors for the local area, are important to the market for attractions. There are many good examples of country-level support for attractions in France and indirectly in the UK through Millennium funds. In contrast, the USA does not directly fund attractions through public funds, since donations, bequests or community efforts are more notable than public-sector subsidies. Where the public sector intervenes directly, employment protection or development is usually justified as the basis for such intervention. In some cases states may seek to help develop an attraction in a destination and so funding for events and festivals can feature as a major element of public-sector intervention in the attraction sector.

Conclusion

The postmodern age has witnessed a large increase in the range of visitor attractions in Britain and globally and the visiting public has to make certain decisions about visiting particular venues based on a complex mix of factors including location, appeal, cost and perceived benefit or a combination of these. Incentives such as free admission may have an impact, as the example of the UK's national museums and galleries illustrated. It is evident that professional approaches to researching visitor satisfaction are necessary as visitors' expectations increase and there is a greater urgency to ensure competitive advantage in the visitor attraction market. One of the major challenges for visitor attractions lies in harnessing new technology whilst market research agencies such as Mintel argue that visitors are seeking good quality facilities at competitive prices in the leisure sector, with which attractions now compete. Visitors are seeking greater interaction at attractions, which involves the integration of technology and 'high-touch' exhibits to develop a greater degree of social interaction at attractions, whilst fulfilling a range of motivations for visiting. Yet, as the example of Dubai illustrated, attractions not only need to excite and surprise visitors, but they also need to have the 'wow' factor if they are to impress visitors and be world class.

References

Gunn, C. A. (1988) *Tourism Planning*, 2nd edn. New York: Taylor and Francis.

Holloway, J. C. (2001) *Business of Tourism*, 6th edn. Harlow: Pearson.

Jansen-Verbeke, M. (1986) Inner-city tourism: Resources, tourists and promoters. *Annals of Tourism Research*, 13 (1): 79–100.

Kotler, P. (1994) *Marketing Management: Analysis, Planning, Implementation and Control*, 8th edn. London: Prentice Hall.

Lennon, J. (ed.) (2001) *Tourism Statistics: International Perspectives and Current Issues*. London: Continuum.

Martin, A. (2003) *The Impact of Free Entry to Museums*. London: MORI (www.mori.com).

Myerscough, J. (1988) *The Economic Importance of the Arts in Britain*. London: Policy Studies Institute.

Parasuraman, A., Zeithaml, V. and Berry, L. (1985) A conceptual model of service quality and its implications for future research. *Journal of Marketing*, 49 (4): 41–50.

Pearce, P. (1991) Analysing tourist attractions. *Journal of Tourism Studies*, 2 (1): 46–55.

Scottish Enterprise/Highlands and Islands Enterprise (2001) *New Horizons: International Benchmarking and Best Practice for Visitor Attractions*. Glasgow: Scottish Enterprise/Highlands and Islands Enterprise.

Stevens, T. (1991) Visitor attractions. In C.P. Cooper (ed.) *Progress in Tourism, Recreation and Hospitality Management Volume Three*. London: Belhaven Press.

Swarbrooke, J. (2001) Visitor attraction management in a competitive market. *Insights*, A41–52. London: English Tourism Council.

Swarbrooke, J. (2002) *The Development and Management of Visitor Attractions*, 2nd edn. Oxford: Butterworth-Heinemann.

VisitScotland (2004) *Scottish Visitor Attraction Monitor*. Edinburgh: VisitScotland.

Walsh-Heron, J. and Stevens, T. (1990) *The Management of Visitor Attractions and Events*. London: Prentice Hall.

Yale, P. (1997) *From Tourist Attractions to Heritage Tourism*. Huntingdon: ELM Publications.

Further reading

The most accessible source is:

Swarbrooke, J. (2002) *The Development and Management of Visitor Attractions*, 2nd edn. Oxford: Butterworth-Heinemann.

Questions

1 Why are visitor attractions so crucial to the tourism sector?
2 What are the main factors associated with the successful management of visitor attractions?
3 Why are visitor attractions complex to categorize and classify?
4 What is the future for the visitor attraction with the growth of technology?

10

The management of tourism

Learning outcomes

This chapter builds on the previous discussion of the tourism industry, reviewing the need to manage tourism businesses. On completion of this chapter, you should be able to understand:

- the principles of management and their application to tourism businesses
- the role of marketing as a management function
- the role of management in establishing standards and systems of service provision
- the significance of small tourism businesses in the tourism sector
- the role of innovation and tourism development as a management function.

Introduction

The previous chapters have highlighted the very fragmented nature of the business which many refer to as 'tourism', being a complex amalgam of businesses that cooperate and work together to supply services and products to tourists as consumers. Each of these businesses and bodies are known as 'organizations', which are formal entities such as businesses or corporations that exist to interact, trade and exchange goods, services and knowledge to create wealth or other outputs through the use of their staff, capabilities and know-how within a tourism context. Profit is the main driver of many businesses operating in the private sector. But there are also organizations within the public sector (see Chapter 11) and voluntary sector which interact in tourism in a regulatory or voluntary sense or as interest groups (i.e. a professional organization such as ABTA, the Association of British Travel Agents), and seek to influence and affect change and represent specific interests or viewpoints. All of these organizations impact upon tourism and its direction, nature and operation (this will be discussed more fully in Chapter 11). For businesses to exist and operate effectively some form of management and organization is needed. This chapter will examine and develop the theme of management already raised throughout the book in each chapter, with a focus on the manager as the conduit for such action.

Managing tourism businesses: Key principles

The vast array of business interests that are interlinked together in the production and delivery of tourism products largely operate for profit. For them to achieve this profit objective, they need management to get things done. In other words, management occurs in a formal sense in organizations, and in most cases, management is about harnessing the organization's resources (especially people, as its most valuable asset) to create services, outcomes or products in line with what the tourist requires as a consumer. In practical terms tourism management involves harnessing the power over resources (i.e. people, finance, technology and the organization) to bring some degree of order to the tasks that must be undertaken for the organization to function and achieve its objectives. This will require a

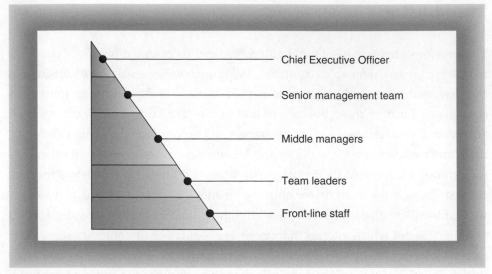

Figure 10.1 Levels of management

manager (or teams of managers) to link with employees to undertake managerial tasks, which comprise managerial work.

Most tourism businesses work towards a set of common objectives. Tourism businesses are often organized internally into specialized functions (e.g. sales, human resource management, accounts and finance). This horizontal form of organization provides a structure for employees. Companies are also organized vertically into a hierarchy, and are characterized by different levels of power, authority and status. Within tourism organizations, managers are grouped by level (see Figure 10.1).

Managers can also be classified according to functional roles and include:

- *functional managers*, who manage specialized functions such as accounting, research, sales and personnel in large organizations;
- *business unit, divisional or area managers*, who exercise management responsibilities at a general level lower down in an organization; their responsibilities may cover a group of products or diverse geographical area and combine a range of management responsibilities;
- *project managers*, who manage specific projects (a project is typically a short-term undertaking) and may require a team of staff to complete it.

The purpose of management in tourism organizations

The goals of managers within organizations are usually seen as profit-driven, but are often more diverse including:

- *profitability*, which can be achieved through higher output, better service, attracting new customers and cost minimization (for example, in 2005–2006, British Airways reduced its middle and senior management by 351 posts to save £50 million in order to reduce costs to try and remain profitable);
- in the public sector, *other goals* (e.g. coordination, liaison, raising public awareness and undertaking activities for the wider public good) that dominate the agenda in organizations;
- *efficiency*, to reduce expenditure and inputs to a minimum to achieve more cost-effective outputs;
- *effectiveness*, (achieving the desired outcome); this is not necessarily a profit-driven motive.

Yet in practical terms, the main tasks of managers are based on the management process, which is how to achieve these goals. Whilst management theorists differ in the emphasis they place on different aspects of the management process, there are four commonly agreed set of tasks: organizing, planning, leading and controlling (see Chapter 1).

The process of management is an ongoing, ever-changing one in which the wide range of managers make decisions which affect the organization and nature of the business. Chief executive officers make decisions which have major impacts on the organization (e.g. the decision to downsize due to a drop in demand or to expand and grow the business) while more junior managers deal with more routine day-to-day decision-making. In managerial decision-making, two prevailing elements have to be balanced: technical skills and human skills. These are vital when interacting and managing people *within* the organization as well as those *outside* it such as clients and suppliers. This balancing of skills is often underpinned by an ability to communicate effectively and confidently with others, as well as an ability to lead and motivate people; it also highlights one other skill set that managers need to possess: cognitive and conceptual skills. Cognitive skills are those which enable managers to formulate solutions to problems and conceptual skills are those which allow them to take a broader view and consider the links with other areas of the business. These skills are apparent from studies of managers and their work.

A study by Carroll (1988) identified clusters of management tasks, which characterized managers as:

1 *representatives* of the organization
2 *investigators*, who research issues and problems
3 *negotiators*, who communicate with one or more people over a transaction to reach a desired outcome, such as a contract
4 *coordinators*, who ensure that the organization's resources are deployed to good effect to ensure flow in work tasks
5 *evaluators*, who observe, examine and control aspects of the organization's activities
6 *staffers*, who control human resource functions
7 *supervisors*, who direct the everyday work of junior staff.

These clusters inherently cause competing roles for managers, requiring them to have a wide range of competencies to be successful.

According to Inkson and Kolb (1995: 32) a competency is:

an underlying trait of an individual – for example a motive pattern, a skill, a characteristic behaviour, a value, or a set of knowledge – which enables that person to perform successfully in his or her job.

The main motivation for organizational interest in competencies is their desire to improve management through education and training, and competencies can be divided into three groups:

1 understanding what needs to be done
2 getting the job done
3 taking people with you.

Quinn *et al.* (1990) examined the skills, competencies and role of managers and concluded that the skill set of a manager often revolved around the following activities: mentoring, innovation, brokerage, as a provider, as a director, coordination, monitoring and facilitation.

The concern with competencies questions the simple notion of management as planning, organizing, leading and control; it emphasizes skills as the basis for management. However, relying upon only competencies may overlook the need for cognitive skills, which are related to personality and individual style, while conceptual skills are based on the natural abilities of individuals.

Above all, managers need to be adaptable and flexible to accommodate and lead change, particularly in fast-moving areas such as tourism. Among the common skills which a range of ecotourism businesses in Australia identified as critical to business performance were:

- business planning, financial planning, business plan skills, research
- general marketing skills, strategic marketing skills, an understanding of price, product, place and promotion
- operational skills, especially in terms of customers and business operations
- personal attributes, especially in dealing with people.

Source: McKercher and Robbins (1998)

This list highlights the diversity of skills and knowledge that business managers need.

Most significantly, change is a key feature for tourism businesses, and they need to be cognizant of a wide range of factors – sociocultural and economic issues (especially the nature of the economy), demographic changes, the role of legal and political changes, technological change (especially information technology), what the competition is doing, the global environment and role of change and uncertainty in markets. Internal resistance to change may be a problem for managers when seeking to move the business in new directions, and various techniques can be used to adapt to change including:

- education and communication
- participation and involvement
- facilitation and support
- negotiation and agreement
- manipulation and co-optation
- explicit and implicit coercion.

The ability to learn to manage in new situations where there are no guidelines or models to follow is, according to Handy (1989), how people grow, especially in a managerial role. In fact managerial behaviour has been studied through the twentieth century, from the early work of Fayol, Mintzberg and others who observed and studied what managers did and why. In terms of how managers react to new challenges and tasks, research has illustrated that much managerial work is mundane, based on establishing ongoing reciprocal working relationships within and between businesses (i.e. networking). A number of stages in managerial responses to work are:

- taking hold of the job, normally three to six months in duration
- immersion, lasting four to eleven months
- reshaping, after a period of intense change, normally three to six months
- consolidation, running for three to nine months
- refinement.

Mintzberg argued that managers often work on a stimulus–response pattern, responding to problems, challenges and issues, and the nature of much of their work is fragmented and discontinuous, often being interrupted.

What do tourism managers manage?

Tourism is widely attributed as a service sector activity that has a high level of customer contact. Despite the wide range of tasks managers undertake, there are three principal management functions which tourism businesses need to be involved in when dealing with people as customers: marketing, operational issues and human resource management. Although other functions are important, these three are crucial where the service output is intangible. In a tourism context, marketing differs from other products because tourism is a service industry, the intangible elements, quality of delivery and evaluation of experiences being difficult to visualize. The heterogeneity (i.e. diversity), perishability (i.e. a tour cannot be stored and sold at a different time) and intangibility of tourism services make marketing a challenge when combined with two other key problems:

1 the customer must travel to the product/resource base to consume it
2 the operator has little influence over the tourism activity (holiday).

The marketing focus belies the fact that tourism consumption is based upon the provision of a service and so marketing as a process acts to link the customer with the supplier, (see the example of the holiday brochure illustrated in Chapter 8). Marketing is also vital to establishing the market research, market needs, specification and nature of service provision in consumer industries (see the example of establishing a tour programme in Chapter 8).

Marketing tourism as a management function

Marketing is widely acknowledged as a vital prerequisite to communicating the product or service offering of businesses or suppliers to the market (as observed in Chapter 9). According to Kotler and Armstrong (1991), marketing is a process whereby individuals and groups obtain the type of products or goods they value. These goods are created and exchanged through a process, which requires a detailed understanding of consumers and their wants and desires so that the product or service is effectively and efficiently delivered to the client or purchaser.

In particular, businesses need to understand, using market research, what markets they wish to serve and the service attributes they wish to offer; to establish the prices to be charged and to tailor the service to meet the clients' needs as closely as possible. They must then develop a communication programme to inform them about the service (e.g. create a brochure, advertisement or other method of communication, such as the internet).

To meet customer needs, a company analyses its own products or services in terms of its own business expertise and how competitors' products and services may affect them. This is frequently undertaken as a SWOT analysis, which considers the Strengths and Weaknesses of, Opportunities for and Threats to its products and services in the business environment.

For those tourism operators who may wish to grow and expand, a number of options exist. Horner and Swarbrooke (1996: 325) indicate these can involve:

- *marketing consortia*, where a group of operators cooperate to create and develop a product
- *strategic alliances*, where different businesses agree to cooperate in various ways (this varies by sector in the tourism industry, and includes such things as marketing agreements or technical cooperation)

- *acquisition*, which is the purchase of equity in other operations
- *joint ventures*, where operators seek to create new businesses
- *franchising*, where major operators use their market presence and brand image to further extend their influence by licensing franchisees to operate businesses using their corporate logo and codes.

However, the actual implementation of marketing for tourism ultimately depends on the 'marketing mix' a company chooses.

The marketing mix

The marketing mix is 'the mixture of controllable marketing variables that the firm [or company] uses to pursue the sought level of sales in the target market' (Kotler cited in Holloway and Plant 1988: 48). This means that in any tourism organization there are four main marketing variables that need to be harnessed:

1 *Product formulation*, which is the ability of a company to adapt to the needs of its customers in terms of the services it provides. Products are constantly being adapted to changes in consumer markets.
2 *Price*, which is the economic concept used to adjust the supply of a service to meet the demand, taking account of sales targets and turnover.
3 *Promotion*, which is the manner in which a company seeks to improve customers' knowledge of the services it sells so that those people who are made aware may be turned into actual purchasers. To achieve promotional aims, advertising, public relations, sales and brochure production functions are undertaken within the remit as promotion.
4 *Place*, which is the location at which prospective customers may be induced to purchase a service – the point of sale (e.g. a travel agent or another point of distribution such as the worldwide web).

These 'four Ps' are incorporated into the marketing process in relation to the known competition and the impact of market conditions. Thus, the marketing process involves the continuous evaluation of how a business operates internally and externally to meet customer requirements.

Managing operational issues in tourism businesses

Operational issues have traditionally dominated the focus of most service organizations centred on tourism, particularly where labour-intensive operations exist (e.g. at an airport). Business operations in tourism assume a major role: the highly seasonal nature of tourism requires seasonal staff at resorts, airports, in hotels and for transport operators. Demand is largely concentrated in six months of the year and this is a key management challenge for many businesses. Seasonality shapes tourism demand from consumers due to a wide range of factors including the climate and environment of the origin area and the attraction of the destination. Pricing is also used by tourism businesses to capitalize upon peak demand in popular summer months. In less popular seasons (e.g. autumn and winter), businesses may seek to leverage support from public-sector bodies to host large-scale events (e.g. the Harbin ice festival in China) and attract visitors out of season. Events in the winter, such as Hogmanay in Scotland and new year celebrations in London (which attracts around 250 000 people) are a way of providing a stimulus to reduce seasonality effects.

Some destinations experience one-peak seasonality (e.g. coastal resorts in the summer season) or two-peak seasonality (a summer and winter season) while many urban destinations experience non-peak seasonality, where the climate and environment do not cause peaks as different international markets' holidaytaking habits shape the pattern of seasonal demand. Seasonality means that individual businesses have to be able to manage the peaks and troughs of demand and supply. For example, in January 2006, British Airways made 1.5 million promotional air fares available for travel up to December 2006 to stimulate demand and fill airline seats so that its scheduled departures met their revenue targets for each flight, in spite of good loadings of around 74 per cent for the last three months of 2005. The timing of travel by different markets is vividly illustrated by patterns of tourism to Iceland. Most of the visitor arrivals from continental Europe are concentrated in the months June to August, and occupancy rates for hotels in the capital exceed 75 per cent in these months. At the same time, the island has been able to accommodate a growth in seasonal visitor arrivals from 70 000 in 1982 to 300 000 in 2003 which required additional hotel capacity if demand was to be met.

Operational issues assume a dominant day-to-day role for many businesses, especially in places where large volumes of tourists are being managed, such as attractions or airports. To ensure the smooth flow and organization of these activities managers must delegate a great deal of responsibility in managing the interactions with visitors to front-line staff. The area is often termed 'operations management' and it focuses on five interrelated areas:

1 *capacity*, which is understanding the ability of the organization to produce something (such as service)
2 *standards*, which are those prevailing within the tourism sector (such as waiting times at an airport check-in or hotel reception)
3 *scheduling*, which is the planning of work and use of the organization's physical and human resources
4 *inventory*, which is understanding the organization's ability to meet supply and demand
5 *control*, which ensures the operations are managed in an efficient and systematic manner and brings the planning, preparation and readiness inherent in the four functions above into action.

Much of this is dependent upon having competent staff to undertake these tasks.

Managing service provision: Human resource issues and service delivery

According to Baum (1993: 4) tourism can be conceptualized as a client purchasing 'the skills, service and commitment of a range of human contributors to the experience that they are about to embark upon' highlighting the importance of human resource management (HRM) issues and the challenge this poses for tourism managers (see Table 10.1). Many of these issues are embedded in some specific problems which the tourism sector faces including:

- demographic issues related to the shrinking pool of potential employees and labour shortages (as discussed in Chapter 7)
- the tourism industry's image as an employer
- cultural and traditional perceptions of the tourism industry
- rewards and compensation for working in the sector
- education and training
- skill shortages at the senior and technical levels
- linking human resource concerns with service and product quality

Table 10.1 Managing human resource issues: Scope and extent for businesses (modified from Baum, 1993)

1 A critical awareness of the scope and nature of the labour market
2 The design of jobs
3 Recruitment, selection, appointment and retention of staff
4 Induction, equal opportunities, training and development
5 Evaluation of staff performance
6 Salaries and incentives
7 Employment termination, grievance and dispute procedures
8 Industrial relations and employment law
9 Motivation of staff

- poor manpower planning
- a remedial rather than proactive approach to human resource issues.

Source: Based on Baum (1993)

In line with management, HRM is concerned with planning, monitoring and control of the human resource as a management process. More complex analyses of HRM identify the concern that the individual human resource system within any organization is able to realize the strategic objectives of the organization (i.e. the delivery of excellent customer service to tourism consumers) as will become evident later in the discussion of the Disney model.

For the medium- or large-sized tourism enterprise, human resource issues and the factors affecting their performance are usually linked to the staff and workforce; therefore, recognizing the role of recruitment and ongoing development of the staff resource to achieve strategic goals becomes essential. The scale of the human resource function will often reflect the size of the organization and specific functions (e.g. training and development) may be allocated to specific individuals whereas in smaller organizations the commitment to core functions (recruitment and retention) may be all that is possible, due to work pressures and constraints on staff time.

The major challenges for the tourism industry in the new millennium are aptly summarized by Cooper *et al.* (1998: 458):

the challenges facing the tourism industry will only be met successfully by a well-educated, well-trained, bright, energetic, multi-lingual and entrepreneurial workforce who understand the nature of tourism and have a professional training. A high quality of professional human resources in tourism will allow enterprises to gain a competitive edge and deliver added value with their service.

People do make a difference in what is undoubtedly a people business.

More sophisticated human resource policies need to be developed and implemented in the following areas for the tourism sector to be responsive to add value to its staff and change the sectors' image as an employer:

• induction of staff
• appraisal and staff performance evaluation
• effective staff communication
• rewarding initiative and excellence
• empowering staff
• improved industry – education collaboration.

Source: Page and Connell (2006)

Therefore, the quality, commitment and effectiveness of human resources can be critical in businesses' competitiveness. Understanding how HRM issues interact and, more importantly, what types of service staff need to provide, are significant elements for managing tourism businesses.

Service provision in tourism: A perennial management challenge?

Service provision can be conceptualized as a system in which elements of the product are created and assembled and delivered to the customer. Whilst parts of the service are visible to the consumer, the manner of delivery is what will entail exposure to the tourist and will impact upon the company's reputation as a service provider. The tourist's satisfaction with the service delivered in tourism will focus upon two critical elements: the technical and the functional quality of the service. The technical quality relates to the measurable elements, such as whether an airline seat of a certain quality was provided and delivered. In contrast, the functional element relates to the impression one wants a client to receive: an overall impression that is more holistic and gauges satisfaction with what was consumed. Whilst the analysis of functional quality is more intangible, as Chapter 8 illustrated in terms of human behaviour in travel agencies, certain factors – such as posture, the use of a smile, voice, attitude, empathy and responsiveness – will have a major bearing. For tourism managers, seeking to achieve consistent levels of service in tourism will be measured by tourist satisfaction. This is a complex phenomenon since satisfaction is linked to a consumer's emotions and level of expectation of the service being consumed. This is partly dependent upon three interrelated factors: the level of equity in the service provided, whether expectations were met, and perception of the actual performance. This requires managers to understand in more detail the technical aspects of service provision in tourism, especially:

- what the final product is
- how it is produced
- the form and shape the service will take
- who ultimately delivers the service.

Therefore, recognizing that customer service is central to the satisfaction levels of tourism services is significant because consumers are often buying something they have high expectations of, based on the marketing mix (the price, product, place and promotion), which is shaped by people, physical attributes (i.e. was the weather good?) and processes of delivery. In a customer contact business, managers need to be aware of the most commonly measured elements that determine service quality. These elements are known among researchers as SERVQUAL determinants:

- tangible elements
- reliability
- responsiveness
- communication
- credibility
- security
- competence
- courtesy
- understanding/knowing the consumer
- access/ease of approach and contact.

These are central in managing the service encounter with tourists and at an operational level will determine how customer expectations/needs are met.

One area which is vital in meeting tourists' expectations is communication. This is important not only in marketing a company but also for the way in which individual companies locate and nurture their customer base. In some sectors of the tourism industry defined standards of service and provision may exist to meet visitor expectations. Three key elements are associated with the staffing of tourism enterprises, based on the SERVQUAL model:

1 *the responsiveness of staff* – their willingness to help promptly (rather than ignore customers and leave them waiting, as many call centres now do with direct sales and the telephone waiting systems)
2 *the assurance of staff* – their ability to evoke images of trust and confidence associated with the company's offerings (as opposed to those staff who bemoan the problems of service delivery and weak elements in the system that have contributed to service failure)
3 *staff empathy* – their ability to provide tourists with individual attention and a commitment to the service they are providing (as opposed to more disaffected staff who do not have a stake in the business they are working for which may reflect poor levels of pay and motivation along with the use of casual staff).

When things go wrong, as they sometimes do when dealing with human behaviour that is not predictable and needs and attitudes to tourism services that are not homogenous, staff and businesses can follow a number of simple principles in handling complaints:

- *act professionally*, remaining calm and confident whilst listening to the nature of the problem raised by the tourist
- *apologize* for the problem and agree to try and resolve it, summarizing what you will do, the time scales involved and the proposed solution
- *ensure the tourist leaves satisfied with the outcome*, but avoid committing to any specific solution or outcome until all the facts and information have been collected and analysed to provide an informed opinion
- *refer the matter to a manager where necessary*, working within the level of responsibility you are empowered to deal with.

Yet there are some businesses such as the Disney Corporation which go far beyond that approach to service provision: their customer service is widely seen as an example of international best practice; a good example whose principles other businesses can emulate to be successful and to improve their performance.

Box 10.1 Case Study: The Disney model of customer care

The Disney Organization is acknowledged as one of the leaders in customer care, employing over 55 000 staff with revenue of US$23 billion in 1999 and profits of US$2 billion. In 2004, the company revenue had risen to US$31 billion, a growth of US$3 billion since 2003, and by 2005 its workforce had expanded to 129 000. The company evolved from the Walt Disney business founded by its owner in 1923 and now encompasses four core businesses:

- *studio entertainment* (including its purchase of Pixar)
- *Disney consumer products* (including the highly successful merchandising activities)
- *Disney media networks*
- *Disney parks and resorts*, launched in 1952 with the opening of Disneyland in Anaheim, California. Disney now has eleven parks and resorts it owns/operates on three continents, together with thirty-five resort hotels and two luxury cruise ships. In 2005, Disney opened Hong Kong Disneyland, with a 43 per cent ownership of the venture. This is widely acknowledged as Disney's initial move towards a globalized strategy towards the theme park sector, as it expands into the growing Asian market. This followed its successful opening of a theme park in Japan. An indication of the scale of Disney's business is illustrated by the 500 million guests which have stayed at the Disney World Resorts in Florida since it opened.

One notable feature of Disney is the level of repeat business in its theme parks which has grown from 50 per cent to 70 per cent in recent years, despite major competition from other parks – a feature that many tourism businesses want to emulate to build a strong customer base. The concepts it uses are interesting in a customer service setting for the tourism industry because it uses a theatrical context – staff are referred to as *cast members*, and play their role *on stage*, which is at the point of customer contact. Staff are allowed to be themselves backstage, when they are not in front of customers, and there is a set of processes and procedures which are part of the Disney magic. The Disney formula for customer service is based on a set of values that come from integrating its commercialism with a quality experience for the visitor. It is based on three elements:

1   a quality staff experience, since each individual staff member impacts on the customer experience
2   a quality customer experience, based on the experience being customer driven; Disney seeks to exceed customer needs and expectations rather than simply meet them
3   a quality set of business practices, where knowledge, marketing, innovation and other elements are blended to ensure commercial success.

In particular, the Disney philosophy is to 'exceed customer expectations and pay attention to detail', with the visitor at the centre of all elements that drive business activities. Many of the failings in service sector provision in the new millennium is just that lack of attention to detail, unless you are purchasing a luxury product. In Disney jargon (which is a common feature of Disney internal communications), 'Guestology' is their approach to customer service, where staff need to know their customers and understand them in terms of psychographics (see Chapter 3 for more detail of psychographics). This requires an understanding of both the quantitative aspects of their visitors, experience and the more qualitative features (i.e. feelings, attitudes and reasoning), since the visitor experience is based upon these intangible elements. On the basis of this information, Disney develops its service theme – the type of service their guests want – which has four key service standards: safety, courtesy, show (to provide a seamless experience) and efficiency (to ensure smooth operations). To deliver these service standards, Disney uses a corporate brand.

A brand is a name, design or symbol (or combination of each) used to identify a service. This enables the customer to identify the product or service easily. For a company, a brand can help to build customer loyalty, since it implies less risk in a purchase – something that can help with further merchandising opportunities, as the Disney brand has achieved through its international retail outlets. Disney recognizes the need for consistency in the way the organization conveys itself via its brand to the public. In one visit, a person may interact with sixty cast members in one day; to achieve consistency and a coherent brand image, Disney seeks to ensure staff are competent, attentive, seamless and trained, with managers providing service support for these cast and identifying how to 'reach out' to guests.

To achieve these goals, Disney has a number of processes and procedures to help the delivery of its service and recognizes that in the real world service breakdowns and interruptions may occur. Putting things right by empowering staff to alleviate the impact of such problems means that a negative event can be shaped into a positive response from staff (perhaps responding to problems with 'How can I help?'). 'Service debugging', as they refer to it, involves seeking solutions to problems so that good communication is achieved between visitor and staff member. One of Disney's major achievements, which is often held out as a model for the tourism industry, is its ability to deal with large flows of visitors at its theme parks: up to 30 000 a day in the case of Hong Kong Disneyland. It has introduced visitor management tools (see Chapter 12 for more discussion of this concept) including *Early Bird Programmes*, to allow early entry before the main visitors; Fast Passes, to avoid waiting; and Tip Boards, which advise people how long a wait is required at a specific attraction. The aim is to optimize the operation of the attraction, guest flow and queue experience so the visitor experience is enhanced.

In seeking to manage the visitor experience at Disney, sending the right message to the visitor is seen as vital, from the entry point until the point of departure. By paying careful attention to detail, Disney seeks to create a positive image (it calculated that an average duration of a visit to Hong Kong Disneyland was nine hours, which is a long time for the visitor attraction sector). It does this by ensuring it creates the right ambience and feeling among visitors by harnessing details such as design, landscaping, lighting (which can affect visitor moods), colour, signage, texture of surfaces, music and ambient noise as well as elements that appeal to the other senses: smell, touch and taste. Above all, tidiness and cleanliness in mass visitor attractions are seen as critical to the image created. This highlights how integrated the visitor experience is at an attraction and that customer service is not just about visitor contact and interaction, but about the entire environment and how service systems are designed and managed to enable satisfaction to be achieved. Above all, Disney is constantly reinventing itself, innovating and seeking to stay in front of the competition. Management research has termed this 'business re-engineering' – seeking to reintegrate processes (i.e. tasks, labour and knowledge) to make continuous improvements to its business performance. In fact some commentators see Disney as the market leader in attraction management.

Whilst many of these Disney principles may seem quite alien to some service organizations, this example highlights a range of experiences that tourism businesses can adapt and develop in understanding how to deliver services to visitors. The culture of the workforce is important in terms of their willingness to embrace such principles to deliver services. However, one of the problems that this poses for tourism operators in many countries is their scale of operation, especially when they are based in the small business sector that has specific managerial concerns, particularly in the early set-up stage.

Developing and managing tourism ventures in the small business sector

There is a tendency to assume that tourism has great potential to stimulate economic development if it is managed well. The basic argument is that the fledgling new business of today could develop and grow into the large international corporation of the future. This may indeed occur in a few cases, such as the rise of the Virgin transport conglomerate which evolved from the Virgin Atlantic airline venture. Many governments have avidly supported small business development in tourism owing to its future employment-generating potential, although they were not overtly concerned until the 1980s with ensuring managers and owners had the skill set needed to manage such enterprises. The small business sector (also known as small- and medium-sized enterprises or SMEs; very small ventures are 'micro enterprises') does play a major role in most countries, not least for its employment role but also because it is a key element of the industry.

According to Morrison (1996: 400):

> a small tourism business is financed by one individual or small group and is directly managed by its owner(s), in a personalised manner and not through the medium of a formalised management structure ... it is perceived as small, in terms of physical facilities, production/service capacity, market share and number of employees.

Morrison goes on to argue that:

> traditionally the tourism industry has been dominated by the small business and this still remains true in the 1990s. Currently in Ireland ... firms with less than fifteen employees account for around 79 per cent of all Irish tourism businesses. (1996: 401)

Indeed, it is notable that the success often attributed to Ireland as a booming tourism destination can be directly related to activity across the tourism sectors, in which SMEs play a role.

However, in terms of small tourism firms, entrepreneurship seems weakly developed because tourism is perceived as having low entry barriers (i.e. you do not need large amounts of capital and investment to start a venture like a bed-and-breakfast establishment). The main management issues affecting tourism SMEs is highlighted by Carter (1996: 4504) who suggested that:

> irrespective of the relative size of each country's small business sector, the main management characteristics of small firms remain similar regardless of nationality. Researchers have consistently noted that small firms play an important role in new product and process innovation and are characterised by their product specialisation … [and] … that these firms are undercapitalised, product-led, family-owned concerns in which the management function is confined to one person or a few key individuals.

The short-term planning horizon of many tourism SMEs, their limited knowledge of the business environment and their owner-managed structure influences the way tasks are managed. SME managers rely upon attitudes, personal qualities (i.e. leadership skills) and experience. The differences between small and large firm management is that the preparation of ongoing business plans and the marketing function in SMEs is seen as peripheral to the management task of running the business. Many of these characteristics are borne out in the studies by Shaw and Williams (2002), where few businesses had formal marketing strategies, skills and knowledge of the tourism business.

Many localities promote tourism business development because it has the potential to form linkages with businesses that supply it ('backward linkages') and with those it supplies ('forward linkages') and so has the potential to generate economic development. An example of a backward linkage is a new hotel sourcing local food supplies. These types of supply chain, using local networks, have attracted a great of attention from public and private-sector organizations seeking to promote local collaboration, where collaborations can also become the basis for expanding regional tourism products and events. This can help to create a distinctive local and regional product offering and when these networks evolve into producer groups they can also add value to the tourist experience.

Research focused on the accommodation sector has shown that many new entrants to this sector have little experience of the business and have a wide range of motives for entering the market. What is interesting in the tourism sector is that the sources of venture capital for new businesses are varied, with a proportion often coming from families and contacts in small business ventures. However, tourism entrepreneurs need to harness managerial skills if their business idea is to work. In Cornwall, research by Williams and Shaw (2002) found that more than 50 per cent of capital came from these sources, especially for older entrepreneurs. The grounds given by over 80 per cent of these entrepreneurs for establishing their businesses included lifestyle reasons (i.e. a better way of life), as they were new migrants to the region. There is also evidence that where these businesses are operated by family members, there are social benefits that are additional to the lifestyle reasons for operation. Similar reasons are also evident in a new form of business venture now appearing in the UK – home-working travel agents.

Home-working travel agents have started to become established as a new form of business venture to offset the decline in the conventional high street travel agent in the face of massive competition from the online agencies discussed in Chapter 8. A number of travel agent companies have set up home-working as a self-employed model of a franchised travel agency where the employee is based at home and works the hours to suit their clients and their lifestyle. Travel Counsellors, Hays Travel and Instant Holidays are three examples of home-working business brands. They support the home-workers with state-of-the-art ICTs, a head office function, advertising and the provision of leads to generate business. This provides many travel agents with the flexibility of working from home as well as the opportunity to operate when clients want to contact them (i.e. out of normal office hours), competing with the way consumers use the internet and plan/book travel. Clients are provided with a dedicated person for each booking and inquiry. In 2005, Travel Counsellors had recruited 560 travel consultants and has recently been licensed to offer dynamic packaging; the company expects to expand its current £150 million turnover in 2006 and plans to recruit further consultants as organizations such as the high street chain Going Places closed 110 locations which were no longer profitable.

The scale of travel agency provision and market share of travel business in the UK in 2006 was still dominated by the four main chains. TUI operated 700 high street travel agencies under the Thomson brand, controlling 16 per cent of the market. Thomas Cook operated 600 shops, 7 travel warehouses and 120 Bureau de Changes (foreign currency exchanges), plus 3 call centres and 40 home-workers, controlling 10 per cent of the market. MyTravel has downsized with the rationalization of its Going Places chain from 624 to 514 shops, which may be further reduced to 500 by late 2006, but it still retains a 10 per cent share of the market. First Choice had around 269 shops, 38 holiday hypermarkets and 2 call centres with a 9 per cent share, while Expedia.co.uk and the Cendant Corporation (with Travelbag, a call centre, eight shops and an online agency) both have a 3 per cent share to provide a comparison with the main high street provision. Yet in 2006, there were also debates among analysts that the low-cost airlines Ryanair and easyJet were likely to sell more accommodation as part of their online travel business than the top four high street chains. This illustrates how the travel market and model of business competition is changing rapidly. Small businesses seeking to compete in the mass market will need to become niche product providers if they are to offer something different from the mass market products now being sold by the low-cost airlines.

With many countries having a strong dependence upon small businesses for the tourism sector, it is not surprising that many government agencies are concerned with improving the performance and managerial skills of new businesses when they do not enter the market for profit-only motives. For example, in New Zealand, 99 per cent of the country's businesses are based in the SME sector, which employ 60 per cent of the working population. Over 85 per cent of these businesses employ fewer than five people and this is replicated through the tourism and hospitality sector, though the hospitality industry tends to employ more staff.

What is apparent is that new business start-ups and small business ventures in tourism have specific management requirements, with a common range of obstacles to improving business performance including:

- high rates of inflation
- high labour costs
- high interest rates
- high rents or rates
- debtors/poor cash flow
- lack of external guidance on business development
- competition from other businesses
- low labour productivity
- lack of skilled employees
- insufficient customer demand
- government regulations and bureaucracy
- limited access to finance
- competition from large firms.

This highlights the scope of management challenges faced by many small tourism and hospitality businesses. Addressing these through good management skills is critical, and in the initial set-up stage of the business venture particular attention should be paid to the obvious financial issues through a feasibility study or business plan. The website www.scotexchange.net, funded by Scottish Enterprise and hosted by the National Tourism Organization VisitScotland, has a page entitled 'Business development' aimed at entrepreneurs seeking to start their own business. The page examines the following points:

- How do I get started?
- Marketing
- Knowing your market
- Networking
- Staff-related issues
- Risks in setting up a business
- Business types.

It has related links to Scottish Enterprise advice through its network of 22 local enterprise companies and its Small Business Gateway site (www.sbgateway.com). Above all, these sites highlight much of the conventional wisdom on small business start-ups in tourism and hospitality, and the importance of developing a good business plan and the role of innovation.

Tourism and innovation

Challenges for tourism managers

Innovation is a often seen as one way in which businesses may seek to gain competitive advantage, especially where innovation in the face of competition leads to growth, survival or enhanced profitability. Innovation implies change of some sort and can be divided into a number of areas: diffusion of new ideas, products or processes; adoption by individual organizations and levels of innovativeness. Much of the existing research on innovation emerged after Schumpeter's study (1952) which identified five principal routes to innovation (demonstrated in Figure 10.2) with a number of tourism applications. What this highlights is that much of the focus of innovation centres on creative thinking and inventiveness. For tourism managers, the challenge is to understand the ways it is adopted, used

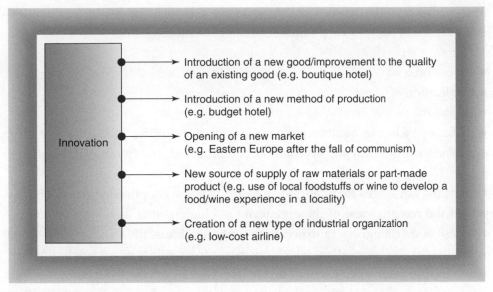

Figure 10.2 Schumpeter's types of innovation and their application to tourism

by organizations and diffused to the business and commercial/non-commercial environment to provide solutions to problems or generate ideas that can make a difference to the way a business operates or functions.

How and why does innovation occur and what is its significance in tourism?

Human actors, environmental factors such as turmoil and crisis, idea champions and external factors such as government intervention and competition can induce innovation. What is not clear in existing research is whether management is necessary to encourage innovation, or whether it will occur without the influence of management. However, managers need to understand the role of innovation and its potential to improve business processes and the client–organization interface and to add value to the business (i.e. it may lead to cost savings). This is important in a people industry such as tourism, which is reliant upon new ideas, experiences and destinations for the generation of new product ideas. Business research highlights that there are pioneer adopters in some organizations who embrace innovation and the change that it may induce, and adapt the innovation to fit the company's needs. In contrast, innovation laggards hold out against innovation and change until the majority of the workforce accepts it. Innovation in organizations is seen to pass through a number of stages including:

- invention
- application
- adoption
- diffusion, where a number of sub-stages exist including: marketing the idea, interest arousal, trial implementation, continued use and full implementation.

One of the key stages for a tourism business is in the adoption stage, which may reflect the receptiveness of the organization – highlighting its degree of innovativeness and willingness to experiment with new ideas. This will often depend upon the level of innovation, which can range from mildly new to radically new (from the producer's perspective), and is also reflected in how the consumer might perceive the innovation. Two contrasting examples can be seen in the field of air travel: a mildly innovative idea is the reduction in the number of cabin crew to reduce costs and service levels; a very radical one is the removal of all in-flight service.

Innovation is critical in tourism, given the sector's fast-evolving nature. Being trend driven means that tourism has to adapt and innovate to meet consumers' needs for improved quality and new products and experiences, a feature recognized in the recent Scottish Tourism Framework for Action 2002–2005 and its successor which runs to 2010 (see Chapter 11). In 2001, a Tourism Innovation Group was formed by the tourism industry to promote such processes to make Scottish tourism more competitive to see the focus of their actions and why they are engaged in such a process as a result of intervention by Scottish Enterprise to promote greater levels of innovation. Much of their work in this area is world leading, since few other public-sector agencies have pursued and championed such an ambitious innovation programme. It embraces:

- *the Tourism Innovation Group*, with its resulting Pride and Passion programme for encouraging new ideas, with passionate people able to promote it
- *Learning Journeys* to destinations deemed to be innovative and able to provide learning experiences for participants, with ideas to introduce into their businesses
- *a Tourism Innovation Day*, where members of the tourism industry can gather to hear about and share new ideas and best practice

- *a Tourism Innovation Toolkit* and training programme to facilitate in-company innovation and training
- *an annual Innovation Development Award* to help fund promising new ideas by financially assisting the development of a feasibility study to implement the idea
- *a Destination Development programme* to help focus resources geographically into leading destinations to foster excellence in key areas
- *an Ambassadors Scheme* aimed at encouraging enhanced product development.

Each initiative is driven by a desire to see innovative businesses fostered to cater for tomorrow's tourists and their changing needs, while also acting as a high-profile model for other businesses to learn from. This approach to tourism intervention is based on the perceived need for leadership in the tourism sector, which is dominated by many SMEs. SMEs are predominantly operationally focused and not renowned for their long-term vision and strategic assessment of how tourism markets are evolving and what new products are needed to cater for these markets.

For small businesses to be innovative, they must often overcome the barriers of size and resources, especially in terms of financial, technical and human resources. They may also be inhibited by a lack of marketing expertise. Yet where innovation occurs, it can be very significant and some researchers have focused on the concept of niche tourism (i.e. new forms of specialized tourism products and experiences) as one outcome of the innovation process. One form of innovation that is constantly evaluated and examined by tourism managers is growth options and the need to pursue new business ideas such as establishing new developments, and the next section examines how managers need to approach such ideas.

Tourism management in action: Designing and developing a visitor attraction

One of the key features inherent in tourism is the tourist's search for something new – a new experience and a new place to visit or new activity. Part of the innovation development process for businesses is how they evaluate the feasibility of new ideas and potential business ventures or developments. This is usually undertaken in two stages: the construction of a business plan that sets out the ideas and then a more detailed feasibility study if investment of external or large sums of money is involved. The formulation of a business plan will usually need to examine the fairly standard set of issues, many of which are listed in Table 10.2 in a simplified form. This is a fairly reflective exercise for a company, entrepreneur or planner and asks a range of questions. Many lending institutions also offer advice to new ventures regarding creating a business plan, and provide software to assist in the development of the final plan to a pre-determined structure. The business plan is the stage where many of the issues are scoped out and identified, and the proposal will identify what might be expected to occur.

However, for a much larger venture, such as the building of a new tourist attraction, or modification and expansion involving the investment of large capital

Table 10.2 The possible structure for a simplified tourism business plan

Executive Summary
- What type of business are you planning? What type of product or service will you provide?
- What do you believe are the critical success factors for this type of business?
- Why does it promise to be successful?
- What is the growth potential?

Market for the Business
- Who are your potential customers and what is the market?
- How will you price your product or service?
- What market share can you expect?
- How will you promote your business?

Management
- Who will manage the business?
- What skills and characteristics will they need?
- How many employees will you need?
- What tasks will they be deployed in?
- What will their remuneration be?
- Are there potential threats to your business?

Financial Elements
- What will the business cost to open?
- What will be your projected assets, liabilities, and net worth?
- What is your total estimated business income for the first financial year?
- What sources of funding will you seek/use?

Many elements of a business plan can now be prepared with the aid of business planning software available from banks and their small business venture/start up units.

sums, a feasibility study will normally be undertaken, which is often contracted out to consultants who can offer specialist advice on certain aspects of the project. It requires detailed research or the compilation of existing research knowledge, and analysis of a range of issues as the example in Box 10.2 will show.

Box 10.2 A feasibility study for a new tourism attraction: The scope and range of issues

The example which follows is a real-world example that has been modified for reasons of commercial confidentiality so that the identity and location are not revealed. The project, which was initially released to three consulting firms as an invitation to tender, consisted of a brief to evaluate the existing business plan for a new attraction on a greenfield site, with no local competition. The brief asked for a detailed project proposal that would outline the expertise of the consultants, timescale in which they could complete the tasks, their track record in previous projects and the costs for undertaking the task. Any area of feasibility work in tourism requires a multidisciplinary team to be assembled. In this case, quantity surveyors, a tourism planner, a tourism development expert with detailed knowledge of the region in which the attraction was to be sited and a managing partner were assembled to work on different aspects of the project. The brief identified certain misgivings with the existing business plan prepared previously, and questioned whether the financial assumptions and model used to base the development on were sufficiently robust. As a result, the project examined:

- the objectives of the visitor centre development
- the business requirements of the visitor centre (i.e. the requirement from the client that it had to be self-financing from visitor numbers and spending)
- planning regulations for new developments in the region
- existing and future tourism trends in the region, to understand if the domestic and international tourism markets would generate enough business for the new project on existing and future forecasts
- local tourism statistics and surveys that illustrated visitor behaviour within the region and their willingness to travel to a new attraction, based on existing travel patterns
- the impact of seasonality in visitor numbers and their impact on the business model
- visitor attraction trends in other countries and experiences of new developments

- infrastructure constraints and opportunities to make the new development less or more accessible, such as road improvements to cut journey times
- the market segments that were likely to use the new attraction, particularly the schools market, tour groups and independent travellers
- methods of revenue generation, including visitor spending among domestic and international visitors as well as day trippers
- financial assumptions and projections for the visitor centre, including ownership structures, assumptions about visitor spending, refined assumptions based on actual experiences at other attractions, and a model of the visitor mix and projected numbers
- construction budgets, space usage and fit-out within the new visitor centre and project programming to show the timelines for completion of each stage of the development and cost implications of different options
- the preferred model of development and likely management model that would work.

This is a typical framework for many feasibility studies. The critical element which has proved so controversial in the UK relates to the availability of Millennium Fund grants to new visitor attraction developments. In many cases, consultants have overestimated the market for these developments and in some cases the developments have run into financial trouble within a year to 18 months of opening; some have closed (see Chapter 9). This highlights the problems that employing consultants can pose for entrepreneurs and businesses: managers need to have a degree of understanding of the business process involved in a business plan and feasibility study. In each case, an impartial view or evaluation by a third party may help managers validate or reject the outcome of the study, rather than simply reiterate the findings which they are looking for simply to secure funding, which may lead to financial problems if the plan is implemented and it is not viable and realistic. In other words, the multiskilled nature of managing a tourism business and new opportunities requires a balance of risk-taking counterweighted by financial prudence and a questioning mind to ensure that any investment is well used.

Conclusion

Managing tourism is a dynamic activity: change, more change and upheaval is a function of managing a fast-changing business. Tourism businesses are subject to the vagaries of consumer tastes and market conditions, and can easily be sent into crisis by catastrophic events such as SARS, avian flu or other disease outbreak; civil disturbances (i.e. riots); and environmental disasters such as hurricanes or floods. There is a growing recognition among large tourism organizations that they need to have contingency plans to plan for such events and to engage in an understanding of crisis management (see Chapter 13). However, this is probably less challenging than day-to-day operational issues and responding effectively in a competitive market where cost, service quality and delivery at a suitable price are now dominant. Nevertheless, there is a growing need for businesses to understand the anatomy of a crisis and its different phases (i.e. pre-crisis; crisis and post-crisis) so they can begin to understand the management challenges it poses at each stage.

Even normal operating conditions can prove challenging as market trends, unforeseen events, structural problems in a business and corporate philosophy can have a substantial bearing on business performance. The following example illustrates the differences of the significance of these respective factors in relation to the airline industry. United Airlines made an operating loss of US$1 360 000 000 in 2003 and US$777 000 000 in 2004. Similarly, Delta had losses of US$785 000 000 in 2003 and US$ 3 308 000 in 2004. Since 2000, the largest six full-service carriers in the USA have incurred losses of US$14 billion. The business travel sector no longer supports the lucrative first-class (business-class) market in the USA, which was a high-yielding segments, causing the companies to rely on less lucrative coach class (economy) in the last five years.

In stark contrast, SouthWest Airlines was one of the world's most profitable airlines after Ryanair. The full-cost service airlines like Delta and United had massive cost and management structures that are out of line with current models of profitable airline production, making it difficult for them to compete with the likes of SouthWest on an equal basis. Therefore, these full-service carriers have sought to restructure to reduce their cost base. At the same time, these airlines have been seeking to reposition, restructure and redesign their major company offerings. The low-cost carriers in the USA have provided many examples of innovative provision, tailoring their products to the changing market. Some analysts have argued that the low-cost carriers have evolved the market so that demand now follows the low-cost supply model, causing full-service provision to be completely overhauled in the USA.

These examples show that the business model airlines use, marketing, operations management and human resource management functions are critical to delivering their service to the tourist. Even in the face of adverse conditions such as 11 September, businesses responded to the market conditions and adapted, innovated and responded to new situations. In the case of the US airline industry, the scope for innovation was limited by negative publicity and a reduction in air travel. But in other sectors of the tourism industry, innovative advertising, moving capacity such as cruise ships to new destinations and routes, and promoting domestic travel, can allow managers to re-orient their business activities to fit with demand. Ultimately, management of tourism in the private sector is about marrying supply with demand, and in managing capacity so that peaked demand through season-ality is accommodated and profitability is achieved. Yet there are various agencies and organizations that work alongside the private sector businesses and act as facilitators of tourism, to ensure it is planned, managed and developed in a man-ner that befits each locality. For this reason, Chapter 11 turns to the role of tourism agencies and the public sector in managing tourism.

References

Baum, T. (ed.) (1993) *Human Resource Issues in International Tourism*. London: Butterworth-Heinemann.

Carroll, S. (1988) Managerial work in the future. In G. Hage (ed.) *Futures of Organisations*. Lexington: Lexington Books.

Carter, S. (1996) Small business marketing. In M. Warner (ed.) *International Enyclopedia of Business and Management*. London: Thomson Learning.

Cooper, C., Fletcher, J., Gilbert, D. and Wanhill, S. (1998) *Tourism, Principles and Practice*. London: Pitman.

Handy, C. (1989) *The Age of Unreason*. London: Business Books Ltd.

Holloway, J. C. and Planr, R. (1998) *Marketing for Tourism*. London: Pitman.

Horner, S. and Swarbrooke, J. (1996) *Marketing Tourism, Hospitality and Leisure in Europe*. London: International Thomson Business Press.

Inkson, K. and Kolb, D. (1995) *Management: A New Zealand Perspective*. Auckland: Longman Paul.

Kotler, P. and Armstrong, G. (1991) *Principles of Marketing*, 5th ed. New Jersey: Prentice Hall.

McKercher, B. and Robbins, B. (1998) Business development issues affecting nature-based tourism oper-ators in Australia. *Journal of Sustainable Tourism*, 6(2): 173–88.

Morrison, A. (1996) Marketing the small tourism business. In A. Seaton and M. Bennett (eds) *Marketing Tourism Products: Concepts, Issues, Cases*. London: International Thomson Publishing.

Page, S. J. and Connell, J. (2006) *Tourism: A Modern Synthesis,* 2nd edn. London: International Thomson Publishing.

Quinn, R., Faerman, S., Thompson, M. and McGrath, M. (1990) *Becoming a Master Manager: A Competency Framework*. New York: Wiley.

Schumpeter, J. (1952) *Can Capitalism Survive?* New York: Harper and Row.

Shaw, G. and Williams, A. (2002) *Critical Issues in Tourism: A Geographical Perspective*, 2nd edn. Oxford: Blackwell.

Further reading

One of the most digestible sources is:
Leiper, N. (1995) *Tourism Management.* Victoria: TAFE.

Questions

1 Why is innovation important to tourism? How do businesses embrace and harness the potential of innovation?
2 Why do tourism managers need to understand the role of management in tourism? How far are good managers 'people persons'?
3 Why do small businesses dominate the tourism sector? What particular management challenges does this pose?
4 Can the Disney model of customer care be widely rolled out to be adopted in tourism firms? Outline the reasons why or why not this may be the case.

Chapter

11

The public sector and tourism

Learning outcomes

This chapter examines the role of the public sector and the ways it facilitates and constrains the development, operation and management of tourism. On completion of this chapter, you should be able to:

- identify the roles and responsibilities of the public sector in tourism
- explain what is meant by tourism policy and why it is developed to guide tourism planning and development in different contexts and destinations
- present a coherent argument as to why the public sector needs to intervene in the tourism sector
- present examples of best practice in developing public sector models of intervention that balance the needs of stakeholders
- recognize why tourism planning is used as a tool and what are its problems in implementation.

Introduction

Chapter 10 introduced the concept of tourism management in relation to the way private sector businesses interact, operate and perform in market economies. It highlighted the importance of management to ensure that for private sector companies profitability is ensured. Yet tourism operates in a wider macroeconomic environment beyond the level of the firm and that environment can be indirectly and directly managed, influenced and directed by government. According to Elliot (1997), there are four main questions that need to be asked in relation to the involvement of government in tourism:

1 Why are governments important to tourism, and why do governments get involved in tourism management?
2 Who are the main participants in the tourism policy system?
3 How is management of tourism policy carried out, and how do such managers manage?
4 What are the effects on tourism – has it led to success or failure?

This chapter will explore these questions and explain how the public sector manages tourism, emphasizing the role of policy-making, the implementation through planning and the impact on the management of tourism.

Governments and tourism

Governments become involved in tourism either through direct action to develop facilities and areas or indirectly by nurturing organizations that foster tourism. To the political scientist, tourism is an interesting phenomenon because for it to thrive, the ideal conditions are political stability, security, a well-defined legal framework and the essential services and infrastructure (roads, water supplies and a suitable environment) that the state is able to provide these services at both the national level and also at a regional and local level, through local councils (see Table 11.1). In addition, national governments are the main organizations, which negotiate on immigration, visa requirements and landing rights for airlines. These statutory responsibilities are often delegated to different government departments and do not take account of more active involvement in tourism. The main factor at work here is *power* – the

Table 11.1 The scope of local authority involvement in tourism in Scotland (adapted from SLAED, 2002; COSLA and Economic Development and Planning Executive Group, 2002)

There are 32 local authorities in Scotland, called councils, and their main area of involvement is in:

- infrastructure provision (e.g. roads, water, refuse collection, food safety and hygiene licensing)
- ensuring visitor facilities are accessible
- provision of information to visitors.

This is largely a tourism-support role.

A lesser-known role for local authorities is in tourism operations. They:

- fund local tourism activity, via partnership agreements with the main tourism organization – VisitScotland
- promote tourism initiatives at the local level
- own and manage visitor attractions (around 900 free admission attractions in Scotland), approximately 21 per cent of the total of Scottish visitor attractions
- engage in tourism development through the planning process as well as in promoting specific initiatives (e.g. city centre renewal strategies)
- promote tourism marketing via promotional campaigns, sponsoring and facilitating events.

---

ability to use influence and authority to effect decisions and change. Whilst governments are expected to perform statutory tasks such as immigration and negotiating aviation rights for the wider public good, it is their degree of involvement and commitment to tourism over and above these statutory functions that is important. In other words, if power is about 'who gets what, when and how in the political system' (Elliot 1997: 10), then the political system is worthy of consideration. This is because it can explain why some countries, regions and localities are characterized by high levels of public sector management (PSM) and involvement and others are not. PSM is how the government influences tourism through actions and policies to either constrain or develop tourism. To governments, PSM is expected to effect change due to intervention, which is being in the 'public interest' and based on principles of accountability, which are determined by the political and legal system and PSM culture. In other words, PSM is the way in which governments manage tourism although few tourism commentators would adopt that perspective, preferring to deny that government has an active role in management directly, since it is often delegated to purpose-designed tourism bodies such as National Tourism Organizations.

Why governments intervene in the tourism sector

At the country level, governments have an interest in tourism because it is an environmentally damaging activity if left uncontrolled, and may affect the people and economies of areas in positive and negative ways (see Chapter 12). In other words, governments have a strong interest in tourism in terms of its benefits to the economy and society. It is usually argued that the government's utilizing of the concept of leverage, namely investment in facilities and infrastructure to promote and stimulate tourism, brings wider benefits of tourism for the well-being of the population (i.e. it can create jobs and raise tax income). This is illustrated by the World Tourism Organization (now UN-WTO) (1998: 29) *Guide for Local Authorities on Developing Sustainable Tourism*, which highlighted the preconditions, benefits and effects of government intervention:

> Tourism requires that adequate infrastructure such as roads, water supply, electric power, waste management and telecommunications be developed. This infrastructure can also be designed to serve local communities so that they receive the benefits of infrastructure improvements. Tourism development can help pay for the cost of improved infrastructure. Tourism can provide new markets for local products ... and thereby stimulate other local economic sectors. Tourism stimulates development of new and improved retail, recreation and cultural facilities ... which locals as well as tourists can use.

The report also acknowledged that tourism can contribute to environmental improvements as tourists seek out unpolluted places, also promoting cultural and heritage protection. In fact Middleton and Hawkins (1998: 6) identified the attraction of state-encouraged tourism in the developing world as being because of its potential to expand rapidly as an economic sector. This shows that it is a global phenomenon, has major economic (e.g. foreign currency) benefits, can promote employment growth and creates value in natural, cultural and heritage resources for visitors. In contrast to other sectors of the economy it has been described as a smokeless industry (i.e. it is perceived as low polluting compared to developing heavy industry) and can contribute to the quality of life of residents and visitors. But there are scep-tics who question the positive reasons behind state intervention, since it can induce social and cultural change amongst the resident population, and alter the character and ambience of places as tourism development is followed by the resort life cycle and mass tourism. Furthermore, the economic benefits of tourism are not necessarily oriented to generating local wealth and employment, as in less developed countries (LDCs) and non-urban areas, the benefits leak out and low-paid, seasonal employment is the norm rather than full employment for all. The economic drawbacks become more serious when external control by multinational companies results in the environmental costs being borne by the locality while the profits are expropriated back to the company, often located overseas.

Jeffries (2001) also pointed to wider political objectives by governments in affecting tourism development:

- In Spain, the Franco regime in the 1960s sought to use tourism to legitimize its political acceptability, as well as recognizing its economic potential.
- Since the 1930s, France has used the concept of social tourism (similar to the for-mer Soviet Union's idea of recreational tourism, to improve the quality of life of workers at resorts, spas and holiday camps), especially among low-income groups, to enhance the welfare role of the state.
- The UK government in the 1980s emphasized the employment potential of tourism to create new jobs and wealth in an era of high unemployment.
- Some countries and transnational bodies such as the EU actively promote grants and aid to the peripheral regions to help develop the tourism infrastructure (e.g. road improvements in the Republic of Ireland and the Highlands and Islands of Scotland) to encourage the expansion of the tourism potential.
- In LDCs, tourism expansion is often politically justified as a means of poverty eradication and a number of developed countries' governments (e.g. the UK, Australia, New Zealand and the EU) provide aid to assist with this objective, as evident in the case of the Pacific islands.

Government intervention and tourism performance

Governments also intervene in the tourism arena because it is perceived to be a complex industry, being an amalgam of different businesses and sectors, where benefits accrue if these businesses are coordinated better to achieve common goals – the development and improvement of the quality of tourism. A more controversial argument for intervention is that it can prevent market failure. Indeed, some commentators argue that when the public sector gets too involved in tourism, such as through major investment in business activities like visitor attractions, failure is never far away. This is because the imbalance with public sector intervention may deter private sector investment if tourism becomes overly bureaucratized with a multiplicity of agencies involved in its management and regulation. In extreme cases, too much public sector investment may lead to a dependency culture where tourism is protected from market forces, becomes uneconomic due to the subsidies, is unattractive to investors and fails to reach its full potential.

But intervention is often politically justified since the highly seasonal nature of tourism activity in some regions and countries means that there is often insufficient business to support all-year-round operation. In extreme cases, there may not be adequate flows of tourists to support a tourist attraction. State subsidies, grants and assistance to the tourism sector in this context is justified, supporters argue, because without support the attraction may not be able to survive, and therefore would not provide a vital element of the region's attractiveness. This is highly controversial in countries wherethe performance of the tourism sector (in terms of visitor arrivals, productivity per business and high levels of seasonality) has been supported by public subsidies to operators and the tourism sector. Critics of such policies point to the obvious advantage of allowing the tourism sector to operate in a market economy with no subsidies or state intervention: it improves competitiveness. They argue that a market forces culture is important to stimulate innovation and new ideas, exciting developments and a dynamic tourism industry. Enterprise, development and innovation may need support and assistance at a fledgling stage, but first ideas on innovation need to be generated. If there is no incentive for such activity due to dependency, and the tourism sector operates in a protective environment and does not have to compete globally, then public sector support may actually dampen vital activity. The result of increased competition may well be the loss of businesses without a viable market to support them in the short-term if subsidies were removed. Yet a decline in the number and range of tourism operators may actually be desirable if it removes marginal and poor-quality operators with low service standards, who may depress the market for other businesses seeking to promote a quality product.

The perceived impact of such changes on marginal tourism regions, which have a heavy dependence on seasonal tourism for local employment, is viewed as politically unacceptable. Removals of subsidies are only implemented where public sector funding for tourism is reduced owing to financial stringencies in central, regional or local government budgets. Yet critics of state subsidies for tourism argue that few other sectors of the economy with significant private and public sector involvement enjoy such levels of state-related support to facilitate economic activity.

Advocates of continued state support, often described as 'lobbying' or 'interest groups' (e.g. the Scottish Tourism Forum in Scotland, the British Hospitality Association in the UK and Tourism Industry Association in the USA, which represents its tourism members) highlight the wider benefits of state involvement in tourism. Even in the USA, where Congress suspended funding of the US Travel and Tourism Administration in 1996 and pushed the marketing and promotion of the US to an industry body (the Tourism Industry Association), it re-intervened in 2005 to provide federal funds for marketing the USA overseas since a combination of problems had damaged the country's attractiveness as a destination. Industry lobby groups argue that improvements to the range of infrastructure (e.g. roads), attractions and business activity may also have benefits for residents of areas. In many local council areas, especially in towns, tourism is seen by residents as a problem in that cleansing, rubbish collection, policing and marketing/promotion that arises from tourism adding to the tax burden. Yet the beneficial effects of tourist spending on the local economy (see Chapter 12) arguably can reduce rating levels, as tourism supports local businesses, which pay business rates, create employment and generate greater revenue for councils, thereby reducing the potential rates burden for local residents.

Such arguments are highly controversial and different facets of each argument are invariably highlighted by interest groups, depending upon the evidence used and points raised to advocate or reject public sector support. There is often a great deal of conjecture, supposition and value-laden arguments used by interest groups and stakeholders when debating tourism. This may explain why some local councils, which periodically change their political complexion, can be described as 'blowing hot and cold' towards tourism, exemplified in the policies and planning approaches they adopt towards tourism. This is one reason why governments have endorsed better research methods to understand, analyse and explain how local economies are impacted by tourism. As Chapter 12 will show, the use of Tourism Satellite Accounts have begun to provide some objective data to support the wider economic arguments on the importance of tourism to national economies. This has started to address the ongoing tension associated with situations where objective tourism data do not exist.

Inevitably, government involvement in tourism at any level is about the resolution of conflict, seeking to achieve a balance between actively promoting tourism and acting as guardians of the public interest in the manner, form, direction, impact and effect of tourism from a national to local level. This conflict resolution process will often mean balancing the protagonists (i.e. the tourism industry) and antagonists (often residents) who are both valid stakeholders in the tourism economy, in seeking to meet the needs of the visitor in a sustainable and locally appropriate manner (see Box 11.1).

Box 11.1 Case Study: Government policy towards tourism in Africa and the role of industry associations in Southern Africa

According to Brown (2000), few countries in sub-Saharan Africa had developed sizeable tourism economies prior to 1980. Even by 1999, over half of all overseas arrivals were concentrated in South Africa, Morocco and Tunisia. South Africa is one of the success stories of African tourism, with growth rates in recent years of up to 20 per cent a year in non-African visitor arrivals and over six million international visitors a year. Many factors can be attributed to this growth, not least a depreciated currency (the rand) which makes it a very attractive destination for European and Asian visitors. It is also ranked highly by luxury travellers who consume ecotourism and wildlife tourism experiences, as the leading long-haul luxury UK travel magazine *Condé Nast Traveller* states. To understand how Africa has embraced tourism, it is interesting to consider policy shifts by African governments that have facilitated such growth.

Brown (2000) argues that, historically, African tourism was based on game reserves and parks, developed to suit expatriate white residents, settler communities and overseas visitors. Most of these visitors came from Eastern and Southern Africa prior to the 1950s. As the independence movement developed in many African countries in the period after 1950, national park systems were created. These largely had a conservation rather than a tourism focus. It was mainly in the Eastern and Southern African countries that tourism ministries were created, with a focus on planning, marketing, developing and administering tourism as a vital economic activity.

In the period since the 1970s, government attitudes towards tourism as an economic activity have evolved, integral to economic reconstruction following independence. Prior to the 1970s, tourism was rightly seen as an exploitative activity, controlled by white colonial interests and multinational enterprises. During the 1980s governments, according to

Brown (2000) identified the link between tourism and economic development as a process that they have more power to control and direct, to avoid purely exploitative relationships. However, many studies have highlighted to governments the capital investment that is needed to develop tourism infrastructure.

Tourism also offers new hope, as many politicians acknowledge, bearing in mind the ongoing problems of promoting agricultural development and the obstacles to fair world trade as development options. Tourism also offers some scope for indigenous entrepreneurship, as the extensive government support schemes in South Africa, post-apartheid, suggest. Many African governments have also begun to recognize that they can manage international investment to build visitor markets, as leading hotel brands provide a customer base loyal to international products. As African governments have embraced more democratic government, and ensured a greater degree of political stability, international investment has begun to help build the necessary infrastructure.

The challenge in South Africa is to build the complementary infrastructure and tourism capacity so that indigenous communities can seize the economic development opportunities. Accompanying the international investment has been a greater investment in tourism organizations and administration together with tourism policies and strategies to set the direction for development. Perhaps the greatest challenge for Africa's fledgling and established tourism industries in those countries that have embraced such activity is ensuring it develops in an environmentally balanced manner. With many fragile environments and ecosystems, government policy has often had a particular focus on this element, especially in relation to ecotourism that has nurtured luxury high-spending markets. Among other challenges for African tourism are:

- generating research data that enable governments to monitor tourism's development and impacts (social, economic and environmental)
- developing indigenous entrepreneurship as a basis for unique product development
- training and equipping the labour force to meet the needs of international visitors
- developing the right tourism organizations to accommodate the industry's growth, with marketing, planning and development capacity
- being able to identify the social and cultural effects of tourism growth and development on the indigenous population, to ensure that local culture, expertise and knowledge are not lost with the greater globalization of tourism experiences.

In South Africa a tourism industry association – the Southern African Association of Tourism Professionals (SAATP) – was formed in 2000. As an expanding sector of the economy,

SAATP sought to 'represent the collective interests of individuals operating at a professional level in Southern Africa' and its objectives are to:

● raise standards of tourism professional within Southern Africa
● attain and maintain regional and international recognition as representative of professional tourism competence within Southern Africa
● speak on behalf of professional people operating within the tourism sector in Southern Africa
● encourage members of the association to strive for professional excellence both academically and in practice
● protect the professional standing of the association and its members by imposing a code of conduct on the membership and ensuring enforcement thereof
● encourage the development of potential tourism professionals through interaction with appropriate education and training organizations
● foster a better understanding of the role of tourism professionals within public, private and civil society
● establish a tourism network that includes information held by members, tertiary education institutions, public, private and other institutions
● contribute intellectual leadership to tourism development in Southern Africa by providing appropriate responses to public domain issues and processes
● provide opportunities for discussion and debate on tourism issues important to the membership
● develop and maintain an information directory of all the members of the association and to implement appropriate distribution strategies regularly for the benefit of members.

Source: www.tourismprofessionals.org

Members are required to adhere to a code of conduct, including the Global Code of Ethics for Tourism produced by the UN-WTO. SAATP has an important role lobbying industry, coordinating and developing the sector. Not only can it provide industry leadership, it can also promote many of the training and development objectives of the tourism industry in line with government tourism policy. It complements the activities of government-funded bodies such as the National Trade Organization, South African Tourism. With forecasts by UN-WTO of an increase of 300 per cent in visitor arrivals by 2020 to the Southern African region (comprising South Africa, Swaziland, Botswana, Namibia and Lesotho) the organization and management of the tourism sector by government and private sector bodies such as SAATP will be critical to take advantage of growth opportunities.

A more active role for governments, and a potential reason for intervention in the tourism economy or markets, is related to strategic objectives aside from the development process. Here one dimension of public sector management has been divided into two perspectives by Jeffries (2001):

1 strategic seasonal redistribution of tourists
2 strategic geographical redistribution of tourism.

In the first instance, seasonal redistribution is a major global issue, given the problems of seasonality in tourism discussed in Chapter 10. Seasonality can lead to a highly skewed pattern of business for tourism operators outside major urban areas but tourism organizations responsible for tourism promotion, development and management may intervene in the market, as the case of Destination Northland (north of New Zealand, www.destinationnorthland.co.nz) suggests. It was able to:

• provide a new series of innovative new products for visitors in the low season that are less weather dependent, by emphasizing the appeal to the domestic market (e.g. through hosting sporting events and promoting sightseeing on the twin-coast highway route, and wine and food tourism based on local products)
• operate marketing campaigns via printed media and the worldwide web to highlight the region's indigenous culture (i.e. the Maori of Tai Tokerau iwi) and the built heritage, at Russell, the country's first capital, as the birthplace of New Zealand. It also recognized the appeal of the marine environment of the Bay of Islands, with the attraction for yacht-based tourists to winter over in the region.

Despite the example of Destination Northland, the tourism industry in many localities remains highly fragmented, lacks cohesion and lacks the ability to have political clout and influence change, since the individual operators are focused on their own activities rather than the strategic development of the region. By seeking to extend the tourist season, and expand the range of opportunities for low season visitation, public sector agencies argue that they will encourage increased business activity and turnover that will lead to greater profitability, as

Table 11.2 Selected eccentric events in the USA (adapted from Friedman, 2004)

- National Cowboy Poetry Gathering, Nebraska
- International Pancake Race, Kansas
- Moose Stompers Weekend, Maine
- World Snow Shovel Race, New Mexico
- Underwater Music Festival, Florida
- Rattlesnake Round-up and Cook-off, Texas
- Mule Day, Tennessee
- Cardboard Boat Regatta, Illinois
- Stink Fest, Pennsylvania
- Redneck Games, Georgia
- International Cherry Pie Spitting Contest, Michigan
- Zuccini Fest, Vermont
- Watermelon Seed-Spitting and Speed Eating Contest, Wisconsin

well as possibly increasing employment and gaining a higher profile as a tourism region.

One widely used tool that tourism organizations use to promote out-of-season tourism is the staging of events. These act as a nucleus for visits, as an attraction (see Chapter 9) but also as a wider catalyst for tourism activity. In some very unlikely locations that have a limited tourism potential, innovative and sometimes bizarre associations or the creation of events may be used to create a unique proposition to attract visitors. For example, in the USA the *Eccentric America Guidebook* (www. eccentricamerica.com) provides over 1000 entries and an annual events calendar of many weird events that sometimes attract visitors to small towns with few other attractions, or to tourist destinations with a highly seasonal industry. Table 11.2 lists a number of these events which the local tourism industry and other bodies promote as unique attractions, and often attract a substantial community involvement in their organization, management and promotion.

In the second instance the public sector directly intervenes in tourism planning and development by seeking directly to achieve a geographical redistri-bution of tourists and the volume of visits. For example, in the 1960s the French government produced a plan to develop a coastal region to the south of Montpellier, known as Languedoc-Roussillon. The initial plan was to develop a resort area with 150 000 bedspaces; this was subsequently revised and expanded in the 1970s and 1980s. This is a widely cited example of state-led tourism development in a peripheral area, and reveals the state's motives: seeking to direct tourism to an undeveloped region to assist with regional development. In contrast, tourism in London, which is the gateway for UK tourism, saw resident views, congestion, overcrowding and high occupancy rates in hotel accommodation result in the London Tourist Board commission the *Tourism Accommodation in London in the 1990s* report (Touche Ross, 1988). This formed the basis for policies to limit further hotel growth in London's West End, while encouraging out-of-town accommodation development. The result was the development of tourism accommodation in the period 1988–2000 in districts adjacent to the West End of London and the expansion of accommodation in London's urban fringe adjacent to Heathrow and Gatwick airports – especially budget accommodation next to the M25 motorway junctions. This policy of constraint and directed development has taken a number of years to evolve, but despite the lead time for new accommodation and even over a 14-year period, changes are notable.

London is a crucial gateway, with 48 per cent of all overseas visitors to the UK entering via London. Other leading cities also handle a high proportion of their country's international arrivals (e.g. Sydney 50 per cent; Dublin 54 per cent; Amsterdam 52 per cent) although this does not apply to all capital cities (Paris only accounts for 12 per cent of all arrivals in France and Rome for 10 per cent of arrivals in Italy). What many public sector analysts recognize is that London is competing globally as a world city and tourism is a necessary component of that globalization. Therefore, policies constraining tourism have had to be replaced with those seeking to facilitate growth 'to create jobs and increase the contribution of tourism to the economy of the capital and the country as a whole' (London Development Agency 2004: 60). This has meant developing a public sector policy of dispersal where

> growth needs to be more evenly spread across London, with new businesses encouraged to develop outside the central London area. This will increase choice and improve value for money for visitors, and help ensure all parts of London can share in the economic benefits of tourism. The Mayor's Culture Strategy has also highlighted the importance of the spatial (geographical)

diversification of London's Cultural amenities. (London Development Agency 2004: 60)

In the wider scheme of tourism, key elements identified in this dispersal strategy are:

- improving the supply of London's accommodation with a further 26 000 rooms as well as improved value for money and quality control
- developing new attractions and accommodation to achieve the dispersal strategy in outer London boroughs
- improving transport and infrastructure to facilitate this dispersal in areas identified for economic growth (as well as safeguarding the West End of London as a key element of London's international appeal as an entertainment district).

One area that has seen considerable growth is the night-time economy in London both for tourist and leisure use, with a rise in restaurant and bars opening since the 1990s. This in itself has been stimulated by a greater provision of all-night buses by Transport for London. However, a number of problems also exist and these can impact upon the tourist image of London. They include crime and antisocial behaviour, and street-cleanliness, all of which are aggravated by the expansion of the night-time city. In 2005 controversial legislation in the UK allowed pubs to open for 24 hours in approved instances, in a bid to address the problems of binge drinking and a yob culture among 18- to 30-year-olds in city centres. Thus, whilst policies to decentralize tourism in London have seen a degree of success, the expansion in central and suburban London's nightlife, where residents and visitors coexist, may prove a major social and environmental nuisance for residents and affect the image of London as a destination for tourists.

More explicit state intervention is evident in many of Europe's small historic towns, where local planning authorities have adopted radical measures to constrain the saturation effects of mass tourism in cities such as Canterbury, York, Stratford-upon-Avon and Cambridge. But how do organizations in the public sector affect such change, and what processes and procedures are used to manage tourism? This begins through the development of tourism policy.

Tourism policy

According to Hall and Jenkins (1995: 2), tourism public policy can help the causes and consequences of policy decisions, since it indicates the way in which policy influences tourism through:

- the political nature of the policy-making process
- the degree of public participation in the tourism policy and planning process
- the sources of power in the tourism policy-making environment, and the choices and decisions made by civil servants towards complex policy issues
- the perceptions of stakeholders as to the effectiveness of tourism policies.

This illustrates that tourism policy-making is inherently a political activity, affected by the formal structures of government. A wide range of forces affects policy-making. According to Hall and Jenkins (1995: 5) public policy in tourism is 'whatever governments choose to do or not to do', and it is a function of three interrelated issues according to Turner (1997):

- the intentions of political and other key actors
- the way in which decisions and non-decisions are made
- the implications of these decisions.

Figure 11.1 illustrates the continuous nature of policy-making, which requires one to understand the nature of the institutions and organizations involved in shaping policy, since policy-making is filtered through a range of different institutions that may seem complex to the uninitiated observer. These institutions help shape policy outcomes because they are involved in negotiation and bargaining to achieve their own organization's objectives. At the same time, interest groups (producer groups such as national tourism associations), non-producer groups (e.g. environmental organizations) and single issue groups (e.g. opponents of an airport project) seek to influence the decision-making element of policy-making.

Tourism policy does not exist in a vacuum because various agencies exist to implement policy. The implementation is, again, a resolution of conflict and attempt to meet the needs of stakeholders whilst meeting national or local tourism development needs. Policy cannot be viewed in isolation from political decision-making, which determines the direction of policy, which is constantly evolving.

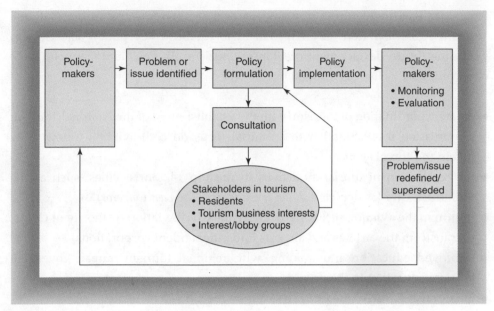

Figure 11.1   The policy-making process in tourism

For example, in the case of China, a series of policy changes post-1978, when the country first opened its doors to tourists, required major policy changes. After 1978, policy success has often been measured through one simple barometer of tourism – international visitor arrivals. In 1978, international visitor arrivals in China were a modest 1.8 million; these subsequently increased to 17.8 million in 1985 and 33.3 million in 1991. Five years later, visitor arrivals exceeded 51 million, and in 1997 some 57.5 million arrivals were recorded. This incredible rate of growth in inbound tourism required a shift in policy from the pre-1978 socialist idea that tourism was a vehicle to educate visitors about the virtues of com-munism to one that was accommodating a large influx of visitors who were only allowed to visit certain areas. A similar rationale characterized inbound tourism policy in the former Soviet Union and pre-1990s Albania.

In the case of China, tourism policy was effectively embodied in the Five-Year National Plans, which controlled a state-command economy. From 1986 to 1991, state policy saw tourism as a lucrative source of foreign exchange. This view evolved from the 1978–1985 period where a general tourism policy with little state interven-tion created major operational problems in terms of a general shortage of supply, an inadequate non-market pricing structure, and ineffective management of tourists and employees, resulting in poor service standards. By developing a

National Tourism Plan, the government tourist agency – the China National Tourism Administration (CNTA) – began to establish key policy objectives to guide the future development of Chinese tourism. As Page and Connell (2006) observed, policy changes resulted in:

- greater coordination of tourism, with the establishment of the National Tourism Commission in 1988 and with an initial focus on civil aviation followed by hotels and travel agencies
- the restoration of tourist attractions in the top 14 tourist cities, such as the Forbidden City (as depicted in the famous film *The Last Emperor*)
- reform in the aviation sector, particularly the Civil Aviation Authority of China, to transform the airlines and airports into independent corporations
- improved education and training, with regional tourism bureau governing tourism education in their region
- greater regulation of the tourism sector by the CNTA
- the promotion of international tourism, with CNTA's budget for overseas marketing increased from US$1.4 million in 1986 to US$3.2 million in 1991 following the decline of tourist arrivals and the impact of the Tiananmen Square incident.

Subsequent policy changes in 1992 were embodied under the new 'market economy under socialism' policy, whereby tourism could move towards a market system without unduly compromising the underlying principles of Chinese socialism. One notable change was the introduction of competition into China's aviation sector (subsequently reversed after safety concerns), a greater use of tourism promotion, and recognition of the diversity of inbound tourism and niche markets as well as the need for state-led regulation of the tourism sector to improve quality standards. In addition, government policy towards the economy may have an indirect and direct effect on tourism. In the period 1986–1996, the government used a growth pole strategy: a key location is chosen and investment and economic development concentrates in less developed areas to pump-prime the economy. The growth pole was located at the town of Yunnan in inland China, which became the basis for economic development fostered around tourism; the aim being to assist in dispersing the current patterns of tourism development from the coastal region and key cities. This was found to help address regional economic inequality where the tourism sector had powerful backward linkages with other economic sectors (e.g. agriculture (see Chapter 12 for more discussion)).

The growth pole strategy helps to spread the effects and benefits of tourism, but equally it can pose planning problems where policy decisions have to be taken over the style of tourism development to pursue (i.e. small-scale versus mass tourism). A similar strategy of growth pole development in tourism has been used and has had a benefit in economically remote areas in Ireland, Scotland and Canada. In each case, the state has invested in the infrastructure and provided incentives for private sector investment in tourism.

Yet it is not just governments which influence tourism policy, but also a range of international non-governmental agencies (NGOs) such as the World Tourism Organization. The UN-WTO, based in Madrid, seeks to assist its member countries to work in a cooperative and collaborative manner to provide statistical information on tourism, and to advise on policies and practices to improve tourism planning and education and training. Other international lobby groups seek to influence the air transport and its industry groups (i.e. the IATA, ICAO, ATAG and ACI – see Chapter 7). These bodies promote the interests of their members, who have vested interests in tourism.

One additional agency that is influential in government tourism policy is the EU. The 25 member countries of the EU represent an important trading bloc, which is mirrored by similar blocs in other parts of the world. The EU seeks to promote tourism as a free-trade activity in and between member states by trying to simplify and harmonize policies and procedures to facilitate the free movement of travellers. The EU also seeks to develop measures to improve the quality of tourism in member states although tourism policy remains the remit of individual governments. The scale and extent of the EU's impact on the wide range of issues which affect tourism are shown in Table 11.3 which highlights the diversity of EU measures affecting tourism (see www.europa.eu.int for more up-to-date information as EU policy and developments in tourism are constantly evolving).

Among the most influential agencies that develop policy for tourism in individual countries are:

- ministries of tourism, which fund or part-fund National Tourism Organizations (NTOs) such as VisitBritain (which replaced the former British Tourist Authority)
- NTOs
- Regional Tourism Organizations which manage the implantation of national and regional policy in their respective areas
- local authorities and other agencies, which set policies at the local area level.

Table 11.3 The range of European Community measures affecting tourism

- Economic policies
- Enterprise policy towards tourism businesses
- Competition issues and mergers
- State aid for tourism (e.g. subsidies)
- The internal market and tourism
- Fiscal policies and tourism (e.g. taxation)
- Employment and social policy (e.g. the minimum wage)
- Enhancing Europe's potential for tourism
- Tourism and employment
- Exchange and dissemination of information
- Training, skills and the workforce
- Education and vocational training
- Qualifications, employability and lifelong learning
- Social rights, social protection, social integration and inequality
- Social dialogue
- Quality issues in tourism destinations
- Improving the quality of tourism products
- Safety in tourism installations, food safety and health
- The environment and sustainable development
- Environmental protection
- Natural and cultural heritage
- Transport
- Energy

The European Commission has produced guidelines or reports for each of these areas, all of which can be accessed at: www.europa.eu.int

This vast array of public sector agencies is complemented by *ad hoc* agencies set up within specific areas such as inner city regeneration projects (e.g. the London Docklands Development Corporation in the 1980s and 1990s). These specific area-based initiatives by local economic development agencies have been reintroduced in England and Wales; they highlight how policy changes can affect the actual structure of provision. In Scotland, Scottish Enterprise's local enterprise companies set out policies for the tourism sector and intervene, using public funds, to meet specific tourism objectives (see Chapter 9) as is explained in considerable detail in Page and Connell (2006).

It is apparent that in many countries, while tourism policy may rest with the Ministry of Tourism or department responsible for tourism, a host of agencies interact to produce a multilayered system of public sector support. Figure 11.2 illustrates this model of support in the UK, a model that has been described as chaotic and extremely bureaucratic. Whilst there is a growing debate over whether governments are still about direct control of tourism, or whether they should be encouraging other agencies to govern the public sector and be more accountable to stakeholders, the UK government is creating an overly complex web of agencies that may have confused, overlapping and competing roles. For example, the UK model is characterized by:

- One national organization, VisitBritain, to market the UK overseas.
- Four country-based NTOs – VisitEngland (incorporating the former English Tourism Council), VisitScotland (formerly the Scottish Tourist Board), the National Ireland Tourist Board and the Wales Tourist Board (which is being disbanded in 2006 and incorporated into the Welsh Assembly). In some cases, these NTOs market each country to domestic and international tourists, which may seem as a duplication of the efforts of VisitBritain, which markets the UK as a united destination overseas.
- Regional tourist boards in England, Wales and Northern Ireland, and the former network of area tourist boards in Scotland which are now part of the VisitScotland area offices. These agencies are funded by grants from the devolved governments in Wales and Scotland. In Scotland, the ministerial review of area tourist boards that reviewed their roles, activities and responsibilities concluded that one agency to manage tourism in Scotland in relation to marketing and promotion would be a more effective use of public resources.
- Local authorities in England of which there are 387 – 34 are non-metropolitan county councils, 238 are non-metropolitan district councils, 36 are metropolitan councils, 46 are unitary councils, 32 are London boroughs, plus the City of London Corporation.

Through their role in managing services for visitors, such as tourist information centres (TICs) (some local authorities undertake this role in other countries), regional and area tourist boards provide a network of contact points for visitors. For example, in Scotland the 148 TICs handled an average of 22000 bookings in a month and five million visitor enquiries. Given the scope and nature of the public sector agencies in tourism, attention now turns to how these organizations plan for tourism.

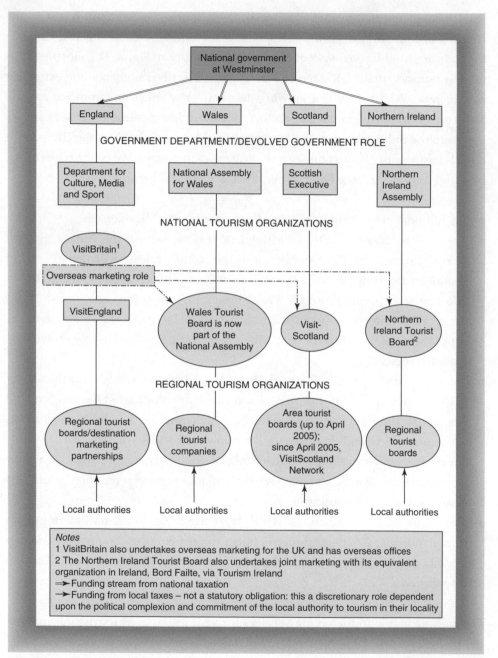

Figure 11.2   The Statutory Framework for the administration of tourism in the UK

How government organizations influence tourism

In the UK, the Department for Culture, Media and Sport (DCMS) is the government department responsible for tourism. Like its counterpart in many countries, it is not seen as a high-profile ministry, since tourism is not accorded a portfolio that reflects its economic role in most countries. As a result, other government departments make a significant contribution directly and indirectly to infrastructure development (e.g. the Department of Transport in terms of roads, ports and aviation). The DCMS has a broad responsibility for leisure, tourism and the cultural industries in the UK, including tourism, the arts, broadcasting, cultural artefacts, film, art, heritage, libraries, museums, galleries, the press, the royal estate, sport and recreation. Whilst such an integrated approach to the leisure industries is intended to achieve the ministry's objectives to improve the quality of life through cultural industries and sporting activities, and by contributing to job creation, there is a danger that tourism is subsumed and lost among so many functions.

Having outlined which organizations and bodies are involved in policy-making for tourism at different levels, attention now turns to how these policies are implemented – through the planning process.

Planning and tourism

So far this chapter has highlighted the tensions that exist in the formulation of policies to guide the development of the tourism sector, as a process of negotiation between stakeholders groups brokered by public sector agencies. At a practical level, the implementation of public sector policies requires an understanding of how agencies plan, manage and use tools in tourism destinations. The context in which agencies involved in tourism planning operate is also important, because underlying principles and ideas shape planning. For example, although the concept of sustainability is not the focus of this chapter, it is an important theme to explain, given its widespread use in tourism planning. In simple terms, sustainability is a common-sense approach to the use, consumption and management of the resources upon which tourism relies (see Chapter 12). In essence, the arguments developed on sustainability, and embodied in the Brundtland Report (World Commission on the Environment and Development, 1987), are that we need to use resources in such a manner that they can be enjoyed today but also conserved and managed for future generations. They question man's historical pursuit of resource depletion in the name of progress and development, with no concern for the future use. This concept, which was guided by environmentalism in the 1960s and 1970s, recognizes that there are limits to the growth of the planet, with many resources being finite and non-renewable (e.g. oil).

In a tourism context, the question of sustainability has emerged as a major debate for planners because of the global growth of tourism. Tourism equates to the consumption of environmental resources and this poses problems for destination areas. In practical terms, planners face the challenge of balancing tourism demand and supply, and of recognizing the future effects of tourism if the concept of sustainability is not considered. The public sector therefore intervenes in tourism and planning terms, to implement tourism policy objectives and to avoid over-development from tourism, as the tourism sector pursues short-term profits. This means that without public sector intervention, the environment and resource base for tourism in destination areas could be irreversibly damaged and the potentially beneficial effects of tourism may easily be lost.

If we return to the basic premise of tourism management, then tourism planning in its practical form is about the public sector leading to organize, plan and control tourism development in relation to policies in each destination area. This requires the complex coordination of stakeholder interests (private sector businesses, public sector agencies, residents and visitors). These tasks also have a time horizon, known as 'the strategic dimension', where tourism planning has a five- to ten-year time frame during which the impact and implications of policies and plans can be monitored and evaluated. This was illustrated above in the case of London's tourism accommodation 1988–2000, where policies directly shaped the nature, form and location of accommodation development. But does tourism planning actually exist and, if it does, how does it operate and how is it organized?

Does tourism planning exist?

There is an ongoing debate amongst tourism professionals as to whether tourism planning exists as a phenomenon, since much of the planning activity for tourism is based upon public sector planning as opposed to planning led by tourism agencies. In many cases, planning exists within regional (i.e. county councils) and local (i.e.

district councils) agencies in the UK and their equivalents in other parts of the world. These bodies typically subsume tourism within economic development departments, which seek to accommodate future demands and change. As Hall (1999) argues, much of the planning for tourism is based on an *ad hoc* approach, lacking continuity, cohesion and strategic vision.

Even so, Getz (1987) has described four traditions that have evolved towards planning tourism:

1 boosterism
2 an economic-industry approach
3 a physical-spatial approach
4 a community-oriented approach.

This can also be extended to give a fifth approach – sustainable tourism planning, which is 'a concern for the long-term future of resources, the effects of economic development on the environment, and its ability to meet present and future needs' (Page and Thorn, 1997: 60) although the implementation and management of sustainable tourism indicators remain problematic for many destinations despite the guidance recently issued by the UN-WTO in a report. The UN-WTO argued that sustainable tourism should:

● make optimal use of environmental resources (while maintaining the essential ecological processes while helping to conserve the natural heritage and biodiversity)
● respect the sociocultural authenticity of host communities (helping to conserve the cultural heritage and traditional values as well as seeking to engender intercultural understanding and tolerance)
● ensure viable, long-term economic operations, providing socioeconomic benefits to all stakeholders.

This illustrates both the environmental focus and the sociocultural and economic dimensions in relation to the nature of tourism and its impact. It is these elements that the UN-WTO argue should be the focus of any planning activity.

Inskeep (1994) has indicated that the effective management of tourism requires certain 'organizational elements'. The most important of these in a planning context are organizational structures, which include government agencies and private sector interest groups as well as local and regional government bodies, which are all involved in planning for tourism activity as well as tourism-related legislation and regulations. These bodies utilize the statutory planning frameworks such as planning acts, government ordinances and directives from central government, which in turn condition the parameters for planning. Where the planning process focuses on tourism, a process akin to the way policy-making is developed is followed.

The planning process for tourism

There is normally a set of pre-defined steps that characterize the planning process for tourism including:

1 *Study preparation*, which is where the planning authority within the local or regional government (although on small island states that do not have a complex planning structure it may be the NTO) decide to proceed with the development of a tourism plan. Normally a statutory body undertakes to prepare the plan but in more complex urban environments, where a local and regional agency both develop a tourism plan, it is important that they are integrated to ensure a unified approach to tourism. This was a problem in London in the 1990s, when the 33 London boroughs each had unified development plans but pursued different approaches to tourism. This meant that some councils promoted tourism development while others positively discouraged it despite the efforts of the London Tourist Board, which sought to coordinate their activities in tourism. The result was a pattern of uneven development across the city.

2 *Determination of objectives*, where the objectives of the plan are identified (e.g. is the agency seeking to promote an explanation of tourism to pump-prime economic development or trying to manage the problems of mass tourism and the associated effects?).

3 *Survey of all elements*, where an inventory of existing tourism resources and facilities are reviewed, requiring the collection of data on the supply and demand for tourism and the structure of the local tourist economy. It will need to recognize which other private and public sector interests are stakeholders in tourism within the destination.

4 *Analysis and synthesis of findings*, where the information and data collected from the previous stage are used to begin formulating the plan. This typically involves

four techniques: asset evaluation, market analysis, development planning and impact analysis (see Chapter 12) to establish the future for tourism.

5 *Policy and plan formulation*, where the data are used and synthesized (i.e. sifted, sorted and organized) to establish development scenarios for tourism. This will invariably lead to the preparation of a draft development plan with tourism policy options. These policies must have three elements to be able to meet the varying needs of the tourism stakeholders – visitor satisfaction, environmental protection and ensuring a pay-back for investors.

6 *Consideration of recommendations*, where the full tourism plan is sent to the organization's planning committee. A public consultation would normally follow after the planning committee's acceptance of the plan. The general public and interested parties are then able to read and comment on the plan. A number of public hearings may also be provided to gauge the strength of local feeling towards the plan. Once this procedure is completed, the plan will then be sent back to the planning authority in a revised form for approval with any changes incorporated, so the final plan can be prepared.

7 *The implementation and monitoring of the tourism plan* then follows, which includes various actions. Legislation may be required in some cases to control certain aspects of development (e.g. the density of development) that need to be implemented as part of the plan. However, the political complexity of implementing such a plan is substantial since the political balance of elected representatives on the statutory planning authority may change and cause the priorities to change. Where an action plan is produced that causes intense political debate over each issue, it may allow for some degree of choice in what is implemented and actioned in a set period of time. At the same time as the plan is implemented, it will also need to be monitored and evaluated, and frequently criticized by commentators. The planning agency will need to assess if the objectives of the plan are being met. The operational timeframe for a tourism plan is normally five years after which time it is reviewed.

8 *The periodic review*, is the process of reporting back on progress after the plan has run its course. When analysing the reasons for the success or, more commonly, failure of the plan to achieve all its objectives a range of reasons may be suggested. These may include a lack of resources to achieve the goals, political infighting by elected members of the planning authority, inadequate transport and infrastructure provision, public opposition to tourism among residents, and a lack of investment by public sector businesses.

Governmental tourism strategies

To guide the multitude of public sector agencies and stakeholders involved in tourism, government departments will often embody many of the policy object-ives in a strategy document. This strategy document will identify what the gov-ernment wishes to achieve in broad terms in tourism, and identifies objectives and action points for other agencies, as the case study in Box 11.2 shows.

Box 11.2 Case study: The Scottish Tourism Framework for Action 2002–2005 and Scottish Tourism – The Next Decade: A Framework for Tourism Change 2006–2015

In 2001 the newly created Ministry of Tourism, Sport and Culture in the Scottish Executive (SE) set out to develop a number of new directions for Scottish tourism. It closely followed the SE's first tourism strategy in February 2000 – *A New Strategy for Scottish Tourism* – with a new strategy in 2002. The initial strategy in 2000 identified five key areas for action in Scottish tourism to improve the performance of the industry, against a decline in over-seas arrivals. These areas were:

1 the effective use of information technology
2 better marketing
3 higher standards of quality
4 higher standards of service
5 the development of the skills base of tourism employees.

In 2002, the new ministry developed its new vision and priorities for Scottish tourism, embodied in *The Tourism Framework for Action 2002–2005*, which set out a vision thus:

> *Scotland* is a must-visit destination where visitors' needs come first, and tourism makes a vital contribution to economic growth.

This identified three specific priorities:

1 To develop a better and stronger market position for Scotland, based on clearly iden-tified brands and products to meet customer needs.

2 To improve the consumer focus to drive forward quality standards, as well as developing new products and services, ultimately to create successful business leadership.

3 To enhance the status of tourism in Scotland, based on understanding the linkages between different elements of the economy and tourism that require businesses and stakeholders to work together collaboratively, particularly through partnerships and alliances to improve sales, competitive position and focus. These objectives and visions are embodied in Figure 11.3; they require actions to be delivered by businesses, public sector agencies and the SE. For example, in 2002 VisitScotland launched a new brand and product portfolio to refocus VisitScotland's marketing focus for Scottish tourism (outlined in Figure 11.4, which shows the key products and segments in the market).

Based on this framework, the SE identified the role of tourism and non-tourism businesses in taking a responsibility for delivering the framework for action. A detailed set of actions is identified in relation to each objective in Figure 11.3 together with the responsibility for implementation. For example, in improving Scotland's market position it outlined the following objectives:

● To achieve high brand awareness amongst target groups, with three actions spread between businesses and public sector agencies.

● To increase the conversion of potential visitors from awareness to sales, with four actions split between public and private sector.

● To increase direct access opportunities for target consumers, with two actions, largely aimed at the SE – to develop the infrastructure and services as well as businesses collaborating to market such improvements.

A similar matrix of objectives and actions was developed for each of the three priorities (Figure 11.3). Interestingly, the framework for action identified the multiplicity of 'relevant' public sector agencies which need to work in partnership to deliver the public sector element of the strategy, including:

● The area tourist boards, particularly in relation to leading marketing initiatives that fit with VisitScotland's objectives, as well as operating TICs, delivering area tourism strategies and advising tourism businesses.

● The former British Tourist Authority (now VisitBritain), working with VisitScotland to market Scotland internationally using the BTA's network of overseas offices as well as its international market intelligence/research.

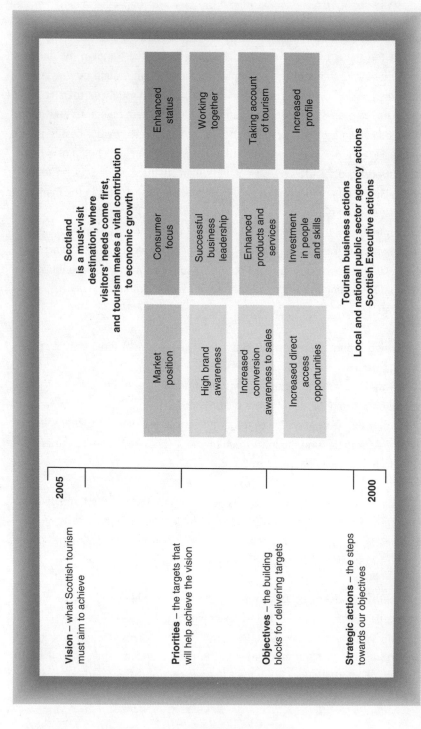

Figure 11.3 Scottish Tourism Framework for Action 2002–2005 (reproduced with permission from the Scottish Executive)

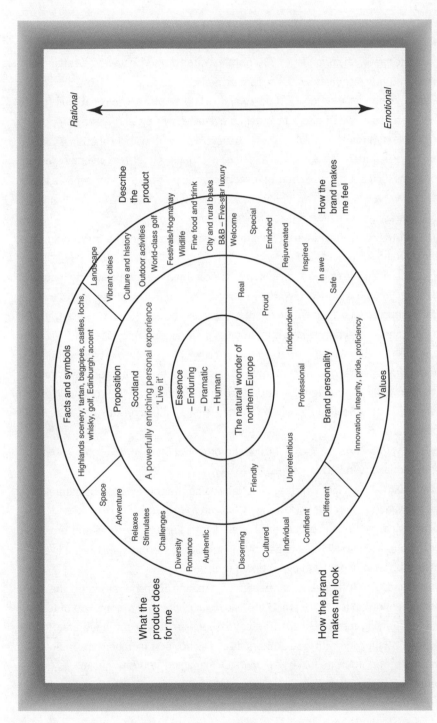

Figure 11.4 The VisitScotland brand essence wheel. © VisitScotland, reproduced with permission

- The Forestry Commission, which manages forestry resources and has a contribution to make to create opportunities for tourism.
- Historic Scotland, which manages 330 historic visitor attractions across Scotland and markets heritage resources to the tourism market.
- The local authorities who develop policy and deliver services within national frameworks for tourism, whilst also administering planning controls and managing publicly owned or leased tourism facilities. These agencies also work with local business associations (e.g. Chambers of Commerce) and trade associations (e.g. local voluntary tourism associations such as Dunblane Tourism Association) and part-fund the former area tourist boards (now part of a seamless VisitScotland organization covering all of Scotland) and actively participate in delivering area tourism strategies.
- The Scottish Arts Council, which supports and promotes the arts and administers lottery funding for the arts in Scotland.
- The Scottish Enterprise Network, comprising the local enterprise companies and Highlands and Islands Enterprise Network, which are involved in formulating strategies for training and infrastructure development and support services such as Small Business Gateway and vital coordination/networking opportunities for local tourism businesses.
- The Scottish Executive, with legislative responsibility for the Scottish economy functions devolved from the UK government in Westminster. It is responsible for direct funding to tourism and support agencies including local authorities, VisitScotland, Scottish Enterprise, Historic Scotland, Scottish Natural Heritage, the Scottish Arts Council and Sportscotland.
- The Scottish Museums Council, which is the organization that represents 200 members in Scotland with 320 museums.
- Scottish Natural Heritage, which provides advice on the conservation of natural heritage, recreation in the countryside and coastal areas.
- Sportscotland, which administers the Lottery Sports Fund in Scotland and promotes sporting opportunities. It has a role to play in relation to the growing interest in sport-related tourism (e.g. golf) and event-based tourism.
- VisitScotland, which formulates strategy for marketing Scotland, based on the 1969 Development of Tourism Act. It is also the lead organization in the promotion of tourism and in identifying research needs for Scottish tourism. It also cofunded area tourist boards (in conjunction with local authorities and its business membership) and advises government on tourism issues as well as managing tourism quality assurance schemes.

To implement the strategy and to evaluate its achievements, the following four steps were introduced in 2002:

1 The SE and VisitScotland were to develop a measurement framework for the required actions, with a series of performance indicators that measure progress.
2 A steering group was created, chaired by the Minister for Tourism, Sport and Culture, to oversee progress with the framework for action.
3 VisitScotland were to chair an implementation group to monitor actions, and to engage the industry to advise the steering group.
4 The hosting of events to engage the Scottish tourism industry to improve the mutual understanding of tourism and to recognize each organization's roles and responsibilities.

What is interesting about the framework is the extended coordination, communication and leadership role needed to drive Scottish tourism forward in the new millennium. It also emphasizes the scope of organizations that must be consulted in relation to tourism policy, and the potential conflicts that exist between agencies with competing objectives (e.g. conservation agencies and business development agencies). It also reinforces the arguments that policy-making is multilayered and involves a large number of interest groups. The progress towards targets set in the 2000–2005 tourism strategy included:

- increased marketing spend by VisitScotland: their budget has been doubled since 2001 and its marketing spend leverages £14.50 in tourism revenue for every £1 spent, up from £12 in 2000
- VisitScotland's brand proposition being demonstrated in research as unique, with its focus on the five key elements (see Figure 11.4) (active, cities, freedom, business, and culture and heritage)
- additional training for businesses being provided by Scotland's Enterprise Network since 2000, to try and raise the standards of provision in the tourism sector (especially food quality)
- business leadership being established by Pride and Passion
- the Scottish Executive Route Development Fund: this has improved accessibility to Scotland by funding 13 new air links and the Rosyth–Zeebrugge ferry service since 2000 as well as ferry services to remote islands.

In November 2005, the draft *Scottish Tourism – The Next Decade: A Framework for Change* was launched for the period 2006–2015. This set a new set of ambitious targets for Scottish tourism:

> To grow the revenue from Scottish tourism by 50 per cent, equivalent to a volume growth of 2 per cent a year.

To achieve this target, the strategy set out its ambition based on 'business entrepreneurship, business leadership and a focus on the consumer, with the public sector strongly supporting businesses and industry bodies to grow the sector'.

Sixteen targets were set out in the strategy for 2006–2015, among which were:

- establishing a tourism research network to ensure approach research is undertaken and disseminated to all stakeholders
- businesses to collect data to 'know their visitor' (who they are, why they have come and what they want out of their trip)
- VisitScotland to increase the proportion of businesses involved in its Quality Assurance schemes
- the Scottish Tourism Innovation Group's Pride and Passion scheme to double the number of friends each year, each of whom will make a commitment to improving the visitor experience
- the organization People First to develop and implement a workforce development plan so as to achieve a more highly skilled workforce by 2006
- managers and business owners to increase the take-up of training
- enterprise agencies (i.e. Scottish Enterprise and Highlands and Islands Enterprise) and the career organization Springboard Scotland to deliver support to businesses to improve recruitment and retention of staff
- the Scottish Executive to help provide affordable homes in locations facing a recruitment problem due a lack of housing for workers who are are priced out of the market
- the Tourism Innovation Group to work with groups of businesses, enterprise agencies and VisitScotland to identify emerging visitor trends, needs and new product opportunities
- every tourism business to become fully e-enabled by 2010 to maximize booking opportunities from VisitScotland.com.

Following on from the *Tourism Framework for Action 2000–2005*, the new strategy seeks to measure 'success' using many non-numerical measures; instead it focuses on more intangible and qualitative measures. Qualitative measures may be easier to use to justify success than existing quantitative indicators such as value of tourism revenue, visitor numbers, visitor satisfaction and expectation surveys. Nevertheless, the headline target established of growing Scottish tourism is unambiguous and clear and can only be evaluated using quantitative measures.

In the Scottish case, concerns with the industry's competitiveness, value for money, travel costs, unfavourable exchange rates and the problems of seasonality are not necessarily issues that a strategy can easily address. Above all, lateral thinking, industry–public sector cooperation and more visionary central government legislation aimed at tackling obstacles to improve business performance are needed to find ways to reposition Scottish tourism. With 50 per cent of overseas and 30 per cent of British visitors to Scotland visiting July–September each year, seasonality adds pressures on businesses and raises costs of production. This illustrates the need to reposition Scotland with new products and experiences to encourage a more even spread of visitation.

The public sector marketing of tourism

The majority of National Tourism Organizations (NTOs) are not producers or operators in a tourism context, but seek to influence the images which visitors and potential visitors may hold of the country or region. There are four models widely used to undertake this task:

1 Full state intervention, where the state promotes the brand image; this is not a common occurrence outside the former Eastern Europe, Africa (excluding South Africa) and South America.
2 A public–private-sector partnership, where the private sector contributes to the marketing, an approach that is widely used in Australia, Europe (excluding Germany, Italy and Greece).
3 A minimalist public sector role, as in the Netherlands, Japan and the USA, where private sector promotion is dominant.

4 Other models that are entirely funded from taxation of tourists and tourism rather than state support for destination marketing as a concept.

Most NTOs are engaged in destination promotion, usually aimed at the international market (though in large countries they may also target the domestic market). NTOs are also involved in the maintenance of a network of tourism offices in key international source markets, though this is more restricted in less developed countries whose budgets are very restricted. The most up-to-date figures on NTO budgets are the 1997 data from UN-WTO, which are based on a self-completion survey; this was cited in Pike's (2004) excellent review of this area. In 1997, European countries only spent 0.5 per cent of the gross receipts from international tourism on NTO marketing, which is considerably higher than 0.3 per cent in the USA. Yet globally it is estimated that NTOs spend US$1.5 billion on marketing which accounts for between half and two thirds of NTOs' total budgets – illustrating the cost of seeking to influence visitors' images of a destination. This can be done by direct advertising campaigns and product launches in target markets. For example, in October 2002, the Danish Tourist Board announced plans to spend £8 million on promoting short breaks from the UK to encourage a desire among Britons to visit Scandinavia, particularly since budget airlines afforded easy access. Similarly Tourism Ireland (the new all-Ireland promotion agency, see www.shamrock.org) announced a short-breaks programme themed around the 'temptation Ireland' idea designed to tempt visitors to visit and experience Ireland in short breaks. This is a coordinated pan-Ireland approach to assist the visitor with a more united approach to Destination Ireland – The Emerald Isle. As Table 11.4 shows, the budgets of NTOs and state/destination marketing organizations are substantial in many larger countries. In addition, the large proportion of their budgets are spent on marketing initiatives (see the figures in Table 11.4 for Australia, Toronto, Tourism Ireland and the US state tourism offices).

Expenditure on marketing is only one of the influences that affect tourism volumes to a country. There is no easy way to link marketing spend to performance in attracting visitors. Marketing of a destination is more about the subliminal changes to visitor perceptions to encourage and shape their interest in a place rather than a direct influencer of demand, in the same way that advertising affects fast-moving consumer goods.

There is new research evidence in tourism that the cultural and psychological association which people develop with a place, known as 'place bonding', may be

Table 11.4 Examples of National Tourism Organizations and destination-specific marketing organization spending on tourism/tourism initiatives (compiled from National Tourism Organization websites and other sources)

Country/Organization	Budget (Year)
Tourism Ireland	€200 million (2005)
(joint marketing of Northern and Southern Ireland	
marketing programme)	
Hawaii Visitor and Convention Bureau, USA	US$27 million (2005)
Reno, Nevada, USA	US$36 million (2005)
Toronto, Canada	US$23 million (2005)
(2006 re-branding campaign)	US$4 million in (2006)
Los Angeles, USA	US$20 million (2005)
New York City, USA	US$14.6 million (2005)
Montreal, Canada	US$14.3 million (2005)
VisitLondon, UK	£21 million (2004)
Miami, USA	US$14.6 million (2005)
Las Vegas Convention and Visitor Authority, USA	US$147 million (2005)
Maison de la France	€60 million (2004)
Tourism Australia	AUS$169.8 million (2004)
(formerly Australian Tourist Commission)	
(Global marketing campaign 2005/2006)	AUS$60 million
VisitBritain	£35.5 million (2004)
VisitScotland	£44 million (2004)
South African Tourism	US$69 million (2005)
Illinois State Tourism	US$47 million (2005)
All state tourism budgets for USA	US$602 million (2005)

important in developing the desire to visit a destination. This is still a relatively new idea in tourism research but has a long history of research in other areas such as recreation, and could begin to help us understand how NTOs and marketing strategies can target the very qualities to which visitors have an emotional attachment in a destination. In this respect, destination marketing is only the first stage in trying to raise the visitor's awareness of the place, and provoking the notion of what bonding associations they have and whether these can be fostered to create an image of a highly desirable and must-see place. There is also a more substantial marketing effort by the tourism industry, much of which has often been led by airlines and tour operators. Indeed, given the low levels of industry membership of tourist boards, NTOs only have a limited influence in developing an industry-led campaign that seeks to send a specific message to potential visitors. Even so, in some countries (e.g. Scotland and Singapore), the efforts are very successful in harmonizing marketing messages where they are directed towards target markets and specific segments with growth potential. This approach recognizes that the NTO has an influence far beyond that of individual businesses and industry-sector groups such as tour operators. Indeed, VisitEngland identified a number of different approaches to domestic tourism marketing to try and influence English people to take holidays in England through its 2006–2007 *Enjoy England Strategy* which had the target of: 'Promoting England within Britain' to leverage an additional £500 million of visitor spending. It sought to encourage one million Britons to take English holidays and short breaks, of which 49 per cent would be targeted at the autumn and winter months. This was designed to spread the seasonal distribution of visitors and was a continuation of VisitEngland's *England Marketing Strategy for 2003–2005*, which had as one of its principles: 'To achieve greater seasonal and rural/urban spread and thus make English tourism more sustainable.'

There are many other marketing initiatives that seek to promote a destination using the conventional print and new forms of media such as the worldwide web. They do this by creating promotional messages and symbols/messages, and using promotional media to provide merchandising opportunities as well as providing incentives to buy. In each case the work of NTOs in place and product marketing is to develop a product substitute role (i.e. come to our destination as opposed to a competitor's), by using advertising opportunities to access the destination's products and thereby provide a purchasing mechanism in some cases. The launch of an e-commerce site is now seen as a vital element of any NTO strategy for destination marketing, since it offers a mechanism for generating a sale and a convenient method of communicating with the customer. It has been evident throughout this book that e-commerce is now a vital element for all sectors of the tourism industry in a rapidly changing business environment. It can be beneficial for NTOs to engage in e-commerce for the wider tourism sector, since tourists select particular place products (i.e. destinations) in their holiday decision-making process. Tourists normally consider a limited set of place products, often on the basis of limited knowledge of the destination and available options. Yet the holiday may be as much the place as the place is the holiday for the tourist. In contrast, the various businesses and organizations associated with tourism focus on specific aspects of the place product (e.g. an attraction or facility). For this reason, NTOs may often seek to address any shortcomings in the destination through the application of more sophisticated marketing techniques that change the visitor's perception of the destination. For example, enjoyengland.com seeks to portray 'England as real, fun, and indulgent, incorporating these into the brand essence that everyone can share' (VisitEngland 2005) to address negative images of England that have arisen because of the cost of being a tourist, the unreliability of the weather and quality issues in tourism provision. The e-commerce strategy of the NTO and the ready provision of visual information and images may help to broker the tourist as purchaser with the business as a seller. It can help to promote an initial interest registered by a potential tourist after they became aware of the destination, and encourage a follow-up visit to a website. This linking the purchaser and seller electronically often requires NTOs and the tourism industry to work collaboratively through a partnership approach, as discussed in Box 11.2 in relation to VisitScotland.com.

The growing collaboration between public and private sector in countries such as Canada and Australia have indicated how powerful these new NTO partnerships can be in marketing a dynamic industry. The Canadian Tourism Commission, which has a remit to seek private sector partnerships, raised its funding for marketing from C\$15 million in 1995 to C\$100 million in 1998/99, with the private sector contributing 50 per cent of the funds. By 2004, this core funding from the public sector had risen to C\$79 million, with matched funding from the tourism sector. The marketing activities of NTOs are outlined in Figure 11.5 which highlights the different options available such as developing a visionary promotional strategy. They may involve branding as a process, though the range and nature of activities will be dependent upon the nature of the budget, and may also be controlled by the NTO's remit, established by legislation (such as the 1969 Development of Tourism Act in the UK). Figure 11.5 also reiterates the coordination and liaison roles the NTOs perform and how tourism businesses interact with the public sector.

Below the level of the NTO, regional or area tourist boards perform a similar function. These bodies emphasize the attributes of their local area and many local authorities seek to promote their city or locality, in a lesser way, to establish a destination as a distinctive and unique place to visit, emphasizing the unique selling proposition

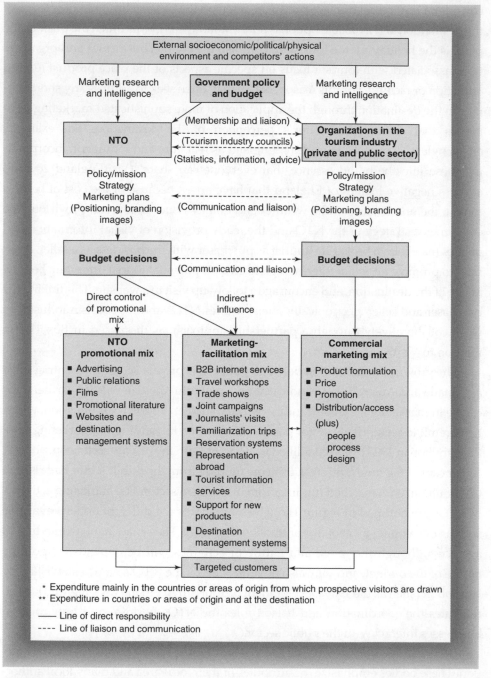

Figure 11.5 The destination marketing process for National Tourist Organizations (reprinted from *Marketing for Travel and Tourism,* V. Middleton and J. Clarke, 338, © 2001 Butterworth-Heinemann with permission from Elsevier)

(USP). In Northern Ireland, there are five regional tourism organizations (RTOs). These are themed to reflect the destination they represent and unique attributes of the area and comprise: Belfast Visitor and Convention Bureau, Derry Visitor and Convention Bureau, Causeway Coast and Glens, Kingdoms of Down and Fermanagh Lakeland Tourism. Each RTO is a company limited by guarantee, with funding from the public and private sectors in line with other parts of the UK. They are largely membership organizations, so businesses have to pay a fee to join and in return they are able to draw upon the RTO's services, which include marketing, advertising, training and research and development. The RTOs have an annual marketing budget of £2 million a year, and have over 1600 members from private sector businesses. The RTOs' income streams are supported by the Northern Ireland Tourist Board (NITB) and local authority contributions as well as through commercial income (e.g. sales of goods to visitors and commissions on sales). This RTO structure was established in 1998, after a strategic review of tourism in Northern Ireland that recommended that the NITB should be more consumer focused, work in partnership and avoid unnecessary fragmentation. This resulted in the 15 former local authority funded marketing consortia with limited private sector involvement being replaced by the RTO network. However, with change never far away, the NITB appointed consultants in 2002 to review this network and the wider support structures for tourism (i.e. regional and local development funding and support) since the establishment of Tourism Ireland Limited to market one Ireland.

The future of the public sector in the management of tourism

At a global scale, there has been a growing consensus among governments that private sector tourism interests (i.e. stakeholders) need to work more closely with the public sector to manage the marketing, planning, control and development of tourism. Part of the marketing logic here is to gain industry ownership of what is being marketed in terms of sales and promotion. The term 'tourism collateral' is now in vogue to describe how the tourism sector get buy-in to the collateral of the destination from the private sector (e.g. the brochures, websites, posters and visual material to promote the destination) so as to feel an integral part of the messages, images and focus of how the area is being sold to tourists. This is part of a withdrawal of central government from direct management of many areas of public activity, reflecting a desire to see a greater use of public–private partnerships to govern the tourism sector, where the private sector are seen as joint owners of the tourism collateral. In many countries, national or devolved government still plays a role in funding NTOs and other tourism-related functions. There is a recognition of the need for the tourism sector to be in charge and responsible for its own destiny. Whilst public sector-led marketing remains the norm in most countries, there is a greater awareness of the need for tourism to be a self-financing activity and debates over the possible value of tourist taxes to fund public sector planning and management of tourism.

In some cases, the withdrawal of central government involvement in tourism and the replacement with quangos (quasi-autonomous government organizations) reflects a changing philosophy that industry-led bodies are more appropriate entities to deliver tourism policy and its implementation as the case study in Box 11.2 highlighted. However, this is not being accompanied by the rationalization of tourism organizations that input into policy and planning. To the contrary, with the growth of tourism associations and interest groups, there is a greater need than ever for the public sector to coordinate, liaise and interact with such bodies to monitor and evaluate the needs and issues that impact upon the performance and management of tourism. However, since policy-making is an inherently political process, the historical role of the public sector as the main agency formulating tourism policy seems set to continue. But tourism policy monitoring and evaluation still remain a neglected area for many public sector agencies, and there is a need for more critical evaluation of the assumptions behind policy.

If the public sector is to play a greater role in tourism, understanding the consequences of specific tourism policies, it requires a more explicit recognition of whether policy is successful or a failure. Indeed, there is a degree of introverted, inward-looking thinking that fails to question the need for government intervention in tourism. Policy analysis and evaluation in the public sector has remained generalized in many tourism contexts, since poorly specified objectives and goals may contribute to perceived failures in policy. If the policy is flawed, its implementation and integration into planning mechanisms will not deal with the issues it originally was intended to address. The growth in the number of agencies involved in tourism inevitably delays the speed at which change in policy and planning can be affected. It is no surprise, therefore, that urban development corporations in the UK in the 1980s, despite criticisms about their lack of accountability, did remove planning obstacles, allowing areas to be regenerated. In many cases the tourism development process was thereby streamlined to remove endless tiers of consultation, strategy development and disagreement over development goals. In 2001, for example, South Africa Tourism (SAT) took a policy decision to shift from a more traditional approach to marketing the destination as a place to visit, to one which was consumer-oriented and aligned to destination marketing objectives (VisitScotland also did this). By adopting a focused and targeted segmentation strategy, SAT has evaluated 'who its tourists are, where they come from and why'. This served as a basis for identifying the range of actions necessary to invest in and develop these markets. As part of a wider global competitiveness study, SAT was able to recognize what marketing it needed to undertake to remain a competitive destination.

Whilst such a radical approach is not advocated for the public sector in tourism, there are compelling arguments for nationally determined tourism policy, strategy and planning to remove some of the layers of administration and bureaucracy. A more centralized approach that avoids a multitude of agencies, each having to review policy and planning at each level, would provide the context for area-based tourism planning and strategies, requiring cooperation at the local level to implement policy and planning. At the national level, the NTO would simply market the destination, with research and market intelligence managed by an agency led and funded by the industry, with regional or area-based tourism organizations driving policy and planning at the local level. This structure for tourism may be radical but is unlikely to be implemented due to politics, as lobby groups and vested interests in the existing system resist change if they perceive it as leading to a loss of power and input in decision-making in relation to policy.

References

Brown, D. (2000) Patterns of attitude change towards tourism development in Africa: A review of the last two decades. *Development Policy Management Bulletin, The Economic Commission for Africa,* 2 (1).

COSLA and Economic Development and Planning Executive Group (2002) *Review of the Area Tourist Boards.* Edinburgh: COSLA.

Elliot, J. (1997) *Tourism, Politics and Public Sector Management.* London: Routledge.

Friedman, J. (2004) *Eccentric America: The Bradt Guide to all that is Weird and Wacky in the USA.* Chalfont St Peter, UK: Bradt Travel Guides.

Getz, D. (1987) Tourism planning and research: Traditions, models and futures. Paper presented at the Australian Travel Research Workshop, Bunbury, Western Australia, 5–6 November.

Hall, C. M. (1999) *Tourism Planning: Policies, Processes and Relationships.* Harlow: Prentice Hall.

Hall, C. M. and Jenkins, J. (1995) *Tourism and Public Policy.* London: Routledge.

Inskeep, E. (1994) *National and Regional Planning.* London: Routledge/World Tourism Organization.

Jeffries, D. (2001) *Governments and Tourism.* Oxford: Butterworth Heinemann.

Middleton, V. and Hawkins, R. (1998) *Sustainable Tourism.* Oxford: Butterworth Heinemann.

Page, S. J. and Connell, J. (2006) *Tourism: A Modern Synthesis*, 2nd edn. London: Thomson Learning.

Page, S. J. and Thorn, K. (1997) Towards sustainable tourism planning in New Zealand: Public sector planning responses. *Journal of Sustainable Tourism*, 5 (1): 59–78.

Pike, S. (2004) *Destination Marketing Organisations.* Oxford: Elsevier.

Scottish Executive (2002) *The Tourism Framework for Action 2002–2005.* Edinburgh: Scottish Executive.

Scottish Executive (2005) *Scottish Tourism – The Next Decade: A Framework for Change.* Edinburgh: Scottish Executive (www.scotexchange.net).

Scottish Local Authority Economic Development (SLAED) Group (2002) *The Role of Scottish Councils in Tourism.* Edinburgh: SLAED.

Touche Ross (1988) *London Tourism Accommodation in the 1990s.* London: Touche Ross.

Turner, J. (1997) The policy process. In B. Axford, G. Browning, R. Huggins, B. Rosamond and J. Turner (eds) *Politics: An Introduction.* London: Routledge.

VisitEngland (2003) *England Marketing Strategy for 2003–2005.* London: VisitEngland.

VisitEngland (2005) *Enjoy England Strategy.* London: VisitEngland.

World Commission on the Environment and Development (1987) *Our Common Future.* Bründtland Commission's Report. Oxford: Oxford University Press.

World Tourism Organization (1998) *Guide for Local Authorities on Developing Sustainable Tourism.* Madrid: WTO.

Further reading

The most digestible overview of tourism policy is:

Hall, C. M. and Jenkins, J. (1995) *Tourism and Public Policy.* London: Routledge.

The most interesting overview of tourism planning with many good examples and case studies is:

Hall, C. M. (1999) *Tourism Planning: Policies, Processes and Relationships.* Harlow: Prentice Hall.

Questions

1 Why does the public sector need to intervene in the tourism market? Are its reasons driven by political concerns or the pressure exerted on it by lobby groups?

2 How does tourism policy get formulated? Who are the main actors and stakeholders in policy formulation in tourism?

3 How does tourism planning occur in practice?

4 Should public support for tourism be driven by arguments surrounding the wider social benefits which accrues to destinations? Or should the public sector support mechanisms for tourism be equally financed by the public and private sector?

12

Managing the visitor and their impacts

Learning outcomes

This chapter examines the practical ways in which visitors and visitor sites are managed by agencies and the tourism sector. It discusses the typical range of economic, social, cultural and environmental pressures that tourism exerts on the resource base on which it depends and the ways management tools may be used to develop a more sustainable resource base. On completion of this chapter, you should be able to understand:

- what the problems induced by visitor activity are
- how researchers approach the study of the economic, social, cultural and environmental impacts of tourism
- what visitor management is and the tools available to address visitor impacts in soft and hard ways
- the role of tourism planning, development and management in the case of Venice, which highlights the economic, social, cultural and environmental problems induced by tourism.

Introduction

Many of the previous chapters have examined how the members of the tourism industry manage and develop their businesses to produce a product or experience for a tourist. In this chapter the consequences of these actions in terms of tourist consumption are considered in relation to destination areas. This requires an understanding of the visitor as an agent of change in destinations due to the impacts induced directly or indirectly by their actions. Quite simply, it discusses where, why and how such impacts occur and with what effects. Promotion and advertising by the tourism sector (i.e. tour operators, NTOs and other promotional organizations) assist in generating tourism demand as a consumptive activity, which culminates in both positive and negative effects for the places it affects. These effects often coexist, making policy-making, planning and management problematic owing to the tendency to create beneficial and undesirable impacts simultaneously. For this reason, this chapter will focus on some of the tools and approaches used in tourism studies to understand how tourism generates impacts, how these can be managed and the lessons that can be learned.

In any discussion of tourism's impacts, these are three principal areas of concern exist: the economic effects of tourism; its social and cultural effects and, of course, the environmental dimension upon which the consumption of tourism experiences is often based. Since many of these impacts are site- or place-specific, it is useful to have some understanding of the geography of tourism to identify who goes where, when and why, and what impacts occur where.

The geography of tourism: Its application to impact analysis

Geography is about the study of the environment, people and the coexistence of man with the environment at different scales, ranging from the international through the national and regional to the local level. More advanced studies of tourism have shown that the contribution of geography can be significant, with its interest in place and space (i.e. how activities are organized in different locations) because tourism is an inherently dynamic activity that requires movement from an origin to destination area. Many studies of geography and tourism are highly

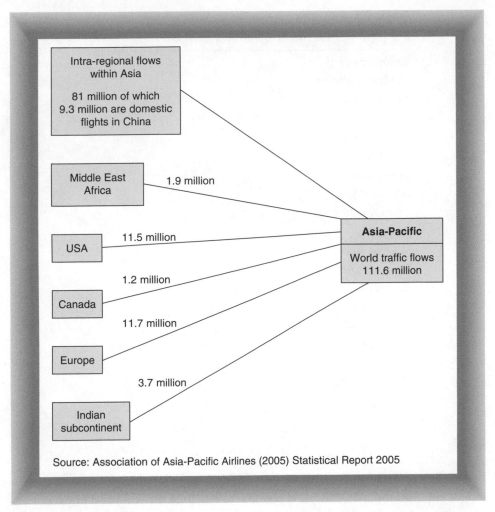

Figure 12.1 Inter-regional passenger flows by air on the Association of Asia-Pacific Airlines April 2004–March 2005

academic and based on theory and concepts to understand the complexity of tourism in time and space (i.e. how it operates at different times and in different places). But there are certain research skills that geographers use, the application of which to tourism can help in understanding why tourists go on holiday to certain locations, when they go, what they do when there, where the impacts of such visitor activity occur and what can be done to minimize the effects. Figure 12.1 is based on international data from the leading airlines which form part of the

Table 12.1 Association of Asia Pacific Airlines (AAPA) Members, 2005 (source: AAPA (2005) *Statistical Report 2005*)

Air New Zealand
All Nippon Airways
Asiana Airlines
Cathay Pacific Airways
China Airlines
Dragonair
EVA Airways
Garuda Indonesia
Japan Asia Airways Limited
Korean Air
Malaysia Airlines
Philippines Airlines
Qantas Airways
Royal Brunei Airways
Silk Airways
Singapore Airlines
Thai Airways International
Vietnam Airlines

Association of Asia-Pacific Airlines (see Table 12.1). Using the data from their passenger volumes for 2004–2005, it is possible to illustrate the scale and impact of visitor traffic on the airlines by region. Figure 12.1 shows that the majority of the airline's traffic is generated as intra-regional traffic (i.e. traffic which is generated and travels within Asia – 81 million passengers carried, of which 9.3 million occurred within China). This shows that 72 per cent of all the traffic occurs within Asia, and only 28 per cent is to other regions of the world. At a rudimentary level, Figure 12.1 begins to at least show the scale of tourist travel within Asia-Pacific, with significant flows to/from the USA and Europe. As geographers look at the scale of travel, it is then possible for them to begin to understand more about the dynamics of tourist travel within a specific region, such as Europe, and the trends in the market, and then to consider these issues as a basis for understanding how tourism operates in the region.

European tourism: Trends and patterns

According to the European Travel Commission (ETC) (2004), France and Spain are the leading tourist destinations in the EU. In Spain, an interesting trend is the tendency for up to half of tourists to make their own travel arrangements using the internet, which reflects the impact of the low-cost airlines in creating demand for seat-only sales. The ETC noted that the low-cost airlines' impact was less pronounced on capital cities than it was on many smaller secondary destinations which have seen major growth. According to the ETC, the scale of tourism growth in 2003 can be gauged from the following facts:

- 338 million Europeans made trips abroad (though not necessarily all by air given the large number of land borders in the EU)
- 86 per cent of these trips (290 million) were for leisure, 14 per cent were for business (which includes attending meetings, incentive travel, conferences and exhibition attendance – the MICE market)
- leisure travel grew at 5 per cent
- travel patterns were influenced by a strong Euro, improved economic performance across the EU, and the growth in low-cost airlines and cheap flights
- 88 per cent of travel by Europeans overseas was intra-regional (i.e. to other EU countries and the Mediterranean)
- 27 per cent of all trips in the top ten outbound markets were booked online.

The geography of European tourism based on air transport: Key trends and impacts

There are two techniques that can be used to address some of these issues surrounding visitor behaviour to understand the geographical patterns of tourism, particularly the nature of tourist flows, so that the scale and extent of tourism can be understood at different scales. The first technique is a simple analysis and mapping of tourism flows between origin and destination countries, to highlight the main flows. At the EU level, the largest tourist flows occur from the UK to Spain whilst the next most important flow is Germany to Spain. Data from airport departures on intra-regional travel (that is travel in and between EU member states) can

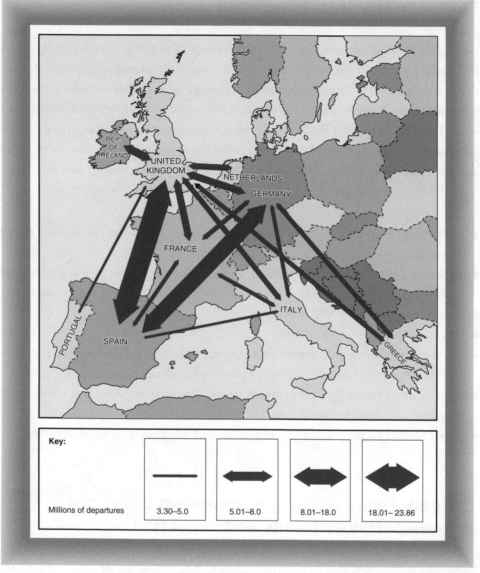

Figure 12.2 Top 15 intra-European country pairs in 1999 (source: Eurostat, based on air departures)

be modelled to produce Figure 12.2. This shows the top city-to-city flows of travellers, which are dominated by holiday and business travel. The top ten city–city pairs account for around 50 per cent of all intra-regional travel in the EU. Here the above-mentioned large numbers of flights from the UK and Germany to Spain and the Mediterranean, including business travel, are clearly shown. In addition markets that are near to a land border and a popular destination (e.g. flows from France to Spain) have a strong propensity to use car-based travel, which results in seasonal effects upon the roads and airports in each respective destination area. Even at such a rudimentary level, such patterns begin to explain the seasonal rhythms of tourism, the effect of mass travel on destination areas and the pressure this causes on infrastructure, the environment and people in the resort areas. Research by Eurostat (the European Statistical Agency) on the stability of tourism flows in the EU based on hotel occupancy data shows that tourism is largely concentrated in the June–September months although this does vary by country. These variations therefore highlight the importance of understanding the timing of tourist trips and where they are destined if one is to begin to identify where impacts will occur.

The second more sophisticated method of analysis used to understand how visitors can impact upon destinations through their activities is to study their activity patterns (what they do when, where, for how long and the variations according to market segment). This can utilize the recent advances in information technology made by geographers in terms of the new Geographical Information Systems (GIS). GIS uses sophisticated computer programs, typically the industry standard ArcInfo and variants, to collect data on tourism with a geographical dimension. The geographical elements of the data (i.e. a tourist's travel pattern and specific activities undertaken at each point on an itinerary) can then be recorded, mapped and modelled to understand how overall patterns of tourist activity exist in a location or region. This was recently undertaken for Loch Lomond and Trosasachs National Park by Connell (2005) as a basis for establishing the nature and hierarchy of visitor destinations that existed in the Park for the new National Park plan. These destinations could then be used to establish how to manage visitor impacts and what planning mechanisms were needed to cope with seasonal demands. On the basis of such an exercise, we can then begin to identify where particular impacts are occurring. We would also be able to identify the geographical patterns of tourism business development, to establish where the main development opportunities exist. The exercise would be useful in identifying what planning measures are needed where and when to constrain or facilitate tourism development and the tools that might need to be used to manage different patterns of visitor behaviour. Not surprisingly, many local authority planning departments use such techniques in their daily work but the application to tourism has been quite limited to date. GIS is a powerful, yet greatly under-utilized research tool in tourism. It has an enormous potential application to assist in managing, developing and understanding the dynamics of tourism.

The integration of different data sources in GIS has a major potential to visually illustrate the dynamics of tourism, and the different impacts that exist, by linking other sources of data together (e.g. records of land degradation, environmental pollution, economic data). This helps us to identify and understand some of the impacts of tourism and where management measures will need to be developed. Therefore, with these issues in mind, attention now turns to the different impacts to understand what relationships exist with tourism, how to measure them and what management tools may be used.

Analysing the impact of tourism

One of the major problems facing planners in assessing tourism impacts is the establishment of an appropriate baseline against which to measure the existing and future changes induced by tourism. This is a problem mentioned in scientific studies of Environmental Assessment (EA) which seek to combine different data sources to understand how tourism development affects the environment. EA acknowledges the practical problems of establishing baseline studies and in disaggregating the impact of tourism from other economic activities since it is hard to isolate tourism from other forms of economic development. Mathieson and Wall (1982) highlight the precise nature of the problem since in many tourist destinations it is almost impossible to reconstruct the environment minus the effects induced by tourism.

While it is widely acknowledged that tourism is a major agent affecting the natural and built environments, isolating the precise causes or processes leading to specific impacts is difficult: is tourism the principle agent of change or is it part of a wider process of development in a particular destination? As Mathieson and Wall (1982: 5) argue:

tourism may also be a highly visible scapegoat for problems which existed prior to the advent of modern tourism. It certainly is easier to blame tourism than it is to address the conditions of society and the environment.

The complex interactions of tourism with the built and physical environments make it virtually impossible to measure impacts with any degree of precision. Even so, impacts may be large scale and tangible (e.g. where a destination is saturated by visitors) or small scale and intangible.

Further factors complicating the analysis of tourism's impact are the extent to which the effect of tourism is necessarily continuous in time (i.e. how seasonal is it?) and the geography of tourism (as tourism activity tends to concentrate in certain locations such as destinations where the supply of services and facilities occurs). At this point, one needs to begin to identify specific indicators of tourism impacts chosen to represent the complex interaction of tourism and the destination to guide the impact assessment. Whilst this involves complex methods of analysis which may be aided by GIS and computer modelling, it is clear that impacts are more than just costs and benefits for specific destinations.

One useful starting point in analysing the impact of tourism in a practical context is to establish how to measure visitation levels as a basis for calculating visitor numbers for a destination. Yet one of the ongoing problems with visitor surveys is their value, as they are often undertaken at visitor attractions or based on accommodation occupancy rates as a means to establish the scale of visitors. Their ability to yield a representative sample of visitation at the destination, and thus their reliability, is debatable. Therefore, where visitor information is collected, it needs to be related to other forms of statistical information to establish the volume of tourism.

An early work by Potter (1978) provided a general framework for impact assessment. This is shown in Figure 12.3 where the impacts incorporate environmental, social and economic issues. Potter's approach has a number of steps, starting with the context of the development and proceeding through making a decision on a particular development that is useful in a planning and management context.

The economic impact of tourism

The economic measurement of tourism has a long history in many countries. The study by Ogilvie (1933), *The Tourist Movement*, is one of the early attempts to illustrate the significance of outbound tourism's impact on the national economy. Ogilvie (1933: 135) compiled tourist expenditure by British residents in Europe and outside Europe in the 1920s and early 1930s (Table 12.2) using Ministry of Labour and other

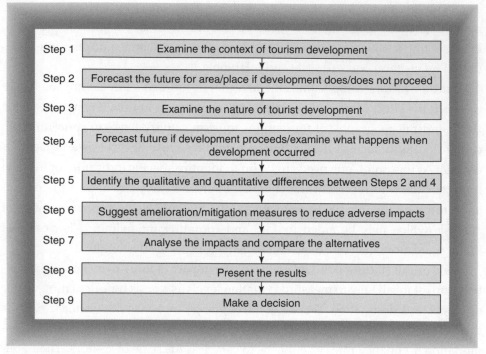

Step 1	Examine the context of tourism development
Step 2	Forecast the future for area/place if development does/does not proceed
Step 3	Examine the nature of tourist development
Step 4	Forecast future if development proceeds/examine what happens when development occurred
Step 5	Identify the qualitative and quantitative differences between Steps 2 and 4
Step 6	Suggest amelioration/mitigation measures to reduce adverse impacts
Step 7	Analyse the impacts and compare the alternatives
Step 8	Present the results
Step 9	Make a decision

Figure 12.3 Potter's impact of tourism framework (after Potter, 1978, Pearce, 1989, Page, 1995)

official statistics. Ogilvie estimated average expenditure by visitors to show that UK residents spent over £24 million in 1921 using an adjusted Cost of Living Index which rose to over £33 million in 1928 but then dropped due to the stock market crash and subsequent recession. What is interesting from Ogilvie's study is that he observed a £10–£11 million deficit in the 1920s and early 1930s in the balance of UK outbound tourist spending and inbound tourism from other countries. This is one of the most notable studies to make the vital point that tourism is important to the economy of many countries.

Ogilvie's innovative and landmark study also compiled a number of European sources to develop this point for many of the world's leading countries in the late 1920s/early 1930s. This not only illustrates the scale of their inbound tourists but also the scale of their outbound markets and the scale of spending, to calculate the impact on national travel accounts as they would later be called. Table 12.3 outlines these features for 24 countries and offers further detail for each

Table 12.2 Expenditure of United Kingdom tourists abroad, 1921–1931 (source: Ogilvie 1933: 136)

Year	British residents		Foreign residents (average £20)	Unadjusted total	Final total, adjusted to Cost of Living Index (Ministry of Labour: 1929 = 100)
	On tour to countries outside Europe and the Mediterranean area (average £100)	On tour to Europe and the Mediterranean area (average £30)			
	£	£	£	£	£
1921	1 948 800	14 405 000	1 205 000	17 558 800	24 231 000
1922	2 009 500	16 679 200	1 222 300	19 911 000	22 300 000
1923	2 233 400	20 284 700	1 190 400	23 708 500	25 131 000
1924	2 192 800	20 946 500	1 068 100	24 207 400	25 902 000
1925	2 645 300	24 118 600	1 065 400	27 829 300	29 777 000
1926	2 717 000	25 044 500	1 072 000	28 833 500	30 275 000
1927	2 926 100	25 486 500	1 020 100	29 432 700	30 021 000
1928	3 193 500	28 546 000	1 029 700	32 769 200	33 097 000
1929	3 271 700	28 548 100	974 000	32 793 800	32 794 000
1930	3 245 100	29 365 800	952 500	33 563 400	32 221 000
1931	2 797 000	26 882 800	848 800	30 528 600	27 476 000

country. Even in the late 1920s, France was established as the leading inbound destination whilst the USA and UK had a travel deficit, features which still exist today.

On the basis of this early economic analysis, one can see why tourism is used by many national and local governments as a mechanism to aid the development and regeneration of economies. Politicians and decision-makers see that it offers renewed opportunities for work, income and revenue for the local economy as places are affected by global, national and local economic restructuring. There is a prevailing perception among national and local governments that economic benefits accrue to tourism destinations, which then create employment opportunities

Table 12.3 International tourist balances, 1928–1930 (source: Ogilvie, 1933: 140–2)

Country and year		£ thousands			
		Receipts from foreign tourists	Expenditure of national tourists abroad	Balance	
				Credit	Debit
Albania	1928	159	12	147	—
	1929	198	12	186	—
	1930	198	32	166	—
Argentine	1928–29	2379	5947	—	3568
(now Argentina)	1929–30	2379	4956	—	2577
	1930–31	1982	3965	—	1983
Austria	1928	9078	1879	7199	—
	1929	7517	1879	5638	—
Bulgaria	1928	74	89	—	15
	1929	74	185	—	111
	1930	74	133	—	59
Canada	1928	54 802	20 671	34 131	—
	1929	61 480	22 870	38 610	—
	1930	57 370	23 281	34 089	—
Czechoslovakia	1928	4689	4263	426	—
	1929	4933	4324	609	—
	1930	4842	4263	579	—
Denmark	1928	551	826	—	275
	1929	826	1377	—	551
	1930	826	1377	—	551
Dutch East Indies	1928	578	8508	—	7930
(now Indonesia)	1929	496	7104	—	6608
	1930	413	5039	—	4626
Finland	1928	881	932	—	51
	1929	984	1140	—	156
	1930	984	1140	—	156

(Continued)

Table 12.3 (*Continued*)

Country and year		£ thousands			
		Receipts from foreign tourists	Expenditure of national tourists abroad	Balance	
				Credit	Debit
France	1928	72 450	12 075	60 375	—
	1929	80 500	12 075	68 425	—
	1930	—	—	68 425	—
Germany	1928	8811	14 685	—	5874
	1929	8811	14 685	—	5874
	1930	13 706(a)	13 706	—	—
Hungary	1928	740	1369	—	629
	1929	787	1880	—	1093
	1930	960	2049	—	1089
Italy	1928	28 100	3600	24 500	—
	1929	26 100	3400	22 700	—
Japan	1928	3851	3831	20	—
	1929	4568	4312	256	—
Jugoslavia	1928	1307	1245	62	—
	1929	1481	1242	239	—
Lithuania	1928	240	286	—	46
	1929	277	312	—	35
	1930	279	436	—	156
New Zealand	1927–28	683	1657	—	974
	1928–29	720	1650	—	930
	1929–30	719	1671	—	952
Poland	1928	2266	3895	—	1629
	1929	3852	3801	51	—
Roumania	1929	615	430	185	—
	1930	492	344	148	—

(*Continued*)

Table 12.3 (*Continued*)

Country and year		£ thousands			
		Receipts from foreign tourists	Expenditure of national tourists abroad	Balance	
				Credit	Debit
Sweden	1928	—	—	—	1542
	1929	—	—	—	1652
	1930	—	—	—	1377
Switzerland	1928	15 700	3200	12 500	—
	1929	—	—	11 100	—
	1930	—	—	9700	—
Union of	1928	1076	4291	—	3215
South Africa	1929	1125	4461	—	3336
United Kingdom	1928	22 108	33 097	—	10 989
	1929	22 445	32 794	—	10 349
	1930	21 622	32 221	—	10 599
United States	1928	33 500	169 000	—	135 500
	1929	37 500	178 000	—	140 500
	1930	32 200	167 000	—	134 800

and stimulate the development process in resorts and localities. This was shown in Figure 9.1, which depicts the economic development process and how tourism is often used to pump-prime regeneration initiatives in declining areas (e.g. the inner city). For the local population, it is often argued by proponents of tourism development that investment in tourist and recreational facilities provides a positive contribution to the local economy. One very controversial illustration of this can be seen in the debate on the impact of casino development on localities: this is very topical, given the reform of legislation governing the development of casinos in the UK. Taxes levied from gambling generate positive economic benefits for localities in terms of visitor spending and employment, and this is being emphasized by proponents of plans for casino development in Blackpool. In Auckland, New Zealand, a casino constructed in the 1990s acts as the city's main drawcard. The scale of the impact on the local economy can be gauged from the 12 000 visitors a day it receives, but around 80 per cent of visitors are residents or New Zealanders. Gaming revenue averages NZ$595 000 a day (including goods and service tax at 12.5 per cent) and the operating company employs 2400 people.

Tourism is not necessarily a stable source of income for destinations because tourists are not noted for their high levels of customer loyalty to tourism destinations. Page and Hall (2002) identify a number of features to support this argument based on urban tourism destinations:

- Tourism if a fickle industry, being highly seasonal, and this has implications for investment and the type of employment created. Tourism employment is often characterized as being low skill, poorly paid and low status, and lacking long-term stability.
- The demand for tourism can easily be influenced by external factors (e.g. political unrest, unusual climatic and environmental conditions) which are beyond the control of destination areas.
- The motivation for tourist travel to urban destinations is complex and variable and constantly changing in the competitive marketplace.
- In economic terms, tourism is price and income elastic, which means that it is easily influenced by small changes to the price of the product and the disposable income of consumers.
- Many cities are becoming alike, a feature described as 'serial reproduction'. This means that once an idea for urban economic development is successful in one location, the concept diffuses to other places. The example of waterfront revitalization is a case in point; many projects are similar in structure and character across the world.

Source: Modified from Page and Hall (2003)

Pearce (1989: 192) argued that 'the objective and detailed evaluation of the economic impact of tourism can be a long and complicated task'. This is because there is little agreement on what constitutes the tourism industry although it is normally classified in relation to:

- accommodation
- transport

- attractions
- the travel organizers' sector (e.g. travel agents)
- the destination organization sector.

Hospitality and ancillary services are also important. Understanding the economic impact of these disparate sectors of the economy requires a method of analysis that allows us to isolate the flow of income in the local tourism economy. This is notoriously difficult because of attributing the proportion of tourist expenditure on goods and services in relation to the total pattern of expenditure by all users of the destination (e.g. residents, workers and visitors). What we usually need to do is identify the different forms of tourist expenditure and how they affect the local economy. Typically these include:

- the nature of the destination area and its products, facilities and physical characteristics
- the volume and scale of tourist expenditure
- the state of the economic development and economy in the destination
- the size and nature of the local economy (i.e. is it dependent on services or manufacturing or is it a mixed economy?)
- the extent to which tourist expenditure circulates around the local economy and is not spent on 'imported' goods and services
- the degree to which the local economy has addressed the problem of seasonality and extends the destination appeal to all year round.

Source: Modified from Page (1995)

On the basis of these factors, it is possible to assess whether the economic impact will be beneficial or have a detrimental effect on the economy. In this respect, it is possible to identify some of the commonly cited economic benefits of tourism:

- the generation of income for the local economy
- the creation of new employment opportunities
- improvements to the structure and balance of economic activities within the locality
- the encouragement of entrepreneurial activity.

In contrast, there is also a range of costs commonly associated with tourism and these include:

- the potential for economic over-dependence on one particular form of activity
- inflationary costs in the local economy as new consumers enter the area, and potential increases in real estate prices as the tourism development cycle commences and tourism competes with other land uses
- depending on the size and nature of the local economy, a growing dependence on imported rather than locally produced goods, services and labour as the development of facilities and infrastructure proceeds
- seasonality in the consumption and production of tourism infrastructure and services leading to limited returns on investment
- leakages of tourism expenditure from the local economy
- additional costs for city authorities.

Source: Modified from Page (1995)

Constructing the economic impact of tourism

In seeking to understand the extent, scale and consequences of tourism on the economies of countries and destinations, a range of analytical methods have been developed by economists. These usually involve collecting data to model the expenditure from tourism and its impact, as information gathered in visitor surveys can be used to identify:

- *Direct expenditure* by tourists on goods and services consumed (e.g. hotels, restaurants and tourist transport services), although this is not a definitive account of expenditure due to leakage of tourist spending to areas and corporations outside the local economy.
- *Indirect expenditure* by visitors is often estimated by identifying how many tourism enterprises use the income derived from tourists' spending. This money is then used by enterprises to pay for services, taxes and employees, which then recirculates in the urban economy. In other words, tourist expenditure stimulates an economic process which passes through a series of stages (or rounds).

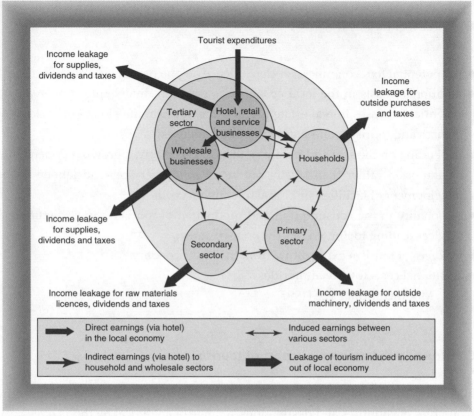

Figure 12.4 The economic impact of tourist spending in an urban area (after Murphy, 1985; Page, 1995)

- *The induced impact*, by calculating the impact of expenditure from those employed in tourism and its effect on the local economy.

Source: Modified from Page (1995)

These three impacts are then used to estimate the nature of tourist spending, as illustrated in Figure 12.4, which highlights the interrelationships that exist between tourism, tourist spending and other sectors of the economy. Figure 12.4 also introduces the concept of leakage, in which expenditure is lost from the local system to other areas. For planners and managers, maximizing local economic linkages (e.g. buying local produce and employing local people) can enhance the benefits of tourism to a locality. Where the local economy is very vulnerable, and dependent upon a large number of imports (e.g. labour, goods and services), leakage will be high and so reducing the openness of the tourism economy will help to improve the impact locally. Many rural areas are characteristically open economies and high levels of leakage in tourism occur there, whereas in urban areas leakage is reduced as the economy is more closed. In many less developed countries and island nations that depend upon tourism, the leakage is also high due to external control by multinational companies and a reluctance of tourism businesses to use local products. Instead, high-volume imports reduce the beneficial local effects of tourism. Economists use various tools to measure tourism demand in local economies; one is Multiplier Analysis, where a formula expresses changes that tourism spending can generate.

More recently, governments have tried to understand how tourism affects the national economy. In conjunction with the UN-WTO and Organization for EconomicCo-operation and Development, some countries have developed tourism satellite accounts (TSA) to measure more precisely the economic impact of tourism. In 1999 the New Zealand government launched the results of its TSA, which used a wide range of economic data to identify six main themes regarding the impact of tourism:

1 The direct impact of tourism on GDP.
2 Tourism expenditure expressed as a percentage of GDP.
3 The level of tourism employment in the economy.
4 The proportion of international travel-related expenditure as a percentage of total travel-related expenditure.
5 Domestic personal expenditure as a percentage of total travel expenditure.
6 Domestic business and government expenditure as a percentage of total travel expenditure.

Using 1995 data, the New Zealand government was able precisely to identify visitor impacts in 2001 using a TSA and this was subsequently updated in 2005. Therefore, in the period 2001–2004:

- international visitors' contribution to the economy from tourism rose from NZ$4.3 billion in 1995 to NZ$7.4 billion in 2004
- domestic tourism expenditure rose from NZ$4.8 billion in 1995 to NZ$9.8 billion in 2004
- the number of tourism employees directly employed in tourism rose from 58 000 full-time equivalent jobs (FTEs) in 1995 to 102 7000 FTEs in 2004.

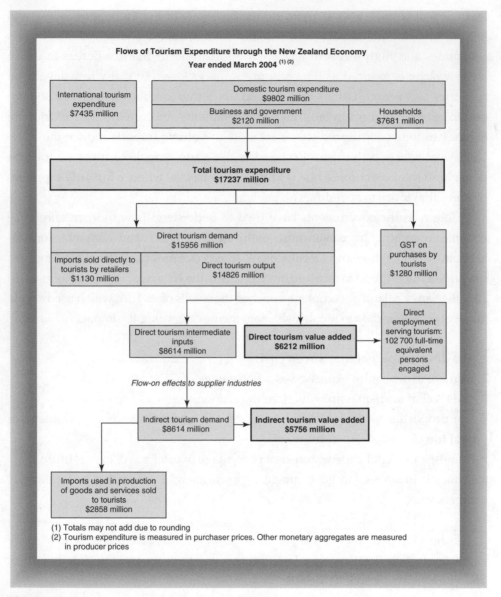

Figure 12.5 Flows of tourism expenditure through the New Zealand economy (source: Statistics New Zealand)

The more complex financial flows generated by tourism in the New Zealand economy are shown in Figure 12.5, which is based on the 2004 TSA and shows that NZ$5.8 billion was added to the tourism economy by industries indirectly supporting the tourism sector whilst NZ$1.3 billion of tax (GST – goods services tax) was generated for the New Zealand Treasury by tourism.

This modelling of the tourism economy is increasingly gaining credence in many governments, since reliable information on the economic impact of tourism is useful:

- for policy-making
- for planning and macro-management of the economy
- for allocating public sector resources towards tourism projects
- for internal government processes to secure additional resources for the Ministry of Tourism and the NTO.

In the New Zealand example, the TSA also helped to raise the profile of the tourism sector, since the magnitude of the economic impacts were far in excess of existing estimates of tourism's effects on the national economy. Yet while it is now becoming easier to gauge the economic effect of tourism, as researchers use more refined methods of analysing its impact, it is much less visible and tangible than the social and cultural impacts which tourism induces.

Social and cultural impacts of tourism

Tourism can emerge as a source of conflict between hosts and visitors in destinations where its development leads to perceived and actual impacts. There has been a wealth of studies of the social and cultural impacts by anthropologists and sociologists, embodied in the influential studies by Valene Smith (1977, 1992). The attitudes of residents towards tourism represent an important way in which this stakeholder group contributes to policy and public support for or dissent towards tourism. At a simplistic level, resident attitudes may be one barometer of an area's ability to absorb tourists. However, the analysis of tourism's social and cultural impacts is related to the way in which it affects or induces change in a number of elements, as Figure 12.6 implies.

The focus of any analysis of host–guest impacts is a function of the interaction between these two groups and will be dependent upon:

- the nature and extent of social, economic and cultural differences between tourists and hosts
- the ratio of visitors to residents

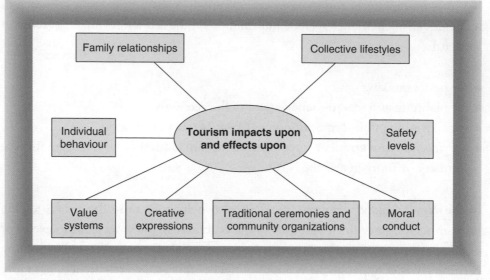

Figure 12.6 The social and cultural impact of tourism

- the distribution and visibility of tourist developments
- the speed and intensity of development
- the extent of foreign and employment.

Source: Douglas and Douglas (1996: 51)

In the context of the Pacific islands, Douglas and Douglas (1996) highlighted the differing ethnic origins of residents, and the history of colonialization and tourism development, which provide a backcloth to any analysis of tourism's socio-cultural impacts. The scale of development varies enormously across the region, with over six million visitors in Hawaii (1.2 million population) through to less than 1000 per annum on Tuvalu (resident population 9000). In each case, the physical presence of tourism is huge and dominates the island. Similarly, high levels of foreign ownership have provoked the indigenous population's antagonism towards tourism in some islands, with some multinational corporations expecting employees to adopt certain behaviour towards visitors. In many of these fragile and ancient cultures, indigenous people's art and culture have been over-commodified, resulting in the derided 'airport art'. Similar criticisms have been levelled at the demand for cultural performances, which create income, but result in indigenous cultures being portrayed as a 'human zoo'. Indeed, in many of these island contexts, tourism has led to host–guest relationships that are:

- limited in duration, and so require distinct behaviour from residents where a service or performance is sold
- transitory in nature, especially where a packaged experience or performance is provided
- geographically isolated, since visitors stay in resort enclaves, where hotel companies meet all their needs and only encourage temporary staged visits to engage with locals. This creates relationships that lack spontaneity, and an unequal and unbalanced experience.

Pearce (1989) cited a range of other social and cultural impacts resulting from tourism including:

- The impact of migration from rural areas to urbanized tourism resort areas to secure employment in service industries due to the higher income levels. This can often modify the population structure in destinations, putting pressure on services.
- Changes in occupational structure, as the demand for low-skill, female and seasonal labour expands.
- Changes in social values, with greater levels of community turnover.
- The impact of gentrification in inner city districts where urban regeneration with a strong tourism element transforms the local housing market, and leads to residents having to move to accommodate development.
- Increased levels of crime when special events and hallmark events, such as the Olympics, are held.
- Potentially negative effects related to the increase in prostitution and gambling to meet visitor needs. In some destinations such as Sydney, Bangkok and Amsterdam a distinct sex zone has emerged, changing the social structure of the area.
- A decline in the use of native language because the universal method of conversation in tourism is in European languages (English and French).

But how do we understand the way these changes affect resident attitudes?

Probably the most widely cited study that sought to explain how residents react, respond and interact with tourism is Doxey's Index of Tourist Irritation. This is based on Doxey's (1975) study, in which resident responses in the Caribbean and Canada were observed to identify a series of stages through which they passed. These were:

- *euphoria*, following the initial development of tourism
- *apathy*, as tourism developed further and becomes part of the local way of life
- *annoyance*, as tourism began to interfere with everyday life and cause a level of disturbance
- *antagonism*, where residents became tourist averse and tensions, conflict and anti-tourism feeling became widespread.

More detailed research by Ap and Crompton (1993) questioned the validity of such an approach, arguing that it was too simplistic. Instead, they pointed to the diversity of views in any community at any point in time, especially the significance of difference stakeholders (i.e. businesses and residents) – which make the Doxey model problematic as minority and majority views will exist. Indeed, a community will not necessarily progress through a simple set of phases, but may well react according to the seasonal impact of tourism and reflect the overall analysis of tourism's general impact on residents' quality of life. A wide range of studies have been published that seek to encapsulate residents' attitudes to tourism, but comparatively few studies have been longitudinal, to try and understand attitude change through time. One notable exception was Getz's (1993) longitudinal study of resident attitudes in Scotland. Without such a framework, it is not feasible to assess how attitudes have changed as tourism development progresses. Many *ad hoc* resident attitude studies are not sufficiently detailed or methodologically sophisticated and are unable to adopt a longitudinal approach to help understand how social values, community feelings and everyday life are affected by tourism.

Attention now turns to the last major impact associated with tourism – the environmental effects of tourism.

Tourism and the environment

Throughout this book, the link between tourism and the environment has been emphasized as one that has been assuming greater significance, particularly with the rise of the sustainability debate. Yet this relationship between tourism and the environment has evolved over a much larger time period, namely the last 50 years. For example,

> In the 1950s it was viewed as being one of coexistence … However, with the advent of mass tourism in the 1960s, increasing pressure was put on natural areas for tourism developments. Together with the growing environmental awareness and concerns of the early 1970s the relationship was perceived to be in conflict. During the next decade this view was endorsed by many others … at the same time a new suggestion was emerging that the relationship could be beneficial to both tourism and the environment (Dowling, 1992: 33).

To foster a beneficial relationship between tourism and the environment requires public sector intervention to plan and manage each element, whilst high-lighting the benefits for the tourism industry. For example, the UK government-led study on *Tourism and the Environment* (English Tourist Board/Employment Department, 1991) examined and established the scale and nature of environmental problems induced by mass tourism at major tourist sites, and produced guidelines on how such problems were to be addressed. The study pointed to the need to maintain the resource base for tourism activities. As part of their study, they identified common problems resulting from tourism, including wear and tear on the urban fabric, overcrowding and social and cultural impacts between the visitors and local communities.

Indeed, other authors have portrayed tourism–environment impacts as running along a continuum where the effects may be positive in inner city environments (that benefit from tourism-led regeneration), but more negative as one passes into other tourism environments (e.g. coastal areas, rural areas, upland and mountain environments). Depicting this dependent relationship between tourism and the environment, Mathieson and Wall (1982: 97) argued that:

> In the absence of an attractive environment, there would be little tourism. Ranging from the basic attractions of sun, sea and sand to the undoubted appeal of historic sites and structures, the environment is the foundation of tourism.

This is nowhere more evident than in the South Pacific, where stereotypical images of palm trees, beaches, lagoons and sun create an impression of an idyllic tourist landscape. Yet many of the Pacific islands encapsulate the environmental problems which tourism creates.

Many Pacific islands are fragile ecosystems, where the impacts of tourism are highly visible, particularly given the tendency for tourism development to concentrate on coastal areas. As Hall (1996: 68) observed:

> because of the highly dynamic nature of the coastal environment and the significance of mangroves and the limited coral sand supply for island beaches in particular, any development which interferes with the natural system may have severe consequences for the long-term stability of the environment.

As a result, inappropriate tourism development on coastal areas creates:

- erosion, where vegetation clearance exposes the beach to sea storms, and building activity on beaches makes sand deposits loose and more vulnerable to erosion
- the salination of fresh ground water sources, which are usually in limited supply
- sewage outfall into shallow waters, which cause nutrients to build up and algal growth that adversely affects coral reefs.

Furthermore, the modification of mangrove swamps on lowland areas to create harbours and marinas, or for land reclamation, leads to loss of ecological diversity and a rich environment for wildlife. It also removes a barrier to sediment build-up. As a result tourism's environmental impacts on Pacific islands create:

- environmental degradation and pollution
- the destruction of habitats and ecosystems
- the loss of coastal and marine resources
- coastal pollution
- impacts on ground water.

As island ecosystems are characterized by limited space and species, the impacts are very obvious, especially where the geographical isolation of an island state is suddenly affected by the rapid development of tourism. Some attempts to address these concerns have been seen with the development of ecotourism. In the South Pacific, Hall (1996) indicated that ecotourism could be construed in two ways:

1 as green or nature-based tourism, with a niche market as part of special interest tourism (e.g. scuba diving)
2 as any form of tourism development that is considered to be environmentally responsible.

Both of these should pay attention to the sustainable use of very fragile resources. In many island microstates (IMS) in the Pacific, the significance of environmental issues in tourism are apparent as a number of common themes characterize tourism's development and the pressures on the resource base:

- scale, where impacts can easily be damaging to fragile resources
- the high levels of dependency on external international tourism interests that do not have a long-term stake in the local environment
- an absence of indigenous sources of capital to develop tourism, removing many opportunities for sustainable tourism development that is community owned and locally managed
- the predominance of colonial patterns of control in the tourism sector limiting the permeation of new ideas such as environmentalism
- an economic system characterized by outward migration, a dependence upon remittances back to families, aid to assist economic survival, and bureaucracy (known as the MIRAB model)
- increasing competition among IMS for tourists in the Pacific and resulting compromises in tourism planning and development to attract visitors.

There is also a growing dependence upon tourism, which is politically promoted as a solution to problems of under-development. The main problem is the consumption of a finite resource – the environment to meet tourism aspirations in IMS in the Pacific.

In many ways the environmental impacts in the Pacific islands can be combined with the more general problems that Mathieson and Wall (1982) identify in resort areas, which include:

- architectural pollution owing to the effect of inappropriate hotel development on the traditional landscape
- the effect of ribbon development and urban sprawl in the absence of planning and development restrictions (as is the case on many Spanish resorts in the Mediterranean)
- the resort infrastructure becomes overloaded and breaks down in periods of peak usage
- tourists become segregated from local residents
- good quality agricultural land may be lost to tourist development

- traffic congestion may result in resort areas
- the local ecosystem may be polluted from sewage
- litter and too many visitors in the peak season.

So how has the tourism industry responded to criticisms over its impact on the environment?

The tourism industry response

A substantial lobby has emerged amongst environmental groups to question the seemingly unstoppable march of tourism as a consumer of environmental resources. The hotel industry has responded with environmental initiatives such as the International Hotels Environment Initiative, which promotes recycling, codes of conduct, best practice among members, accreditation schemes and improved standards of energy efficiency (features of this were discussed in Chapter 7). In some hotels, waste minimization strategies have resulted from environmental audits of the tourism and hospitality operations to reduce costs. They may include purchasing more eco-friendly products, waste reduction (i.e. not laundering guests' towels every day), reusing resources and packaging and adopting a green policy towards operational issues. In the Balearic islands, the development of an ecotax in 2002 has been introduced to fund environmental improvements to address decades of tourist development. Yet this has had a negative impact on one market – the Germany package holiday market. In Germany the ecotax has been called 'limonadenstener', a lemonade tax, because hotel owners have been giving guests drink vouchers in lieu of the tax. It has also been dubbed a 'Kurtax' (a cure tax) that has raised ecological issues among visitors. This approach to attempting to remedy the impacts of mass tourism development is at least beginning to move the sector towards a greater understanding of its effect on the environment. So how does the tourism industry manage the impacts of visitors?

Visitor management

The tourism sector, even if it seeks to be socially inclusive and permit access to different resources, has to address an ongoing problem: it needs to permit access to sites and yet needs to protect the resource base upon which tourism is based. This requires a wide range of management tools to balance the needs of the visitor, the place (i.e. the resource base), the host community and other tourism stakeholders (e.g. the industry) in providing a quality tourism experience. As a result the area known as 'visitor management' has emerged in a tourism context. Visitor management develops and adapts many of the principles and practices used in the outdoor recreation and leisure areas. There are two types of measures which are usually used – 'hard measures', which are place extensive and place permanent restrictions on visitor activity, and 'soft measures', which involve improving marketing, interpretation, planning and visitor coordination. These are summarized in Table 12.4.

An example of a country taking hard measures is the kingdom of Bhutan in the eastern Himalayas, which places major restrictions on tourism. It only allows a limited number of visitors to enter on organized packages as independent travellers and backpackers are discouraged. Visitors have to spend US$200 a day during their visit to Bhutan. The majority of the population (Drukpa) follow an ancient Bhuddist culture which has been conserved by the king, and a policy of limited modernization has been followed since the 1970s (radio broadcasting was introduced in 1973 and internet provision was permitted in 1999). Tourism has been developed as a means of deriving foreign revenue for the country. Bhutan's ecological diversity has made it a major nature tourism destination and it also has a rich heritage and culture among the population combined with a traditional lifestyle (including the wearing of traditional dress). Bhutan has a population of 870 000 and visitor numbers have grown from 287 in 1974 to 2850 in 1992, 7000 in 1999 and 6261 in 2003, rising by 30 per cent to 9249 in 2004. The government's ninth Five-Year Plan set a target of around 15 000 tourist arrivals in 2007 which were forecast to rise to 20 000 arrivals in 2012. In 2004 the market was largely dominated by high-spending tourists from the USA (35 per cent), Japan (11.8 per cent), UK (10.3 per cent) and Germany (7.3 per cent). This model of the strict control of tourism has been accompanied by examples of community-based tourism development, where those who benefit from tourism are local people. One good example is the Jigme Singye Wangchuck National Park which has a trekking trail and opportunities for local people to benefit from provision of services (e.g. portering, providing refreshments and cultural activities, and guiding). However, current concerns about managing tourism are associated with the effect of external influences upon Bhutanese culture and the possible change to cultural values that increased numbers of visitors and increased modernization measures may have on the population.

Table 12.4 Examples of visitor management techniques in tourism (modified and developed from Hall and McArthur, 1998)

Technique	Examples
Regulating access by area	Excluding visitors from sacred sites such as aboriginal lands
Regulating access by transport	Park and ride schemes to prevent in-town use of cars, or car-free environments and pedestrianization schemes as part of town centre management programmes
Regulating visitor numbers and group size	The use of group size restrictions in Antarctica
Regulating types of visitors permitted	Discouraging certain groups through marketing and products on offer
Regulating visitor behaviour	Zoning of visitor activities in marine parks in Western Australia to allocate certain activities to certain areas
Regulating equipment	Prohibiting off-road driving except in permitted areas (e.g. in Forest Enterprise's four-wheel drive track in the new Loch Lomond National Park)
The use of entry or user fees	Charging visitors to Kenya's National Parks and Reserves so that some of the fee is used for conservation
Modifications to sites	Constructing hardened paths to direct visitors
Market research	To identify reasons for visiting, to understand how to develop tools to modify visitor behaviour
Promotional marketing campaigns	The provision of alternative destinations in the Lake District, UK to relieve pressure on congested sites
Provision of interpretation programmes	Provision of guided tours or guides to avoid congestion at key sites

In a heritage tourism context, Hall and McArthur (1998: 123) review the value of these management tools to achieve the twin goals of conserving the resource and contributing to improving the quality of the visitor experience. Table 12.5 is a qualitative assessment of each approach they identified, and suggests that hard measures to regulate visitor activity are the dominant mode of control. The table also illustrates the need for managers and planners to consider ways of integrating these approaches to manage tourism. One approach is to develop visitor

Table 12.5 Qualitative assessment of visitor management techniques (source: Hall and McArthur, 1998: 123; reproduced with permission from the authors)

Visitor management techniques	Ability to address heritage management paradox		Create support for heritage management	Other aspects of performance	
	Conservation of heritage	Improve quality of visitor experience		Proactiveness	Reliance by management
Regulating access	◆◆◆	◆	◇	◇	◇
Regulating visitation	◆◆◆	◆◆	◇	◇	◇◇
Regulating behaviour	◆◆◆	◆	◇	◇	◇
Regulating equipment	◆◆◆	◆◆	◇	◇◇	◇◇
Entry or user fees	◆◆◆	◆	◇	◇◇	◇◇◇
Modifying the site	◆◆◆	◆◆	◇◇	◇	◇◇◇
Market research	◆◆◆	◆◆	◇	◇◇◇	◇
Visitor monitoring and research	◆◆◆	◆◆◆	◇	◇◇◇	◇
Promotional marketing	◆◆◆	◆◆	◇◇◇	◇◇◇	◇
Strategic information marketing	◆◆◆	◆◆◆	◇◇◇	◇◇	◇◇
Interpretation	◆◆◆	◆◆◆	◇◇◇	◇◇◇	◇◇
Education	◆◆◆	◆◆	◇◇	◇◇◇	◇
Profile of heritage management	◆◆◆	◆◆	◇◇◇	◇◇	◇
Alternative providers – tourism industry	◆◆	◆◆◆	◇◇◇	◇◇◇	◇
Alternative providers – volunteers	◆◆	◆◆	◇◇◇	◇◇◇	◇
Favoured treatment for accredited bodies bringing visitors to a site	◆◆	◆◆	◇◇◇	◇◇◇	◇

Performance in relation to heritage management paradox: ◆, Limited; ◆◆, Reasonable; ◆◆◆, Good. Performance in relation to other criteria: ◇, Limited; ◇◇, Reasonable; ◇◇◇, Good

management models that seek to assess the capacity of a site or location and the types of management needed to ensure a maximum visitor experience without affecting the sustainable use of the resource and its long-term appeal. A number of technical models have been developed and applied in visitor management contexts across the world, as Table 12.6 shows. Each approach is reviewed in terms of its key characteristics and its ability to meet the varying needs of different stakeholders and be applied in practical contexts. As Table 12.7 suggests, these models (widely used and understood in the recreation and tourism management literature – see Pigram and Jenkins, 1999, for more detail) adopt different management approaches which are useful in illustrating the diversity of tools available to managers. The case study of Venice is examined in Box 12.1 and illustrates the practical problems that visitor management poses.

With the global spread of tourism, the growth in the demand for domestic and international travel is creating an insatiable demand for leisure spending in the new millennium. As new outbound markets such as China and India develop, there will be a huge increase in the rate of tourism growth in certain regions such as Asia-Pacific. The consequences of such growth if it is allowed to develop in an unplanned, unconstrained and unmanaged manner is clear: the continued impact on the environment, people and ecosystems that will be irreversibly damaged by tourism consumption. Since tourism is a powerful force in many economies, some degree of planned intervention by the public sector, as well as the increasing number of public–private-sector partnerships, will be essential in terms of implementing visitor management plans and tools. If the example of Venice tells us one thing, it is that the excesses of tourism can quickly destroy the visitor experience, the resource base and the potential for sustainable tourism if it goes unchecked.

Future issues for visitor management

In the future, the impacts of tourism will continue to pose ethical dilemmas for planners and managers. On the one hand, governments are seeking to develop more socially inclusive societies, where principles such as 'Tourism for All' are pursued to facilitate a greater inclusion of special needs by tourism businesses and agencies, argues against management measures to limit access to those with the purchasing power. Running counter to such ideological arguments on tourism is the recognition that visitor management needs to limit rather than expand the

Table 12.6 Applications of visitor management models (source: Hall and McArthur 1998: 123; reproduced with permission from the authors)

Visitor management models	Applications across the world
The Recreation Opportunity Spectrum (ROS)	• In Australia ROS has been developed for Knarben Gorge, Fraser Island National Park • In an innovative study ROS was applied to the urban parklands around Newcastle, Australia • ROS has been an underlying principle behind the development of management strategies for national parks in New Zealand and the USA
Carrying Capacity Model	• Yosemite Valley, Yosemite National Park, USA – implemented by the United States Parks Service • Boundary Waters Canoe Area, USA – investigated but not fully implemented by the United States Parks Service • Angkor World Heritage Site, Siem Reap Province, Cambodia – the Angkor Conservation Office implemented an annual and daily capacity, as well as a capacity for any one moment in time • Green Island, Queensland, and the Queensland Department of Environment and Natural Heritage, Australia – implemented an annual and daily capacity, as well as a capacity for any one moment in time • In the early 1990s, the New Zealand sub-Antarctic islands had a limit of 500 visits per year • Waitomo Caves in New Zealand have a carrying capacity set at 200 persons at any one moment in time • Bermuda in the USA has set a capacity of 120 000 cruise-ship passengers during the peak visitation period • Lord Howe Island in the Tasman Sea has a limit of 800 visitors at any time
Visitor Activity Management Programme (VAMP)	• Cross-country (Nordic) skiing in Ottawa, Canada – partially implemented by the Canadian National Parks Service. • Mingan Archipelago National Park Reserve, Canada – implemented by the Canadian National Parks Service to help establish the new park

(Continued)

Table 12.6 (*Continued*)

Visitor management models	Applications across the world
	• Point Pelee National Park, Canada – implemented by the Canadian National Parks Service with an interpretation focus. • Kejimkijik National Park, Canada – partially implemented by the Canadian National Parks Service
Visitor Impact Management Model (VIMM)	• Florida Keys National Marine Sanctuary, Florida, USA – pilot implemented by the US Travel and Tourism Administration and the US Environmental Protection Agency • Netherlands – pilot explored for expansion by the World Tourism Organization • Buck Island Reef National Monument, Virgin Islands, USA – implemented but discontinued by United States National Park Service • Youghiogheny River, Western Maryland, USA – implemented but discontinued by Maryland Department of Natural Resources • Price Edward Island, Canada – pilot implemented by Parks Canada and the World Tourism Organization • Los Tuxtlas, Veracruz, Mexico – pilot implemented by the World Tourism Organization • Jenolan Caves, New South Wales, Australia – fully implemented and monitored by the Jenolan Caves Management Trust • Villa Gesell, Buenos Aires Province, Argentina – pilot implemented by the Buenos Aires Province Tourism Authority and the World Tourism Organization • Peninsula Valdes, Northern Patagonia, Argentina – pilot implemented by the World Tourism Organization
The Limits of Acceptable Change (LAC)	• Bob Marshall Wilderness Complex, Montana, USA – tested and implemented by the United States Forest Service • Selway-Bitteroot Wilderness, Idaho, USA – tested by the United States Forest Service • Cranberry Wilderness Area, West Virginia, USA – tested by the USDA Forest Service and West Virginia University

(*Continued*)

Table 12.6 (*Continued*)

Visitor management models	Applications across the world
	• The Wet Tropics World Heritage Area, Queensland, Australia – prepared for but never fully implemented by the Wet Tropics Management Authority
	• The Nymboida River, New South Wales, Australia – prepared for but never fully implemented by the New South Wales Department of Water Resources
	• Wallace Island Crown Reserve, New South Wales, Australia – developed but never implemented by the Wallis Island Reserve Trust and New South Wales Department of Water and Land Conservation
Tourism Optimization Management Model (TOMM)	• Kangaroo Island, South Australia, Australia – implementation in progress by the South Australian Tourism Commission, Department of Environment and Natural Resources and Tourism Kangaroo Island

access to many tourist sites and resources. The introduction of charging to enter religious sites such as Canterbury Cathedral in the face of problems caused by unlimited access is one example that raised many moral issues. The dilemma pricing as a management tool introduces is that political arguments on allowing all members of society to engage in tourism and leisure trips became redundant. Instead a caveat has to be added – participation for all in a defined range of activities and events. Tourism only becomes accessible if one has the disposable income.

Globally, the application of sophisticated management tools used in niche markets such as ecotourism is beginning to permeate other destinations and sites. As Page and Dowling (2002) noted, soft measures in ecotourism management designed to influence visitor behaviour, in order to mitigate impacts, seek to change users' attitudes and behaviour, and even out the distribution of visits between heavily and lightly used sites. An intermediate category of visitor management seeks to lower usage levels by balancing decisions on whether to concentrate or disperse visitors. Last, hard measures seek to ration use by controlling tourist

Table 12.7 Qualitative assessment of visitor management models (source: Hall and McArthur, 1998: 123; reproduced with permission from the authors)

Visitor management models	Key characteristics of visitor management models	Level of sophisti-cation	Range of contributing stakeholders	Actual application by heritage managers
The Recreation Opportunity Spectrum (ROS)	• Determines the threshold level of activity beyond which will result in the deterioration of the resource base • Its main dimensions are biophysical, sociocultural, psychological and managerial • Used for planning, site design and development, and administration	✓✓	✓✓	✓✓✓
Carrying Capacity Model	• Creates a diversity of experiences by identifying a spectrum of settings, activities and opportunities that a region may contain • Helps to review and reposition the type of visitor experiences most appropriate to a heritage site	✓	✓✓	✓✓

(Continued)

Table 12.7 (*Continued*)

Visitor management models	Key characteristics of visitor management models	Level of sophisti-cation	Range of contributing stakeholders	Actual application by heritage managers
Visitor Activity Management Programme (VAMP)	• Is a planning system that integrates visitor needs with resources to produce specific visitor opportunities • Is designed to resolve conflicts and tensions between visitors, heritage and heritage managers • Requires heritage manager to identify, provide for, and market to designated visitor groups	✓✓✓	✓✓✓	✓
Visitor Impact Management Model (VIMM)	• Focuses on reducing or controlling the impacts that threaten the quality of heritage and visitor experience • Uses explicit statements of management objectives and research and monitoring to determine heritage and social conditions, then generates a range of management strategies to deal with the impacts	✓✓	✓✓	✓✓

(Continued)

Table 12.7 (*Continued*)

Visitor management models	Key characteristics of visitor management models	Level of sophisti-cation	Range of contributing stakeholders	Actual application by heritage managers
The Limits of Acceptable Change (LAC)	• Focuses on the management of visitor impacts by identifying, first, desirable conditions for visitor activity to occur, then how much change is acceptable • A monitoring programme determines whether desirable conditions are within acceptable standards • A decision-making system determines management actions required to achieve the desired conditions	✓✓✓✓	✓✓✓	✓✓
Tourism Optimization Management Model (TOMM)	• Instead of limiting activity, it focuses on achieving optimum performance by addressing the sustainability of the heritage, viability of the tourism industry and empowerment of stakeholders • Covers environmental and experiential	✓✓✓	✓✓✓✓	✓

(*Continued*)

Table 12.7 (Continued)

Visitor management models	Key characteristics of visitor management models	Level of sophisti- cation	Range of contributing stakeholders	Actual application by heritage managers
	elements, as well as characteristics of the tourist market, economic conditions of the tourism industry and sociocultural conditions of the local community			
	• Contains three main parts; context analysis, a monitoring programme and management response system			

✓, Low; ✓✓, Moderate; ✓✓✓, High; ✓✓✓✓, Very high

numbers; this often requires advance reservations, different pricing strategies and queuing.

These tools and techniques will begin to gather momentum at many tourist sites and destinations, with taxing tourists as the most radical measure being seriously considered by destinations under extreme pressure. This tool is really a manager's last resort to control tourism. The World Travel and Tourism Council (WTTC) does not want to see its industry members saddled with massive tourist taxation, since it is seen that this may stifle growth. It objected to unfair measures like tourism taxation, fees and levies in its 2002 report *Taxing Intelligently*. Yet the WTTC is not faced with managing tourism in Venice. Venice illustrates what happens in a free-market economy, where pricing and taxation may be the only tools left to radically manage the destination. In locations such as Venice debates on issues such as 'Tourism for All' may be arcane, given the fact that tourism is not a

Box 12.1 Case study: Managing the tourist impact in Venice
(by *Stephen J. Page and C. Michael Hall*)

Venice is acknowledged as one of the world's leading cultural and art cities with its acclaimed fifteenth-century Renaissance art (Plate 12.1). It is a magical place for many visitors, with its elegant architecture, ambience and artistic qualities. Many of its buildings have iconic qualities, not least due to their association with poetry, writing and the work of different artists (e.g. Canaletto). Indeed Canaletto popularized many images of Venice as a place to visit in his picturesque, almost idealized, cityscapes that have contributed to the pursuit of cultural and heritage consumption by visitors. Venice is located on a series of islands in a lagoon with 117 islets, and is the capital of the Veneto region of Italy. The impact of tourism has resulted in continued population loss from the historic city of Venice. The resident population dropped from 175 000 in 1951 to 78 000 in 1992 and 65 000 in 2001; the city receives 47 000 commuters daily. The age and condition of many of Venice's buildings are under constant threat. The environment in Venice is suffering from:

- a sinking ground level
- a rising sea level
- pollution of the lagoon in which it is located
- atmospheric pollution
- congestion on the main canals from motorized traffic
- over-saturation at key locations for tourists
- increased flooding: in the 1970s and 1980s there were 50 high tides a year; in 1996 there were 101, and in 2000 some 80. This illustrates the range and extent of environmental concerns amidst a booming visitor industry.

Visitor arrivals have developed greatly. In 1952 50 000 tourists spent 1.2 million bednights in the historic city of Venice. By 1987 these figures had risen to 1.13 million tourist arrivals and 2.49 million bednights; by 1992, to 1.21 million arrivals and 2.68 million bednights. The average length of stay was 2.21 nights in 1992. These visitor numbers are swelled by a large day visitor market from other parts of Italy, especially the Adriatic beach resorts and Alpine areas. In 1992, the day tripper market was estimated to be six million visitors, providing a total market in excess of seven million visitors a year. In 2005 some estimates placed a figure of 13 to 15 million visitors, deluging the city.

Plate 12.1 1908 Tour of Italy and Venice to fulfil the renewed interest in the Grand Tour

Russo's (2002) study of tourism in Venice highlighted tourists' motivations for visiting cultural attractions and described Venice as being in the latter stage of the resort life cycle – nearing stagnation and decline. Montanari and Muscara (1995) recognized that Venice was saturated at key times in the year (e.g. Easter) and that the police have had to close the Ponde del Liberta when the optimum flow of 21 000 tourists a day has been exceeded (60 000 at Easter and 100 000 in the summer). There is increased competition between residents and visitors in the use of space within the historic city. Up to 34 per cent of the public space in the historic square is used by visitors and 49 per cent by residents. During special events, the use by visitors increases to 56 per cent and this adds to congestion in the city, competition for facilities and a declining visitor and resident experience.

Since 1987, on selected spring weekends, the land route from the mainland to Venice has been closed to visitors as an extreme form of crisis management. Montanari and Muscara (1995) developed a ninefold classification of tourists based on differences in their spatial behaviour (i.e. where and what they visit in the city), perception and spending power, which can be summarized thus:

- the first-time visitor on an organized tour
- the rich tourist
- the lover of Venice
- the backpacker camper
- the worldly wise tourist
- the return tourist
- the resident artist
- the beach tourist
- the visitor with a purpose.

This large number of different categories reflects Venice's unique tourism environment and the diversity of motivations for visiting the city.

Yet Russo (2002) argues that the city does not manage visits prudently. The time tourists spend on queuing at well-known attractions leads to lost opportunities to see lesser-known cultural attractions, heightened by poor marketing and communication with the visitor. This is complicated by the existence of ten agencies responsible for museums in the city. Venice is dominated by excursionists (83.1 per cent) in comparison to tourists (16.9 per cent), with a very even pattern of distribution throughout the year: January–March 14 per cent of visitors arrive; 30 per cent come in April–June; 32 per cent in July–September and 24 per cent October–December. Russo (2002) noted that the average duration of a visit was eight hours, with many tour operators promoting day trips rather than overnight stays. The destination's accessibility has also been increased with the recent advent of low-cost airlines in Europe. Venice's tourist market is comprised of 26.3 per cent of arrivals from within Italy, 36 per cent from the rest of Europe, 17.7 per cent from the USA, 11.1 per cent from Japan and 8.8 per cent from other countries/regions.

The social impact of the existing patterns of demand led van der Borg, Costa and Gotti (1996) to calculate the visitor to resident (host) ratios for Venice and a number of other European heritage cities. In Venice's historical centre, a ratio of 89.4:1 existed while for the wider Venice municipality this dropped to 27.6:1. This level of visitor pressure reflects the scale of the problem facing Venice. Incoming visitors have also purchased holiday properties which have driven up prices and excluded the local population at a time when this has dropped to fewer than 70 000 Venetians.

Venice's capacity for tourism

To assess the capacity of the historic centre of Venice, Canestrelli and Costa (1991) undertook a complex mathematical modelling exercise to examine the parameters to consider in any future visitor management plan. This established what is called the 'carrying capacity' (i.e. how many visitors can the historic city accommodate). The optimal carrying capacity for the historic city of Venice would be to admit 9780 tourists who use hotel accommodation, 1460 tourists staying in non-hotel accommodation and 10857 day trippers on a daily basis. Even if the 4.1 million day trippers who currently visit Venice were evenly spread this would still amount to 11 233 trippers a day. In fact it is estimated that an average of 37 500 day trippers a day visit Venice in August. Canestrelli and Costa (1991) argued that a ceiling of 25 000 visitors a day is the maximum tourist capacity for Venice.

There are important implications for the environment and its long-term preservation if the tourist capacity is being exceeded. Once the capacity is exceeded, the quality of the visitor experience is eroded and the physical fabric may be damaged; extra strain is placed on the infrastructure. Yet the large volume of visitors which descend on Venice each year not only exceeds the desirable limits of tourism for the city, but also poses a range of social and economic problems for planners. For example, over 1.5 million visitors go to the Doge's Palace each year while small numbers visit lesser-known attractions, illustrating the massive congestion at flagship and iconic attractions and areas such as St Mark's Square. As van der Borg *et al.* (1996: 52) observed:

> the negative external effects connected with the overloading of the carrying capacity are rapidly increasing, frustrating the centre's economy and society … excursionism [day tripping] is becoming increasingly important, while residential tourism is losing relevance for the local tourism market … [and] … the local bene-fits are diminishing. Tourism is becoming increasingly ineffective for Venice.

Thus, the negative impact of tourism on the historic centre of Venice is now resulting in a self-enforcing decline. Excursionists, who contribute less to a local tourism economy than staying visitors, supplant the staying market as it becomes less attractive to stay in the city. Up until 2000, changing the attitude of the city's tourism policy-makers was difficult: the pro-tourism lobby heavily influenced it. Since 2000 a number of positive measures have been enacted to address the saturation of the historic city by day visitors including denying access to the city by unauthorized tour coaches via the main coach terminal.

In 2001 a new mayor was elected and introduced a number of emergency measures to safeguard the future of tourism by:

- the introduction of a tourist tax to recover some of the external costs of tourism
- plans to impose a strict control on motorized traffic in the canals to reduce the wash effects on gondolas and buildings
- the introduction a multi-million pound mobile flood barrier, despite protests from ecologists, to reduce the regular flooding.

Another serious issue that impacts upon the quality of the tourist experience is the effluent problem in the city: the absence of sewers results in algal growth and a notable stench in the summer season.

Environmental processes that affect both the local and tourist population must also be recognized – such as flooding. Flooding in Venice now means that St Mark's Square, an icon for visitors, floods forty to sixty times a year compared to four to six times a year at the beginning of the twentieth century. As a result, tourism must be balanced with measures of environmental protection and management. Positive steps are needed to provide a more rational basis for the future development and promotion of tourism in the new millennium. Glasson *et al.* (1995: 116) summarized the problem of seeking to manage visitors and their environmental impact in Venice:

> every city must be kept as accessible as possible for some specific categories of users, such as inhabitants, visitors to offices and firms located in the city, and commuters studying or working in the city. At the same time, the art city needs to be kept as inaccessible as possible to some other user categories (the excursionist/day-trippers in particular).

The behaviour of visitors combined with the volume of visits has led the Mayor's office to introduce a Tourist Code of Conduct based on a range of principles including some of the following:

- Visitors should obtain a map and look beyond the iconic attractions (although visitors visit to see these very features); this is to try and geographically disperse visitors around the city. It is widely argued that overcrowding due to tourists has affected the residential ambience of the city, which is why many residents have left. If this trend continues Venice could become a living museum with a minimal resident population – at worst a cultural Disneyland.
- Tourists should keep to the right in the streets to help reduce congestion and to improve the flow of people.

In addition, new laws have been passed to regulate tourist behaviour in St Mark's Square (Articles 12, 23 and 28 of the Regulations of the Metropolitan Police of the City of Venice) which prohibit visitors from:

- lying down in public places
- sitting or lingering on the street, or eating picnic lunches
- throwing litter on the floor
- swimming in the canals or in the St Mark's Bay area
- riding bicycles or other vehicles in the city
- performing unsafe or bothersome activities
- undressing in public places
- walking about the city shirtless or in bathing costumes.

Any breach of these rules will be receive a 50 euros fine.

Source: www.commune.venezia.it

The example of Venice shows that, while tangible economic benefits accrue to the city, social and environmental costs are substantial. Montanari and Muscara (1995) argued that Venetian water transport plays a major role in tourism within the city and could be used to manage visitors, while the city needs to plan to separate the access, circulation and exit of the resident/commuting population and tourists. Russo (2002) expanded this debate, and argued that the better matching of tourism demand (i.e. visitors) with the available supply of attractions through improved marketing and information would bring some economic benefits to the city. It would also assist in geographically spreading the impact of visitors. But a much more visitor-focused management strategy is also needed, with policies and actions to:

- increase the attraction potential in some areas
- place access restrictions in some areas.

This could be achieved through a range of visitor management measures listed in Table 12.8. These combine soft and hard controls, listing the problem (causation), reviewing the context of addressing it and suggesting potential interventions. In some respects, the recent growth in cruise-ship traffic (short-term high-volume day trippers) has also placed additional strains on the city's tourist infrastructure. The introduction of the Venice Card in 2004 to give pre-booked visitors priority entry to attractions has been a move in the right direction, as it allows the city to limit the number of visitors to 25 000 on peak days when up to 50 000 people can descend on the city. Russo's (2002) advocacy of greater taxation/tariffs to 'disincentivize' excursions is likely to be implemented. Russo rightly advocates tourism management as a starting point to plan the future for tourism in the city, to raise the industry from saturation and stagnation. The continued growth in the numbers of day trippers has led to a deterioration in the quality of the tourist experience. This case study is significant in that it highlights the prevailing problems affecting many historic cities and both the political and policy issues that must be addressed to manage the impacts so that tourism does not destroy its vital resource – the environment.

Venice may be an extreme example of a city under siege. The management of visitor numbers and flows of these visitors is central to the long-term management of the destination. Venice has long passed any level of what might naively be called 'sustainable' tourism, meaning that tourism management must adopt a model of crisis management and deploy a radical solution.

Table 12.8 The problems, causes, measures and future actions needed to manage tourists in Venice (reprinted from *Annals of Tourism Research*, vol. 29, A. Russo, The 'Vicious Circle' of Tourism Development in Heritage Cities, 165–82: 2002 with permission of Elsevier)

Causation	Context	'Hard' interventions	'Soft' interventions
1 Increase of tourist demand → enlargement of tourism region, shorter visits	Difficult expansion of tourism supply, irreproducible heritage (*small centres, islands*)	Zoning, regional planning, enlargement of accommodation capacity in the city centre	Entrance ticket, incentives based on advance booking, discrimination policies, tariffs, creation of a supra-local 'tourism authority'
2 Shorter visits → increasing congestion costs, asymmetric information	Many cultural resources, difficult mobility (*medium-sized art cities*)	Zoning, access regulation, closing of portions of city centre, infrastructure policy, decentralization of cultural supply	Information and discrimination policies, promotion, creation of 'alternative routes'
3 Asymmetric information → decline in the quality of tourism supply (primary and complementary)	Limited competition, low controls, scarce homogeneity of cultural institutions (*mature destinations, transition countries*)	Licensing regulations, law enforcement, police controls in central areas, interpretation and welcome centres	Integral management of the cultural system, incentive to start ups, quality labels, virtual access to cultural products, tourism e-commerce
4 Decline in quality → incentive to commuting and disincentive to cultural visits	Sensitiveness to reputation, international attention, prevalence of tour-operated holidays, presence of alternatives in the hinterland (*mature metropolitan destinations, high accessibility*)	Regional–national planning	Reputation policies, promotion, diversification of tourism supply, fidelization, marketing, rejuvenation of products

basic human need, but a consumer good purchased in a free market. Reducing costs of access such as the low-cost airlines have done has actually placed additional stresses on locations such as Venice. Making them potentially more accessible to a larger range of people due to price will conversely add problems for visitor management.

In an ideal world, Page and Dowling (2002) identify the value of environmental planning for ecotourism that destinations can extend and apply in other locations. Here the principles of identifying discrete planning zones, with well-defined conservation values that also accommodate tourist activities and development, require a detailed classification of visitor activity in relation to the need for protection and compatibility with the resource base. This involves identifying types of zones for tourism where ecotourism or environmental issues are critical, such as:

- sanctuary zones, with special preservation provisions
- nature conservation zones, where protection and conservation are balanced
- outdoor recreation zones – natural areas where a wide range of outdoor activities are accommodated
- tourism development zones, with clusters of tourist activities and attractions/ infrastructure
- other land uses to accommodate social and economic activity.

This approach allows tourism management to combine the reduction of environmental impacts with enhancing the visitor experience.

These principles can be modified and refined for application in resorts and urban tourism destinations to achieve a more coordinated and rational approach to tourism. In sum, the activities and freedom of tourists will have to be curtailed in the future as resorts, destinations and sites realize the imperative of visitor management tools to implement a more rational and managed use of resources. This is to maintain a viable and dynamic tourism industry. To do this will require more innovative thinking and planning, partnerships between stakeholders and good communication to explain to visitors the rationale and need for such measures. The resolution of conflict, balancing tourism, non-tourism and other interests, will require planners and tourism managers to cooperate in the best interests of the locality in an increasingly competitive marketplace. With these issues in mind, attention now turns to the discussion of future management challenges for tourism in Chapter 13.

References

Ap, J. and Crompton, J. (1993) Residents' strategies for responding to tourism impacts. *Journal of Travel Research*, 32 (1): 47–50.

Canestrelli, E. and Costa, P. (1991) Tourist carrying capacity: A fuzzy approach. *Annals of Tourism Research*, 18 (2): 295–311.

Connell, J. (2005) Analysing coach tourism in Scotland: trends and patterns. In S. J. Page, *Transport and Tourism: Global Perspectives*. Harlow: Prentice Hall.

Douglas, N. and Douglas, N. (1996) The social and cultural impact of tourism in the Pacific. In C. M. Hall and S. J. Page (eds) *Tourism in the Pacific: Issues and Cases*. London: International Thomson Business Press.

Dowling, R. (1992) Tourism and environmental integration: The journey from idealism to realism. In C. Cooper and A. Lockwood (eds) *Progress in Tourism, Recreation and Hospitality Management,* Vol. 4. Chichester: John Wiley and Sons.

Doxey, G. V. (1975) A causation theory of visitor–resident irritants: Methodology and research inferences. In *Proceedings of the Travel Research Association 6th Annual Conference*. San Diego, CA: Travel Research Association.

English Tourist Board/Employment Department (1991) *Tourism and the Environment: Maintaining the Balance*. London: English Tourist Board.

Getz, D. (1993) Impacts of tourism on residents' leisure: Concepts, and a longitudinal case study of Spey Valley, Scotland. *Journal of Tourism Studies*, 4 (2): 33–44.

Glasson, J., Godfrey, K. and Goodey, B. with Absalom, H. and Van Der Borg, J. (1995) *Towards Visitor Impact Management: Visitor Impacts, Carrying Capacity and Management Responses in Europe's Historic Towns and Cities*. Aldershot: Avebury.

Hall, C. M. (1996) Environmental impact of tourism in the Pacific. In C. M. Hall and S. J. Page (eds) *Tourism in the Pacific: Issues and Cases*. London: International Thomson Business Press.

Hall, C. M. and McArthur, S. (1998) *Integrated Heritage Management*. London: The Stationery Office.

Mathieson, A. and Wall, G. (1982) *Tourism: Economic, Physical and Social Impacts*. Harlow: Longman

Montanari, A. and Muscara, C. (1995) Evaluating tourist flows in historic cities: The case of Venice. *Tijdschrift voor Economische en Sociale Geografie*, 86 (1): 80–7.

Ogilvie, I. (1933) *The Tourist Movement*. London: Staples Press.

Page, S. J. (1995) *Urban Tourism*. London: Routledge.

Page, S. J. and Dowling, R. (2002) *Ecotourism*. Harlow: Prentice Hall.

Page, S. J. and Hall, C. M. (2003) *Managing Urban Tourism*. Harlow: Prentice Hall.

Pearce, D. G. (1989) *Tourism Development*. Harlow: Longman.

Pigram, J. and Jenkins, J. (1999) *Outdoor Recreation Management*. London: Routledge.

Potter, A. (1978) The methodology of impact analysis. *Town and Country Planning*, 46 (9): 400–4.

Russo, A. (2002) The 'vicious circle' of tourism development in heritage cities. *Annals of Tourism Research*, 29 (1): 165–82.

Smith, V. (ed.) (1977) *Hosts and Guests: The Anthropology of Tourism*. Philadelphia: University of Pennsylvania Press.

Smith, V. L. (ed.) (1992) *Hosts and Guests: An Anthropology of Tourism*, 2nd edn. Philadelphia: University of Pennsylvannia Press.

Van der Borg, J., Costa, P. and Gotti, G. (1996) Tourism in European heritage cities. *Annals of Tourism Research*, 23 (2): 306–21.

World Travel and Tourism Council (2002) *Taxing Intelligently*. London: WTTC.

Further reading

This is probably one of the most comprehensively documented subject areas in tourism. A number of good books exist on the impacts of tourism, notably:

Wall, G. and Mathieson, A. (2006) *Tourism: Change, Impacts and Opportunities*. Harlow: Pearson Education.

And with reference to the less developed world:

Schyvens, R. (2002) *Tourism for Development: Empowering Communities*. Harlow: Prentice Hall.

And with an urban bias:

Page, S. J. and Hall, C. M. (2003) *Managing Urban Tourism*. Harlow: Prentice Hall.

Questions

1 Why does tourism create impacts?

2 How can tourism impacts be managed?

3 In what situations does a tourism manager decide to use 'hard' and 'soft' visitor manager approaches?

4 What would you do, as Mayor of Venice, to address the problems and potential of tourism?

13

The future of tourism: Post tourism?

Learning outcomes

This chapter discusses the future range of management problems that the tourism industry will have to address in the new millennium. On completion of the chapter, you should be able to understand:

- why the tourism industry needs to be proactive in managing its impacts
- how tourism has developed to a point where it may be uncontrollable in relation to the snowball concept
- what are the main drivers of change in the tourism sector in the next decade
- the significance of crises for tourism managers.

Introduction

Throughout the book, there has been only a limited discussion of the way in which the global growth of tourism will change, develop and require new forms of planning and management to control its effects. One of the most pressing concerns for planners, decision-makers and businesses is: will tourism stop growing and will it stop spreading across the globe?

The spread of tourism

Earlier chapters examined the way in which tourism has evolved from classical times through to the post-war period. One of the enduring themes in the history of travel is the pursuit by individuals, ruling elites and, latterly, the increasing numbers of leisure travellers, of unique, special and unspoilt locations to visit. For example, Figure 13.1 shows the scale of international tourism development now occurring in less developed and developing countries (where data exist to chart these trends). It also confirms the increasing geographical spread of tourism across the world to many countries that now embrace it as a method of stimulating economic activity, particularly where global trade barriers have frozen many developing countries out of engaging with lucrative trading blocs as a means of generating foreign currency. The problem, however, is that some of these new tourist destinations have not been able to control tourism to retain their vital unique elements. The result is what was described in the earlier chapters as the resort life cycle concept, where the growing popularity (demand) and supply by the tourism sector create a vibrant and dynamic business activity that begins to expand and develop. At that point, planning and policy issues need to be explicitly stated so that sustainable development is implicit in the future rationale for the destination. In 2003 the World Travel and Tourism Council (WTTC) launched a *Blueprint for New Tourism* which recognized that all stakeholders involved in tourism (including tourists, the tourism industry and destination communities) need to adopt a longer-term planning horizon as opposed to taking the short-termist commercial perspective that dominates the tourism sector approach globally (with some exceptions). Implicit in the WTTC's approach to tourism was a concern for sustainable tourism so that everything associated with tourism and the environment in which it is developed remains in balance.

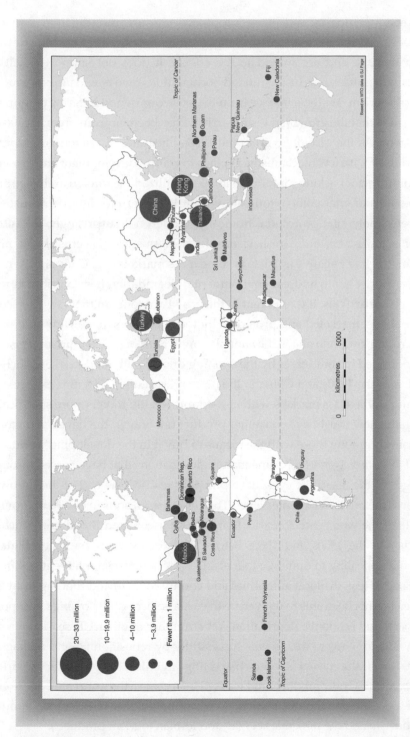

Figure 13.1 International tourism development in developing countries

This seemingly logical and phased approach to tourism destination management by WTTC assumes that tourism will continue to grow, and that the destinations can manage and accommodate the effects. It does not support a halt to tourism growth as it is an industry-funded body with its own agenda to continue to grow global tourism. Yet the evidence from the post-war period in terms of tourism development is that the growth in visitor arrivals has been far from orderly, phased and consistent. As the case of Spain in the 1960s illustrates, mass tourism rapidly established itself with few mechanisms in place to control development and growth. Indeed, public sector backing for tourism in Spain utilized the foreign exchange and political benefits of international tourism with little concern for long-term sustainability or environmental protection. Ironically, though not surprisingly, the introduction of a tourist tax in Spanish resorts to address such concerns in the new millennium, has had negative impacts in some mass markets (e.g. Germany), where images of a tourist tax to address environmental degradation has contributed to a decline in visitor arrivals. It is apparent in the growth of tourism that newly discovered destinations, marketed and promoted by tour operators, have witnessed phenomenal growth, over and above the annual growth rates of global tourism. This has been compounded in some cases by the opening of new outbound markets, such as South Korea in the 1990s and China in the new millennium. Growth is expected in other Asian middle-class markets with new-found wealth: travel (more specifically tourism) is the new must-have consumer product not only in the developed world but increasingly among those with the means to buy it in the developing world.

So will tourism stop growing? Some mature destinations that have passed through all the stages of the resort life cycle have probably reached the end of their growth period unless the public sector intervenes. The UK coastal resorts in east Kent provide an example of the worst-case scenario. Margate, Ramsgate and Broadstairs reached their heyday in the 1950s and 1960s before low-cost overseas package holidays became more appealing to domestic tourists. Despite substantial interventions from the public sector (e.g. the local authorities and county council) and funding from the EU, the area has not been able to rejuvenate the resorts successfully owing to the post-tourism social and economic deprivation. Yet a number of other UK seaside resorts have been able to reinvent themselves successfully by repositioning and reimaging themselves (to use the current in-vogue marketing jargon): in simple terms, these destinations have found new products and ways to intervene in the resort life cycle to create a new demand for the destination. An example of this is Brighton, through business tourism and the pink market (gay and lesbian tourism products).

In many urban areas, new destinations have been created and the towns reimaged and remodelled to generate a new economic sector based on tourism and the cultural industries (e.g. Glasgow after hosting European City of Culture in 1990, Bradford and East London's Docklands area, and Liverpool is currently seeking to redevelop the city based on hosting the 2008 European City of Culture). In each case of urban regeneration, visitor growth has been significant although the public sector cost of stimulating these regeneration schemes has been massive, as the case of London's Olympic Bid illustrated in Chapter 4. At a time of scarce public resources, with endemic poverty in some areas of major cities seeking to regenerate their future based on pleasure and leisure, there have been few attempts to stop and question whether this is the most appropriate economic strategy. Tourism is seen almost unquestioningly within the public sector, in a naive and simplistic manner, as a good development option: it can always be justified if visitors are generated. What consultants and analysts prefer not to say to these public-sector bodies is that tourists will visit many major cities irrespective of their massive infrastructure development, although exceptions to this exist such as the case of Bilbao in Spain where the construction of a flagship project – the Guggenheim Museum – put the city on the international culture map.

Coastal resorts created in the 1980s and 1990s across the Mediterranean and Asia-Pacific (e.g. Pattaya in Thailand) have experienced growth in excess of 10 per cent per annum when many other destinations and countries have been content to receive growth of around 3–4 per cent per annum. Given the time lag involved in new tourism supply coming onstream, this has often had major impacts on local infrastructure, the environment and residents. Likewise, developing countries facing problems of a lack of clean water, scarce water supplies for agriculture and a fragile environment have seen inappropriate forms of tourism developed following public policy decisions. One example, is the development of golf tourism in South East Asia and Goa, southern India: the maintenance of golfing greens requires large quantities of water and fertilizers, resulting in pesticides leaking into the water table, which pollutes the ground water and compromises its drinking quality.

The snowball and amoeba concept in tourism

The resort life cycle was used above to explain the linear growth of tourism through a series of stages of development ending in either stagnation or rejuvenation to stimulate the development process once again. This linear growth is best described as a snowball (see Figure 13.2), which begins to gather momentum as it rolls down a hill. The agents of change that have the idea of stimulating tourism development as a small snowball (i.e. the public and private sector) do not envisage the rapid transition to mass tourism. Initial visions of tourism are rapidly compromised, despite the best intentions of the public sector to control it. The pressure exerted by entrepreneurs, tour operators and other stakeholders takes precedence in early stages of development. Through time, these interest groups impact upon policy and the growing economic dependence upon tourism in the resort adds further pressure. The snowball gathers momentum, almost unstoppable and out of control; public sector interventions become less effective, only able to work around the edge of the problem to try and control an uncontrollable phenomenon that takes on a prominent role in the resort or locality. Although local antagonism grows, tourism cannot be restricted due to the inevitable political fall-out because of employment dependency issues. Yet as the development process continues, it may saturate and destroy the destination and its resource base. This means that the destination will be unable to sustain tourism any longer in that form. The destination becomes unattractive, over-developed and an environmentally

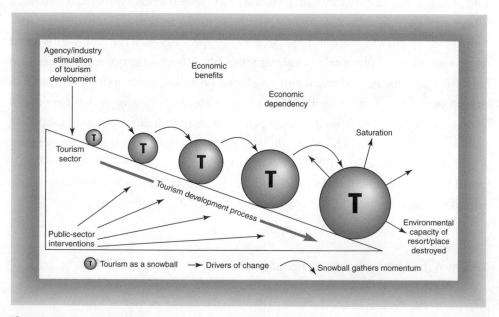

Figure 13.2   Tourism growth and development – snowball concept

compromised location (i.e. visual and physical pollution prevail). Images of saturation lead tour operators to use it as a low-cost, mass resort while high-spending visitors seek more attractive locations.

Although this is a gross simplification of the public and private sector role in
tourism development, the basic principles have been replicated across the world.
Locations have embraced tourism without really appreciating how complex and
powerful it can be – or become – once vested interests begin to drive it forward so
that they can reap potentially short-term profits.

One explanation of the way tourism grows and expands might be described as
the 'amoeba effect'. The amoeba, as a single-cell, simple form of life has the ability
to reproduce itself. Tourism is not dissimilar because once the initial amoeba is
introduced to a locality, and finds a welcoming home that embraces it as a mechanism to help stimulate economic activity, the process has begun (see Figure 13.3).
The ability of tourism to replicate itself, but then adapt and change to meet customer needs in certain cases means that the amoeba keeps dividing and producing
new entrepreneurs, as innovation and change lead to more development. If one
takes the example of London's tourism accommodation stock, constraints in central
London led to development elsewhere as the amoeba looked for a new niche where
it could survive and prosper. This simplistic explanation of tourism as a development process makes control, planning and management extremely difficult since

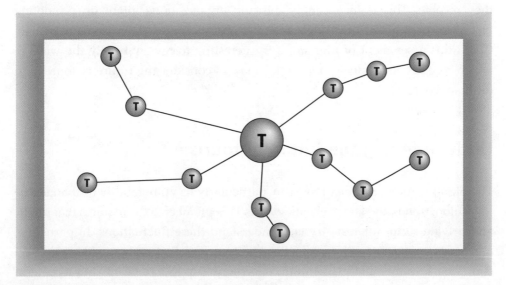

Figure 13.3 The 'amoeba' concept of tourism

the ground rules keep changing as tourism assumes a new form and nurtures new visitors. It is only at the point when the resort or destination reaches total saturation and is destroyed as an attractive location that the amoeba moves to a new home and the process begins again. However, there are good examples of public sector interventions managing tourism and seeking to encase the amoeba and prevent it growing any more, especially at sensitive environmental sites. The amoeba's ability to thrive beyond a controlled level is shifted. Unfortunately, these are the exceptions rather than the rule.

So to re-examine the question: *will tourism continue to grow*? If one considers the snowball and amoeba analogies, then there will almost certainly be tourism growth at a global scale. At a national and regional/local level, growth will largely be dependent upon the attractiveness of the locality in providing a conducive location for tourism to root itself and begin developing. The example of tourism and regeneration in Chapter 9 explained how this might occur. The challenge for the public and private sector stakeholders is to try and control and direct tourism – constrain it if necessary – to meet local social, environmental, economic and political objectives while ensuring it does not escalate too quickly and get out of control. Yet with governments positively encouraging the boom in low-cost air travel (which is artificially subsidized due to an absence of fuel tax on aviation fuel), questioning the efficacy (i.e. the rationale) of continued tourism growth is problematic: too many vested interests wish to see it grow due to the economic benefits they receive. This is increasingly difficult: organizations intent on promoting global tourism growth do not want to see limits imposed on tourism growth. Given this assessment of tourism, it is interesting to review briefly the ways in which researchers, analysts and policy-makers consider the future of tourism in different contexts.

Understanding the future of tourism

The highly variable nature of tourism, particularly its vulnerability to change due to fashion, trends and shock events such as 11 September 2001, requires that public and private sector interests try and understand these fluctuations. In particular, one needs to understand how tourism activity, especially trends, are likely to affect countries, localities and places in the short-term (up to five years) and long-term (up to ten years). To try and envisage how tourism will perform, analysts attempt to forecast the future of tourism, but they must be aware of underlying trends that may pose problems as well as crises and disasters. Glaeßer (2006) observed that natural disasters and shock events are becoming more common in tourism and thus there is a greater demand for crisis management tools to manage their effects. It is not surprising to find tourism analysts utilizing research techniques such as scenario planning, which seeks to construct a number of scenarios of how future trends might play out. This involves:

- framing the issues involved
- identifying people who may be involved in providing input and critical reviews of the scenarios
- drawing a picture or pictures of the future using trends, themes, critical relationships and issues associated with the problem that is being considered (i.e. how would we respond as a destination to three different severities of earthquake?)
- providing known uncertainties that could impact upon the scenarios and upset the status quo, and factors that are critical in moving a scenario from a pre-crisis, to crisis and post-crisis stage (i.e. tipping points)
- identifying possible paths for different scenarios
- testing the plausibility of the scenarios
- anticipating how people and organisations associated with tourism might respond during the different scenarios
- identifying strategies to manage the future scenarios.

Whilst critics of such approaches argue that such 'crystal gazing' exercises may never result in accurate predictions of how the future may evolve, there is a growing acceptance in public and private sector organizations of the need for such exercises. The July 2005 terrorist bombings in London are a case in point: rapid responses and the mobilization of a disaster plan had already been tested after a scenario planning exercise and dry run of the crisis some months previously. Concerns over tourist safety, terrorism, sustainability, climate change and the impact on future configurations of tourist travel have made such exercises all the more valuable. A recent example of such an exercise was the joint project between the author and VisitScotland to assess the possible impact of avian flu and a flu pandemic on Scottish tourism, with one outcome being a contingency plan for the management of Scottish tourism. The scale and significance of avian flu as a crisis that could affect global tourism flows is shown in Figure 13.4, which illustrates the

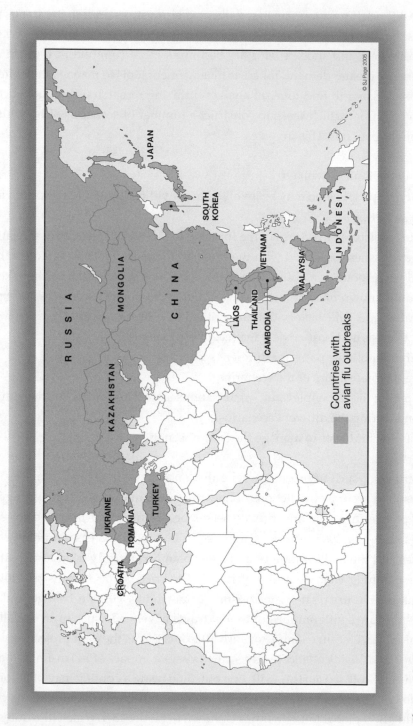

Figure 13.4 Avian flu outbreaks between 2003 and early 2006

outbreaks between 2003 and early 2006. Whilst these outbreaks have certainly caused health risks to tourists, who have been advised to avoid contact with live poultry and poultry markets, the most significant threat is if the H5N1 bird flu virus mutates and leads to human-to-human transmission which could trigger a world influenza pandemic. This would lead to a major shock wave on world tourism, with curtailed travel, interruptions to service provision and other impacts that could see tourism activity slow down or halt in some contexts.

One other tool which is far more commonly used by managers in tourism is forecasting. Forecasting in tourism is far from an exact science. This is because of the effect of so many unknown factors (e.g. exchange rates, fuel prices, the cost of travel, political stability in the origin and destination area and impact of inflation). Yet forecasting still helps planners to measure the order of magnitude of potential change that may occur in tourism. This will be important in a commercial context in trying to match future supply with likely demand (i.e. will an airline need to invest in additional capacity to meet demand?), and in maximizing revenue and profits through the optimum efficiency in resource or asset use. This has been sum-marized by Archer (1987: 77) in a management context as:

> no manager can avoid the need for some form of forecasting: a manager must plan for the future in order to minimise the risk of failure or, more optimistic-ally, to maximise the possibilities of success. In order to plan, he must use forecasts. Forecasts will always be made, whether by guesswork, teamwork or the use of complex models, and the accuracy of the forecasts will affect the quality of the management decision.

In essence, forecasting is about the assessment of future change in the demand for tourism, estimating future traffic and a range of possible scenarios to gauge likely changes in the scale of demand. This invariably involves looking at past tourism trends to statistically model future demand, using a variety of models, formulae and developments in the sub-field of economics known as 'econometrics'. In con-structing these models, the analyst will normally build in key tourism variables such as a number of tourist trips, tourist expenditure, market shares of tourism and tourism's share of gross domestic product. The resulting models will look at the factors that are likely to have a bearing on demand, to develop the forecasts. For example, the UN-World Tourism Organization has produced forecasts for global tourism to 2020, which anticipates 1.5 billion international visitor arrivals.

However, when examining any tourism forecast, one needs to look at the assumptions used by the analyst, what data sources are being used and what the analyst is intending to produce. Regardless of forecasts there will always be pressures for tourism to change.

The pressures for tourism to change

At a global scale, and particularly in the industrialized Western countries, there is evidence from consumer attitudes towards tourism that the self-destructive nature of tourism causes some visitors to question the impact of where they travel. A greater consciousness of the effects of tourism is now permeating both the consumer and the more environmentally responsible tour operators. This is a slow and gradual process of change, and there is always likely to be a role for the mass packaged, low-cost, high-volume, sun, sea and sand holidays. However, at the upper end of the market, a greater demand for environmentally sensitive and conservation-oriented niche products may begin to permeate the activities of the tourism sector, as airlines, tour operators and accommodation providers introduce environmental products to recognize these consumer tastes. The factors involved in pressurizing tourism to change can be divided into those that are external to tourism and beyond its control (e.g. exchange rates) and those that are within its grasp.

An ageing travelling public

In many of the Western industrialized countries, tourism markets are becoming characterized by an ageing population. This has been termed the 'senior market', which, internationally, exceeds 100 million arrivals, or 1 in 6 of all international trips. The senior market is particularly notable in the USA, Europe and Japan, which are major contributors to outbound travel globally. In many European countries, the over-55s now comprises 25 per cent of the total population – although, statistically, the likelihood of travel decreases with increasing age. Senior markets are less seasonal, able to utilize high disposable incomes in those cases where mortgage payments are negligible, and require more attention to their needs. This is reflected in the growth of specialist tour operators (e.g. Saga in the UK and Elderhost in the USA). What is evident is the continued growth in this market and the potential for tourism businesses to adapt to meet these consumers' needs. For example, the revival of coach tourism for long holidays in many parts of Europe reflects one niche product that is particularly favoured by the grey market, since it is perceived as safe and convenient and meets the travellers' needs.

New social trends

New social trends have emerged over the last decade in developed outbound markets. For example, women are playing a more dominant role in the labour market than they were 20 years ago. People in the 20- to 40-year age bracket are marrying later and deferring having children; as a result they have more disposable income, making them a lucrative expanding niche market. This niche market and much of the senior market places a renewed emphasis on the consumption of luxury tourism products. Whereas luxury products in the 1970s and 1980s were often associated with consumer goods and a house, now travel products have become far more fashionable among both the elite and the general population, who are willing to spend more money on a luxury experience.

New outbound markets

In global terms, the rise of the Chinese outbound market and the growth in outbound middle-class travellers in Asia are yet to be fully understood in terms of their impact on tourism trends. Many tourism commentators are watching to see whether these markets create new outbound opportunities, and what are the perceived needs of the market and their likely global travel patterns, given the international family and kinship ties with all parts of the world. What is certain is the scale of such markets are huge and have the potential to change dramatically the nature of international travel patterns towards Asian outbound markets – China has been described as the 'sleeping giant' which is about to awaken. This reflects the importance of political changes, such as allowing outbound and inbound travel, which are notable in shaping future tourism trends: governments can constrain, facilitate and prevent tourism according to the policies they promote in terms of domestic and international tourism.

Crises and disasters in tourism

One of the principal external factors that can affect tourism and is highly unpredictable for organizations and countries is a crisis or disaster (man-made or natural). The challenge of coping with catastrophic events poses many issues for an organization's ability to adapt to change, as reflected in the Foot and Mouth crisis in the UK in 2001, 9/11, the 2004 tsunami and the hurricanes that affected the USA in 2005.

Crises in tourism and business response: A management challenge?

Although such crises may be short-term in nature, the exposure of the tourism sector is significant and apparently stable business activities can be transformed into chaos. However, such crises may also have the potential to stimulate innovation as Chapter 10 highlighted. Ultimately, crises and chaos illustrate tourism's highly volatile nature and indicates how adaptable organizations need to be to change. In a management context, Faulkner and Russell (1999) identified the typical modes of operation for entrepreneurs in tourism, who instituted chaos and change, and for those who were planners and regulators of change. This has important implications for how tourism ventures are managed. Chaos makers were characterized by being:

- individualistic
- flexible
- innovative
- experimental
- intuitive
- risk-takers.

Regulators were characterized by being:

- risk-averse
- rational
- controlled
- planners

- rigid in their outlook
- concerned with reaching consensus on decision-making.

Therefore, the profitability of tourism organizations is increasingly being linked to the ability to:

- innovate
- manage and adapt to change and crises
- manage, recruit and retain high-quality human resources
- develop competitive business ventures by understanding the economic, social, political and managerial challenges of operating tourism enterprises
- react to public policy, and influence its formulation and implementation
- think creatively and globally, with an ability to apply international best practice in a local context
- understand how tourism trends affect one's day-to-day business operations.

In order to react and embrace change, many tourism organizations need to be able to understand and implement technology.

Technology and tourism

Technology is globally connecting tourism businesses and clients together. In tourism environments, the harnessing of technology to achieve entertainment and enhance fun has been widely embraced in the theme park sector. In the USA, the theme park industry generates over US$11 billion a year, while globally over 120 large theme parks exist, each attracting over a million visits a year. Indeed, from a management perspective, the creation of man-made tourism environments such as theme parks may fill a niche in the market for accommodating mass tourism without compromising the local environment. Theme parks allow large numbers to be accommodated, using technology, fantasy, escapism and a safe, monitored and highly managed experience (as the Disney model illustrated in Chapter 10). This is certainly a trend which will continue, as continuous improvements and innovation help these tourism environments to adapt to new consumer tastes and trends.

At an individual business level, information communications technology or ICT is the main driver of change, requiring better management for tourism operations to harness their potential. ICT provides up-to-date, managed client data and the scope to search and select a wide range of products and experiences. ICT has enabled forward-looking businesses to respond to the demand for more up-to-date information and tailor-made products. The worldwide web also allows the customer to undertake this process themselves (dynamic packaging software makes this much easier), challenging the supply chain and its traditional role in selling tourism products, some industry analysts suggest. The rapid growth in online booking may have stabilized in terms of large corporations, but it continues to make inroads into traditional travel agent business. ICTs are now widely adopted in the tourism sector, and innovation is likely to push further developments that allow tourism products to reach a wider audience. Above all, ICTs are making society, and the consumer, more demanding and more conscious of getting value for money. Yet technology will not address all the future processes likely to shape tourism trends, especially environmental issues such as climate change.

Climate change, tourism and the environment: Its impact on future tourism trends

There is major concern among scientists that the world's climate is changing. Global warming resulting in climate change could affect the climate and weather in many of the world's major tourism destinations by 2050. Many of these longer-term changes are also likely to have some shorter-term effects including:

- temperature increases of up to 0.5°C per decade causing many destinations with Mediterranean and African climates to become too hot for normal tourist use in the peak summer season, thereby changing the likely use of many coastal resorts in the long-term
- a drop in summer rainfall in many arid locations, such as small islands, making technological solutions to water supply (e.g. desalination) critical, ensuring that tourism growth is dependent upon the viability of technology
- global warming will lead to sea level rises and many vulnerable islands located around sea level, many of which have thriving tourism industries, will be lost unless expensive flood protection schemes are put in place

- changes to weather patterns, such as an increased severity of storms, may make access to many island destinations problematic, if sea access is the only viable option
- the possible removal of snow cover by global warming in locations dependent upon winter sports, reducing their appeal and attraction
- the need for destinations to think more strategically about the risk assessment associated with climate change in terms of their physical environment as a context and attractor of tourism activity, whilst changes to weather patterns may cause significant disruption to tourism and alter visitors' perception of resorts and areas.

These environmental concerns will certainly begin to feed into the changing nature of tourism as a business activity, as consumers start to recognize how important climate change and environmental risks associated with global warming become.

New business trends

Change is rapid in the tourism sector: today's trends are redundant tomorrow. Tourism has gathered momentum since the 1980s as technology has increased the scale, extent and rate of communication across the tourism sector. ICT has forced many tourism businesses to scrutinize their operations, to assess whether they are operating in an efficient and profitable manner. Greater industry concentration through mergers and acquisitions will certainly continue, premised by perceived economies of scale and efficiency gains. This also reflects competition strategy in the tourism sector, with larger players seeking to dominate certain sectors (e.g. retailing, aviation and tour operation) or adopt integrated operations to raise profitability (e.g. TUI in Europe). This leads to a new operating environment in which evolving trends can create recognition of the need to participate in certain products if businesses are to compete. The announcement in August 2002 that British Midland was replacing its standard airline service from its East Midlands hub with services operated by its BMIbaby budget airline is a recognition of the need to reduce costs and re-orient its business towards an expanding sector of the market, which has been very successful in identifying a niche.

In an ICT context, software launched by RWA - its 'sell it' software package – is also allowing more tour operators to compete for the online market by allowing clients to search by destination, departure point and holiday type. Canadian research on travel since 11 September 2001 noted that these new trends have seen changes in travellers' behaviour, including demands for increased evidence of security, more road-based trips, shorter trips and cruises, a growth in the demand for safer destinations and a larger number of discounted travel offers to stimulate demand.

Furthermore, new business processes, called hypercompetition, now characterize the fast growing tourism sector. D'Aveni (1988) cited in Page and Connell (2006) characterized hypercompetition in this sector of the tourism industry in terms of:

- rapid product innovation
- aggressive competition
- shorter product life cycles
- businesses experimenting with meeting customers' needs
- the rising importance of business alliances
- the destruction of norms and rules of national oligopolies such as state-owned airlines which still dominate South American and South East Asian aviation.

D'Aveni (1988) identified four processes that are contributing to the hypercompetition. These are:

1 Customers want better quality at lower prices.
2 Rapid technological change, enhanced through the use of ICT.
3 The expansion of very aggressive companies who are willing to enter markets for a number of years with a loss leader product (e.g. low-cost airlines), with a view to destroying the competition so that they will harness the market in the long term.
4 The progressive removal of government barriers towards competition throughout the world.

Hypercompetition changes how competitors enter the marketplace and how they disrupt the existing business:

- by redefining the product market, by offering more at a lower price
- by modifying the industry's purpose and focus by bundling and splitting industries

- by disrupting the supply chain by redefining the knowledge and know-how needed to deliver the product to the customer
- by harnessing global resources from alliances and partners to compete with non-aligned business as competition becomes more global.

But given such changes, will tourism be limited by governments in the future – and if so, how?

Limiting tourism: The beginning of the end?

With global concerns for environmental impacts generated by the pollution tourism induces, environmental management has emerged as a new buzzword for the tourism sector. This has also been embodied in a much larger debate on the ethical issues involved in how and what form of tourism governments will allow to develop. For example, legal and moral issues surround the exploitation that sex tourism causes in many countries has produced a great deal of debate on how tourism fuels such activity. NGOs such as the UN-WTO and End Child Prostitution and Trafficking have pursued a campaign since 1996 to eradicate this unacceptable element of tourism. One notable development has been the introduction by the tourism industry of voluntary codes of conduct (see www.world-tourism.org for the UN-WTO view on these codes and its own Ethical Code of Conduct). This is seen as one attempt by the industry to try and reform some of its bad practices and impacts.

Similar debates are also emerging concerning the impact of air travel and transport on global warming, as illustrated by the 2002 World Summit in South Africa. Global warming highlights the interdependencies that exist between different ecosystems and man's damaging effects through tourism. If tourism continues to make a major contribution to such environmental problems, then it will be one more economic activity that is self-destroying. Tourism as a consumer activity is also accentuating the socioeconomic extremes between the 'haves' and 'have-nots' in society at a local, national and international scale, especially in less developed countries. This has led to a greater interest in community-based tourism development which has been rebranded to widen the role for tourism in poverty reduction in less developed countries (called pro-poor tourism).

Proponents of peace have argued that tourism can aid understanding between cultures and societies. Yet the visits of Westernized travellers to less developed areas simply highlights the poverty and income gap, further fuelling discontent, envy and, in some cases, crime and political upheaval – failing to generate peace. Human nature is such that the real impact of tourism and the wealth and consumption of visitors on places with low levels of development can be psychologically and culturally damaging. At the same time, it may bring economic benefits. This highlights the conundrum – tourism's internal tension and tendency to be both positive and negative. In this context, more forceful policy and public sector management will be required to manage these relationships if potentially damaging effects are to be limited.

But should tourism be allowed to spread to all parts of the planet in an uncontrolled or even planned manner?

The evidence is that tourism's growing influence is set to impact on every corner of the globe. Even pristine wilderness areas and very fragile environments such as Antarctica are not immune from the visitor phenomenon. Attempts to license and manage visitors to such pristine environments and charge premium prices have not limited their impacts: they have simply accentuated the demand for visits. For example, the first recorded overflight (i.e. a scenic flight) of Antarctica was by the Chilean national airline (Linea Aerea Nacional) in 1957 and the first commercial ship visited in 1958. By 1998, tourism had expanded to 15 000 ship-borne visits per annum, concentrated in the November–February period. Some forecasts suggest that this could grow to 20 000 by 2010. Various policies exist to limit the development of commercial tourism in Antarctica, such as the 1999 Madrid Protocol, the 1994 Antarctic Treaty Consultative Meeting in Kyoto and a voluntary Code of Practice among the Association of Antarctic Tour Operators (formed in 1991). Yet it is patently obvious that tourism has developed: it exists as a business activity if only as scenic flights and ship-borne visits by Western visitors who are typically prosperous, well educated and professional. Antarctica highlights both the amoeba principle and the evolution of the snowball concept: attempts by vested interests (i.e. tour operators) and conservation agencies to limit visits are slowly being eroded – though arguably limitation is in their interest, as restricting supply keeps the prices high.

The tourism industry's pursuit of the next business opportunity has led to even those countries that limit visitors, such as Bhutan, allowing in more visitors to gain additional foreign currency. It would appear that tourism knows no bounds. Planning and self-management by industry codes of conduct have only had a superficial effect on visitor damage in sensitive environments. Rather than being phrased in restrictive ways, they need to be phrased in positive ways (e.g. 'Do not dump your rubbish here' might be replaced with 'Please take your litter home to help minimize your impact on the environment'). To the critic, however, this is the industry policing itself – and this usually only kicks in when serious problems begin to emerge. For example, in New Zealand, such a debate emerged following the aftermath of numerous adventure tourism accidents. The policy debate focused on whether the state should intervene and regulate operators or whether it should be self-regulating through a wider use of codes of conduct? The latter prevailed in a climate of minimal state intervention as major accidents were covered by a no-fault accident compensation legislation, although there is evidence that legal challenges are now questioning whether this will continue. Is it not time that commentators and researchers began to make a stand and pose some of the following questions in order to engage in a greater debate about tourism, now that the impacts are so important to all of our lives?

- Is there a real need now to make certain parts of the world 'tourism-free'?
- Should not certain pristine areas be kept pristine and be free of the vagaries of tourism?
- Is there not an opportunity to retain Antarctica as a natural wilderness?
- Should nature have some respite from the continuous pressures of tourism?

The notions implied in these questions seem to be common sense, as well as making a stance on environmental preservation, but they remain controversial. This is because the very implementation of such a position would limit the personal freedom of the affluent tourist and, more importantly, prevent business from exploiting the tourism potential of an area. Yet surely with the introduction of virtual reality, these environments can be experienced in more novel ways than in the manner that destroys the resource base? In visionary destinations, tourism revenue has been used to protect and conserve nature and heritage, but these examples are not the norm. One of the problems that tourism development has posed in China, is a tension in areas of environmental sensitivity where there is demand for economic revenue for development from large-scale tourism when the area is better suited to small-scale, locally owned and operated ecotourism developments.

Given the scale of demand for domestic and international travel, tourism can only really be described as an uncontrollable process once the basic elements of economic development become established and drive the ideological development of the sector: therefore, where tourism gets out of control it becomes a destructive force. There is just not enough public debate or academic discussion regarding the justifications for halting tourism or even making a stance and saying – *no tourism here please*. This may have major political overtones, but in public policy contexts, alternative economic development options will be required if tourism is not the solution. It is not necessary to be anti-tourism, but it should be realistically understood what a future committed to tourism means for people, their locality and environment, and to consider the measures to control it.

Although there is a growing sophistication among some travellers, understanding the link between travel, environmental damage, personal consumption and development remains limited. If tourism is not subjected to greater control in many destinations, self-destruction will lead to *post-tourism*, destinations suffering *tourism trauma*, where they are deluged by demand and stretched to a point where they cannot cope effectively with visitors or the demands placed on the resource base. Such a scenario exists in many destinations, which look forward to the shoulder season to allow the area to recover from 'tourist shock', so that psychologically and environmentally the local population once again feel they are not marginalized and pushed out by the influx of visitors. This is noticeable in many small historic cities in Europe that experience such pressures. Post-tourism and tourism trauma should be developed as a new element of the resort life cycle. Here, the loss of attractiveness and damage induced has led to over-development, and the tourist seeks new pastures once the destination goes past its sell-by date. Tourism is a free-market activity, where price, affordability and appeal remain the determinants of consumer demand. If the destination loses its appeal, it may have an economic crisis to address. As examples in this book have shown, many destinations have never returned to their tourism heydays and the redundancy that is now apparent in many former coastal resorts is a permanent reminder of what happens when the resort cycle hits decline. Therefore, striking the right balance between development, sustainable use and destination or tourist appeal is a dynamic element that needs constant review given the ability of tourism to change rapidly. This is why an understanding of tourism, how to manage it and how to take action quickly when things go wrong is fundamental to a healthy, prosperous and enriching tourism environment for all stakeholders. One suggestion may be to rethink how we manage tourism – and one possible and quite radical approach might be the development of a new concept of *managed tourism*.

Towards a new tourism management concept: Managed tourism

Given the increasing cynicism from tourism analysts about the green lobby and the unwillingness of almost every government globally (with the exception of Bhutan) to limit tourism growth, a more radical approach is needed. The 1990s have seen an excessive amount of research activity associated with the notion of sustainable tourism but few examples exist of where this has been developed with the degree of sophistication needed for it to work properly. The concept of sustainable tourism is quite simply too vague, imprecise and lacking in detailed measures for an assessment to be made of how it should be implemented and monitored in different contexts so that limits and thresholds of tourism activity can be established. The tourism industry does not want to see anything implemented that could damage their commercial viability (e.g. limits to growth), and without decrying the validity of much of the academic research activity on sustainable tourism, it has not led to wide-scale changes in the way tourism is developed or promoted. The theory of sustainable tourism has not been widely applied in practice, and so it is probably time for a more radical concept to be introduced that governments and policy-makers can understand in simple terms: it is *managed tourism* (MT).

There are global processes at work in terms of both tourism demand and tools by which tourists can begin to assess and understand their own impact on the environment. One of these, as Table 13.1 shows, is a new tool: *ecological footprinting* (EF), which now allows us to measure and assess how resource consumption occurs in terms of our pleasure and leisure time. It also highlights how unnecessary some forms of excessive consumption of the earth's finite resources are when compared with the effects this may have on the planet. For this reason, and given the prior discussion on the snowball concept in tourism, there is a real need for MT to develop a number of principles to manage such activity in the future. Figure 13.5 illustrates how these principles are starting to arouse interest from tourists in terms of growing numbers of people becoming aware of the effects of tourism on climate change and resource use. Yet the key element in Figure 13.5 is the

Table 13.1 Ecological footprinting

There is a growing interest among environmental researchers on developing measures and indicators capable of accounting for the tourist's impacts on the environment. One technique now being developed and debated in tourism is the ecological footprint (EF). EF is a tool by which an estimate of resource consumption and waste generated by an economic activity, such as tourism, can be generated in a given area.

The technique examines the consumption of energy, foodstuffs, raw materials, water, transport impacts, waste generated and loss of land from development. While criticisms do exist over the methods of analysis used to calculate the EF, it is now being used by public sector agencies to highlight issues of tourist resource use as one approach to assessing tourism and its sustainability in terms of resource use.

Gössling (2002) used this technique to illustrate the EF for tourism in the Seychelles per tourist, using the common unit of measurement 'gha' (global hectares), which is the way demand of an activity on natural resources results in its consumption. In the Seychelles, values of 1.9 gha per year for the EF were 90 per cent the result of air travel.

For a typical two-week holiday in the Mediterranean, a World Wildlife Fund for nature study observed that a gha of 0.37 resulted in Majorca and 0.93 in Cyprus. In each case, air travel was the contributor to over 50 per cent of the EF. The value of the EF technique is that it allows comparison of the overall ecological impact of tourism products on global biological resources.

willingness of governments to see an alternative path to tourism development through policies that may embrace MT and, for this reason, some of the following principles and ideas may need to shape how MT is implemented in different contexts:

- EF needs to be developed more extensively across the tourism sector to show consumers exactly what the environmental costs of their activity are for destinations and the environment. This may need to be introduced as a legislative requirement in the same way that foodstuffs now have to be labelled with their contents or cigarettes carry a warning on their impact on your health.
- Holidaymakers need to be taxed more fully to reflect their impact and use of resources: this may raise issues of equity and social inclusion/exclusion, but with growing environmental problems, there is a need once again to make

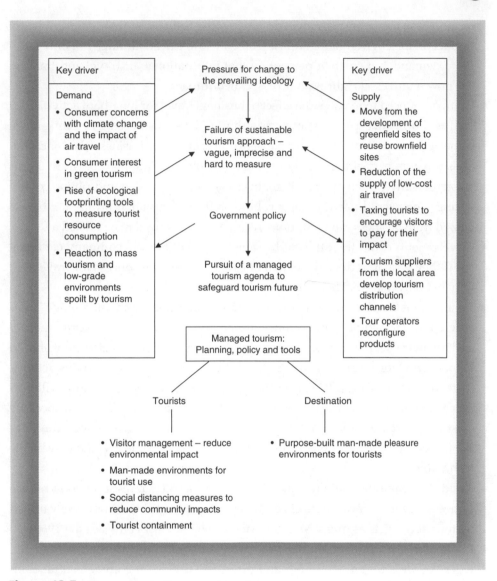

Figure 13.5 The concept of managed tourism

international tourism more of a luxury than a mass product. It should also be emphasized that tourism is not a basic human need such as food, water and shelter. We do not need it to survive, but only to enrich our lives and as a consumer product.

- Governments need to reconsider the ill-advised and short-termist view that low-cost airlines are major contributors to tourism growth and development: in simple terms, these transport providers do not pay the full cost of their environmental impact on the environment, and ridiculously low-priced air fares not only stimulate demand, but create a perception that international air travel and tourism are now a universal right with no associated impacts.

- Companies need to reassess the effect of business travel for long-haul activities (as well as short-haul trips using low-cost airlines). Governments could easily remove some of the tax incentives for companies to offset excessive business-class and first-class travel as part of the perks of being an employee, limiting the nature of this wasteful activity: many good alternatives exist such as video and phone conferencing. This would need a major culture shift but legislation on the tax breaks gained from business travel in company accounts may need to be looked at.

- Governments could treat this in the same way that they tax company car benefits if they wish to reduce the extent of excessive use of resources for travel that may net only marginal benefits to business.

- Destinations need to delimit precisely areas in resorts and man-made areas where tourism activity can be concentrated and so that they are *tourist-resilient* and not in fragile natural environments: no new greenfield development should be permitted for tourism, given the loss of the earth's resources to this activity. Instead, tourism should be concentrated on brownfield sites (i.e. those with former tourism or industrial developments that are no longer in use), especially existing resort areas that can be environmentally improved. This would reduce the impacts on the natural environment as far as is possible given the available technology.

- Residents should be sheltered and socially distanced from resort areas to reduce unnecessary impacts and effects on their culture; they should not be swamped by tourist districts as many Mediterranean resorts have been since the 1960s.

- Local tourism suppliers should be developed from the existing business networks in areas to remove unfair and externally dominant commercial relationships that favour global companies which then take control of the tourism sector.

- Government policies need to reflect a commitment to strongly control MT and the way tourism develops. Without a very active involvement, MT will not be a reality. This commitment would require the use of planning tools that are able to protect destinations, contain tourism and prevent it spilling over to other areas.

- Where governments choose a path based on mass tourism, the future development will need to utilize a wide range of visitor management tools so that the tourist experience is provided in a way that the resource base can easily maintain. This may involve demolishing and rebuilding brownfield tourism sites or upgrading infrastructure rather than allowing resorts to keep expanding whilst other parts become rundown and redundant. This points to a need for resort renewal and regeneration using the existing land area of the resort as opposed to new landtake.

Whilst many of these principles may seem draconian, they are based on many of the tools and principles of visitor management and efficient resource use. They question the logic of constantly expanding tourist resort areas and districts without really looking at an area's capacity to absorb visitors. Managers of destinations need realistically to assess what visitors they can accommodate, limit the numbers and develop a tourism industry based around more rational principles, rather than allowing it simply to grow and mutate along the lines of the amoeba concept. The aim of MT is to tightly control and manage tourism activity given its propensity for resource consumption, while controlling the places where it takes root. A more definite and practical approach to tourism management is needed that is not shrouded in the vagueness and mystery of 'sustainable tourism'. Many sectors of the tourism industry have harnessed this term for marketing purposes to make tourism look more attractive in certain destinations, yet have done little to implement it. Sustainable tourism is also seen as making the tourist feel more environmentally responsible when in fact the very pursuit of tourism to many sensitive environments is the least responsible and sustainable activity in which a consumer can engage. Whilst some examples of genuine sustainable activity exist in sensitive environments, they are not the norm in tourism and this is why it is time for a new approach, radically rethinking how governments perceive and manage tourism. Tourism may seem like a panacea to solve all our ills in economic terms, but the environmental and social costs may be too great in the long term without a stronger commitment to radical principles of MT that require substantial state intervention to direct and manage the tourism sector.

There is no doubt that the new millennium is a very testing time for tourism. The pressure to continually pursue tourism growth is unrelenting from business interests and government agencies. The challenge for the tourism sector, policymakers and governments is to ask a number of very fundamental questions:

- Why do we want tourism?
- What does it mean for our locality or country?

- How will it impact upon our society?
- How will it be managed to make a win–win situation for all stakeholders?

A further dimension to the public policy-making process on the future of tourism in a locality or destination is posed in countries with a substantial indigenous population with ancient rights over tourism resources. In Australia, New Zealand, the Pacific Islands and many parts of Asia, the indigenous people are an integral part of the cultural tourism product. Being sensitive and able to accommodate their needs is assuming a higher priority for many governments that have belatedly recognized how integral these groups of people are to the tourism industry. If integrated and managed in a sensitive manner, such cultural diversity can actually provide destinations with a competitive edge by offering the unique and memorable element in the tourist experience. If managed badly, it can destroy any tourism development potential.

Ultimately many destinations and businesses will seek to develop a 'sustainable tourism industry' – it is good for the marketing of the destination, businesses and may appeal to the environmentally conscious traveller. For very sensitive environments the best form of tourism may be *no tourism*, unless the benefits are reinvested back in protection and preservation, such as in some of Africa's game reserves. Arguably, the best way to manage mass tourism is to concentrate it in purpose-built man-made developments. Many of these developments have already degraded the environment and are now experiencing measures to improve their impact and image. At least, from a planning perspective, this keeps the destructive effects of tourism in one place – but it then limits the economic benefits to the wider population. Some countries are seeking to appeal to a specific type of market and not to drive ahead for large numbers. All too often, however, the efforts of industry supercede such plans, because ultimately tourism remains a free-market activity with few major constraints on incremental growth. Limits are the exception rather than the rule. There is no doubt that tourism is a dynamic industry. Yet the rhetoric of using the latest buzzwords and jargon to appeal to tourists can only be judged by actions. Can tourism really be developed in a way in which profits and demand are balanced by long-term needs of the environment and people it affects? That is the future challenge for tourism.

References

Archer, B. (1987) Demand forecasting and estimation. In J.R.B. Ritchie and C.R. Goeldner (eds) *Travel, Tourism and Hospitality Research.* New York: Wiley.

D'Aveni, R. (1988) Hypercompetition closes in. *Financial Times*, 4 February (Global Business Section).

Faulkner, B. and Russell, R. (1999) Chaos and complexity in tourism: In search of a new perspective. *Pacific Tourism Review*, 1 (2): 93–102.

Glaeßer, D. (2006) *Crisis Management in the Tourism Industry*, 2nd edn. Oxford: Butterworth Heinemann.

Gössling, S. (2002) Global environmental consequences of tourism. *Global Environmental Change*, 12 (4): 283–302.

Page, S. and Connell, J. (2006) *Tourism: A Modern Synthesis*, 2nd edn. London: Thomson Learning.

Further reading

The best starting point are the websites of the World Tourism Organization, World Tourism Council and National Tourism Organizations to assess market trends and future strategies for tourism growth and development.

A number of good sources exist to examine future tourism scenarios including:

Future Foundation (2005) *The World of Travel in 2020*. London: Futures Foundation (www.futures-foundation.net).

And a wide range of scenario planning and futures research can be accessed at VisitScotland's website (www.scotexchange.net, by accessing Know your Market and following the links to scenario planning and Tomorrow's Tourist).

Questions

1 What are crises in tourism? And how should individual businesses respond to them?

2 What is the future growth potential of tourism in relation to the earth's resource base?

3 What are the principal management problems facing tourism managers in the new millennium?

4 How would you develop an action plan for managing tourism in a destination area you know or have recently visited? Will you need to take radical action to limit or prohibit tourists?

Index